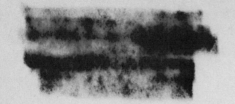

由之龍送于华山

Computers: Programming and Applications

Computers: Programming and Applications

HERBERT MAISEL

Professor of Computer Science
Director, Academic Computation Center
Georgetown University

SCIENCE RESEARCH ASSOCIATES, INC.
Chicago, Palo Alto, Toronto
Henley-on-Thames, Sydney, Paris, Stuttgart

A Subsidiary of IBM

ACKNOWLEDGMENTS

We would like to acknowledge the use of material supplied by:

Figure 6.1, courtesy of the Rockwell International Corporation
Figures 6.5, 6.20, and 14.1, courtesy of the Univac Division, Sperry
    Rand Corporation
Figures 6.6, 6.7, 6.8, 6.12, and 6.16, courtesy of the IBM Corporation
Figure 6.17, courtesy of the California Computer Products
    Corporation
Figure 6.18, courtesy of the Teletype Corporation
Figure 6.19, courtesy of the Data Products Corporation

Library of Congress Cataloging in Publication Data

Maisel, Herbert, 1930–
    Computers: programming and applications.

    Bibliography.
    Includes index.
    1.   Electronic digital computers — Programming.
2.   Programming languages (Electronic computers)
I.   Title.
QA76.6.M352   001.6'42   75–30547
ISBN 0–574–21070–9

To my students, who have taught me as much as I have taught them, and who have contributed so much to this book.

Preface

GENERAL OBJECTIVES

This book is intended as a text for a first course in computers at the undergraduate level. It is designed to emphasize programming with some discussion of applications, or applications with some discussion of programming. Specific recommendations on ways to use this book in either kind of introductory course are given later in this preface.

This book is designed for students from a variety of disciplines. Students majoring in mathematics and the physical sciences, as well as quantitatively oriented students majoring in business, the social sciences, and the health sciences, should find this book's treatment of computers appropriate to their capabilities and interests. The treatment also may be especially appropriate for management and accounting majors in a business curriculum because it provides insights into programming efficiency and effectiveness, business applications, and computer centers; and because there are many data-processing examples from business as well as from other areas.

So many introductory books are available that a new book should offer an instructor some special features. This book permits an instructor to introduce programming very early in the course, and to continue assigning programming exercises thereafter. This format benefits the instructor because it develops the students' programming skills in stages, and because it motivates them—by asking them to write simple programs to fulfill the exercises associated with the various topics—to cope with topics such as the representation of information, algorithms, and flowcharts. Also, the preparation, running, and debugging of programs are easier to schedule if programming is carried out over the whole semester. A second special feature of this book is a descriptive summary of computer applications that is especially readable and appropriate for an introductory course, and that can be introduced anywhere in the course.

The major objectives of this book are to enable the student to:

1. Formulate algorithms and write computer programs;
2. Appreciate the ways in which computers are used and their current and future impact; and
3. Understand the ways in which computers work.

The third objective is best met if programming is discussed in terms of machine and assembly languages. Unfortunately, if this approach is taken in a one-semester, introductory course, the first two objectives must be compromised to some extent. Therefore, this book emphasizes high-level languages. Machine languages and assembly languages are defined and briefly discussed in terms of the machine language for an old computer—the IBM 1620. This choice was made for pedagogical reasons: it enables students to grasp the essentials of machine languages more easily, since the essential concepts of a machine language exist independently of the language actually used. A few elementary examples and exercises are provided; however, these topics are discussed to a lesser degree than they might be in an introductory course whose major purpose or sole objective was to teach students how computers work. An excellent text that covers this subject is: Freedman, M. D. 1972. *Principles of Digital Computer Operation.* New York: John Wiley and Sons, Inc.

Special attention has been given throughout the book to the importance of programs (i.e., sets of instructions) as a computer component. These programs are called *software* and are discussed as a computer component in Chapter 6.

Annotated supplementary bibliographies are included in most chapters for the reader seeking further information. They are intended both as a guide to supplementary reading and as a reference in later years. Keywords and phrases are italicized within the context in which they are defined, and boldface type is used in the index of the page reference corresponding to these italicized words or phrases. These aids are provided in lieu of a glossary; too often, definitions offered in a glossary are incomplete, inadequate, or not illustrated. Especially difficult sections of the text and exercises are marked by asterisks before the section and problem numbers.

From another point of view, this book was written with the recommendations of the Association for Computing Machinery (ACM) for an introductory course in mind, and is "designed to provide a student with the basic knowledge and experience necessary to use computers effectively in the solution of problems." It also can be used as a text in a "service course for students in a number of other fields." The emphasis is on "algorithms, programs, and computers." The recommendations, from which these quotes are taken, describe the topics in this book, and thus they are quoted in full.

> Basic programming and program structure. Programming and computer systems. Debugging and verification of programs. Data representation. Organization and characteristics of computers. Survey of computers, languages, systems, and applications. Computer solution of several numerical and non-numerical problems using one or more programming languages.

OUTLINE OF THE BOOK

This book is divided into four major parts. Part 1 introduces the subject of computer programming by first describing how computers work and then by giving the student a start in programming in each of three languages: FORTRAN, using WATFIV; PL/I, using PL/C; and BASIC. (Ordinarily, only one language from among these three will be covered.) This permits the student to write programs very early in the semester.

Part 2 covers a variety of fundamental subjects that should be mastered before more complex programs can be written. These include a description of the components of a computer, how information is represented in and structured for processing by a computer, and the construction of algorithms and flowcharts.

In Part 3 we return to the three programming languages first described in Part 1. The language is described more fully so that the student can implement more complex algorithms. The discussion of FORTRAN attempts to preserve as many standard features as possible. Thus, for example, the H format code is used for annotating outputs rather than quotes. A discussion of the effectiveness, efficiency, and documentation of programs in Chapter 12 concludes this section.

In Part 4, computer applications are described, which can be introduced at any time during the course. The tedious and somewhat annoying programming details which authors frequently include in descriptions of applications are not given here. Instead, the reader is encouraged to digest each description in order to gain a clear understanding of the application and of the computer's contribution to it. The special importance and the modular nature of this part of the book have been indicated by "tabbing" (dark bars in margin of pages) for easy reference. Part 4 concludes in Chapter 16 with a description of the computer center and its organization.

POSSIBLE COURSE CONTENT

All of this book cannot, nor should it, be covered in a one-semester introductory course. As noted above, only one of the three higher-level languages is likely to be covered. In addition, some of the applications may not be discussed, depending on the interests of students.

The effectiveness of this book depends upon its use as a text for one of two general introductory courses: 1) one that emphasizes programming in one of the three languages that are covered; or 2) one that emphasizes applications. Specific recommendations for the content of each of these courses, based on the author's experience in teaching them, are given below. An instructor's guide is available that contains detailed outlines for each of these courses, along with the solutions for most problems, recommendations regarding examinations, laboratory work, and so forth.

Chapters that might be covered in an introductory course:

Emphasizing Programming	*Emphasizing Applications*
Chapter 1	Chapter 1
One chapter from among Chapters 2–4	One chapter from among Chapters 2–4
Chapter 5	Chapters 5 and 6
Selections from Chapter 6	Chapters 13–16
Chapters 7 and 8	
One chapter from among Chapters 9–11	
Chapter 12	
Selections from Chapters 13–16	

The author wishes to express the appreciation that he sincerely feels to the following for the contributions they have made to this book:

Ms. Marilyn Bohl, Dr. Franklin Prosser, Ms. Fran Gustavson, Dr. Allen B. Tucker, Jr., and Dr. Peter Calingaert for their helpful comments. A special thank-you is due Ms. Bohl; her comments were extensive, effective, and of maximum assistance.

My wife, Millie, for her clerical assistance.

My family—my wife, Millie, and my sons, Scott and Raymond—for the tolerance they have shown and the sacrifices they made while I worked on this book.

The staff of Science Research Associates: Steve Mitchell, Paul Kelly, and Alan Lowe, the senior editors; and Kay Nerode and Jim Budd, the project directors for this book. Special thanks also to Naomi Steinfeld, for copyediting, and Alex Teshin for artwork.

Contents

PART 1   PROGRAMMING: A BEGINNING   1

1. How Computers Work   3

1.1	A View of Calculations	3
1.2	Information Flow in a Computer	4
1.3	The Computer and the User	6
1.4	A View of Calculations Revisited	7
1.5	Information Flow in a Computer Servicing Remote Terminals	10
1.6	Procedures and Algorithms	13
	Exercises	14

2. The Elements of FORTRAN Programming and WATFIV   15

2.1	Introduction	15
2.2	A WATFIV Program	16
2.3	Integers, Floating-point Numbers, and Variables	18
	Exercises	18
2.4	The Assignment Statement	19
2.5	Input and Output	20
	Exercises	22
2.6	The STOP and END Statements	22
2.7	Looping and Branching	23
2.8	A Second Example	23
2.9	The IF Statement	25
2.10	Some Extensions and Generalizations	25
2.11	Debugging a WATFIV Program	28
2.12	Setting up a WATFIV Run	28
	Exercises	30

3. The Elements of PL/I Programming and PL/C   33

3.1	Introduction	33
3.2	A PL/C Program	33
3.3	Integers, Floating-point Numbers, and Variables	35
	Exercises	36
3.4	The Assignment Statement	36
3.5	Input and Output	37
	Exercises	39
3.6	Looping and Branching	39
3.7	A Second Example	40

3.8   The IF Statement   41
3.9   Some Extensions and Generalizations   42
3.10   Debugging a PL/C Program   44
Exercises   44

4. The Elements of BASIC Programming   47

4.1   Introduction   47
4.2   A BASIC Program   48
4.3   Constants and Variables   49
Exercises   50
4.4   The Assignment or LET Statement   50
4.5   Input and Output   51
Exercises   52
4.6   Looping and Branching   53
4.7   A Second Example   53
4.8   The IF Statement   55
4.9   Some Extensions and Generalizations   55
4.10   Debugging a BASIC Program   57
4.11   Programming from a Terminal   58
Exercises   61

PART 2   FUNDAMENTAL TOOLS   63

5. The Representation and Structuring of Information   65

5.1   Introduction   65
5.2   Positional Notation—Bases 2, 8, and 16   65
5.3   Conversion Among Bases 2, 8, and 16   67
5.4   Floating-point Representation   68
Exercises   68
5.5   EBCDIC and ASCII   69
5.6   Integer Representation in a Computer   70
5.7   Floating-point Representation in a Computer   72
Exercises   73
5.8   Fields, Records, Files, and Data Bases   74
5.9   Arrays   75
Exercises   79
Annotated Supplementary Bibliography   80

6. The Components of a Computer   81

6.1   Introduction   81
6.2   Processors   82
6.3   Main Storage   83
6.4   The Nature of Machine Languages   87
6.5   Auxiliary Storage   90
6.6   Input/Output—An Overview   95

6.7   Punched Cards and Card-processing Equipment   97
6.8   Printers   100
6.9   Plotters   104
6.10   Remote Terminals   105
6.11   Other Input Devices   109
6.12   Communication and its Impact   110
6.13   Software—An Overview   113
6.14   The Computer as a Translator   114
6.15   An Overview of Higher-level Languages   116
6.16   Application Packages   127
6.17   A Checklist for Application Packages   128
Exercises   130
Annotated Supplementary Bibliography   132

7. Algorithms   137

7.1   Introduction   137
7.2   Definition   138
7.3   Connection with Computer Programming   138
7.4   The Calculation of Accumulated Savings   139
7.5   The Sieve of Eratosthenes   141
Exercises   142
7.6   Looping and Iteration   142
7.7   An Algorithm for Obtaining Square Roots   144
7.8   End-of-File   147
7.9   Character String Manipulation   148
7.10   Testing Algorithms   150
7.11   A Test Set for the Square-root Algorithm   152
Exercises   153
7.12   Errors in Implementing Algorithms on a
       Digital Computer   153
Exercises   154
References   156
Annotated Supplementary Bibliography   157

8. Flowcharts   158

8.1   Introduction   158
8.2   System versus Programming Flowcharts   159
8.3   Detailed and General Flowcharts   159
8.4   Flowchart Symbols for Input and Output   161
8.5   The Decision Symbols   162
8.6   Terminal Symbols   163
8.7   Connectors   163
8.8   Processing   164
8.9   Annotations   164
Exercises   165
8.10   Flowchart for the Sieve of Eratosthenes   166

8.11	The Payroll Problem	166
	Exercises	177
	References	178
	Annotated Supplementary Bibliography	179

PART 3   PROGRAMMING REVISITED   181

9. FORTRAN IV Using WATFIV   183

9.1	The Character Set	183
9.2	Constants	184
9.3	Variables and Arrays	185
9.4	Specifications for Variables and Arrays	186
9.5	A Program to Calculate Tuition Due	188
	Exercises	189
9.6	Operations, Expressions, and FORTRAN Library Subprograms	191
9.7	The END Option in the READ	193
9.8	Annotating Output—The WRITE and FORMAT Statements	194
9.9	FORMAT Codes	197
	Exercises	198
9.10	The Computed GO TO and Logical IF Statements	200
9.11	The DO Statement	201
9.12	Input and Output of Arrays	207
9.13	A Program to Compute Means and Standard Deviations	208
9.14	Subprocedures—Statement Functions, Function Subprograms, and Subroutine Subprograms	209
	Exercises	215
9.15	Debugging a WATFIV Program	215
	Exercises	219
	Annotated Supplementary Bibliography	219

10. PL/I Using PL/C   221

10.1	The Character Set	221
10.2	Identifiers	222
10.3	Statement Labels	223
10.4	Keywords	223
	Exercises	224
10.5	Constants	225
10.6	Variables and Arrays	226
10.7	Specifications for Variables and Arrays	227
10.8	A Program to Calculate Tuition Due	228
	Exercises	231
10.9	Operations and Expressions	231
10.10	Annotating Outputs—Edit-directed Output	233
10.11	Format Items	234

Exercises		237
10.12	The ON ENDFILE Statement	238
10.13	The DO Group and DO Loops	240
10.14	Input and Output of Arrays	243
Exercises		244
10.15	A Program to Calculate Means and Standard Deviations	244
10.16	Procedures within Procedures	245
10.17	Debugging a PL/C Program	250
Exercises		253
Annotated Supplementary Bibliography		255

11. BASIC

11.1	The Character Set	256
11.2	Variables and Arrays	257
11.3	The DIM Statement	258
11.4	Operations and Built-In Functions	258
11.5	A Program to Calculate Tuition Due	260
Exercises		262
11.6	Annotating Outputs	263
11.7	Annotating Inputs	263
11.8	The READ and DATA Statements	265
Exercises		267
11.9	The FOR and NEXT Statements	268
11.10	The Input and Output of Arrays	270
Exercises		270
11.11	A Program to Compute Means and Standard Deviations	271
11.12	Subroutines in BASIC—The GOSUB and RETURN Statements	271
11.13	Debugging a BASIC Program	274
Exercises		276
Annotated Supplementary Bibliography		277

12. Program Effectiveness, Efficiency, and Documentation | | 278 |

12.1	Definition and Debugging	278
12.2	Structured Programming, Program Proof, and Maintenance	279
12.3	Program Effectiveness	280
12.4	Documentation	282
12.5	An Example	285
Exercises		292
12.6	More on Efficiency	293
Exercises		294
References		295
Annotated Supplementary Bibliography		295

PART 4   APPLICATIONS   297

13. Cultural Impact   299

13.1   Introduction   299
13.2   The Second Industrial Revolution   299
13.3   Information Systems, Privacy, and Efficiency   301
13.4   Computers in the Federal Government   302
13.5   Education and Teaching Machines   304
13.6   The Potential Impact on Health Care   305
13.7   Computers and the Law   306
13.8   Urban Impact—The Wired City   306
13.9   Intelligent Machines and their Implications   307
Topics for Discussion   309
References   309
Annotated Supplementary Bibliography   310

14. Applications in Business and Management   312

14.1   Introduction   312
14.2   Hospital Information Systems   313
14.3   National Parts Wholesaler   317
14.4   Simulation—General Considerations   319
14.5   Simulation of the Operations of a Social Security
       District Office   322
Annotated Supplementary Bibliography   328

15. Applications in Engineering and the Sciences   330

15.1   Introduction   330
15.2   Ballistic Calculations   330
15.3   Monitoring Sewage Pumps   331
15.4   Numerical Taxonomy   332
15.5   Medical Diagnosis   335
15.6   Function Fitting—Least Squares   337
15.7   Content Analysis   341
References   342
Annotated Supplementary Bibliography   343

16. Computer Centers   344

16.1   Introduction   344
16.2   Business Computer Centers   344
16.3   Scientific and Academic Computer Centers   347
16.4   Staffing Qualifications   349
16.5   The User's View   350
Exercises   353
References   354
Annotated Supplementary Bibliography   354

Appendix   356

Part 1

Programming: A Beginning

In this part of the book we introduce computers, programming, algorithms, and programming languages. The first principles of these topics are defined and discussed at a basic level. After the reader has covered Chapter 1, he is expected to read only one chapter from among Chapters 2 through 4, after which he should be able to write programs. Thus, programming can be introduced quite early.

Chapter 1

How Computers Work

1.1 A VIEW OF CALCULATIONS

The computer is an extremely fast and reliable manipulator of information. To understand how computers work, we will first discuss a much simpler and more easily understandable data manipulation system—a desk calculator, its operator, and his supplies.

Suppose that a series of calculations are to be made and that the operator of the calculator is unfamiliar with them. A table can be prepared to describe the sequence of calculations to be made, and to record the results of these calculations.

Consider, for example, the calculation of a schedule of annual amortization payments corresponding to a principal of $10,000, an annual interest rate of 8 percent, and a five-year amortization period. A table something like that in Figure 1.1 might be used. The amount of the annual payment is input; it is in the table at the start of the calculations. The outstanding principal at the end of year zero is also input. The values that are input are in italics in Figure 1.1. These values are in the table when it is given to the operator. The operator calculates all the other values in the table using these inputs. The final outstanding principal of four cents results from rounding all calculations, including the annual payment, to the nearest cent. The last payment might be increased to $2504.60 in order to complete amortization of the principal.

The operator must complete each calculation and make the appropriate entries in the appropriate columns. He needs both the directions for making the calculations, which are contained in the column headings, and sets of inputs for the calculation. He produces the output— the information desired by the person requesting the calculations,

3

End of Year	Interest Due at 8%(I=.08 OP)	Annual Payment (A)	Principal Repaid (P=A—I)	Outstanding Principal (New OP=Old OP—P)
0				10,000.
1	800.00	2504.56	1704.56	8,295.44
2	663.64	2504.56	1840.92	6,454.52
3	516.36	2504.56	1988.20	4,466.32
4	357.31	2504.56	2147.25	2,319.07
5	185.53	2504.56	2319.03	0.04

Fig. 1.1 Form for completing an amortization table using a desk calculator

in this case, the series of entries in the second, fourth, and fifth columns of the table that the operator calculated. The output is the interest due each year, the part of the payment credited to reducing the principal, and the amount of the outstanding principal that remains at the end of each year after year zero.

What are the elements of this process? Some of them have already been identified: the directions for carrying out the calculations, the input, and the output. The operator of the desk calculator needs other, less explicit capabilities to solve this problem: he knows how to interpret the formulas given in the column headings (i.e., he can translate the instructions given him); he also knows how to execute these instructions (i.e., he knows which keys to press on the calculator to produce the desired results); and he understands where to record the results of his calculations and how to determine what to do next. Each of these functions must be explicitly provided in the computer. Figure 1.2, shows the computer's *central processing unit,* which interprets and executes the instruction, and its *storage* or *memory* unit, which records intermediate and final results. The storage unit in a computer also contains the instructions themselves, which are called the *program.* Input and output are handled by devices such as card readers and printers. In the next section, we will describe more precisely what a computer does and how it does it.

1.2 INFORMATION FLOW IN A COMPUTER

Computers are merely a collection of electrical circuits that are wired together, packaged in pastel-colored boxes, and linked to electromechanical devices that provide input or output or additional storage facilities. A computer cannot perform any calculations until it is programmed — that is, supplemented by sets of instructions that cause the

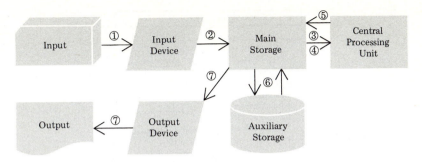

Fig. 1.2 The flow of information in a computer

machine to function in a special way. These sets of instructions are called the *software*. If computers are to be used intelligently, the patterns of information flow must be understood. In this section, we shall describe information flow in a computer from two points of view: first, we. will describe the overall flow; then we will focus on the activities of the central processing unit.

Figure 1.2 describes the flow of information in a computer. The program and data are loaded by the computer operator into an input device (1). The computer carries out the remaining steps automatically, first transferring this information to main storage (2). Instructions are brought into the central processing unit from main storage and are decoded and executed (3). If the execution involves the processing of data, the data are brought from main storage to the processor (4). A result is obtained and entered in main storage (5). Output is obtained as needed (7), and exchanges with auxiliary storage devices are made (6) if the computer's main storage cannot hold all the information needed to complete the calculations. Also, additional inputs may be obtained as necessary during the course of the calculation (2).

Figure 1.3 depicts the sequence of internal computer activities that occur in the central processing unit (CPU). *The CPU functions by alternating instruction cycles with execution cycles.* The CPU has a control unit and a processor. In an *instruction cycle,* a sequence of digits called a *machine language instruction* is obtained from main storage and treated as an instruction; the control unit breaks this sequence down into its component parts, decodes the digits specifying the operation to be performed, and initiates the execution cycle. In the *execution cycle,* the control unit causes the processor to obtain data from main storage, execute the instruction, and return the result to main storage for those operations — such as arithmetic processes — that do more than transfer data. The processor need not be involved if the operation involves only the transfer of data. However, such transfers do require the execution of a series of instructions, as does

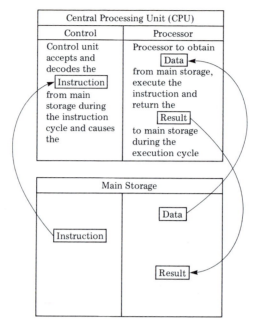

Fig. 1.3 Internal activities of the central processing unit

stopping the computer. The alternating sequence of instruction and execution cycles continues as long as there is an instruction to be interpreted and executed.

This flow sequence illustrates one of the major difficulties that a computer user faces: the solution to a problem must be reduced to a sequence of individual, elementary operations, each given in a single machine-language instruction. These operations include a single addition of one number to another, a single transfer of data, or a single modification of the contents of main storage. Many of these individual operations are required in order to solve a problem. A single error in their construction or ordering can make it impossible to determine the final result. Fortunately, the situation is not that grim: the computer itself can help a user by permitting him to write one instruction that results in many machine-language instructions. The computer translates from the easier language to the machine language by means of a computer program called a *compiler.*

1.3 THE COMPUTER AND THE USER

From the point of view of the user, the computer is a tool, one which places special demands on its users. The computer is a reliable, fast, and willing slave, but it must be told precisely what to do and given the material on which to work. The user of a computer must see to it that a computer program (a series of instructions that satisfies the user's needs) and the inputs to this program are available. The problem is like trying to converse with someone who does not understand your language. You must learn a new language—or at least part of a new language—to satisfy your communication needs. If your only need is to order meals from waiters, you can soon master the limited vocabulary and grammar for this purpose. If, however, you wish to live for an extended period of time among people speaking another language, you need a more complete mastery of the language.

Similarly, if you plan to use the computer infrequently, it may not be necessary to master a programming language. Your time might better be spent chatting with the staff of the computer center and contacting people with similar interests to find out what programs are available. If, however, you want to be a computer science specialist, or will use the computer extensively or in a novel way, then you certainly should master at least one programming language.

1.4 A VIEW OF CALCULATIONS REVISITED

We return to the more easily understood data manipulation system—the desk calculator, its operator, and his supplies. Consider once again the calculations outlined in Figure 1.1, but from a somewhat different point of view. Note that the table is set up in such a way that the operator proceeds from left to right, and from one row to the next. Thus, it is possible, with the one set of instructions contained in the table headings and with the understanding that the operator has developed a procedure to obtain all the entries in the table in a single sitting. This illustrates the process of *looping*. The procedure returns to earlier steps repeatedly to obtain new results from the same sequence of instructions. This is an important technique in the construction of such procedures, and we shall see it used over and over again.

The operator easily recognizes when he is finished—there are no more rows in the input table. The number of rows was limited by the amortization period. The procedure must come to an end.

Let us consider a somewhat different problem to illustrate other aspects of computing systems. The calculation is a simple one: the computation of arithmetic means (averages). This involves the summation of a series of values, and then the division of this sum by the number of values. Suppose that we have very large sets of values and that we do not know how many values there are in each set. We must both count the number of values (*enumeration*) and obtain their sum to calculate the mean. Suppose also that the source for the values is a series of ledger sheets contained in a notebook to be taken from a file. The instructions to the operator might be:

1. Go to the file and obtain notebook 376.
2. For each set of entries in the notebook, calculate their sum, say T, and the number of values in the set, say N. Note these results on a worksheet.
3. Calculate $\bar{x} = T/N$ and write $\bar{x}$ in the upper right-hand corner of each page in the notebook on which a set of values begins. Label this result by writing MEAN = before the result.

This calculation is simple to carry out, since many desk calculators produce the number of operands as a by-product in calculating the sum. The operator probably will proceed by obtaining the notebook, setting up a worksheet, and then carrying out the calculation, recording each result in the notebook as it is obtained.

The major difference between this procedure and the one for obtaining the amortization table is that the input for the amortization problem was completely known to the operator, since it was incorporated in the instructions that were given him. This is not the case for the calculation of means. This discrepancy has at least three important implications: first, the number of values, their form, and their magnitude are not known when the instructions are written. This permits the processing of a greater variety of input, but it also means that the operator must be able to handle anything that might come up. Second, by merely modifying the first instruction, the operator can be made to calculate the mean of sets of values in any notebook available to him. Third, the notebook must contain some clear indication of when one set of data ends and another begins.

This ability to refer to sets of data outside of the main body of instructions (data in the notebook rather than data on the worksheet) is also important in carrying out calculations on an electronic computer. Such extra storage, or auxiliary storage capacity, is provided in decks of cards, on magnetic tapes, on magnetic discs, and on magnetic drums. We shall say more about these media and the devices used to process them in Chapter 6. Their availability substantially broadens the range of problems that a computer can work on.

It now should be clear why procedures that modify their own instructions can be useful. In this example, the modified instructions contain a definition of the data set which is to be processed. The same can be said of some instructions for computers. Repeated modification and looping permits a whole set of inputs contained in auxiliary storage to be processed.

CALCULATING GROSS PAY				
EMPLOYEE			GROSS PAY, G	
ID#	HRS. WORKED, H	HOURLY RATE, R	IF H ≤ 40 G = HR	IF H > 40 G = (1.5H − 20)R
12347	40.00	2.40	96.00	
12351	40.00	2.80	112.00	
12353	45.00	2.40		114.00
12356	40.00	3.10	124.00	

Fig. 1.4 Form for calculating gross weekly pay on a desk calculator

The boundaries of the data sets must be defined clearly. This is done in different ways, with different auxiliary storage media. Cards are accumulated in decks, so that the end of a data set might be indicated by the end of the deck. Also, special entries might be made on a card to indicate that we have come to the end of a data set. Gaps are left between data sets on magnetic tapes, and the boundaries of data sets on discs are indicated by the addresses of the data that are referenced.

Consider a third example of a desk calculation: determining an employee's gross weekly pay. A worksheet for this calculation is given in Figure 1.4. Of course, this would be just one step if actual payrolls were being calculated, in which case gross pay would be combined with the calculation of deductions and the determination of net pay.

Suppose that the operator of a desk calculator is instructed as follows:

1. Call extension 3107 to obtain the input—i.e., to obtain a list of employees and their identification numbers, and the number of hours each employee worked last week.

2. Enter the employee's identification number and the number of hours he worked in the preceding week in the first two columns of the calculation table and in Form A.

3. Go to ledger 314 to determine the hourly rate paid to each of these employees. Enter these figures in the third column of the calculation table.

4. Calculate the weekly gross pay due each employee and enter this result in the last column of Form A.

5. Send Form A to Department 21 via the special messenger.

We now have introduced a special form in which results are recorded and forwarded, Form A (illustrated in Figure 1.5). In addition, we have introduced an important auxiliary source of data—Ledger 314—and

FORM A REPORT OF GROSS PAY Dept. 21		
EMPLOYEE		GROSS PAY
ID#	HRS. WORKED	
12347	40.00	96.00
12351	40.00	112.00
12353	45.00	114.00
12356	40.00	124.00

Fig. 1.5 Form used in reporting gross weekly pay

the need to obtain inputs from a remote location via telephone and to return the output to some remote location via messenger.

Many applications of computers require that the results of the calculation be recorded on special forms. In fact, when computers are used to calculate payrolls, the paychecks are printed directly by the computer. Inputs are frequently obtained directly from the remote location where they are generated, to reduce the chances for error in preparing data for the computer. Information that is passed from hand to hand and transcribed from form to form is subject to more error than information that is entered directly at its source. Finally, outputs ultimately must be routed to where they are utilized, whether via a messenger or a printer located in or near the office where the output is required.

This illustrates the way many applications of computers are implemented today. Information flow in a computer facility serving remote locations is described in the next section.

Clearly, this same layout can be used to calculate and report the gross pay for employees in each of several departments. We need only change the phone extension, 3107, to the extension of the next department to be processed; the ledger number, 314, to the ledger number that has the corresponding hourly rates; and the department number, 21, to the corresponding number of this next department.

1.5 THE FLOW OF INFORMATION IN A COMPUTER SERVICING REMOTE TERMINALS

We now consider the flow of information in a computer facility that has input and output devices located some distance away from the computer. These remote terminals may be hundreds or even thousands of miles, or only hundreds or thousands of feet, away.

This type of input/output means that:

1. The information must be passed over communication lines; and
2. The computer operator can no longer control the operation of the input/output devices.

Because of the need for communication lines, the computer user must be aware of the state of the art in this area. Since the operator cannot control all the input/output terminals, provision must be made in the computer for effectively servicing these terminals. In permitting input via remote terminals, the computer center commits itself to the immediate servicing of these remote users. Since ongoing work may take a great deal of time to complete, the inputs from the remote terminals are permitted to interrupt this work. The terminals are serviced, and the computer returns at a later time to the program that was interrupted. This is the kind of system we shall discuss in this section, concentrating first on the flow of information in this system when no interrupt occurs.

A special series of programs, called an *operating system,* undoubtedly would be required to implement this system, and the description of the information flow that follows assumes the presence of this software component. An operating system is a set of programs that permits the computer to function with a minimum of operator intervention. These programs:

1. Maintain a smooth flow of work to be processed;
2. Call up special programs as they are needed;
3. Perform administrative and accounting functions such as keeping track of the amount of computer time used by each job; and
4. Provide facilities for processing interrupts and otherwise handling remotely located input and output devices.

Consider work loaded from an input device at the computer center which is processed as it is loaded (refer to 1 in Figure 1.6). The instructions need not be loaded from an input device; a request to retrieve the proper instructions from a library of programs that is part of the operating system can be loaded instead. In the latter case, the input consists of data plus this request. The presence of the request causes the operating system to signal the CPU (2 in the figure), to obtain instructions from auxiliary storage (3), and to execute the library program. Main storage must contain some of the operating system at all times. The transfer and the interpretation and execution of instructions

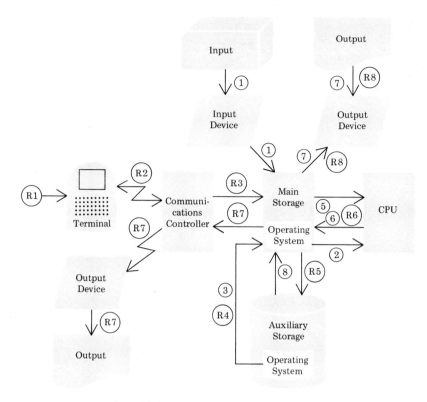

Fig. 1.6 Flow of information in a computer with remote terminals

(5 and 6) proceed as usual. Exchanges with input/output (7) and auxiliary storage (8) are carried out as necessary. When the job is completed, control is returned to the operating system. Either other jobs awaiting processing will be serviced, or there will be a pause in the operation of the system.

Next, consider a job coming in via the remote terminals. In most cases, the terminal itself and the operator are so slow — when compared with the speed of the computer — that many remote terminals can be serviced simultaneously without causing serious delays in the response to these terminals. Users, not the computer, operate simultaneously. This simultaneity is called *time sharing* of the computer. The users operate their terminals simultaneously, but the computer processes the work sequentially. Some operating systems also contain features that permit the computer to process several jobs concurrently, by overlapping the input/output activities of one job with the execution of another job. This is called *multiprogramming.* A computer can be time shared without multiprogramming, or it can be multiprogrammed without being time shared. It also may be both multiprogrammed and time shared.

Referring again to Figure 1.6, we see that the job is now input from a remote terminal (R1). The information is passed over a communication line (R2) to a device called the *communications controller,* which links the computer and the remote terminal. This device can cycle from one remote terminal to another, picking up signals from the communication lines, translating them into the types of signal required by the computer, and holding them for transmission to main storage (R3). The transmission of an inquiry from a remote terminal causes the operating system to initiate a series of exchanges among the operating system in auxiliary storage, the operating system in main storage, and the other contents of auxiliary storage (R4, R5, and R6). The exchanges permit interruption of the ongoing work; storage in auxiliary storage, if necessary, of the information required to resume the the work that was interrupted; and initialization of the work generated from the remote terminal. This job is processed in the usual manner, except that output to the remote terminal is permitted (R7), as is output to a device such as the printer in the computer center (R8). Upon completing the work for the remote user, the operating system restores the previously ongoing work, which continues to completion or until it is interrupted again. When people operate a computer in this way, they assign priorities to the different jobs, and only a job of higher priority can interrupt ongoing work. The operating system is able to recognize priorities and maintain continuous job processing as long as there is work to be done.

1.6 PROCEDURES AND ALGORITHMS

The computer is a willing slave that must be told what it is to do in no uncertain terms. Although it requires a different and generally more detailed set of instructions than a desk calculator, the procedures discussed in connection with the desk calculating systems introduce the subject of procedures for solving problems on a computer. Such procedures are called *algorithms,* and are of great importance to computer users. We shall define and discuss English-language algorithms in Chapter 7. Flowcharts, another way to describe algorithms, are discussed in Chapter 8. Alogrithms are implemented on computers by writing programs. Three languages for writing computer programs will be discussed in Chapters 2 through 4.

Exercises

1. Set up a worksheet for use in connection with the calculation of means discussed in Section 1.4.

2. Modify the procedure given in Section 1.4 for the calculation of means to calculate the means of all data sets contained in notebooks No. 21 through 33, inclusive.

3. Describe as many data sets as you can for which an operator could not get the mean using a desk calculator. (Hint: Consider both unusual kinds of numbers and numbers with so many digits that they exceed the capacity of the desk calculator.)

4. Modify the procedure given in Section 1.4 for calculating gross pay so that the gross pay of employees in any department could be calculated. Do this by 1) adding an instruction that would require the operator to obtain the identity of the department, its phone number, and the ledger in which its hourly rates are stored from some other source; and 2) by modifying the calculation table, Form A, and the other steps in the procedure as required to use this information.

5. Describe the information that would flow through a computer system (structured as in Figure 1.2) in calculating the amortization table. Assume that both the instructions and the inputs are given in a deck of cards. Also assume that the output is to appear on the printer.

6. Describe the information that would flow through a computer system (structured as in Figure 1.2), in calculating means. Assume that the instructions are given in a deck of cards and that the data sets are stored on magnetic disk. Assume also that the output is given on the printer.

Chapter 2

The Elements of FORTRAN Programming and WATFIV

Writing programs is a form of communication; the programmer is trying to tell the computer what to do by means of a language. Since most early users of the electronic digital computer were scientifically oriented, substitutions in elaborate formulae frequently were required. As might be expected, the first popular compiler was developed to make formula programming easy. FORTRAN (FORmula TRANslation), developed in the late 1950s by the IBM Corporation, does just that.

FORTRAN comes in a variety of dialects and versions within dialects. FORTRAN II was developed early; FORTRAN IV, later. For example, FORTRAN II was the dialect implemented on IBM 1620 computers; and FORTRAN IV was implemented on IBM System/360 and System/370 computers. However, each dialect may be available in several versions. There is a standard version of FORTRAN called ANSI FORTRAN, which is very much like FORTRAN IV. The language described in this chapter is a version of FORTRAN IV called WATFIV. It was developed at the University of Waterloo and has several important advantages over other versions of FORTRAN IV. Most significantly for colleges and universities, it can process many jobs very rapidly and produce error messages that are more easily understood than those produced by other versions of FORTRAN.

This chapter emphasizes the elementary features of WATFIV that permit programming to be initiated with a minimum of explanation and practice. A more complete description of WATFIV will be given

15

in Chapter 9. The reader interested in learning more about FORTRAN should refer to the Annotated Supplementary Bibliography at the end of that chapter.

2.2 A WATFIV PROGRAM

A WATFIV program is introduced at this point to describe its general appearance and to discuss some general considerations in writing these programs. The program is given in Figure 2.1; it is designed to find the sum of three numbers that are input.*

Note that the program in Figure 2.1 is presented on a special coding form. These forms are useful because the writing of WATFIV programs is rather stereotyped, with respect to use of the punched card. Individual statements appear on individual cards. The statement is actually entered in columns 7–72 of the card. Columns 1–5 are reserved for the statement number, which serves as a cross reference to the statement.

Column 6 of the card is used to indicate continuation cards. This column ordinarily is blank, but if more than one card is required to record a single statement, something other than zero must be punched in column 6 in all cards after the first one. A good practice is to punch successively greater digits in column 6, beginning with a one on the first continuation card.

Column 1 of the card also serves a special purpose: the letter C is entered in this column to identify a card as a *comment card,* and to make the FORTRAN compiler ignore the remainder of the card. Thus, comment cards—easily inserted in FORTRAN programs—are used to annotate programs and to make them more readable.

Finally, columns 73–80 of the card always are ignored by the compiler. The programmer can use these in any way he sees fit; he might enter his name in these columns, or he might use them to number the cards sequentially.

Two final introductory comments: first, only capital letters are used in WATFIV programs; there are no lower case letters in WATFIV. Second, computers are very intolerant. If there is even a minor error, such as a missing comma or a misspelled word, the program either will not be executed or it will be executed incorrectly.

---

*Cross-references to Chapters 3 and 4 will be avoided in this chapter because Chapters 2, 3, and 4 should be studied independently. However, those who are interested in contrasting the languages will find that the chapters are developed in a similar way. For example, a PL/C program to solve the same problem can be found in Section 3.2, and a BASIC program to solve this problem can be found in Section 4.2.

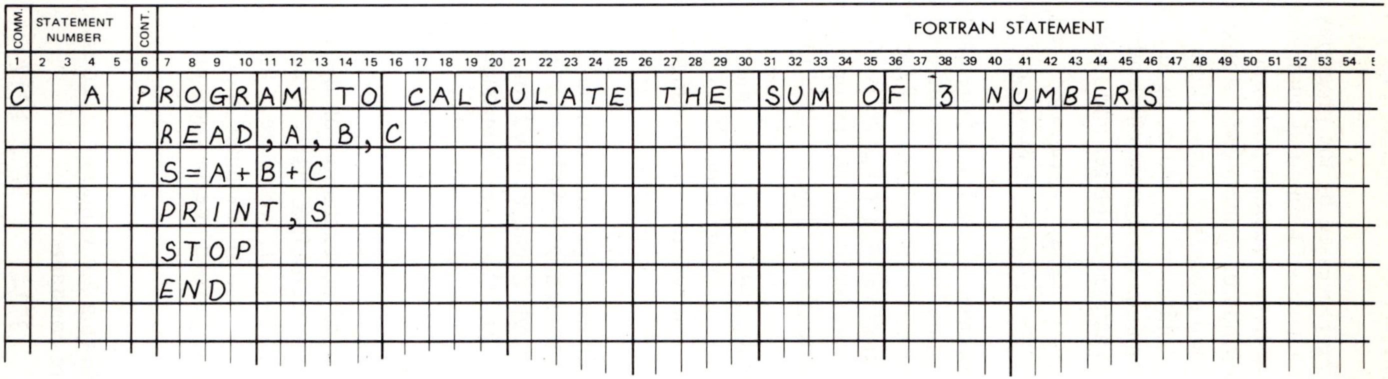

FORTRAN STATEMENT

COMM	STATEMENT NUMBER	CONT	FORTRAN STATEMENT
C			A PROGRAM TO CALCULATE THE SUM OF 3 NUMBERS
			READ, A, B, C
			S = A + B + C
			PRINT, S
			STOP
			END

Fig. 2.1 A program to calculate the sum of three numbers

2.3 INTEGERS, FLOATING-POINT NUMBERS, AND VARIABLES

The values that will be processed by the programs described in this chapter will be either integers (the natural numbers) or floating-point numbers (numbers that have a decimal point and may have fractional portions). These two kinds of numbers are stored in different ways inside computers, and are processed using different machine-language instructions. In general, integers should be used if they are appropriate, since they can be manipulated more efficiently.

The following are examples of integer and floating-point numbers:

    integer: 1674, −214, 0, −44, 476234
    floating-point: 3.1416, −.002634, 1726489.88

A name, called a *variable,* is used in a program to denote the contents of a storage location. Values always must be assigned to variables, one way or another, in a program. In fact, from one point of view, the principal objective of a program is to change the values stored for the diverse variables until the appropriate values have been stored in the appropriate places. These values then are output to the user.

A variable can be used to store either integers or floating-point numbers. A final choice must be made: if a certain variable will be assigned integer values sometimes and floating-point values at other times, it should be considered floating-point. This is because integers can be represented by floating-point notation, but floating-point numbers cannot be represented by integer notation.

A variable can be denoted in WATFIV by a letter. The letters A through H and O through Z can be used for variables that denote floating-point numbers, and the letters I through N for variables that denote integer numbers. Thus, for example, X or A or S could be used to denote floating-point variables, and K or I or N to denote integer variables.

A number that is used just as it appears in the program and is fixed at that value throughout the execution of the program is called a *constant.* Floating-point constants have a decimal point; integer constants do not. Therefore, 1. would be a floating-point constant; 1 would be an integer constant. Commas should not appear in constants; thus, 3,247 is not a valid integer constant.

Exercises

1. Which of the following are valid integer constants and which are valid floating-point constants?

        0.3   3724.   67,274.217   −143
        98235   0   7,172   −20.20

2. Which of the following are integer variables and which are floating-point variables?

E L Q J M U H

2.4 THE ASSIGNMENT STATEMENT

One way to assign a value to a variable is to use the assignment statement. First the variable appears, then an equal sign (=), and then something that looks like a mathematical formula. This mathematical formula is called an *arithmetic expression*. It contains variables, constants, and operations. It also may contain parentheses in order to correctly fix the order in which the operations are to be executed. For example:

$$Y=(A+B)/C$$

assigns a new value to Y. It is obtained by adding the value stored in location A to that stored in B, and then dividing the result by C. We see, then, that expressions in parentheses are executed first and that + is used to denote addition and / to denote division. Also, − is used to denote subtraction and * to denote multiplication. These are the only operations which we will use in this chapter.

In the absence of parentheses, division and multiplication are executed before addition and subtraction. Otherwise, operations are carried out from left to right in the order in which they appear in the expression. The numbers under the operations in the expression below indicate the order in which these operations are executed.

$$A+B/C*D-E$$
$$3 \quad 1 \quad 2 \quad 4$$

If, for example, A = 1.5, B = 5., C = 2.5, D = 2., and E = 5.3, then the result of evaluating this expression would be:

5. divided by 2.5 times 2. plus 1.5 minus 5.3, which is 0.2.

Expressions that involve only integer variables and integer constants can take on only integer values. This presents no problem as long as no divisions take place. However, although dividing one integer by another (e.g., 8 divided by 3) does not necessarily result in an integer, in FORTRAN, when the numerator and denominator are integers, the result is always an integer. The answer is obtained by discarding, or *truncating,* the fractional portion of the result. This means that the statement

$$I=8/3$$

assigns a value of 2 to I.

2.5 INPUT AND OUTPUT

Values also can be assigned to variables by reading them from a card in the input. If a variable is to be assigned values by the user of the program, that variable must be assigned a value via input. Thus, for example, if we write a program that can calculate and output the sum of any three numbers provided by a user, the three numbers must be input. Similarly, the results that interest a program user must be output. In the example, the sum—which first must be calculated using an assignment statement—should be output (refer to Figure 2.1).

Input is requested by a READ statement and output by a PRINT statement.

A READ statement (see Figure 2.1) looks like:

`READ, A,B,C`

It begins with the word READ, which is followed by a comma, and then by a list of the variables to which values are being assigned. The variables are separated by commas. The READ statement will attempt to assign values to all the variables in the list. If there are three variables in the list and only one number on the first input card, then the second input card will be read, and so on until all the variables in the list have been assigned values. Figure 2.2 illustrates what happens if all three values appear on one input card, or if just one value appears on the first card and two appear on the second card. The values punched on the input cards should be in the correct sequence, separated by blank spaces or commas. Otherwise they may occur in any column on the card.

A PRINT statement (see Figure 2.1) looks very much like a READ statement. For example,

`PRINT,S`

The statement begins with the word PRINT, which is followed by a comma and then by a list of the variables from which values are to be printed. The result obtained in executing the program given in Figure 2.1, using the input in Figure 2.2, is:

`0.1016000E 04`

When the PRINT statement is used, the computer prints a floating-point number in a standard way—called *scientific notation*. The letter E stands for exponent, and the number following E is the power of 10 by which the digits preceding E should be multiplied to determine the equivalent, familar form for the value. Therefore, 0.1016000E 04 means .1016 multiplied by 10^4, which equals 1016.

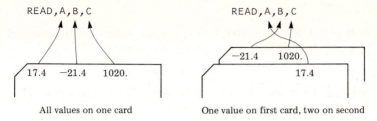

All values on one card   One value on first card, two on second

Fig. 2.2   How values are assigned to variables using the READ statement

A few rules should be kept in mind when using the READ and PRINT statements:

1. Numbers that are input to a floating-point variable can be either integers or floating-point constants, but numbers that are input to integer variables must be integer constants (i.e., a number that is to be input to an integer variable cannot have a decimal point).

2. Numbers that are to be input cannot be continued from one card to the next.

3. Each READ statement will begin to READ a new card, and each PRINT statement will result in one line of printed output (unless there are too many values to fit on a single line). If results are to be printed on different lines, then distinct PRINT statements should be used. Figure 2.1 shows that, if we intended to print the input values on the next line after the line on which the sum is printed, we would need the following successive PRINT statements in the program:

```
PRINT,S
PRINT,A,B,C
```

If we had used the statement

```
PRINT,S,A,B,C
```

then the sum and the values all would be printed on the same line.

The input and output discussed in this section is called *format-free I/O* (not available in all versions of FORTRAN). As the term *format-free* implies, the programmer cannot specify the layout of the printed result, nor can he be flexible in handling the input. For example, it would be very difficult to print a table such as that given in Figure 1.1 for the amortization problem. Also, values that appear on input cards cannot be skipped.

Exercises

3. If R = 3.8, S = 1.9, and T = 4.4, what value will be assigned to X when the following statement is executed?

$$X=T+R/S$$

4. If I = 2, J = 4, and K = 5, what value will be assigned to M when the following statement is executed?

$$M=I*K/J$$

5. What values will be assigned to I, R and T by the statement

$$READ, R, I, T$$

If the following appear in the input cards?

Card	Cols.	Entry	Card	Cols.	Entry
1	1–50	blank	2	1–10	blank
	51–55	3.456		11	4
	56–80	blank		12–78	blank
				79–80	4

6. Referring to Exercise 5, suppose that the entry in cols. 51–55 of the first card were 34567. What values would be assigned to the variables?

7. Referring again to Exercise 5, suppose that the entry in cols. 11–13 of the second card were 4.1. What values would be assigned to the variables?

2.6 STOP AND END STATEMENTS

The last statement in a WATFIV program must be an END statement. It tells the compiler that no more WATFIV instructions follow. It is *nonexecutable* — that is, it does not cause a series of corresponding machine-language statements. The STOP statement, which *is* executable, signals that the execution of the algorithm has been completed. The computer must be told when execution of a procedure is complete. The STOP statement results in a series of machine-language instructions that will return control of the computer to the operating system when execution of the program has been completed.

The last statement in the sample program is an END statement, of course, and the next-to-last statement is a STOP statement. STOP statements also may appear elsewhere in a WATFIV program, not necessarily as the next-to-last statement.

2.7 LOOPING AND BRANCHING

The procedure used to add three numbers is simple indeed. It could be described as: input, sum, output, stop. Real problems, however, are more complicated than this. Suppose, for example, that we wish to calculate the sum of many numbers; we could add them together one at a time, much as is done on a desk calculator. In finding a sum on a desk calculator, we enter the next number in the keyboard, and add it to the sum of the preceding numbers. This result is stored in an accumulator that we can see (usually in a display found at the top of the calculator). Much the same thing can be done in a computer. The process of adding eight numbers by repeatedly adding the next number to the preceding sum could be described as follows: input, sum, input, sum, input, sum, input, sum, input, sum, input, sum, input, sum, input, sum. Or we could say, more succinctly: input, sum, repeated eight times—thereby indicating that a certain procedure is to be repeated over and over again. The use of a loop can implement this procedure by going back to an earlier statement repeatedly, until the loop has been executed the correct number of times. Then we would go ahead to a new statement. This means that we must check, after each execution of the loop has been completed, to be sure that we proceed to the next correct step. We do not necessarily execute all statements in the order in which they appear: it may be necessary to branch to a different step at certain points in the program. *Branching* is another important basic technique.

2.8 A SECOND EXAMPLE

These additional techniques now put us in a position to work on a more difficult problem: adding ten numbers. A WATFIV program for this purpose, and the input submitted and output obtained, are given in Figure 2.3. It is assumed that the numbers are punched one to a card. In this program we read them in one at a time into the same storage location, B. We then add B to the previous sum, S. Note that the first thing we do, just as with the desk calculator, is to clear the accumulator before using it. Otherwise we might not be adding the first number to zero. Note also the use of a *counter*, N, that is cleared to zero. This counter will keep track of the number of values that have been accumulated. The *initialization* of storage locations is another important technique in writing computer programs, as is the use of counters.

Input

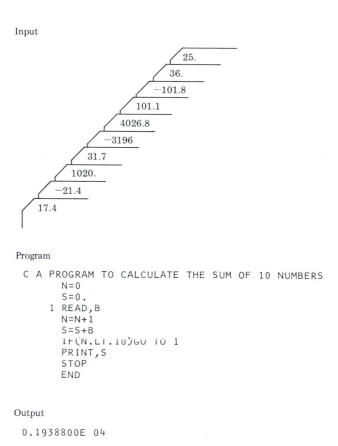

Program

```
C A PROGRAM TO CALCULATE THE SUM OF 10 NUMBERS
      N=0
      S=0.
    1 READ,B
      N=N+1
      S=S+B
      IF(N.LT.10)GO TO 1
      PRINT,S
      STOP
      END
```

Output

```
0.1938800E 04
```

Fig. 2.3   A program to calculate the sum of ten numbers and the input submitted, as well as output obtained in a run of this program

The program proceeds by reading in the next number, B. B is added into S, using the statement S = S + B. This should clarify the distinction between an assignment and an equation. We are not saying that S is equal to S + B; this is nonsense if B is not zero. We are saying that the previous contents of the storage location that we call S should be added to the contents of the storage location that we call B, and this new result put in S. This is just what happens in the desk calculator, if we call the number in the keyboard B and the number in the accumulator S. The counter that keeps track of the number of values we have added into the accumulator then is incremented by 1 in N = N + 1. (Many desk calculators also contain a dial that does this.) Then comes the IF statement—a critical conditional statement that permits branching back to statement 1 if the counter, N, is less than ten.

2.9 THE IF STATEMENT

The IF statement that appears in Figure 2.3 is performed by first making the comparison that appears in the parentheses. The comparison either will be true or false. If the comparison is true (in this case if N is indeed less than ten), the program executes the command following the parentheses. Here, the program branches to statement 1. If the expression is false (if N is greater than or equal to ten), the program goes directly to the next statement. If N is not less than ten, the PRINT statement is executed. In executing this program, N should never exceed ten.

Some other comparisons that can be made, and the code used to indicate them in the IF statement, are:

equal to	.EQ.
greater than	.GT.
less than or equal to	.LE.
greater than or equal to	.GE.

Frequently, as in the example, the command that appears after the comparison is a GO TO. That is, the IF statement looks like:

IF (comparison) GO TO statement-number

Now we can see how this statement is used to implement a loop. As long as the comparison is true, the loop is executed by branching back to its beginning (the statement labeled 1 in the example). As soon as the comparison is false, we exit from the loop by going on to the next statement, PRINT, S in the example.

2.10 SOME EXTENSIONS AND GENERALIZATIONS

The techniques and examples introduced in this chapter will be discussed further, both to illustrate how more general programs can be written with just a few minor extensions, and to introduce some important concepts and techniques of implementing programs.

Consider first the program in Figure 2.3. Suppose that we wished to add an unspecified number of values. Analysis of this program indicates that the element which controls the number of values that are added is the constant 10 appearing in the IF statement. If we changed 10 to some other number, we could add a different number of values. We could develop a more useful and more general result by permitting the first number in the input to indicate how many values are to be added. The set of values to be added would begin with the second number in the input. To do this, we would modify the program given in Figure 2.3, as shown in Figure 2.4. Note that the first two

Input

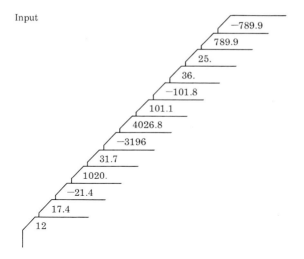

Program

```
C A PROGRAM TO CALCULATE THE SUM OF A VARIABLE NUMBER OF VALUES
      N-0
      S=0.
      READ,K
    1 READ,B
      N=N+1
      S=S+B
      IF(N.LT.K)GO TO 1
      PRINT,S,K
      STOP
      END
```

Output

```
0.1938800E 04                12
```

Fig. 2.4 A program to calculate the sum of a variable number of values and the input submitted, as well as output obtained in a run of this program

statements are unchanged; we still must initialize N and S. There are now two READ statements. (This is because the sequence of statements in the loop must not include the statement READ, K that determines how many times the loop will be executed.) The number of values is read in once; then we proceed to the loop. In developing algorithms for use in computer programs, we must always distinguish those steps that are to be executed inside loops from those that are to be executed outside loops.

Since the first card of the input deck contains the number of values, we must execute this READ first. From this point, the program is much like the one given in Figure 2.3. The only other modification is that we now compare N to K rather than to 10, and we output the number of values along with the answer, the sum. The input submitted and output obtained in a run of this program also are given in Figure 2.4.

So far, we have been discussing programs as if no one makes mistakes. However, now and then someone may mispunch the number of values he wishes to add. He might say that there are 90 values when actually there are 89 or 91 values, or he might say that there are zero values to add. There are programming techniques to check for errors of this kind as well as other kinds. To illustrate, we will indicate how one kind of error could be detected and how an appropriate response could be made.

The error we will check for is whether K, the number of values, is less than or equal to zero. An IF statement is used. The program is terminated without any output if an erroneous value for K is detected. This program is given in Figure 2.5, along with an input set. Note that since zero was input for K, no output was obtained.

Input

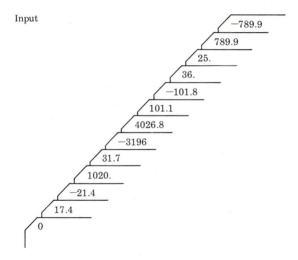

Program

```
C A PROGRAM TO CALCULATE THE SUM OF A VARIABLE NUMBER OF VALUES
C THAT CHECKS FOR NONPOSITIVE ENTRIES FOR THE NUMBER OF VALUES
      N=0
      S=0.
      READ,K
      IF(K.LE.0)GO TO 2
    1 READ,B
      N=N+1
      S=S+B
      IF(N.LT.K)GO TO 1
      PRINT,S,K
    2 STOP
      END
```

Fig. 2.5 A program to calculate the sum of a variable number of values that checks for nonpositive entries for the number of values (no output is obtained with the input shown)

2.11 DEBUGGING A WATFIV PROGRAM

Errors frequently appear in a program despite the programmer's best efforts. This is true of programs written by experienced programmers as well as those written by beginners. Trying to correct these errors is called *debugging* the program.

Two types of errors can occur: syntactical and logical. *Syntactical* errors happen when a rule of the language is broken—a comma is omitted, a word is misspelled, an expression cannot be evaluated, a statement begins in column 6 rather than column 7. Even though the error does not permit the program to be executed, compilation is attempted and the program itself is printed out along with messages that attempt to describe the error. A printout of this type is called a *program listing*. Figure 2.6 contains a listing of an erroneous version of the program to compute the sum of three numbers. Note how the compiler diagnosed the four errors that were present and what messages were printed. In this case, the error messages, especially the first and last ones, may be misleading, and expert assistance may be required to help interpret them. Unfortunately, this is true of many error messages that are generated by compilers.

Logical errors result from a mistake in the procedure. Each statement is syntactically valid, but either the answer is not obtained, or a wrong answer is obtained, because the procedure is not correct. Logical errors are more difficult to detect than syntactical ones. We will postpone the discussion of debugging logical errors until after we have discussed algorithmic formulation and the WATFIV language more fully in later chapters. The programs that are given in this chapter and that the student will be required to write in the exercises are all simple enough that logical errors probably will not occur—or, if they do occur, they should be easy to correct.

2.12 SETTING UP A WATFIV RUN

Ordinarily, a user will supply only a program and two control cards, called a $JOB and $ENTRY card when submitting a WATFIV program. These control cards are messages to the WATFIV compiler. The $JOB card precedes the program and the $ENTRY card is placed immediately after the END card. Since the layout of these control cards, especially the $JOB card, varies from one installation to another, they will not be described here.

The programs submitted by the users are combined with other WATFIV programs after input data and other control cards have been added. In some instances, the user may provide the input data

```
      C  AN ERRONEOUS PROGRAM TO CALCULATE THE SUM OF  3  NUMBERS
   1        READ A,B,C
:::::ERROR::::  VARIABLE FORMAT MUST BE AN ARRAY NAME.  A      IS INVALID
   2        S=A++C
:::::ERROR::::  ILLEGAL SEQUENCE OF OPERATORS IN EXPRESSION
   3        PINT,S
:::::ERROR::::  UNDECODEABLE STATEMENT
   4        STOP
            END
:::::ERROR::::  INVALID CHARACTER(S) ARE CONCATENATED WITH THE FORTRAN KEYWORD.  UNEXPECTED ND
:::WARNING:::  MISSING END STATEMENT;END STATEMENT GENERATED
```

Fig. 2.6   An erroneous program to calculate the sum of three numbers

as well. Figure 2.7 contains a description of the layout of the deck that is submitted when using WATFIV.

Exercises

8. Write a program that adds five numbers without using a loop.

9. Modify the program written in answer to Exercise 8, so that it uses a loop and branching in calculating the sum of five numbers. Assume that each number appears on a single card on input.

10. Write a program to calculate the difference between two numbers. Assume that the numbers appear on the same card and that the second number is to be subtracted from the first.

11. Modify the program written in answer to Exercise 10 to calculate and output the difference between K pairs of numbers. Assume that K is input on the first card. This means that you will have to introduce a loop.

12. Modify the program written in answer to Exercise 11 to detect values of K that are not positive and to end the program if such values are found.

13. Suppose that the value for K in either the summing or the differencing programs was 50, and that the number of values that were input was 49 or 51. How might we detect errors of this kind? (Hint: Consider adding a card to the end of the input deck which would contain a value that could never appear in the input; for example, -9999999. This value would mark the end of the data. After reading this card, we always would know precisely how many numbers actually were input.)

14. Write a program that calculates and prints out the mean (average) of a set of values (see Section 1.4). Assume that the number of values, say K, appears in the first input card, and that the values themselves appear one to a card thereafter.

15. Write a program that calculates and prints out the gross pay for each of a set of employees, given the hourly rate and number of hours worked for each employee (see Section 1.4). Assume that the number of employees to be processed is given in the first card, and that the hourly rate and number of hours worked by each employee, in that order, appears on each successive card. (Note that we did not identify the employees in either the input or the output.)

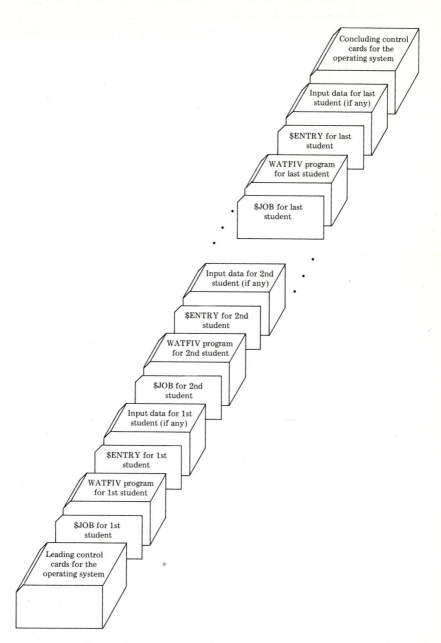

Fig. 2.7 Layout of a typical input deck for WATFIV jobs

16. Modify the program written in solving Exercise 15 so that it also accepts as input an identification number (assume that it is an integer number) for each employee, and outputs this number along with the employee's gross pay. Assume that the identification number is entered first in each input card after the first card, followed by the hourly rate and number of hours worked. Print out the identification number and then the gross pay for each employee.

Chapter 3

The Elements of PL/I
Programming and PL/C

3.1 INTRODUCTION

In the late 1950s and early 1960s, many users of IBM computers wished to have a more general-purpose language than FORTRAN. PL/I was developed by the IBM Corporation to satisfy this demand. The specifications were established, for the most part, by a committee made up of members of SHARE, user's group for medium- and large-sized IBM computers.

The language described here is a version of PL/I called PL/C, which was developed at Cornell University especially for use at colleges and universities. PL/C produces error messages that are more easily understood than those produced by PL/I, and it also can process jobs more quickly than PL/I.

There are a few facilities in PL/C that are unavailable in PL/I (just as there are facilities in PL/I that are unavailable in PL/C). However, since we will not discuss any of these facilities in this book, the PL/C capabilities and programs that we will discuss include PL/I capabilities and programs as well.

This chapter emphasizes the elementary features of PL/C that permit programming to be initiated with a minimum of explanation and practice. A more complete description of PL/C will be given in Chapter 10. A reader interested in learning more about PL/I should refer to the Annotated Supplementary Bibliography at the end of that chapter.

3.2 A PL/C PROGRAM

At this point, we introduce a PL/C program to expose the reader to its general appearance and to discuss some general considerations in

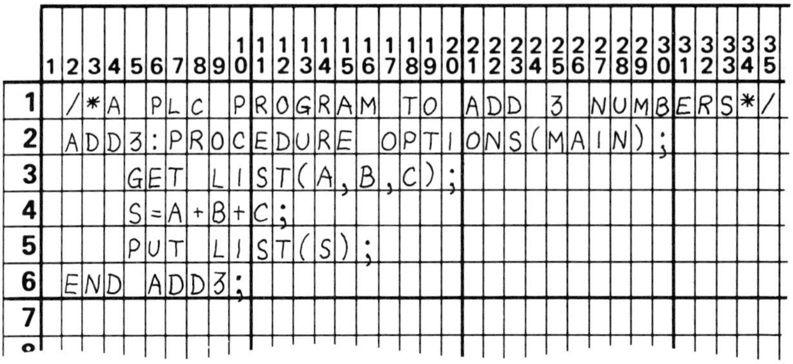

Fig. 3.1 A program to calculate the sum of three numbers

writing these programs. The program, given in Figure 3.1, is designed to find the sum of three numbers that are input.*

PL/C programs are made up of a sequence of commands called *statements*. Statements are ended with a semicolon and ordinarily are punched on cards for input to the computer. The statements should be entered in columns 2 through 72 of the card; several statements may be entered on the same card. An approach which makes the program more readable is to punch only one statement on each card, to begin the first and last statements in column 2, and to indent the other statements a few columns.

The first entry in the program in Figure 3.1 — the one that begins with a slash and an asterisk and ends with an asterisk and a slash — is not a PL/C statement. It is a comment that is ignored by the PL/C compiler and so does not affect the execution of the program. Comments should be used to annotate programs and to make them more readable. They may be entered anywhere in a PL/C program, but they must be enclosed, as in Figure 3.1, within slashes and asterisks.

PL/C statements may be labeled by entering the label first, then a colon, and then the statement. The *label* can be any sequence of letters and numbers; however, the first character must be a letter. It is desirable to limit the length of a label to seven characters.

Only the first statement in the program in Figure 3.1 is labeled. A PL/C program should begin with a labeled PROCEDURE OPTIONS(MAIN); statement. The label in this first statement can be

---

*Cross-references to Chapters 2 and 4 will be avoided in the text of this chapter because Chapters 2, 3, and 4 should be studied independently. However, those who are interested in contrasting the languages will find that the chapters are developed in a similar way. For example, a WATFIV program to solve the same problem can be found in Section 2.2, and a BASIC program to solve this problem can be found in Section 4.2.

thought of as the name for the program; thus, the program in Figure 3.1 is called ADD3. The program concludes with an END ADD3 statement. This indicates that the procedure labeled ADD3 — that is, the program — has concluded. PL/C programs are structured as follows:

```
label:PROCEDURE OPTIONS(MAIN);
    statement;
    statement;
        .

        .

        .

    statement;
    END label;
```

3.3 INTEGERS, FLOATING-POINT NUMBERS, AND VARIABLES

The values that will be processed by the programs described in this chapter either will be integers (the natural numbers) or floating-point numbers (numbers that have a decimal point and may have fractional portions).* These two kinds of numbers are stored in different ways inside computers and are processed using different machine-language instructions. In general, integers, if appropriate, should be used, since they can be manipulated more efficiently.

The following are examples of integer and floating-point numbers:

integer: 1, 674, −214, 0, −44, 476234

floating-point: 3.1416, −.002634, 1726489.88

A name, called a *variable*, is used in a program to denote the contents of a storage location. Values always must be assigned to variables, one way or another, in a program. In fact, from one point of view, the principal objective of a program is to change the values stored for the various variables until the appropriate values have been stored in the appropriate places. These values then are output to the user.

A variable can be used to denote either integers or floating-point numbers. A final choice must be made: if a certain variable will be assigned integer values sometimes and floating-point values at other times, it should be considered floating-point. This is because integers

---

*Actually, this is a simplification of the elaborate characterizations that are possible for the values processed by PL/C programs. We shall see in Chapter 10 that floating-point numbers in PL/C are defined somewhat differently. However, since the simplification will help us to write PL/C programs quickly and more easily, it will be retained in this chapter. Other simplifications also will be introduced for the same reason.

can be represented using floating-point notation, but floating-point numbers cannot be represented using integer notation.

A variable can be denoted in PL/C by a letter. The letters A through H and O through Z can be used for variables that denote floating-point numbers, and the letters I through N for variables that denote integer numbers. Thus, for example, X or A or S could be used to denote floating-point variables, and K or I or N to denote integer variables.

A number that is used just as it appears in the program and is fixed at that value throughout the execution of the program is called a *constant*. Commas should not appear in constants; thus, 3,247 and −1,684,101.04 are not valid constants.

Exercises

1. Which of the following are valid constants?

    0.3   −143   7,243.08   6.07945   −831,816

2. Which of the following are integer variables and which are floating-point variables?

    E L Q J M U H

3.4 THE ASSIGNMENT STATEMENT

One way to assign a value to a variable is to use the assignment statement. The variable appears first, then an equal sign (=), and then something that looks like a mathematical formula. This mathematical formula is called an *arithmetic expression*. It contains variables, constants, and operations. It also may contain parentheses in order to correctly fix the order in which the operations are to be executed. For example:

$$Y=(A+B)/C$$

assigns a new value to Y. It is obtained by adding the value stored in location A to that stored in B, and then dividing the result by C. We see, then, that expressions in parentheses are evaluated first, and that + is used to denote addition and / to denote division. Also, − is used to denote subtraction and ∗ to denote multiplication. These are the only operations which we will use in this chapter.

In the absence of parentheses, division and multiplication are executed before addition and subtraction. Otherwise, operations are carried out from left to right in the order in which they appear in the expression. The numbers under the operations in the expression below indicate the order in which these operations are executed.

$$A+B/C*D-E$$
$$3\ \ 1\ \ 2\ \ 4$$

If, for example, A = 1.5, B = 5., C = 2.5, D = 2., and E = 5.3, then the result of evaluating this expression would be:

5. divided by 2.5 times 2. plus 1.5 minus 5.3, which is 0.2.

If a value is being assigned to an integer variable, the fractional portion of the result is discarded, or *truncated*. This means that the statement I = 8/3; assigns a value of 2 to I.

3.5 INPUT AND OUTPUT

Values also can be assigned to variables by reading them from a card in the input. If a variable is to be assigned values by the user of the program, that process must occur via input. Thus, for example, if we write a program that can calculate and output the sum of any three numbers provided by a user, the three numbers must be input. Similarly, the results of interest to a program user must be output. In the example, the sum—which first must be calculated using an assignment statement (refer to Figure 3.1)—should be output.

Input is requested by a GET LIST statement (see Figure 3.1) and output by a PUT LIST statement.

A GET LIST statement looks like

GET LIST(A,B,C);

It begins with the words GET LIST, which are followed by a list of the variables to which values are being assigned via input. The list is enclosed in parentheses and the variables are separated by commas. The GET LIST statement will attempt to assign values to all the variables in the list. If there are three variables in the list and only one number on the first input card, then the second input card will be read, and so on until all the variables have been assigned values. Figure 3.2

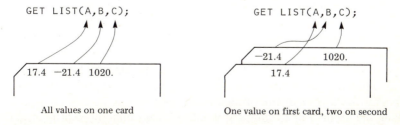

All values on one card   One value on first card, two on second

Fig. 3.2 How values are assigned to variables using the GET LIST statement

illustrates what happens if all three values appear on one input card, or if just one value appears on the first card and two appear on the second card. The values punched on the input cards should be separated by blank spaces or commas.

A PUT LIST statement (see Figure 3.1) looks very much like a GET LIST statement. For example,

PUT LIST(S);

The statement begins with the words PUT LIST, which are followed by a list of the variables from which values are to be printed. The result obtained in executing the program given in Figure 3.1, using the input in Figure 3.2, is:

1.01600E+03

The computer prints a floating-point number in a standard way when the PUT LIST statement is used. This way of representing a number is called *scientific notation*. The letter E stands for the exponent, and the number following E is the power of ten by which the digits preceding E should be multiplied to determine the equivalent, familiar form for the value. Therefore, 1.01600E+03 means 1.016 multiplied by 10^3, which equals 1016.

A couple of rules should be kept in mind when using the GET LIST and PUT LIST statements:

1. Numbers which are input to integer variables will be truncated; thus, for example, if we used:

GET LIST (I,J,K);

to read in the first card in Figure 3.2, the value stored for I would be 17, for J would be −21, and for K, 1020.

2. The printed output generated by PUT LIST statements is laid out in a standard way, which may vary from installation to installation. At the computer center where the programs in this book were executed, the first value was printed in the first 24 print positions of the first line of output; the next in the following 24 print positions; and so on. (Six values are printed on each line.) An example of the result obtained when two values are printed out is given in Figure 3.4.

The input and output discussed in this section are called *format-free I/O*. As the term *format-free* implies, the programmer cannot specify the layout of the printed result, nor can he be flexible in handling the input. For example, it would be very difficult to print a table like that given in Figure 1.1 for the amortization problem.

Exercises

3. If R = 3.8, S = 1.9, and T = 4.4, what value will be assigned to X when the following statement is executed?

$$X=T+R/S$$

4. If I = 2, J = 4, and K = 5, what value will be assigned to M when the following statement is executed?

$$M=I*K/J$$

5. What values will be assigned to I, R, and T by the statement:

$$GET\ LIST\ (R,I,T);$$

if the following appear in the input card?

Card	Cols.	Entry	Card	Cols.	Entry
1	1–50	blank	2	1–10	blank
	51–55	3.456		11	4
	56–80	blank		12–78	blank
				79–80	4

6. Referring to Exercise 5, suppose that the entry in cols. 51–55 of the first card were 34567. What values would be assigned to the variables?

7. Referring again to Exercise 5, suppose that the entry in cols. 11–13 of the second card were 4.1. What values would be assigned to the variables?

3.6 LOOPING AND BRANCHING

The procedure used to add three numbers is simple indeed. It could be described as: input, sum, output, stop. Real problems, however, are more complicated than this. Suppose, for example, that we wish to calculate the sum of many numbers; we could add them together one at a time, much as is done on a desk calculator. In finding a sum on a desk calculator, we enter the next number in the keyboard and add it to the sum of the preceding numbers. This result is stored in an accumulator that we can see – usually in a display found at the top of the calculator. Much the same thing can be done in a computer. The process of adding eight numbers by repeatedly adding the next number to the preceding sum could be described as follows: input, sum, input, sum, input, sum, input, sum, input, sum, input, sum, input, sum. Or we could say, more succinctly: input, sum, repeated eight times – thereby indicating that a certain procedure is to be repeated over and over again. The use of a loop can implement this procedure by going back to an earlier statement repeatedly, until the loop has been executed the correct number of times. Then we would go ahead to a new statement. This means that we must check after each execution of the loop has been completed to be sure that we proceed to the next correct step. We do not necessarily execute all statements in the order in which they appear. It may be necessary to branch to a different step at certain points in the program. *Branching* is another important basic technique.

3.7 A SECOND EXAMPLE

With these additional techniques, we are now in a position to work on a more difficult problem: adding ten numbers. A PL/C program for this purpose, and the input submitted and output obtained in a run of the program, are given in Figure 3.3. It is assumed that the numbers are punched one to a card. In this program, we read them in one at a time into the same storage location, B. We then add B to the previous sum, S. Note that the first thing we do, just as with the desk calculator, is to clear the accumulator before using it so that we add the first number to zero. Note also the use of a *counter*, N, that is cleared to zero. This counter will keep track of the number of values that have been

Input

```
17.4  −21.4  1020.  31.7  −3196  4026.8  101.1  −101.8  36.  25.
```

Program

```
/*A PROGRAM TO CALCULATE THE SUM OF 10 NUMBERS*/
ADD10:PROCEDURE OPTIONS(MAIN);
        N=0;
        S=0;
    ONE:GET LIST(B);
        N=N+1;
        S=S+B;
        IF N<10 THEN GO TO ONE;
        PUT LIST(S);
END ADD10;
```

Output

```
1.93879E+03
```

Fig. 3.3 A program to calculate the sum of ten numbers and the input submitted and output obtained in a run of this program

accumulated. The *initialization* of storage locations is another important technique in writing computer programs, as is the use of counters.

The program proceeds by reading in the next number, B. B is added into S, using the statement $S = S + B$;. This should clarify the distinction between an assignment and an equation. We are not saying that S is equal to $S + B$; this is nonsense if B is not zero. We are saying that the contents of the storage location we call S should be added to the contents of the storage location we call B, and this new result put in S. This is just what happens in the desk calculator example, if we call the number in the keyboard B and the number in the accumulator S. The counter that keeps track of the number of values we have added into the accumulator then is incremented by 1 in $N = N + 1$;. (Many desk calculators contain a dial that does this too.) Then comes the IF statement—a conditional statement that permits branching back to the statement labeled ONE if N is less than ten, or proceeding if N is greater than or equal to ten. Note that we punched the statement labeled ONE on the card so that the label clearly stands out to the left of the statement when the program is printed. This improves the program's readability but does not affect the way it is executed.

3.8 THE IF STATEMENT

A PL/C IF statement always contains two important words: *IF* and *THEN*. The phrase that appears between the words IF and THEN is evaluated as either true or false. (In the example, this phrase is $N < 10$; either N is less than 10 or it isn't.) This phrase frequently contains mathematical symbols which are used in comparing numbers. Some of these symbols are:

$<$	less than	$>=$	greater than or equal to
$>$	greater than	$<=$	less than or equal to
$=$	equal to	$\neg=$	not equal to

The phrase after the word THEN is a statement that is to be executed if the first phrase is true. However, if the first phrase is false, the following statement in the program is executed instead. Frequently, as in the example, the statement that appears after the word THEN is a GO TO. Thus, the IF statement looks like:

IF comparison THEN GO TO label;

Now we can see how this statement is used to implement a loop. As long as the comparison is true, the loop is executed by branching back to its beginning (the statement labeled ONE in the example). As soon as the comparison is false, we exit from the loop by going on to the next statement—PUT LIST(S,K);—as illustrated by the example.

3.9   SOME EXTENSIONS AND GENERALIZATIONS

The techniques and examples introduced in this chapter will be discussed further, both to illustrate how more general programs can be written with just a few minor extensions of these programs, and to introduce some important concepts and techniques of implementing programs.

Consider first the program in Figure 3.3. Suppose that we wished to add an unspecified number of values. Analysis of this program indicates that the element which controls the number of values that are added is the constant 10, appearing in the IF statement. If we changed 10 to some other number, we could add a different number of values. We could develop a more useful and more general result by permitting the first number in the input to indicate how many values are to be added. The set of values to be added would begin with the second number in the input. To do this, we would modify the program given in Figure 3.3, as shown in Figure 3.4. Note that the first two statements are unchanged; we still must initialize N and S. There are now

Input

```
 12  17.4  −21.4  1020.  31.7  −3196  4026.8  101.1  −101.8  36.  25.  789.9  −789.9
```

Program

```
/*A PROGRAM TO CALCULATE THE SUM OF A VARIABLE NUMBER OF VALUES*/
ADDVAR:PROCEDURE OPTIONS(MAIN);
        N=0;
        S=0;
        GET LIST(K);
  ONE :GET LIST(B);
        N=N+1;
        S=S+B;
        IF N<K THEN GO TO ONE;
        PUT LIST(S,K);
END ADDVAR;
```

Output

```
1.93879E+03
```

Fig. 3.4   A program to calculate the sum of a variable number of values and the input submitted and output obtained in a run of this program

two GET LIST statements, because the sequence of statements in the loop must not include the statement GET LIST (K); that determines how many times the loop will be executed. The number of values is read in once; then we proceed to the loop. In developing algorithms for use in computer programs, we must always distinguish those steps that are to be executed inside loops from those that are to be executed outside loops.

Since the first card of the input deck contains the number of values, we must execute this GET LIST first. From this point, the program is much like the one given in Figure 3.3. The only other modification is that we now compare N to K rather than to 10, and we output the number of values along with the answer, the sum. The input submitted and the output obtained in a run of this program also are given in Figure 3.4.

So far, we have been discussing programs as if no one makes mistakes. However, now and then someone may mispunch the number of values he wishes to add. He might say that there are 90 values, when actually there are 89 or 91 values; or he might say that there are zero values to add. There are programming techniques to check for this as well as other kinds of errors. To illustrate, we will indicate how one kind of error could be detected and how an appropriate response could be made.

The error we will check for, using an IF, is whether K, the number of values, is less than or equal to zero. The program, terminated without any output if an erroneous value for K is detected, is given in Figure 3.5. No output is obtained with the input shown.

Input

```
0  17.4  −21.4  1020.  31.7  −3196  4026.8  101.1  −101.8  36.  25.  789.9  −789.9
```

Program

```
/*ADD A VARIABLE NUMBER OF VALUES WITH AN INPUT CHECK*/
ADDVCH:PROCEDURE OPTIONS(MAIN);
      N=0;
      S=0;
      GET LIST(K);
      IF K<1 THEN GO TO TWO;
  ONE:GET LIST(B);
      N=N+1;
      S=S+B;
      IF N<K THEN GO TO ONE;
      PUT LIST(S,K);
TWO:END ADDVCH;
```

Fig. 3.5 A program to calculate the sum of a variable number of values that checks one of the input values (no output is obtained with the input shown)

3.10 DEBUGGING A PL/C PROGRAM

Errors frequently appear in a program despite the programmer's best efforts. This is true of programs written by experienced programmers as well as those written by beginners. The effort directed toward correcting these errors is called *debugging* the program.

Two types of errors can occur: syntactical and logical. *Syntactical* errors happen when a rule of the language is broken—a semicolon is omitted, a word is misspelled, an expression cannot be evaluated. The PL/C compiler usually will give messages that are quite effective in locating the error and helping to correct it. The computer even may attempt to correct the error and execute the program. Even though the error does not permit the program to be executed, compilation is attempted and the program itself is printed out, along with messages that attempt to describe the error. A printout of this kind is called a *program listing*. Figure 3.6 contains a listing of an erroneous version of the program to compute the sum of three numbers. Note how the compiler diagnosed the four errors that were present and what messages were printed. Two of the errors were correctly diagnosed and the statements were corrected (the omission of parentheses in the GET LIST statement and the omission of the semicolon in the END statement). One error was not detected (the omission of the variable, B, in the assignment statement), and a second error was incorrectly diagnosed (the misspelling of LIST in the PUT LIST statement). The error messages associated with this last error are misleading. Although PL/C usually diagnoses errors better than other languages do, expert assistance can sometimes be helpful in interpreting PL/C error messages.

Logical errors result from a mistake in the procedure. Each statement is syntactically valid, but either the answer is not obtained, or a wrong answer is obtained, because the procedure is not correct. Logical errors are more difficult to detect than syntactical ones. We will postpone our discussion of debugging logical errors until after we have discussed algorithmic formulation and the PL/C language more fully in later chapters. The programs which are given in this chapter, and which the student will be required to write in the exercises, are all simple enough that logical errors probably will not occur— or, if they do, they should be easy to correct.

Exercises

8. Write a program that adds five numbers without using a loop.

9. Modify the program written in answer to Exercise 8, so that it uses a loop and branching in calculating the sum of five numbers.

```
              /:: AN ERRONEOUS PROGRAM TO SUM THREE NUMBERS::/
              ADD3:PROCEDURE OPTIONS(MAIN);
         1    1          GET LIST A,B,C;
IN      2    1    ERROR  SY02 MISSING (
IN      2         ERROR  SY04 MISSING )
PL/C USES                GET LIST (A,B,C);

IN      3    1           S=A+ +C;
IN      4    1           PUT LIT(S);
IN      4         ERROR  SY22 IMPROPER I/O PHRASE
IN      4         ERROR  SY02 MISSING (
        4         ERROR  SY04 MISSING )
PL/C USES                PUT LIST (LIT (S));

IN      5    1           END ADD3
IN      5         ERROR  SY08 MISSING SEMI-COLON
PL/C USES                END ADD3;


IN STMT    4   ERROR  SM50 NAME NEVER DECLARED, OR AMBIGUOUSLY QUALIFIED
IN STMT    4   ERROR  SM4E $UFIXVAR HAS TOO MANY SUBSCRIPTS. SUBSCRIPT LIST DELETED
PL/C USES             PUT LIST ($UFIXVAR);
DECLARED IN BLOCK                    0
```

Fig. 3.6 An erroneous PL/C program to calculate the sum of three numbers

10. Write a program to calculate the difference between two numbers. Assume that the numbers appear on the same card and that the second number is to be subtracted from the first.

11. Modify the program written in answer to Exercise 10 to calculate and output the difference between K pairs of numbers. Assume that K is the first number that is input. This means that you will have to introduce a loop.

12. Modify the program written in answer to Exercise 11 to detect values of K that are not positive and end the program if such values are found.

13. Suppose that the value for K in either the summing or the differencing programs was 50, and that the number of values that were input was 49 or 51. How might we detect errors of this kind? Hint: Consider adding a value to the end of the set of input data that could never appear in the input; for example, -9999999. This value would mark the end of the data. After reading this value, we always would know precisely how many numbers were actually input.

14. Write a program that calculates and prints out the mean (average) of a set of values (see Section 1.4). Assume that the number of values, say K, appears first.

15. Write a program that calculates and prints out the gross pay for each set of employees, given the hourly rate and number of hours worked for each employee (see Section 1.4). Assume that the number of employees to be processed is given first, and that the hourly rate and number of hours worked by each employee, in that order, appear in pairs thereafter. (Note that we did not identify the employees in either the input or the output.)

16. Modify the program written in solving Exercise 15 so that it also accepts as input an identification number (assume that it is an integer number) for each employee, and outputs this number along with the employee's gross pay. Assume that the first value input is the number of employees, and that the indentification number is entered first for each employee. This means that the input for each employee is the indentification number, followed by the hourly rate and number of hours worked. Print out the identification number and then the gross pay for each employee.

Chapter 4

The Elements of
BASIC Programming

4.1 INTRODUCTION

More and more users of computer systems are gaining access to them through remote terminals. A remote terminal lets the user receive an immediate response from the computer. For example, a program can be written one statement at a time. Each statement is diagnosed as it is input, and errors are indicated immediately after the statement has been input. This is called *interpretive* computer programming. Another advantage is that the user can converse with the computer. For example, a program may be written in such a way that the user is asked to supply each set of input, as the program requires it, by means of an English-language request addressed to him at the terminal. This *interactive* use of the computer became available in the 1960s, when time-shared computers came into use.

One of the first time-shared computer systems, developed by the Rand Corporation in California, used a programming language called JOSS (Johnniac Open Shop System). Not long afterward, a time-sharing system was developed at Dartmouth College that incorporated another programming language called BASIC (Beginner's All-Purpose Symbolic Instruction Code). BASIC, modeled after JOSS but containing some new features, was the first programming language widely used at remote terminals. Today, it is still among the most widely used.

BASIC is discussed in this chapter to accommodate the user who has access to remote terminals.* The scope of the discussion is limited

---

*BASIC programs can be submitted and processed at the computer center. Since we are discussing BASIC to accommodate users at a remote terminal, we will assume that access to the computer is from a remote terminal.

```
   1 REMARKS A PROGRAM TO ADD 3 NUMBERS
  10 INPUT A,B,C
  20 LET S=A+B+C
  30 PRINT S
9999 END
```

Fig. 4.1 A program to calculate the sum of three numbers

to those features that are especially important when programming from a remote terminal. This chapter emphasizes the elementary features of BASIC that permit programming to be initiated with a minimum of explanation and practice. A more complete description of BASIC will be given in Chapter 11. The reader interested in learning more about BASIC should refer to the annotated supplementary bibliography at the end of that chapter.

4.2 A BASIC PROGRAM

A BASIC program is introduced at this point to show the reader its general appearance and to discuss some general considerations in writing these programs. The program, given in Figure 4.1, is designed to find the sum of three numbers that are input.*

Each line of the BASIC program is numbered. Statement numbers are limited to four digits on some versions and five digits on others. We will limit our statement numbers to four digits. These numbers are both necessary and useful. They permit the programmer to correct a single line in the program by simply re-entering that line. The new line automatically replaces the old one. For example, if statement number 10 had been typed:

```
10 INPT A,B,C
```

it could be corrected immediately by going to the next line and typing:

```
10 INPUT A,B,C
```

The new version of the statement replaces the old one, and the error is corrected immediately.

---

*Cross references to Chapters 2 and 3 will be avoided in the text of this chapter because Chapters 2, 3, and 4 should be studied independently. However, those who are interested in contrasting the languages will find that the chapters are developed in a similar way. For example, a WATFIV program to solve the same problem can be found in Section 2.2, and a PL/C program to solve this problem can be found in Section 3.2.

Statement numbers, rather than the order in which the statements are typed, determine the order in which the statements are executed. For example, if we type:

```
10 INPUT A,B,C
```

and then on the next line type:

```
2 LET S=A+B+C
```

statement 2 would be executed before statement 10.

Remarks may be entered in a BASIC program on any line of the program. A line number is entered, followed immediately by the word REMARKS (sometimes abbreviated REM). Since the compiler then ignores the remainder of the line, the programmer may annotate his program in any fashion to improve its readability.

Ordinarily, a single command, or statement, is placed on each line. There is no provision for continuing a statement from one line to the next. If a teletypewriter is used, a line is limited to 75 characters. The collection of commands — the program — is executed in the order of the statement numbers. Because it frequently is necessary to insert statements in BASIC programs, the statements should be numbered in multiples of ten: 10, then 20, then 30, and so on. This facilitates the insertion of additional statements.

In a BASIC program, an END statement can be used to terminate the execution of the program; it marks the last statement in all BASIC programs. Since statement numbers are limited to four digits, and since the END statement should be the last statement, it is a good idea to number the END 9999.

4.3 CONSTANTS AND VARIABLES

The operands in BASIC statements are either constants or variables. We can denote BASIC *constants* merely by entering their values in the program. A constant is used just as it appears in the program, and is fixed at that value throughout the execution of the program. Commas should not appear in constants; thus, although 3, 214.21 is not a valid constant, 3214.21 is a valid form of this same constant. *Scientific notation* can be used to represent a constant. In this notation, a number is represented in two parts, called a *mantissa* and an *exponent*. For example:

$$.321421E4$$

The exponent appears to the right of the letter E. It is the power of ten by which the number preceding E, the mantissa, should be multiplied to determine the equivalent familiar form. Therefore .321421E4 means .321421 multiplied by 10^4, which equals 3214.21.

A name, called a *variable,* is used in a program to denote the contents of a storage location. Values always must be assigned to variables, one way or another, in a program. In fact, from one point of view, the principal objective of a program is to change the values stored for the various variables until the appropriate values have been stored in the appropriate places. These values then are output to the user. A variable can be denoted in BASIC using a letter.

Exercises

1. Which of the following are valid and which are invalid constants in BASIC?

21.74	−88	1.2E3	6,871	2,417,110.21
−6.44E5	27	−6,321.1E1	444	21.111

2. What are the equivalent, familiar values of the following numbers which are expressed in scientific notation?

    $$1.2E3 \qquad -6.44E5 \qquad 244.24E-3$$

4.4   THE ASSIGNMENT OR LET STATEMENT

One of the ways to assign a value to a variable is to use the assignment, or LET, statement. The statement number appears first; then the word LET. This is followed by the variable to which a value is being assigned; then an equal sign; and then something that looks like a mathematical formula. This mathematical formula may contain variables, constants, and operations. It may also contain parentheses to correctly fix the order in which the operations are to be executed. For example:

```
10 LET Y=(A+B)/C
```

assigns a new value to Y. It is obtained by adding the value stored in location A to that stored in B, and then dividing the result by C. We see, then, that expressions in parentheses are executed first and that + is used to denote addition and / to denote division. Also, − is used to denote subtraction and * to denote multiplication. These are the only operations which we will use in this chapter.

In the absence of parentheses, division and multiplication are executed before addition and subtraction. Otherwise, operations are carried out from left to right in the order in which they appear in the expression. The numbers below the operations in the following expression indicate the order in which these operations are executed.

$$A+B/C*D-E$$
$$3\ \ 1\ \ 2\ \ 4$$

If, for example, $A = 1.5$, $B = 5$, $C = 2.5$, $D = 2$, and $E = 5.3$, then the result of evaluating this expression would be:

5. divided by 2.5 times 2. plus 1.5 minus 5.3, which is 0.2.

4.5   INPUT AND OUTPUT

A program user sitting at a terminal can assign values to variables via input. Thus, for example, if we write a program that can calculate and output the sum of any three numbers provided by a user, the three numbers must be input. Similarly, the results of interest to a program user must be output. In the example, the sum should be output. Of course, it first must be calculated using a LET statement (refer to Figure 4.1).

Input is requested using an INPUT statement, and output using a PRINT statement. Once it has been executed, the INPUT statement makes the computer print a question mark at the terminal, thus asking the user for input. At the terminal, the user enters a sequence of constants, separated by commas or blank spaces, that are to be assigned one by one to the variables in the INPUT statement. For example, the execution of the statement

```
10 INPUT A,B,C
```

will cause a question mark to be printed at the terminal. The user then should enter the three constants which are assigned to A, B, and C. This is illustrated in Figure 4.2.

As indicated in the example, the form of the INPUT statement is simple—a statement number, the word INPUT, and then a list of variables to which values are being assigned from the terminal.

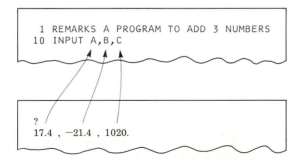

Fig. 4.2   How values are assigned to variables using the INPUT statement

The PRINT statement looks like the INPUT statement and functions in a similar way. For example, when the statement

```
30 PRINT S
```

is executed, the value currently stored in S is printed at the terminal.

The form is: a statement number, the word PRINT, and a list of variables, separated by commas, from which values are to be output. The output obtained in executing the program in Figure 4.1, using the input in Figure 4.2, is:

```
1016
```

There are several rules which should be kept in mind when using the INPUT and PRINT statements.

1. Numbers that are to be input should not be continued from one line to the next at the terminal.

2. Each PRINT statement will result in one line of printed output (unless there are too many values to fit on a single line). If results are to be printed on different lines, then distinct PRINT statements should be used. Referring to Figure 4.1, for example, if we intend to print the input values on the next line after the one on which the sum is printed, we must have the following successive PRINT statements in the program:

```
30 PRINT S
31 PRINT A,B,C
```

If we had used the statement

```
30 PRINT S,A,B,C
```

then the sum and the values would all be printed on the same line.

The input and output discussed in this section is called *format-free I/O*. As the term *format-free* implies, the programmer cannot specify the layout of the printed result, nor can he be flexible in handling the input. For example, it would be very difficult to print a table such as that given in Figure 1.1 for the amortization problem. Also, we cannot annotate the request for input to give the user a clue as to which values are being sought. We shall see how these things are done when we discuss BASIC in greater depth in Chapter 11.

Exercises

3. If R = 3.8, S = 1.9, and T = 4.4, what value will be assigned to X when the following statement is executed?

```
40 LET X=T+R/S
```

4. What values will be assigned to I, R, and T by this statement?

   60 INPUT R, I,T

   if the following is entered at the terminal?

   ?3.456,4,4.

5. Referring to Exercise 4, what assignments are made if the following are entered?

   ? 3456.E-3,.4E1,40.E-1

4.6 LOOPING AND BRANCHING

The procedure used to add three numbers is simple: input, sum, output, stop. However, real problems are more complicated than this. Suppose, for example, that we wish to calculate the sum of many numbers; we could add them together one at a time, much as is done on a desk calculator. In finding a sum on a desk calculator, we enter the next number in the keyboard, and add it to the sum of the preceding numbers. This result is stored in an accumulator that we can see, usually in a display found at the top of the calculator. A computer can do the same thing. The process of adding eight numbers by repeatedly adding the next number to the preceding sum could be described as: input, sum, input, sum, input, sum, input, sum, input, sum, input, sum, input, sum, input, sum. Or we could say, more succinctly: input, sum, repeated eight times—thereby indicating that a certain procedure is to be repeated over and over again. The use of a loop can implement this procedure by going back to an earlier statement repeatedly, until the loop has been executed the correct number of times. Then we would go ahead to a new statement. This means that we must check after each execution of the loop is completed to be sure that we proceed to the next correct step. We do not necessarily execute all statements in the order in which they appear: it may be necessary to branch to a different step at certain points in the program. *Branching* is another important basic technique.

4.7 A SECOND EXAMPLE

These additional techniques put us in a position to work on a more difficult problem: adding ten numbers. A BASIC program for this purpose, and the output obtained in a run of the program, are given in Figure 4.3. It is assumed that the numbers are entered one at a time. Each time the statement

   30 INPUT B

```
   1 REM A PROGRAM TO ADD 10 NUMBERS
  10 LET N=0
  20 LET S=0
  30 INPUT B
  40 LET N=N+1
  50 LET S=S+B
  60 IF N<10 THEN 30
  70 PRINT S
9999 END

   ?
  17.4
   ?
  -21.4
   ?
  1020.
   ?
  31.7
   ?
  -3196.
   ?
  4026.8
   ?
  101.1
   ?
  -101.8
   ?
  36.
   ?
  25.
    1938.80
```

Fig. 4.3 A BASIC program to calculate the sum of ten numbers and the entries made and output obtained in a run of this program

is executed, a question mark appears at the terminal. A number then should be entered, which is assigned to B. We then add B to the previous sum, S. Note that the first thing we do, just as with the desk calculator, is to clear the accumulator before using it so that we add the first number to zero. Note also the use of a *counter*, N, that is cleared to zero. This counter will keep track of the number of values that have been accumulated. The *initialization* of storage locations is another important technique in writing computer programs, as is the use of counters.

The program proceeds by reading in the next number, B. B is added into S, using the statement 50 LET S = S + B. This should clarify the distinction between an assignment and an equation. We are not saying that S is equal to S + B; this is nonsense if B is not zero. We are saying that the contents of the storage location we call S should be added to the contents of the storage location we call B, and this new result put in S. This is just what happens in the desk calculator example, if we call the number in the keyboard B and the number in the accumulator S. The counter that keeps track of the number of values we have added into the accumulator then is incremented by 1 in 40 LET N = N + 1. (Many desk calculators contain a dial that does this too.) Then comes the IF statement — a conditional statement that permits branching back to statement 30 if N is less than ten, or going ahead to the next statement (statement 70), if N is not less than ten.

4.8 THE IF STATEMENT

A BASIC IF statement always contains two important words: *IF* and *THEN*. The phrase that appears between the words IF and THEN is evaluated as either true or false. (In the example, this phrase is N < 10; either N is less than 10 or it isn't.) This phrase frequently contains mathematical symbols which are used in comparing numbers. Some of the symbols are:

< less than	>= greater than or equal to
> greater than	<= less than or equal to
= equal to	<> not equal to

A statement number is given after the word THEN. This statement is to be executed next if the phrase is true. If it is false, the next statement in the program is executed instead. In general, then, the form of the IF statement is:

number IF comparison THEN number

Now we can see how this statement is used to implement a loop. As long as the comparison is true, the loop is executed by branching back to its beginning (statement 30 in the example). As soon as the comparison is false, we exit from the loop by going on to the next statement (statement 70 in the example).

4.9 SOME EXTENSIONS AND GENERALIZATIONS

The techniques and examples introduced in this chapter will be discussed further, both to illustrate how these programs can be minimally extended to write more general programs, and to introduce some important concepts and techniques of implementing programs.

Consider first the program in Figure 4.3. Suppose that we wished to add an unspecified number of values. Analysis of this program indicates that the element which controls the number of values that are added is the constant 10, appearing in the IF statement. If we changed 10 to some other number, we could add a different number of values.

We could develop a more useful and more general result by permitting the first number in the input to indicate how many values are to be added. The set of values to be added would begin with the second number in the input. To do this, we would modify the program given in Figure 4.3, as shown in Figure 4.4. Note that the first two statements are unchanged; we must still initialize N and S. There now are two INPUT statements, because we do not want to read in the number of values inside the sequence of statements that is executed repeatedly, i.e., inside the loop. The number of values is read in once; then we proceed to the loop. In developing algorithms for use in computer programs, we must always distinguish those steps that are to be executed inside the loops from those that are to be executed outside.

Since the first number to be input is the number of values to be summed, we must execute this input first. From this point on, the pro-

```
   1 REM A PROGRAM TO SUM A VARIABLE NUMBER OF VALUES
  10 LET N=0
  20 LET S=0
  25 INPUT K
  30 INPUT B
  40 LET N=N+1
  50 LET S=S+B
  60 IF N<K THEN 30
  70 PRINT S,K
9999 END

   ?
  12
   ?
  17.4
   ?
  -21.4
   ?
  1020.
   ?
  31.7
   ?
  -3196.
   ?
  4026.8
   ?
  101.1
   ?
  -101.8
   ?
  36.
   ?
  25
   ?
  789.9
   ?
  -789.9
   ?
  1938.80          12
```

Fig. 4.4 A BASIC program to calculate the sum of a variable number of values and the entries made and output obtained in a run of this program

```
   1 REM VARIABLE SUM WITH A CHECK
  10 LET N=0
  20 LET S=0
  25 INPUT K
  28 IF K<1 THEN 9999
  30 INPUT B
  40 LET N=N+1
  50 LET S=S+B
  60 IF N<K THEN 30
  70 PRINT S,K
9999 END
```

Fig. 4.5   A BASIC program to calculate the sum of a variable number of values that checks the first number that is input

gram is much like the one given in Figure 4.3. The only other difference is that we now compare N to K rather than to 10, and we output the number of values along with the answer, the sum. The entries made in running this program and the output that was obtained are also given in Figure 4.4.

So far, we have been discussing programs as if no one makes mistakes. However, now and then someone may mispunch the number of values that he wishes to add. He might say that there are 90 values when actually there are 89 or 91 values; or he might say that there are zero values to add. There are programming techniques to check for errors of this kind as well as other kinds. To illustrate, we will indicate how one kind of error could be detected and how an appropriate response could be made.

The error we will check for is whether K, the number of values, is less than or equal to zero. An IF statement is used. The program, terminated without any output if an erroneous value for K is detected, is given in Figure 4.5.

4.10   DEBUGGING A BASIC PROGRAM

Errors frequently appear in a program despite the programmer's best efforts, whether he is experienced or a beginner. Trying to correct these errors is called *debugging* the program.

Two types of errors can occur: syntactical and logical. *Syntactical* errors occur when a rule of the language is broken—if, for example, an expression cannot be evaluated. The BASIC compiler usually will give messages that are quite effective in locating the error and helping to correct it. Even though the error does not permit the program to be executed, the statement is analyzed and a message is printed that attempts to tell the programmer what went wrong. Figure 4.6 contains a listing of an erroneous version of the program to compute the sum of

```
 1 REMARKS AN ERRONEOUS PROGRAM TO ADD 3 NUMBERS
10 INPUT A,B,C
20 LET S=A++C
30 PRINT S
   END
```

```
::::DIAGNOSTICS::::
LINE  0004  STATEMENT  00020  BFR01 NO OPERATOR AFTER STATEMENT NUMBER
LINE  0006  STATEMENT  00000  BFR44 NO STATEMENT NUMBER
LINE  0006  STATEMENT  4040   BFR52 NO END STATEMENT
```

Fig. 4.6   An erroneous BASIC program and the error messages obtained in attempting to run it

three numbers. Note how the compiler diagnosed the two errors and the messages that were printed. These messages were printed at the terminal immediately after the program was entered. They can be corrected at the terminal by entering the statement number for the incorrect statement, followed by the correct statement.

Logical errors result from a mistake in the procedure. Each statement is syntactically valid, but either the answer is not obtained, or a wrong answer is obtained, because the procedure is not correct. Logical errors are more difficult to detect than syntactical ones. We will postpone the discussion of debugging logical errors until after we have discussed algorithmic formulation and the BASIC language more fully in later chapters. The programs which are given in this chapter, and which the student will be required to write in the exercises, are all simple enough that logical errors probably will not occur—or, if they do, they should be easy to correct.

4.11   PROGRAMMING FROM A TERMINAL—
       SOME PRELIMINARY CONSIDERATIONS

To write a program at a terminal, a user must gain access to the computer system. Several steps ordinarily are required, which include:

1. Dialing up the computer system;
2. Gaining access to the computer by means of an appropriate user identification code, and
3. Gaining access to the BASIC compiler.

Most remote terminals are connected to the computer system via telephone lines. In order to gain access to the computer system, a user ordinarily dials a telephone number which connects him with that system. When the proper signal is heard, he returns the receiver to its cradle. At that point, the terminal is connected to the computer system.

In some installations, this may not be necessary; the terminal may be linked directly to the computer either by means of a dedicated telephone line that is always connected to the computer system, or by means of connections that are made independently of the telephone system.

Once the telephone has been connected to a computer system, the user will be asked by the computer system either to provide a code or to initiate communication with the computer by inputting a code of some kind. This code serves to identify the user. In reality, it serves two purposes: 1) it permits the computer to determine whether a person requesting services is a legitimate user of the facility; and, 2) if this is a legitimate user, it permits the computer to assign time and charges to that user. Each user has his own appropriate code, whether it is a number followed by the user's name, or something more elaborate.

Once the user has gained access to the system and been identified as a legitimate user of the facility, he must tell the computer which capability he wants of those available to the terminal user (in this chapter, that capability usually will be the BASIC compiler), and send the computer a message to that effect.

Figure 4.7 contains an example of a sequence of inputs and outputs obtained in accessing the BASIC compiler available on a UNIVAC 1108 computer system. The sequence is annotated, and the notes indicate whether the user or the computer initiated the messages.

We already have noted that it is sometimes possible for the user to write one instruction at a time and have the computer analyze that instruction before proceeding to the next one. The programmer then can correct the instructions as he goes along. This is especially convenient, and many users prefer to work in this mode. However, it does tend to be expensive. There is usually a charge for *connect time* — that is, for the time during which the terminal is connected to the computer system. When we write a program one line at a time and make corrections one line at a time as errors are uncovered by the computer, a great deal of connect time is used. If the terminal accepts either punched paper tape or punched cards as input, then the user may find it considerably more economical to punch up a program off-line and read it in to the remote terminal all at once. This is especially true for those users who do not key quickly and accurately.

Anyone who does a great deal of programming in BASIC should get a copy of the appropriate manual for his installation. These manuals vary from installation to installation, depending on the version of BASIC in use. It is virtually mandatory for a programmer to have a manual handy when he is writing a BASIC program at a terminal, particularly if the terminal is connected to the computer while the program is being written. It is not advisable to waste time at a terminal trying to guess the correct form of a BASIC statement.

Typed Message at the Terminal	Originator of Message	Comments
AUCRMAL	User	Makes initial contact after dialing up
UNIVAC 1108 TIME/SHARING EXEC VERS 2720143L08	Computer	Computer identifies system in operation
@RUN,/TPC A8900X,211DD	User	User code
DATE:04067 TIME:130109	Computer	Computer supplies date and time
@BASIC A✕P1//WKEY,	User	BASIC compiler is accessed

Fig. 4.7 Annotated sequence of access statements

Exercises

6. Write a program that adds five numbers without using a loop.

7. Modify the program written in answer to Exercise 6 so that it uses a loop and branching in calculating the sum of five numbers. Assume that the numbers are input one at a time.

8. Write a program to calculate the difference between two numbers. Assume that the two numbers are input at the same time and that the second number is to be subtracted from the first.

9. Modify the program written in answer to Exercise 8 to calculate and output the difference between K pairs of numbers. Assume that K is input first. This means that you must introduce a loop.

10. Modify the program written in answer to Exercise 9 to detect values of K that are not positive and to end the program if such values are found.

11. Suppose that the value for K in either the summing or the differencing programs was 50, and that the number of values that were input was 49 or 51. How might we detect errors of this kind? (Hint: Consider adding a value to the end of the input that never would actually occur; for example, −9999999. This value would mark the end of the data. After it was input, we would always know precisely how many valid sets of values were input.)

12. Write a BASIC program that calculates and prints out the mean of a set of values (see Section 1.4). Assume that the number of values, say K, appears first and that the values themselves are input one at a time thereafter.

13. Write a program that calculates and prints out the gross pay for each of a set of employees, given the hourly rate and number of hours worked for each employee (see Section 1.4). Assume that the number of employees to be processed is given first and that the hourly rate and number of hours worked by each employee is given, in that order, in pairs thereafter. (Note that we did not identify the employees in either the input or the output.)

14. Modify the program written to solve Exercise 13 so that it also accepts as input an identification number (assume that it is an integer number) for each employee, and outputs this number along with the employee's gross pay. Assume that the identification number is entered first in each set of input after the first one (the number of employees is still input first). That is, after the number of employees has been entered, values will be input

three at a time. The first of these three numbers is the employee identification number; the second, the hourly rate for that employee; and the third, the number of hours worked by that employee. Print out the identification number and then the gross pay for each employee.

Part 2

Fundamental Tools

Now that we have an elementary view of programming, it should be clear that solving a problem with the aid of a computer cannot be undertaken lightly. A foundation is needed to cope with realistic, complex problems. This foundation includes how information is represented in a computer and what computers are like, as well as how to develop and implement procedures on a computer. These subjects are discussed in Part 2.

The representation and structuring of information on a computer is discussed in Chapter 5. Some of the sections in Chapter 5 are marked with an asterisk to indicate that they may be especially difficult, because some actual computer representations of information were described in a precise manner. These sections can be skipped without sacrificing the continuity of the discussion.

The components of a computer are described in Chapter 6, with an emphasis on their appearance, capabilities, and function. Algorithms and flowcharts are discussed in Chapters 7 and 8. These chapters include several asterisked sections which, once again, can be skipped if necessary.

At the conclusion of Part 2, the reader should understand how procedures for solving problems are developed, recorded, and transmitted to the computer. However, until he has mastered at least one of the languages for transmitting these procedures, he will not be able to do all of these things himself. Mastering a programming language is the main objective of Part 3 of this book, in which three languages are discussed.

Chapter 5

The Representation and Structuring of Information

5.1 INTRODUCTION

The raw materials with which a computer works are sets of digits that represent characters to be processed by the computer. This chapter discusses certain conventions used in representing, processing, and structuring these sets of digits.

Everything that is processed by a computer is encoded. Codes are used to represent both numeric and non-numeric information. A variety of codes for representing alphabetic or numeric, or—more succinctly, *alphanumeric* information—have been developed. Different computers represent information in different ways. Digital Equipment Corporation's PDP computers, for example, use the ASCII code to represent alphanumeric information, whereas the IBM 360/370 family of computers use the EBCDIC code. (Both these codes will be described later in this chapter.) As long as a selected code is rigidly maintained, and as long as the devices (such as the card reader and printer that interpret inputs and prepare outputs) translate this code into the appropriate characters, the nature of the code used in the computer need not be mastered by humans.

5.2 POSITIONAL NOTATION—BASES 10, 2, 8, AND 16

The number 437 is understood to mean:

4 hundreds plus 3 tens plus 7 ones.

Multipliers of successive powers of ten are used to represent a number. That is, multipliers of $10^0 =$ one, $10^1 =$ ten, $10^2 =$ one hundred, and so on are used. The multipliers can be of any of the ten digits 0 through 9; thus, $437 = 4 \times 10^2 + 3 \times 10^1 + 7 \times 10^0$.

Numbers also can be represented by multipliers of powers of some other number. *Binary representation* uses powers of 2, and allows only two multipliers: 0 and 1. This means that we can represent a number by means of only two symbols.

How would the number 437 be represented in binary notation? A table of powers of 2 (Appendix A) shows us that the greatest power of 2 that is less than or equal to 437 is $2^8 = 256$. Thus we would use 1 times 2^8. Since $437 - 256 = 181$, we must now represent 181 using smaller powers of 2. From the table, we see that $2^7 = 128$; thus, 1 times 2^7 also would be used. Since $181 - 128 = 53$, $2^6 = 64$, and $2^5 = 32$, we see that 0 times 2^6 and 1 times 2^5 would be used. By this means, we arrive at the representation:

$$
\begin{array}{rr}
1 \text{ times } 2^8 = & 256 \\
1 \text{ times } 2^7 = & 128 \\
0 \text{ times } 2^6 = & 0 \\
1 \text{ times } 2^5 = & 32 \\
1 \text{ times } 2^4 = & 16 \\
0 \text{ times } 2^3 = & 0 \\
1 \text{ times } 2^2 = & 4 \\
0 \text{ times } 2 = & 0 \\
1 \text{ times } 2^0 = & \underline{1} \\
& 437
\end{array}
$$

or

$$110110101_2 = 1 \times 2^8 + 1 \times 2^7 + 0 \times 2^6 + 1 \times 2^5 + 1 \times 2^4 + 0 \times 2^3$$
$$+ 1 \times 2^2 + 0 \times 2^1 + 1 \times 2^0.$$

The subscript 2 is used to indicate that this is a binary representation. We shall omit the subscript for decimal numbers. Note that 437 and 110110101_2 are two different ways of representing the *same* quantity.

The number that is raised to the power and appears as a subscript in the representation is called the *base* or *radix* of the representation. Decimal numbers use base 10; binary numbers use base 2. We also shall use numbers which have a base of 8, called *octal representation*, and those which have a base of 16, called *hexadecimal representation*. The multipliers in octal representation are the digits 0 through 7. Hexadecimal notation uses 16 multipliers, the first 10 of which are the digits 0 through 9. Symbols other than these digits are used for multipliers that are equal to 10 through 15. A common practice is to use the letters of the alphabet — A for 10, B for 11 and so on, up to F for 15. This notation shows us that:

$$437_{10} = 6 \times 8^2 + 6 \times 8^1 + 5 \times 8^0$$
$$= 665_8, \text{ and}$$
$$437_{10} = 1 \times 16^2 + 11 \times 16^1 + 5 \times 16^0$$
$$= 1B5_{16}$$

Conversion from base 2, 8, or 16 to base 10 is made directly from the definition of the representation. Thus, for example

$$724_8 = 7 \times 8^2 + 2 \times 8^1 + 4 \times 8^0 = 468$$
$$1D4_{16} = 1 \times 16^2 + 13 \times 16^1 + 4 \times 16^0 = 468$$

This means that just as 437, 665_8, $1B5_{16}$, and 110110101_2 all represent the same quantity, so too do 468, 724_8 and $1D4_{16}$.

Since the digits of a numeral represent multipliers of different powers of a base, depending upon their position in the number, we use the term *positional notation* to describe this convention for representing values. The two digits, 0 and 1, used for representing binary numbers are called *binary digits* (or *bits* in ordinary usage).

5.3 CONVERSION AMONG BASES 2, 8, AND 16

Numbers written in base 8 or 16 can be converted to base 2 directly, digit by digit, with the aid of the table given in Figure 5.1. For example, to convert $1B5_{16}$, we note from the table that $1_{16} = 0001_2$, $B_{16} = 1011_2$, and $5_{16} = 0101_2$. The answer, therefore, is 000110110101_2, and if we delete the superfluous leading zeros, we get 110110101_2. Similarly, to convert 762_8, we note that $7_8 = 111_2$, $6_8 = 110_2$, and $2_8 = 010_2$. This means that $762_8 = 111110010_2$. Each octal digit is always represented by three bits, and each hexadecimal digit by four bits.

We also may use this table to convert from base 2 to either base 8 or base 16 by grouping the numbers written in base 2 from the right

Base 16	Base 2	Base 16	Base 2	Base 8	Base 2
0	0000	8	1000	0	000
1	0001	9	1001	1	001
2	0010	A	1010	2	010
3	0011	B	1011	3	011
4	0100	C	1100	4	100
5	0101	D	1101	5	101
6	0110	E	1110	6	110
7	0111	F	1111	7	111

Fig. 5.1 Tables for converting between bases two and sixteen and bases two and eight

in sets of three bits (to convert to octal), or four bits (to convert to hexadecimal). If we wished to write 11001_2 in octal, we would note that:

$$\underbrace{11}_{3} \quad \underbrace{001}_{1}$$

to get 31_8. Similarly, if we wished to write 11001_2 in hexadecimal, we get:

$$\underbrace{1}_{1} \quad \underbrace{1001}_{9}$$

to get 19_{16}.

*5.4 FLOATING-POINT REPRESENTATION

Scientific notation, which uses a mantissa and an exponent, was introduced in Chapters 2–4. The computer can store numbers in this two-part form, called *floating-point representation.** In most computers, it is conventional for the mantissas of floating-point numbers to have no leading zeros and for the decimal point to be immediately to the left of the first digit in the mantissa. This is called the *normalized form*. For example, the normalized form of 186,000 is given uniquely by: .186E6.

In general, normalization proceeds by first rewriting the mantissa so that it has no leading zeros and is less than 1, and then adjusting the exponent appropriately. For example, .000274 should be written as .274 times the appropriate power of 10. This power is -3; therefore, the normalized form of .000274 is .274E-3.

Since zero cannot be represented in a computer in this normalized way, it must have a special representation. Each computer has a specific representation. For example, in the IBM System/360 and 370, a floating-point zero is represented by a mantissa and exponent which are both zero.

Exercises

1. Write 273 in bases 2, 8, and 16.

2. Write 10111_2 in bases 10, 8, and 16.

---

*We did not define floating-point numbers this way in Chapters 2–4. In Chapter 2 we said that 21.7 is a floating-point constant in WATFIV. In fact, a constant written in this way in a WATFIV program will be stored in floating-point format in the computer. The user need not write it as .217E2 in order to get the computer to do so.

3. Write $2F_{16}$ in base 10 and base 2.

*4. Write each of the following in normalized floating-point form:

$$.00421 \qquad 893.24 \qquad .0021E\text{-}4$$

5. Write a program in one of the languages that you learned in Part I which accepts a two-digit number written in base 8 as input, and outputs the corresponding base-10 number. Assume that the input will be the two digits — the multiplier of 8^1 first and the multiplier of 8^0 next. Assume also that these two digits will be separated by commas in the input.

6. Write a program in one of the languages that you learned in Part I that accepts a single, base-10 digit as input, and that outputs the equivalent number in base-2. The output should be a sequence of bits, each on a separate line. The first bit should be the multiplier of 2^3, the second of 2^2, and so on.

5.5 EBCDIC AND ASCII

Alphameric is another term used for the alphabetic characters, decimal digits, and special characters which the computer can store and process. This term is synonymous with the term *alphanumeric* introduced in Section 5.1. Alphameric data usually are represented in a computer in either of two forms. One form, called the *American standard code for information interchange* (ASCII) is a modification of a code that previously was used with other machines, especially teletypewriters. The other form is called the *extended binary coded decimal interchange code* (EBCDIC). In this section we will present a summary of some EBCDIC and ASCII representations and briefly discuss the way EBCDIC is implemented on the IBM System/360 and 370 computers.

The 360/370 family of computers groups its representations into sets of eight bits. Each set of eight bits is called a *byte*. The EBCDIC code uses a byte to represent a character. The code for the principal alphabetic, numeric, and special characters is summarized in Figure 5.2, which shows representations for 89 characters. Since eight bits can be used to represent $2^8 = 256$ characters, other characters can be represented. For the most part, these are special control characters associated with the operation of input and output devices. Also, there are unused combinations among the 256 possibilities.

The ASCII code is the American National Standard seven-bit code. It is also called USASCII; the US stands for United States and indicates that it has been standardized. Since it is a seven-bit code, it is possible to represent $2^7 = 128$ distinct characters using it. The code is

Letter	Code	Letter	Code	Special Character	Code	Numeric Character	Code
A	11000001	a	10000001	¢	01001010	0	11110000
B	11000010	b	10000010	.	01001011	1	11110001
C	11000011	c	10000011	<	01001100	2	11110010
D	11000100	d	10000100	(	01001101	3	11110011
E	11000101	e	10000101	+	01001110	4	11110100
F	11000110	f	10000110	|	01001111	5	11110101
G	11000111	g	10000111	&	01010000	6	11110110
H	11001000	h	10001000			7	11110111
I	11001001	i	10001001	!	01011010	8	11111000
				$	01011011	9	11111001
J	11010001	j	10010001	*	01011100		
K	11010010	k	10010010	)	01011101		
L	11010011	l	10010011	;	01011110		
M	11010100	m	10010100	¬	01011111		
N	11010101	n	10010101	–	01100000		
O	11010110	o	10010110	/	01100001		
P	11010111	p	10010111				
Q	11011000	q	10011000	,	01101011		
R	11011001	r	10011001	%	01101100		
				—	01101101		
S	11100010	s	10100010	>	01101110		
T	11100011	t	10100011	?	01101111		
U	11100100	u	10100100				
V	11100101	v	10100101	:	01111010		
W	11100110	w	10100110	#	01111011		
X	11100111	x	10100111	@	01111100		
Y	11101000	y	10101000	'	01111101		
Z	11101001	z	10101001	=	01111110		
				"	01111111		
				space	01000000		

Fig. 5.2 The EBCDIC for eighty-nine selected characters

summarized in Figure 5.3, in which codes for 85 of the 89 characters (shown in Figure 5.2) are presented. As with EBCDIC, the other characters are largely associated with input and output operations.

*5.6 INTEGER REPRESENTATION IN A COMPUTER

Thus far, we have talked about the representation of alphabetic characters, decimal digits, and special characters in the computer. In carrying out computations, the operands usually are numbers rather than characters. Both integer numbers and floating-point numbers can be represented in a computer. We shall discuss the representation of integer numbers in terms of the IBM 360/370 computer family. In the next section, we will discuss the representation of floating-point numbers in terms of the Burroughs B-6500 computer.

Integer numbers are represented in the 360 and 370 computer family by means of either two or four bytes. In either form, the left-most bit contains the sign and the remaining bits are used for the

Letter	Code	Letter	Code	Special Character	Code	Numeric Character	Code
A	1000001	a	1100001	!	0100001	0	0110000
B	1000010	b	1100010	"	0100010	1	0110001
C	1000011	c	1100011	#	0100011	2	0110010
D	1000100	d	1100100	$	0100100	3	0110011
E	1000101	e	1100101	%	0100101	4	0110100
F	1000110	f	1100110	&	0100110	5	0110101
G	1000111	g	1100111	'	0100111	6	0110110
H	1001000	h	1101000	(	0101000	7	0110111
I	1001001	i	1101001	)	0101001	8	0111000
J	1001010	j	1101010	*	0101010	9	0111001
K	1001011	k	1101011	+	0101011		
L	1001100	l	1101100	,	0101100		
M	1001101	m	1101101	−	0101101		
N	1001110	n	1101110	.	0101110		
O	1001111	o	1101111	/	0101111		
P	1010000	p	1110000				
Q	1010001	q	1110001	:	0111010		
R	1010010	r	1110010	;	0111011		
S	1010011	s	1110011	<	0111100		
T	1010100	t	1110100	=	0111101		
U	1010101	u	1110101	>	0111110		
V	1010110	v	1110110	?	0111111		
W	1010111	w	1110111	@	1000000		
X	1011000	x	1111000	space	0100000		
Y	1011001	y	1111001				
Z	1011010	z	1111010				

Fig. 5.3 The ASCII code for eighty-five selected characters

number. The sign bit is 1 if the number is negative, and 0 if it is positive. For example, the number 6 is represented in two bytes, as follows:

$$0000000000000110$$

The use of two bytes means that $2^{15} - 1 = 32767$ is the largest integer that can be represented using this form. If four bytes are used, then $2^{31} - 1 = 2147483647$ is the largest integer that can be represented. In each case the largest integer is represented by a zero bit (positive), followed by a sequence of either 15 or 31 ones. Just as a sequence of nines in base 10 represents a power of 10 less 1, a sequence of ones in base 2 represents a power of 2 less 1.

Negative integers are represented by subtracting the number from 2^{15} for the shorter form, or 2^{31} for the longer form. For example, -6 is represented in two bytes, as follows:

$$1111111111111010$$

This is obtained by subtracting 6 from 2^{15}, i.e.:

$$1000000000000000$$
$$- \ 000000000000110$$
$$\overline{111111111111010}$$

This result has 15 bits; and, because −6 is a negative number, a leading 1 bit must be added, resulting in the representation given above.

Subtracting a number from a power of a base is called *complementing;* in this case, since the base is 2, we say that negative integers are represented in a twos complement form. Negative numbers are stored as complements to facilitate subtraction, which is carried out using complements.

*5.7 FLOATING-POINT REPRESENTATION IN A COMPUTER

Recall that a floating-point number consists of two parts: a mantissa and an exponent. Each of these parts of the number may be positive or negative. The exponent is an integer, and the leading digit of the mantissa is not zero if the number is expressed in normalized form. Also, the radix point is immediately to the left of this leading digit for normalized floating-point numbers in most computers.

We will illustrate how floating-point numbers are represented in a computer in terms of a Burroughs B-6500 computer. This Burroughs computer groups its representations into sets of 51-bit words. Floating-point numbers can be represented using one word (single precision) or two words (double precision). Figure 5-4 shows how the 51 bits of a single-precision floating-point number are used. Note that the

Bits	Significance
50-48 (leftmost)	A tag. Single-precision floating-point numbers have a tag of zero, i.e., these three bits are 000.
47	Unused
46	The sign of the number (1 for negative, 0 for positive)
45	The sign of the exponent (1 for negative, 0 for positive)
44-39	The exponent
38-0 (rightmost)	The mantissa

Example: The number $+.000001_8$ would be represented as follows (the octal configuration is shown):

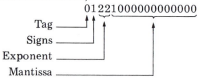

Fig. 5.4 How fifty-one bits are used to represent a single-precision floating-point number in the Burroughs B-6500 computer

mantissa contains 39 bits. This should be thought of as 13 octal digits, because the exponent is assumed to represent a power of eight; that is, the point is moved three bits at a time. Also, although the left-most octal digit is not zero, the leftmost bit may be zero.

The B-6500 deviates from standard normalized form in one respect: the octal point is assumed to be to the right of the least significant digit in the mantissa in single precision (i.e., the mantissa of a single-precision number is an integer). Since six bits are used to represent exponents, the octal exponent may vary from -63 to 63. As a result, the largest number that can be represented in single precision is $(8^{13} - 1) * 8^{63}$. The smallest positive number that can be represented is $1 * 8^{-51}$, since the leading digit of the mantissa cannot be zero, and therefore the smallest mantissa is $1 * 8^{12}$ and $(1 * 8^{12}) * 8^{-63} = 1 * 8^{-51}$.

Consider, for example, 437. We first must convert this to octal to get 665_8. Then it must be written using 13 octal digits (bits 38-0 in the mantissa), with the point to the right to get 6650000000000_8 with an exponent of -10, in order to get a result of 665_8. Note that $-10_{10} = -12_8$.

From Figure 5.4, we see, then, that to represent 437 we have:

Bits	Octal digit	Significance
50–48	0	tag
47	0	unused
46	0	number is positive
45	1	exponent is negative
44–39	12	this is the exponent (-12_8)
38–0	6650000000000	this is the mantissa

Exercises

7. How would 321 be represented in EBCDIC?

8. Indicate how your last name would be represented using the ASCII code. (Capitalize and use punctuation marks wherever it is appropriate.)

9. Write a computer program in the language that you learned in Part I that will translate an integer which uses four bits to the equivalent decimal number. That is, write a program that accepts as input four integer numbers that are all zeros or ones, and produces as output the equivalent decimal number. You may assume that the first bit that is input is the multiplier of 2^3; the second the multiplier of 2^2; the third of 2^1; and the fourth of 2^0. Also assume that the bits that are input will be separated by commas.

*10. Express +94 and −94 as they would appear in the two-byte integer representation in the IBM System/360 and 370 computers.

*11. Express −94 as it would appear in octal notation (for bits 0 through 44) and in bits (for bits 45 through 47) in single-precision floating-point representation in the Burroughs B-6500.

5.8   FIELDS, RECORDS, FILES AND DATA BASES

So far, we have been discussing the representation of single characters and numbers in a computer. However, characters ordinarily are grouped and structured in some way when they are stored.

There are different ways of arranging information. This section goes into a hierarchical structure which is used in business applications. This structure consists of characters, which are grouped into fields, which make up records, which are collected into files, which in turn may be consolidated into a data base. A *field* is the smallest item of information, and is usually made up of a series of adjacent characters. All items of information about a single element in the organization are grouped into *records*, and the complete collection of records used in an application is called a *file* or *data set*. A *data-base* usually contains parts of one or more files referred to for all the information about one whole aspect of the organization.

Consider, for example, information relating to the processing of a payroll. The fields contain such data as employee name, social security number, and rate of pay. Each record contains items of information (i.e., fields) relating to a single employee. The payroll file consists of all records for the employees of the organization. In a small company, the payroll for all employees might be processed in one run; in a large company, the payroll might be processed for only a subset of the employees in one run. For example, there might be separate payroll files for hourly and salaried employees in a large manufacturing company, or separate files for faculty and non-faculty employees at a university. The data base might be all the information about employees that is in any of the files. This would mean that the separate payroll files would be consolidated to make up the employee data base. In addition, information about employees from other sources also would be consolidated into this data base. So, for example, the employee personnel file and health file might be consolidated with the information in the payroll file to make up the employee data base. There could be other data bases relating to areas, such as customers, physical facilities, and company products.

This information could be regarded as organized into a *hierarchical* structure. If the major structure were the whole file or the whole data base, this could be thought of as the first level. If the file were the major structure, there then would be subsets consisting of records (the second level), which in turn might contain subsets consisting of fields (the third level). Fields themselves could be further subdivided. For example, an employee name (a field) could consist of several other fields, such as first name, middle initial, and last name. An example of a specific structure for the records in a payroll file is given in Figure 5.5.

Two operations that frequently occur in processing the information structures discussed in this section are sorts and merges. A *sort* is the ordering of the records in a file, in accordance with the entries in a prescribed field. A *merge* is the combining of two or more files into a single file, in accordance with some specified criteria.

Consider payrolls again. We might sort all records in a payroll file according to social security number, or alphabetically by last name. Sorting is an important computer process which shall be discussed further, along with algorithms and programs.

Another important procedure in file processing is *updating*. We will illustrate file processing and merging by discussing a way to develop payrolls (refer to Figure 5.6). One approach is to construct a master file that contains all information needed to determine the employees' pay (lower left corner of the figure). Such data as regular pay, deductions, accumulated pay and accumulated deductions for the year, and leave information would be contained in this file, along with identification information. The master file would be kept in the computer center. In processing a payroll, a working file also could be used.

Let's assume that we process our payroll weekly; we will call this working file a weekly file. This weekly file would contain specific information on what the employee did in that pay period (i.e., that week), along with identification information. Suppose also that each working file was prepared separately in each plant and transmitted via telephone lines to the computer. The separate files would be sorted and then merged into a single working file for processing. The merged weekly file and the master file would be used to determine which employees should be issued paychecks and, after some processing, how much each should be paid. The output of the payroll run would be a paycheck, a report to the employee, and a revised master file that incorporated the result of this weekly payroll. The updating procedure would be the revision of the master file to reflect the last week's activities.

5.9 ARRAYS

An *array* consists of a collection of homogeneous items that are arranged in some geometric pattern. Thus, we can speak of arrays of

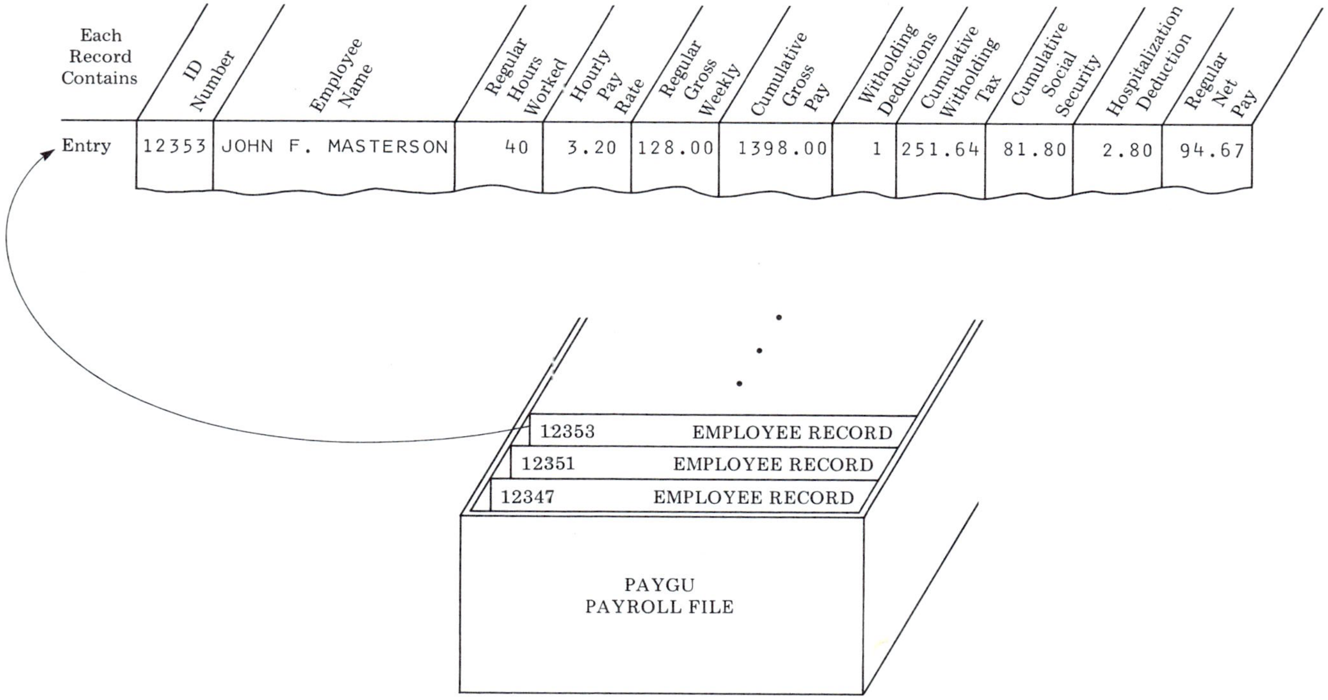

Each Record Contains	ID Number	Employee Name	Regular Hours Worked	Hourly Pay Rate	Regular Gross Weekly Pay	Cumulative Gross Pay	Withholding Deductions	Cumulative Withholding Tax	Cumulative Social Security	Hospitalization Deduction	Regular Net Pay
Entry	12353	JOHN F. MASTERSON	40	3.20	128.00	1398.00	1	251.64	81.80	2.80	94.67

PAYGU
PAYROLL FILE

EMPLOYEE RECORD 12353
EMPLOYEE RECORD 12351
EMPLOYEE RECORD 12347

Fig. 5.5 A payroll file

Input and
Output at
the Center

Computer
Processing
Step

Organizational and Computer Center Activities

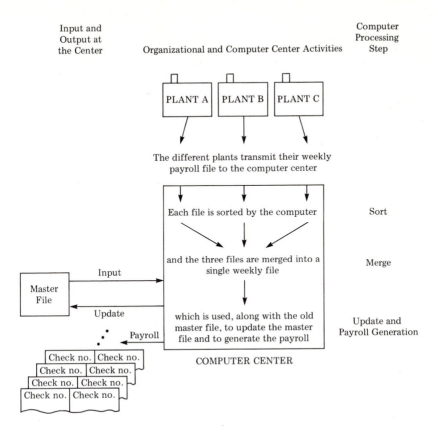

Fig. 5.6   An overview of payroll processing at an organization with three plants

one dimension, two dimensions, three dimensions, and so on. A one-dimensional array is called a *vector* or a *list*. A two-dimensional array is a rectangular arrangement—a *matrix* or a *table*—of items. Two-dimensional arrays frequently are encountered in applications, and special attention will be devoted to them in the following discussion.

Note that we say that an array consists of homogeneous items—that is, the items in the array are identical in nature. For example, the items in the array might all be names, or all be floating-point numbers, or all be decimal numbers. The hierarchical structures discussed in the preceding section were not all homogeneous: some of the elements in these structures were names, some numbers, and some merely collections of characters.

Two examples of rectangular arrays, i.e., matrices, are given below. In one example, the homogeneous items are decimal integers; in the other, they are names. Suppose that we had the following three equations in three unknowns:

$$6x_1 + 22x_2 - 13x_3 = 4$$
$$-3x_1 + 16x_2 - x_3 = 7$$
$$x_1 + 2x_2 - 101x_3 = 26$$

The coefficients of x_1, x_2, and x_3 can be arranged in an array in which the rows are the equations and the columns the variables. Thus, there would be three rows (since there are three equations), and three columns (since there are three variables). The array would be:

6	22	−13
−3	16	−1
1	2	−101

As a second example, consider a manufacturing plant that has three assembly lines. Suppose that there are five stations in each line and that one employee works at each station. We can describe the assignment of employees to stations succintly in the form of an array, in which each row represents an assembly line and each column the corresponding stations in the lines. The matrix might be:

Golden	Harrington	O'Rourke	Thomas	Washington
Smith	Boston	Klein	Dettali	Ferguson
Harris	O'Neil	Siegel	Feurst	Dayton

From this matrix, we see that Golden, Smith, and Harris service the same stations in the different lines, and that O'Rourke works at the third station of the first line.

Individual elements in an array are identified by using the array name, followed by a series of *subscripts*. There is one subscript for each dimension; thus in a one-dimensional array, a single subscript is used to indicate the position of the element in the array. Two subscripts are used in a matrix: the first designates the row and the second, the column.

If, for example, we name the array of coefficients COEF, then the coefficient of x_1 in the third equation above would be called $COEF_{3,1}$. In fact, $COEF_{3,1} = 1$. Similarly, we see that if we call the above array of employee assignments to assembly-line stations WORK, the statement that O'Rourke works at the third station of the first line can be more succinctly expressed by saying: $WORK_{1,3}$ is O'Rourke.

It may be useful to label the rows or columns of a matrix in an unusual way. For example, suppose that the WORK matrix really refers to stations 7 to 11 in the assembly lines. It would be more convenient to use these numbers than the numbers 1 to 5 in the subscript referring to the stations. Now we could say that the $WORK_{1,9}$ is O'Rourke. This tells us that O'Rourke works at station 9 in the first line.

It sometimes is desirable to allow a subscript to vary. Suppose that we wish to study the make-up of the first assembly line. We could use $WORK_{1,J}$ to denote the Jth station in the first line. We then could manipulate the value assigned to J to move from one station in the first line to another station in the same line.

Exercises

12. Consider the process of recording grades for students at a university. Let's say that the master file is the collection of all grades for all students who are currently attending the university. List some of the fields that would appear in the records in this file. When would the master file be updated, and for what purposes? What working files would be used in these updates? What might the data base consist of in this case?

13. Construct the array of coefficients for the following set of equations.

$$36x_1 - 2x_2 + 5x_3 = 27$$
$$88x_1 + 14x_2 - 9x_3 = 14$$
$$x_1 - 16x_2 + x_3 = 4$$

14. A manufacturing plant has two assembly lines and seven stations in each line. The assignments to the stations in this plant will be made from those in WORK. The assignments in the new plant are called NEW, and the assignments are as follows:

$NEW_{1,J}$ = $WORK_{1,J}$ and $NEW_{2,J}$ = $WORK_{2,J}$ for J=1 through 5
$NEW_{1,6}$ = $WORK_{3,1}$, $NEW_{1,7}$ = $WORK_{3,2}$, $NEW_{2,6}$ = $WORK_{3,3}$
and $NEW_{2,7}$ = $WORK_{3,4}$.

Construct the array of NEW assignments.

*15. A matrix also can be used to help refer to cards in a deck of ordinary playing cards. For example, we could use the rows for suits (there would be 4 rows) and the columns for card values (there would be 13 columns). If we call the matrix CARD and use 1 to designate the spades suit, 2 for hearts, 3 for diamonds, and 4 for clubs; and 1 to designate ace, 2 for deuce, 3 for trey, and so on up to 11 for jack, 12 for queen and 13 for king; then the element $CARD_{3,11}$ is the jack of diamonds, and the element $CARD_{1,1}$ is the ace of spades. Suppose that we dealt a hand of 13 cards and used this matrix to specify which cards were in the hand. We would construct a matrix consisting of ones and zeros. A one would appear whenever that card was in the hand; a zero would appear if that card were not in the hand. This is

```
             SPADES:     ACE, FIVE, SEVEN , KING
HAND:        HEARTS:     NONE
             DIAMONDS:   TWO, FOUR, SIX, TEN, JACK, QUEEN
             CLUBS:      ACE, EIGHT, NINE


MATRIX:   1 0 0 0 1 0 1 0 0 0 0 0 1
          0 0 0 0 0 0 0 0 0 0 0 0 0
          0 1 0 1 0 1 0 0 0 1 1 1 0
          1 0 0 0 0 0 0 1 1 0 0 0 0
```

Fig. 5.7   Using a matrix to designate the contents of a hand of thirteen cards

illustrated in Figure 5.7. Using this approach, construct the matrix that would correspond to the hand:

```
SPADES:     DEUCE, FOUR, QUEEN, KING
HEARTS:     ACE, FIVE, SIX
DIAMONDS:   SEVEN, EIGHT
CLUBS:      SIX, TEN, JACK, QUEEN, KING
```

ANNOTATED SUPPLEMENTARY BIBLIOGRAPHY

Most references on computers or computer programming discuss the representation of numbers in a computer. Rather than merely listing as many of these as we can recall, we are citing only references to standards for representation and coding.

The two most important sources for standards in the United States are the International Organization for Standardization (ISO) and the American National Standards Institute (ANS).

ISO standards are published in Geneva, Switzerland. One of the standards that they have published for coding is:

- Six- and seven-bit coded character sets for information processing interchange. ISO recommendation R646, 1967.

   ANS standards are published in New York, New York. They have many standards for coding on a variety of computer-related media, including the following relating to codes mentioned in this or the next chapter:

- Standard code for Information Interchange, ANS X3.4-1968.

- Character structure and character parity sense for parallel-by-bit communication in the ASCII. ANS X3.25-1970.

- Hollerith punched-card code. ANS X3.26-1970.

- Code extension techniques for use with seven-bit coded character set of ASCII. ANS X3.41-1973.

Chapter 6

The Components of a Computer

6.1 INTRODUCTION

We already have noted that computers are merely a collection of circuits wired together, packaged in pastel-colored boxes, linked to other electronic and mechanical devices that provide input/output or additional storage facilities, and supplemented by sets of instructions that cause the hardware to function in a special way. In this chapter, the appearance and functioning of these pastel-colored boxes and their supplements will be discussed. No one computer will be covered in full; however, many particular devices will be mentioned to illustrate the material discussed.

Electronic digital computers have wide ranges of capacities, speeds, and prices. There are small, medium, and large computer systems, as well as minicomputers which are even smaller than the small ones. In this chapter we shall attempt to describe the nature and implications of this range, in particular by discussing processors and main storage. The remainder of this chapter is divided into separate sections, each of which discusses a particular type of computer component. Because there is an especially wide variety of input/output devices, several sections are exclusively devoted to them. Additional sections discuss software, an important component of computer systems. Immediately after the discussion of processors and main storage comes a discussion of machine languages, because they are closely related in function. Other software components are discussed at the end of the chapter.

The electronic computer makes extensive use of *bistable elements*. These are elements that can assume one of two states and that remain in one of these states until modified from the outside. Vacuum tubes and transistors either conduct or do not conduct current; relay switches either are open or closed; punched cards and paper tapes either do or do not have a hole in a given row and column; magnetic tapes and discs either do or do not have a prescribed location magnetized in a prescribed direction. The bistability of computer components leads to a representation of information that requires only two symbols. This accounts for the importance of base 2 in representations of numbers, and for the use of sequences of bits in encoding other information.

6.2 PROCESSORS

The heart of the computer is its processor, the unit that interprets and executes instructions. Processors contain circuits that reduce a machine-language instruction to its component parts and interpret these parts during the instruction cycle. If the instruction requires it, this unit also fetches the values that the instruction will possess, the *operands,* from main storage, carries out the required operation during the execution cycle, and returns the results to main storage.

The speed of the processor, the rate at which it interacts with main storage, and the versatility of its instruction repertoire, are critical to the performance of the whole computer system. The cost of the processor, which is related to the cost of its components and the complexity of its circuitry, is another critical consideration for the user. Consider, for example, the instruction repertoire. In general, a greater variety of instructions makes it easier to write programs. A single instruction may do what a whole series of simpler instructions would have to do otherwise. This is true of floating-point calculations, for example. However, each additional machine-language instruction adds to the complexity of the design of the processor and the cost of its manufacture (and hence its cost to the user).

The rate at which the processor interacts with main storage is affected both by: 1) the amount of information that is exchanged with main storage in a single transfer; and 2) the time required to carry out this transfer of information (called *cycle time*). For most computers, the amount of information exchanged is called a *word.* One of the ways in which minicomputers are distinguished from other computers is by their small word size (usually 12 to 16 bits). Slow processors are distinguished from fast ones by the differences in their cycle times — ranging through as much as two orders of magnitude from 100 nanoseconds to 10 microseconds. A *nanosecond* is one-billionth of a second, and a *microsecond* is one-millionth of a second.

Execution time, the time required to complete the execution of an instruction once the operands are available, also helps to characterize the speed of the processor. The times required to complete arithmetic operations vary greatly. In many computers, addition is carried out in not much more than a single unit of cycle time. Multiplication and divi-

Fig. 6.1 A microelectronic chip

sion often are much slower operations. Calculations with floating-point numbers usually are slower than those with integer numbers.

The circuits used in processors originally were made of individual elements such as relays, vacuum tubes, and capacitors and their connections. These components were assembled in much the same way as other electronic devices. As the technology improved, circuits became smaller and assembly techniques became more sophisticated. The transistor replaced the vacuum tube, and whole circuits were assembled on the surface of a ceramic tile as small as one-sixteenth-inch square. These large-scale, integrated (LSI) circuits or microelectronic circuits resulted in extremely compact processors. Figure 6.1 compares a microelectronic circuit to a penny. This technology has progressed even further, and will be discussed in the next section in connection with the use of circuits in main storage.

6.3 MAIN STORAGE

The processor is connected to a storage facility with which it interacts directly. This storage facility is called *main storage,* as opposed to

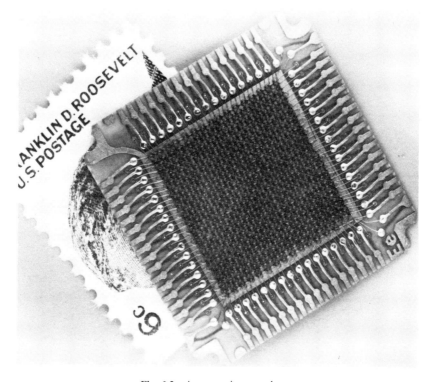

Fig. 6.2 A magnetic-core plane

auxiliary storage which is used to supplement the storage capacities of main storage. In carrying out its instructions, the processor views auxiliary storage devices, such as drums, disc drives, and tape drives, as a type of input/output device. Main storage is linked directly with the processor; the contents of auxiliary storage must be passed through main storage to be accessible to the processor.

Several media and devices have been used as main storage for computers. By the end of the 1960s, magnetic cores were the most widely used main storage medium. In the 1970s, this medium was supplemented by circuits and, to a lesser extent, by such things as plated wires.

Magnetic core storage will be discussed here, both to indicate one way in which bistability is implemented in computers, and because magnetic cores are an important main storage medium. In addition, one of the new techniques, the use of circuits in main storage, will be discussed briefly. This section concludes with some remarks on the cost, speed, and capacity of main storage and its effects on computer productivity.

Magnetic core storage consists of stacks of matrices, or planes of core elements. A typical *magnetic-core plane* is shown in Figure 6.2.

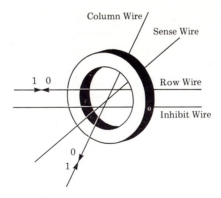

Fig. 6.3 A magnetic-core element

A single *magnetic-core element* in the plane is depicted in Figure 6.3. Note that the elements in the plane are connected by a series of wires strung through them. Each element has four wires* passing through it—one oriented along the rows of the matrix, another along the columns, and a third, called the *inhibit wire,* running parallel to the row wire. The fourth wire, called the *sense wire,* is diagonally oriented and passes through every element in the core plane (as does the inhibit wire). The row and column wires are used to write to the element, and the diagonal wire is used to read from it. The inhibit wire is used in restoring information to the element after reading from it.

Magnetic cores are bistable. They are little magnets which may be polarized in either of two directions. When the core is polarized in one direction, a zero is represented; when it is polarized in the other direction, a one is represented.

Writing is accomplished by sending half the current required to orient the polarity of an element through a row wire, and half the current through a column wire. This means that only the element at the intersection of these wires receives the unit of current required to write to the element. The zero state is obtained by sending current in one direction along each wire; the one state by sending current in the other direction.

Reading from the elements is accomplished by attempting to write a zero. This is called a *destructive read* because it has the effect of erasing core. If the unit has been in a zero state, no current is induced in the diagonal wire because the polarity of the element did not change. If it has been in a one state, a current is induced in the diagonal wire which is sensed, read, and used to restore the one state in the element. If it were not for the restoration of the one state, the process of reading

---

*Some cores use only two wires.

could be disastrous. (If you were performing an extensive desk calculation which required you to store intermediate results by noting them on a scratch pad, and a number was erased as you read it from the scratch pad and not restored, the calculations would suffer.) Only one element in a plane is read at any one time, although elements in each of several planes may be read simultaneously.

Magnetic cores are used as a main storage medium because of their great speed and reliability. They have access times of about a microsecond. (*Access time* is the time interval between the instant at which the data are called from, or requested to be stored in, a storage device, and the instant at which delivery, or storage, is completed.) However, they are expensive. Magnetic cores cost about 10 cents per bit of storage capacity, whereas circuits used in main storage cost about 4 cents per bit. Auxiliary storage is even less expensive: drums cost about .3 cents per bit, and discs and magnetic tape about 0.01 cents per bit. These estimates include the cost of interfacing the drums, disc, and tape units with the computer, and are based on the prices for supplying this equipment with the computer quoted by computer manufacturers. Prices quoted by companies which specialize in the manufacture of these devices tend to be somewhat lower. Larger-capacity, slower drum devices are available at a cost of about .1 cent per bit.

The circuits used in main storage in some of the IBM 370 series of computers use what IBM calls *monolithic system technology*. In these storages, a one-sixteenth-inch-square chip contains a hundred or more components. These chips are then assembled on a one-half-inch-square ceramic tile. A pair of these half-inch squares is assembled into a single storage module. A module has a capacity of 512 bits.

These storages are non-destructive; however, they are circuits, so a current is required to maintain the contents. Since the contents are destroyed when the current is turned off, the storage is said to be *volatile*.

Main storage circuits are somewhat faster than core storage because they are more compact and non-destructive. They also are less expensive and easier to maintain because they have diagnostic capabilities which are available for circuit analysis. However, since they use more current and generate more heat, they require more air conditioning capacity.

The capacity of main storage is an important characteristic because it determines the amount of work that can be done per unit time (the *throughput*) of a computer system. The speed of the computer's processor, the access times of the various storage devices used, and other factors also affect throughput. This is partially because as storage capacity increases, work on one job can be overlapped to a greater extent with work on other jobs (recall the discussion of multiprogramming in Section 1.5).

*6.4 THE NATURE OF MACHINE LANGUAGES

We have already seen, in Section 1.2, how the computer alternates repeatedly between instruction and execution cycles to complete its work. The instruction that the computer processes is a sequence of digits, much like other information that it stores. However, this sequence of digits is structured and interpreted in a very special way by electronic circuits. This permits the computer to carry out hundreds of thousands, even millions, of such instructions in a single second. In this section we shall try to explain what machine languages do and how they do it. We will use an actual machine language for a computer, the IBM 1620. Although it was more widely used in the 1960s than currently, its relative simplicity makes it easy to learn.

The computer expects to find in the instruction it is to execute the answers to certain questions. These may include:

1. What is to be done; i.e., what operation is to be performed?
2. Where are the operands?
3. What should be done with the result?

and, in order to maintain the continuous flow,

4. What should be done next?

The computer is organized to give the answers to the last three questions in the form of addresses—i.e., where to go for the answer, rather than the answer itself. More specifically, it gives the addresses of the operands rather than the operands themselves, the address at which we wish to store the result, and the address of the next instruction.

It might be helpful to imagine that the storage of the computer contains a series of boxes which are labeled with their addresses (i.e., their locations in storage), much like a set of post office boxes. An instruction tells the computer in which box to look for an operand. By modifying the instruction reference, the same sequence of instructions can be used to solve many different problems. The contents of some of the boxes are provided as input; the contents of others are modified during the execution of the program. But no matter what the input or intermediate data are, the procedure goes along in the same way. Similarly, no matter what the contents of the post office boxes are, the postman always responds to an instruction to transfer these contents to a properly identified owner of a box.

The actual structure of the *instruction word* varies from computer to computer. We shall assume that we are dealing with a two-address computer; that is, a computer whose instruction formats comprise an operation and two addresses. More specifically, let's assume that the instruction consists of a 12-digit number, set up as follows:

1. The first 2 digits designate the operation to be performed.
2. Digits 3–7 contain the address of the first operand, called the *P address,* and digits 8–12 contain the address of the second operand, called the *Q address.*

Implicit in this approach is the assumption that our addresses consist of five-digit numbers. Thus we have, at most, one hundred thousand distinct addresses (numbers 00000 to 99999). This means that the instruction word is structured. Figure 6.4 indicates this, and also contains a dictionary of some of the instructions available for the IBM 1620 computer. The dictionary lists operation codes and the significance of the P and Q addresses. Unless otherwise stated, the address of the next instruction is found automatically by adding 12 to the address of the previous instruction.

Each digit in main storage is associated with the presence or absence of a special indicator called a flag. In writing the contents of storage, a bar is placed over the digit to denote the presence of a flag.

Each digit is individually addressable, but the contents of an address (except for an instruction) are found by starting at the address specified and going back to lower-numbered addresses until a flag is found. If the digit stored at the specified address has a flag, a minus sign is attached to the number; however, the computer proceeds to the next lower digit to find the end of the contents. This means that there are no one-digit contents. In the case of instructions, the computer goes to the digit addressed during the instruction cycle and automatically reads the next 12 digits as the instruction, proceeding forward rather than backward, and ignoring flags.

It is customary to denote the contents of a location by placing parentheses around an address. Thus, for example, if we write $(12234) = \overline{1}23\overline{7}$, it means that $\overline{7}$ is stored in address 12234, 3 in address 12233, 2 in 12232, and $\overline{1}$ in 12231. We still say that the contents of address 12234 is minus 1237.

If $(11234) = \overline{1}234$, $(11236) = \overline{9}6$, $(11241) = \overline{0}0001$, and $(11246) = \overline{1}2212$ before the following instruction has been executed, what are their contents afterwards?

INSTRUCTION: 21 11234 11236

From the dictionary, we see that this instruction says:

> Add (11234) to (11236) and store the
> answer in location 11234.

This means that the computer would add 1234 to 96 to get 1330. Since 1330 is stored in 11234, we see that this instruction changes only (11234), which becomes $\overline{1}330$.

Operation P address   Q address

$$\boxed{X\,X}\boxed{X\,X\,X\,X\,X}\boxed{X\,X\,X\,X\,X}$$

Instruction Operation		Meaning of Five Digits	
Meaning	Code	P Address	Q Address
Add	21	address of first operand and address where the result is stored	address of second operand
Subtract	22	address of first operand and address where the result is stored	address of second operand
Multiply	23	address of first operand	address of second operand*
Transmit the contents of Q to P	26	contents of Q address are transferred to this address	contents of this address are transferred to P address
Put a flag at P	32	address of operand	Ignored
Remove flag from P	33	address of operand	Ignored
Go to P only if there is no flag at Q	44	branch to this address, maybe	address of operand used to test for branching
Halt	48	Ignored	Ignored

*Results of a multiplication are automatically stored in location 00099, 00098, and so on, back as far as required. Locations 00080 to 00099 are called the *product area* and are automatically cleared to zeros before the multiplication is executed. If the product contains more than 20 digits, provision must be made by the programmer to clear locations 00079 and back; otherwise, an incorrect result may be obtained.

Fig. 6.4   The structure of an IBM 1620 machine-language instruction and a dictionary of some instructions

Suppose that the instruction executed above is followed by the instruction given below. What are the contents of 11234, 11236, 11241, and 11246 after this second instruction has been executed?

INSTRUCTION: 21 11246 11234

This second instruction says to add (11246) to (11234) and store the answer in 11246. Also, since this instruction is to be executed after the first instruction, $(11234) = \bar{1}330$. We see then that since (11246) $= \bar{1}2212$, the sum is $12212 + 1330 = 13542$. This result is stored in 11246; thus, after this second instruction, $(11234) = \bar{1}330$, (11236) $= \bar{9}6$, $(11241) = \bar{0}0001$, and $(11246) = \bar{1}3542$.

Two exercises at the conclusion of this chapter will be used to illustrate the effects of the other instructions given in the table in Figure 6.4.

6.5 AUXILIARY STORAGE

The principal auxiliary storage devices are drums, disc drives, and tape drives. A *magnetic drum* is a steel cylinder in a coated copper sleeve. The surface of the copper sleeve is coated with a magnetizable iron or nickel compound. Specific locations — actually tiny spots — on the surface of the drum are designated as storage locations for bits. Each spot is magnetized in one of two directions. The drum revolves continually, and each spot can be passed under a read-write head, which can either reorient or sense the direction of magnetization. The process of reading is non-destructive, and restoration is not necessary. The speed of magnetic-drum units is slower than that of main storage, but faster than that of tapes or discs. Access times for the drums are about 5 to 20 milliseconds, more than a thousand times slower than cores. The delay is caused by the need to wait until the desired information is positioned under the read-write head.

Magnetic tape drives were the first widely used auxiliary storage devices. Magnetic tape is a strip of flexible plastic material, such as mylar, that is coated with a thin layer of iron oxide. The oxide can be magnetized, and spots on the tape are designated as storage locations for bits. A reel of tape is from 50 to 2400 feet long, and the longer tapes are more commonly used.

Figure 6.5 shows a magnetic-tape drive. Tape is fed from one reel to another, passing over the read-write heads. (They are just below the tape reels and behind the dark plate in the magnetic drive pictured in the figure.) The operation is like a tape recorder's, except that these tape speeds are much faster — roughly several feet per second; and the density of information on the tape is much greater — as great as 1600 characters per inch.

Access times for magnetic-tape units vary a great deal, depending on where the reel of tape is currently positioned under the read-write head, and where we wish it to be. Though tape can be moved quickly, it can take a relatively long time to position the desired section of a 2400-foot tape under the read-write heads. If you watch the operation of tape drives at a computer center, you will see that a great deal of time is devoted to spinning tapes. Access times of several minutes

Fig. 6.5 A magnetic-tape drive

can be required in some cases. In addition, you should note the amount of time required to mount and dismount tapes.

Suppose that we cut the tape into 20 strips and add 20 read-write heads, operating one for each strip. In addition, suppose that the tapes are continually in motion, so that each location on each strip is positioned under a read-write head at frequent intervals. It is easy to see that this would substantially reduce the need for lengthy tape operations. This is the primary reason for the growth of *magnetic disc*

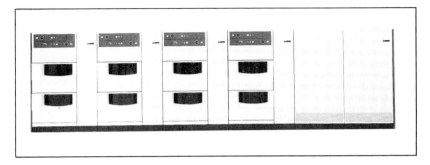

Fig. 6.6 A set of six disc drives

storage. A set of disc drives is shown in Figure 6.6. The disc drive contains a disc unit or pack (which looks like a stack of phonograph records—see Figure 6.7), a read-write head, and a motor to provide the required motion of its parts. The discs rotate continuously while the unit is being used. The read-write heads can either remain stationary over the surface of the disc, or move in and out to the center and edge of the discs. The information is stored in the form of magne-

Fig. 6.7 A typical disc pack

Fig. 6.8 Close-up of a disc drive showing a pack ready for replacement (note the read-write heads in the upper-left corner)

tized spots at designated locations on the disc surfaces. Groups of spots are used to represent characters.

The information on most discs is organized into tracks and cylinders. On some discs, a track is further subdivided into sectors. A *track* is that portion of a disc surface that can be read from or written on by a single read-write head in one revolution of the disc. A *cylinder* is all the vertically aligned tracks on a disc.

Typical access times for discs range from 5 to 100 milliseconds. Disc drives are available with removable media—that is, disc packs that can be removed from drives so that others can be mounted (see Figure 6.8)—or fixed media. Generally, the removable-media type is used more widely. Some have capacities of about 200 million characters. Since several such drives can be linked to a single computer, discs provide very large auxiliary storage capacities.

The storage capacities of magnetic cores currently have an upper limit of 2 million or more characters, and a single reel of high density, 1600-character-per-inch tape can hold about 40 million characters. Since several tape drives can be linked to a single computer, a disc and tape auxiliary storage system permits capacities of billions of characters.

Some of the information that is stored in a computer may be so important to one of the users or to the function of the computer itself that it should be protected from potential erasure or replacement by other facility users. This can be done in a variety of ways. Users may specify in their programs that a storage area containing a particular set of information should not be written on. The messages to the operating system, called *job control statements,* may specify special handling and protection of the information that is stored. The operating system may prevent a user from replacing a particular set of information unless that user is identified as one who is allowed access to that information. Sometimes this identifying is done by requiring the user to provide a special code word or number; this has been called a *password protection* system. Finally, the hardware itself may be so designed that it is almost impossible to write over some of the contents of storage. The storage that is protected in this way is called *read-only storage.** For example, some computers have a special, replaceable disc facility that helps establish the basic characteristics of the computer. These characteristics can be modified by replacing the disc on this facility and then loading the contents of this disc into a reserved section of main storage. The special disc is a read-only storage, and the operating system protects the reserved section of main storage by means of passwords and other more sophisticated protection devices.

Before concluding our discussion of storage media and devices, we should mention two promising media that are still being developed — *thin film memory* and *photographic film.* Thin film consists of thin spots of magnetic material deposited on an insulated base. The deposit is only one or a few millionths of an inch thick. The magnetizable medium on discs, tapes, and drums is continuous, whereas the medium in thin films is not. A matrix of spots is deposited on a plane of insulator material. A memory consists of a stack of these planes. Thin film memories have even shorter access times than magnetic core memories, but their fabrication is more difficult and their reliability has not yet been established.

Photographic-film storage, because it is multistable rather than bistable, offers much promise. A small, 1/64th-inch square could hold 16 or more distinguishable shades of grey. If color coding is permitted, then several hundred distinguishable colors might be permitted. The ability to store a great deal of information in small space makes photographic film particularly desirable as an auxiliary storage medium. Because film storage devices can be read photoelectrically, they also have potential for shorter access times than other auxiliary storage devices. In this case, however, the sensor is difficult to manufacture, and reliability also is a problem. An even more critical diffi-

---

*Read-only storage is also faster and cheaper than read-write storage.

Fig. 6.9 A keypunch station

culty is that photographic storage is not erasable, and therefore cannot be used in applications requiring the frequent substitution of new information for old. However, the increased demand for read-only storages to hold relatively permanent information and protect it from erasure may provide the impetus necessary to develop film storage devices.

6.6 INPUT/OUTPUT—AN OVERVIEW

Computers must communicate effectively with people. The burden of this communication is placed on the computer's input/output devices. Because of the great variety of users' needs, a correspondingly great

Medium	Devices Associated with Medium	Comments
Printouts	Prepared and output via printer, plotter or remote terminal	This is certainly the principal output medium. Finished products such as payroll checks, mailing labels and engineering drawings can be printed by a computer.
Punched cards	Prepared by a keypunch, or a card punch, input via a card reader and output via a card punch	The keypunch may be operated by an optical scanner or a magnetic tape drive. (See reference to these devices below.)
Paper tape	Prepared by a Teletypewriter terminal or a Flexowriter or industrial or laboratory equipment, input via a paper tape reader or a Teletypewriter and output via a paper tape punch	A widely used remote terminal, the Teletypewriter, can prepare and process punched paper tape. This significantly increased the use of punched paper tape as an input medium in recent years.
Magnetic tape	Prepared by a magnetic tape drive or a key to tape device; input and output via a magnetic tape drive	In preparing inputs, the magnetic tape drive may be operated by industrial or laboratory equipment. For output, a magnetic tape drive linked to a printer or a plotter may produce the final result offline.
Disc	Prepared by a disc drive or a key to disc device, input and output via a disc drive	Disc drives may also be operated by industrial or laboratory equipment and may be used to produce printed results offline. Disc drives are less widely used in this way than tape drives.

Fig. 6.10   Devices associated with input/output media

variety of input/output devices has been developed. Each device is associated with a medium — the material through which the person interacts either directly or indirectly. Figure 6.10 summarizes the media used with computer systems, the devices used to prepare them, and those used to input or output them. The most important input media are certainly punch cards and keyboards, and the most important output medium is printouts. This chapter will emphasize the devices used to prepare and process punch cards, those used to prepare printouts, and the more important devices associated with keyboard entry into the computer. This last group will be discussed under the heading

Medium	Devices Associated with Medium	Comments
Face of a cathode ray tube	Prepared and input via keyboards and/or light pens (See Section 6.9) associated with television-like terminals that contain cathode ray tubes. Output via the tubes on these terminals.	Television-like terminals and associated keyboards are being increasingly used for input to and output from computers.
Sound	Input and output via a telephone	Pre-recorded messages can be selected by a computer for response to an inquiry. The inquiry would probably have been made using the keyboard of a touch-tone phone. Sound inquiries are not widely used.
Mark-sense forms	Prepared manually and input via an optical reader (also called an *optical scanner*)	Most mark-sense inputs are put on specially designed forms (see fig. 6.21) and processed by optical scanners. At one time, inputs were put on cards and special devices were available to convert mark-sense cards to punched cards.
Checks	Identification and other information preprinted using magnetic ink, input via magnetic ink reader	Magnetic ink readers are also used to process other banking and credit-related forms.
Hand-written forms	Prepared manually; input via an optical scanner	Optical scanners can reliably recognize only a limited number of block-printed, handwritten characters.
Type-written forms	Prepared on a typewriter; input via an optical scanner	A few special typewriter fonts can be recognized by optical scanners.

Fig. 6.10 (continued)

of remote terminals. Since such terminals also provide output capabilities, the output facilities associated with them will be discussed. An increasingly important output medium is the face of a cathode-ray tube, which also will be discussed under the heading of remote terminals.

6.7 PUNCH CARDS AND CARD-PROCESSING EQUIPMENT

Until quite recently, the punch card was by far the most widely used primary source for computer input. In recent years, keyboards and optical scanners have become more important. Because of the widespread use of punch cards, a number of devices have been developed to provide special handling services for them. The Punch card and two of the devices used to prepare and handle them (a keypunch and a sorter) will be discussed in this section. A computer system component, the card reader/punch, also will be discussed. Keypunches and sorters ordinarily are not connected to computers; the card reader/punch is.

Figure 6.11 contains a picture of the 80-column punch card with a code, called the *Hollerith code,* that is used for recording numeric, alphabetic, and special characters. The card contains 80 columns and 12 rows. Each column ordinarily is used to record a single character. (Several characters may be recorded in a single column by special input formats.) The top three rows are called the 12, 11, and 0 rows. A hole punched in one of these rows is called an *overpunch.* Note that a coded character consists of at most one overpunch combined with one or two punches in rows 1 to 9. These cards can be prepared using a keypunch, such as the one shown in Figure 6.9.

The *keypunch* is a typewriter-like device which permits the entry of one character in a column by pressing a single key. The keypunch then will automatically punch the correct combination of holes in the card. The code need not be memorized; the keypunch operator need only be familiar with the numbers, letters, and special symbols on the keypunch. In fact, the keypunch is as easy to operate as a typewriter. Keypunch operators can prepare about 100 to 150 cards per hour.

The *sorter* separates a deck of cards in accordance with the entry in a specified column. This permits cards with identical entries to be grouped in stacks. When the cards are removed from the sorter in the prescribed order, they can be ordered according to the entry in the column being tested. In addition, by repeating the process, a deck of cards can be ordered in accordance with the entries in several columns. Processing speeds accommodate 500 to 2000 cards per minute. A sorter is shown in Figure 6.12.

Most computer manufacturers offer *card readers* and *card punches,* or *card reader/punches,* which are housed in a single device as a part of their equipment line. Card-reader speeds vary from several hundred to 2000 or more cards per minute, while punch speeds vary from 100 to 500 cards per minute. In addition, it is possible to both read and punch cards at a location remote from the computer. Generally, the speed of remote devices is comparable to that of card readers and card punches located at the computer facility.

The punch card has one inherent limitation: a physical break in the information occurs every 80 characters. Punched paper tapes—as well as magnetic tapes—do not have this limitation. Of course, the absence of this break in information is not entirely advantageous. For example,

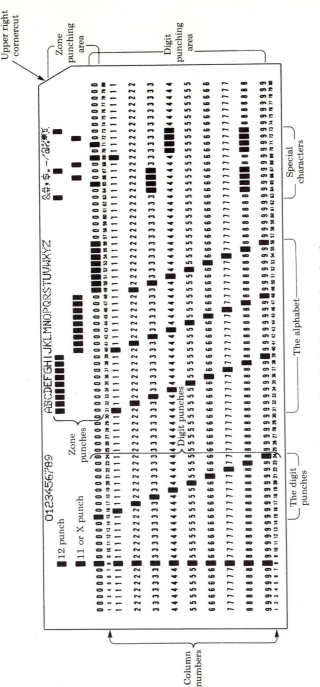

Fig. 6.11 The Hollerith punched-card code

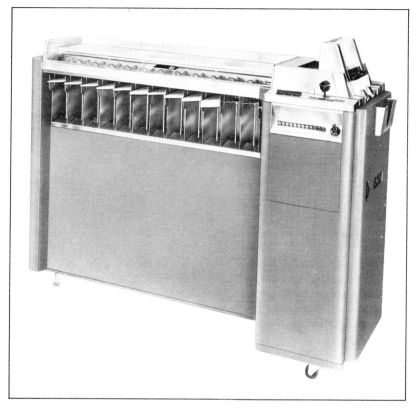

Fig. 6.12 A sorter

on paper tape or magnetic tape, artificial breaks must be inserted in such forms as end-of-line characters on paper tape and record marks on magnetic tape. Cathode-ray tubes have a break in the data which is determined by the maximum number of characters that can be displayed on the face of the tube at any one time. This may vary from as few as 64 to as many as several thousand. Special input forms are limited by the number of characters that can be displayed on a single form. This, too, varies a great deal, but the maximum capacity of a form rarely exceeds several hundred characters.

6.8 PRINTERS

The *printer* is an important computer output device. The ability to produce large volumes of output which are readily intelligible to humans is essential to the extended application of computers to nonscientific problems. Today, thousand-line-a-minute printers are commonplace in computer installations; and address labels, checks, employee report forms, and elaborate tables, as well as complete reports, are being prepared by computers using printers.

Most printers in use today are *impact printers*. These include character, chain, and cylinder printers. Matrix printers and printers using photo-duplication techniques also are used. Matrix printers usually are either thermal or electrostatic.

A *character printer* is really a typewriter-like device that is operated by a computer. It operates at speeds of about 15 to 80 characters per second. It can be used as either an input device — a keyboard ordinarily is associated with a character printer — or an output device. All other printers are only output devices. Character printers, frequently found at remote locations, will be mentioned again under the heading of remote terminals.

The *chain printer* uses a continuously moving chain of type slugs that contain several replications of the character set available for printing. Printing actually is done by firing a set of hammers from behind the paper against the chain. The paper is pressed against the ribbon and type slug, and a character is imprinted (see Figure 6.13).

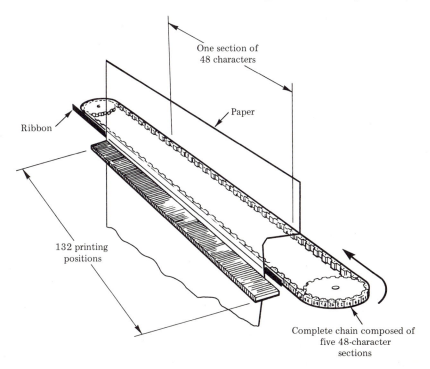

One section of
48 characters

Ribbon

Paper

132 printing
positions

Complete chain composed of
five 48-character
sections

Fig. 6.13 A schematic representation of a chain printer

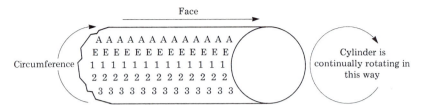

Fig. 6.14 A schematic representation of the action of the cylinder in a cylinder printer

The critical element in the printer's operation is proper timing in the firing of the hammers. This requires sophisticated equipment to interpret the computer's printing command.

The speed of the chain printer is closely related to the size of the character set required. Since the chain is moving at a constant speed, the more sets of the same characters that can be incorporated into a single chain, the faster the operating speed of the printer. Less physical movement is required to position characters for printing. Users who require only a limited set of characters—for example, only the ten numerals and a decimal point—should take advantage of this and order an appropriate chain.

The *cylinder printer* uses a continuously rotating cylinder, containing around its circumference the set of characters that can be printed. Each character is repeated across the face of the cylinder as many times as there are print positions (see Figure 6.14). Printing speeds in excess of 1000 lines per minute are common. Again, the firing of the hammer against the paper, ribbon, and character causes the imprint. Cylinder printers also are called *line printers* because all the entries of a single character of a line are printed simultaneously. For example, if the sentence, "He went to the store," were to be printed on a line, the hammers in the second, fifth, fourteenth, and twentieth print positions would fire as the row on the cylinder containing the letter *e* appeared opposite them. Again, complex equipment is required to analyze the lines which are to be printed, and to fire the appropriate hammers at the right time.

Matrix printers use a series of dots to construct a character. Typically, a five-by-seven matrix of dots is used to print each character. The combination of dots that actually is printed determines which character is displayed. Figure 6.15 illustrates the combination used to print the numeral 5.

A *thermal matrix printer* uses either heat-sensitive paper or wax-coated dark paper as the medium for printing. The heat-sensitive paper undergoes a chemical change when subjected to heat, which produces a visible image. Speeds of 15 to 300 lines per minute are common for

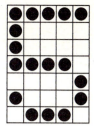

Fig. 6.15 Matrix of dots used to represent the digit 5

thermal printers. The quality of the result is poor—either pale blue dots on a yellowish background or black dots on a pastel-colored, waxy background—but thermal printers are inexpensive. Purchase prices of a few hundred to a few thousand dollars are common. It also should be noted that thermal printers usually give off an unpleasant odor and that thermal printers using wax-coated paper accumulate wax debris.

Electrostatic printers are among the fastest and most versatile printers available. The matrix printing approach accounts for their versatility and also, incidentally, for the poor quality of the printed results. Their exceptional speed results from their use of electrical rather than mechanical impact techniques, and from the fact that printing is completed in several stages. In addition, electrostatic printers can combine the basic 5-by-7 matrix into a 10-by-14 or even finer matrix. This results in better printed images and permits a greater variety of characters.

One of the most recent developments in printing is the use of a laser to write the printed output on the light-sensitive surface of a drum and then to transfer the image on this surface to paper. Printers of this kind can print at speeds of up to 13,350 lines per minute.

Refer to Figure 6.16, in which the operation of a laser-based IBM 3800 printer is illustrated. As the drum rotates (upper right portion of the figure), it first is charged in order to prepare the light-sensitive surface. A special form on which entries are to be printed then can be written on the drum at the forms-overlay station. A film negative that was prepared in advance is loaded in, and a light is flashed through the negative in order to write the form. The laser beam is passed through a modulator and reflected off a mirror onto the drum; this is where the printed output is transferred to the drum. Toner adheres to the lightened areas, and the contents of the surface of the drum are printed on paper at the transfer station. The residual toner then is cleared off the drum, and another cycle begins. The printing is fixed onto the paper at the preheat and fuser stations.

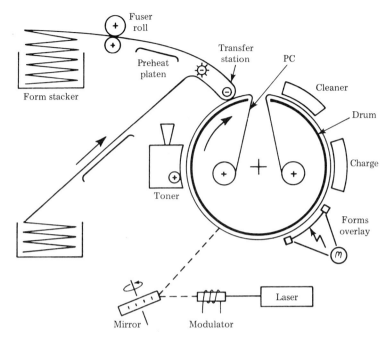

Fig. 6.16 Schematic description of an IBM 3800 laser-based printer

6.9 PLOTTERS

Plotters are becoming an increasingly important output device. They can produce not only finished graphs and illustrations (including labels and scales), but also standard output.

Most plotters use a pen mounted on wires strung over a sheet of paper. The paper is attached to the surface of a horizontal plate or cylinder. The pen writes directly on the paper; its motion is controlled by the wires that draw it across or up and down the paper. In some plotters, the cylinder on which the paper is mounted also moves. Movements can be made in increments as small as 0.01 inch, so that even though a curve is drawn as a sequence of straight lines, a reasonably good-looking product can be obtained. However, on close inspection, curves look like step functions. A picture of a popular Calcomp plotter that uses a cylinder for the mounting is shown in Figure 6.17.

Plotters are extremely versatile output devices. They frequently are used *off-line* from the computer — that is, the plot is not generated directly by the computer. Instead, the information required to generate the plot may be written on an auxiliary storage medium, such as mag-

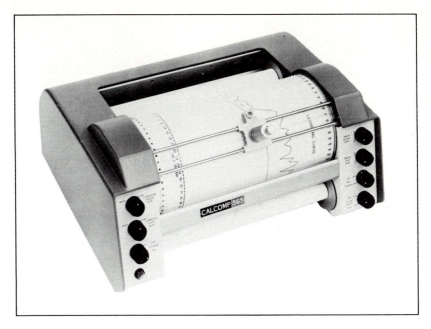

Fig. 6.17   A plotter

netic tape. The reel of tape then is transferred to a special unit that is not connected to the computer. This unit will accept the tape as input, control the plotter, and produce the desired outputs. This approach makes it possible to generate many plots using very little computer time.

6.10   REMOTE TERMINALS

The practice of using a computer from remote locations is increasing. The major facilities in use at remote locations are remote job entry stations, teletypewriters, cathode-ray tubes and keyboards, and typewriter-like devices (character printers).

In some instances, high-volume users are submitting their jobs via remote job entry stations that include a card reader, a printer, and perhaps a small computer that acts as a buffer between the reading and writing operations and the communications lines. The user can function as if he has his own general-purpose computer at his local site. Such remote job entry stations are popular at large universities and companies. In fact, a visitor at a large university who asks for the computer center is apt to be directed to the nearest remote job entry station rather than to the large computer facility that is servicing the station.

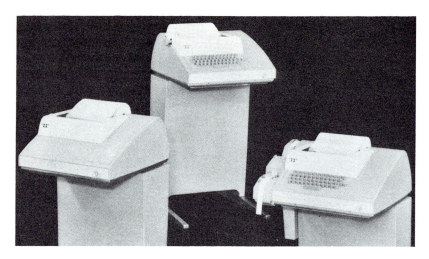

Fig. 6.18 Teletype terminals

Initially, the most widely used terminal was a *teletypewriter* because it was readily available and could be linked to an established communications network. The remote user now has available special-purpose keyboards, cathode-ray tubes and light pens, touch-tone phones, punched card and punched paper tape readers, printers, and even slide projectors and sound tape playbacks controlled by the computer. Finally, smaller computers located some distance away can be attached as satellites on larger computers.

The teletypewriter played a prominent role in the first time-sharing systems. It has the advantage of being able to provide punched paper tape as a by-product of its operation. However, as special terminals are being developed, the importance of the teletypewriter as a terminal is diminishing. A teletype terminal is shown in Figure 6.18.

Little more need be said about *typewriter-like terminals*. They are the equivalent of the character printer that can be found near the console in some computer centers. The portability of these terminals may be their major attraction in the future. These portable terminals may allow computer input/output to be set up at any telephone with an appropriate headset. A portable terminal in operation, with the telephone headset in its cradle, is pictured in Figure 6.19.

Special-purpose keyboard devices are available for providing inputs to a computer. Among them are the *touch-tone input devices*. These allow the transmission of the equivalent of ten or more distinct signals which, with appropriate codification, can permit an inexpensive input of a relatively small set of characters. These devices are being used to process banking transactions. For greater versatility, a more general-

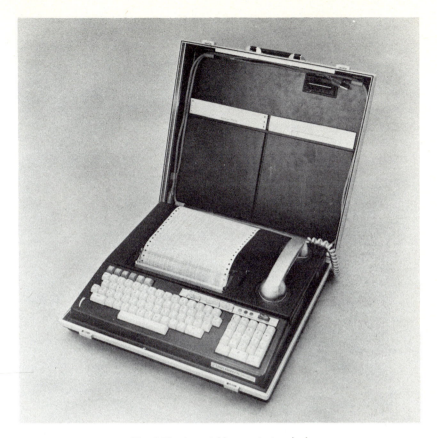

Fig. 6.19 A portable remote terminal

purpose keyboard can be used. Frequently, such keyboards are used with a cathode-ray tube.

The face of a cathode-ray tube is an important medium at remote terminals. The response to an executive's inquiry, a plot of a mathematical relation, or a question for a student to answer as part of an instruction course are readily displayed on the face of a cathode-ray tube. The cathode-ray tube resembles a television picture tube in its functioning characteristics. Numbers are converted to voltages, which then are used to control the writing of lines and dots on the face of the tube. The face of the cathode-ray tube can be photographed if a permanent copy of the output is desired. A cathode-ray terminal is pictured in Figure 6.20.

A light-sensitive cell can be installed in a small pencil-like device, permitting communication with a cathode-ray tube. These small devices are called *light pens*. An engineer can develop new designs

Fig. 6.20 A cathode-ray-tube remote terminal

readily by using a light pen to pinpoint the components of a circuit diagram displayed on the face of the tube, and a keyboard to request
modification of the diagram. Similarly, an army officer engaged in a war
game can use a light pen and keyboard to specify troop movements in
a convenient way.

Many special remote devices are available. For example, there are
terminals that permit the input of punched cards and punched paper
tape to be combined with keyboard entries. There also are terminals
that permit slide projectors and sound tape recorders to be operated by

signals from a computer. When combined with the usual keyboard input and cathode-ray tube and/or typewriter-like output, this capability can be especially useful as a student station in teaching applications.

6.11   OTHER INPUT DEVICES

Optical readers and keyboards linked to magnetic tape cartridges are becoming increasingly important input devices.

Checks, gasoline credit slips, and cash register tapes have been read into computers for several years. Checks first used *magnetic ink printing,* but more recently optical techniques have been employed. Account numbers on gasoline credit slips have been read optically for some time. The *optical scanner* is developing rapidly, and many computer manufacturers offer one as part of their equipment line. The scanner senses differences in the light reflected off the surface of the page being read, by means of one or more optical photo-detectors associated with the appropriate optical and mechanical components. Since the variety of patterns that can be sensed is still quite limited, special type fonts and input forms may be required. Optical scanners are rather expensive: purchase prices for most scanners range from $5000 to $100,000. Scanners are especially useful when the input form can be prepared as a by-product of the organization's regular operations. Survey questionnaires, applications forms for insurance policies, and employment interview forms are typical kinds of forms that can be input via optical scanners. An example of a form used to prepare an insurance application is given in Figure 6.21.

Key-to-tape devices and *key-to-disc devices* also are used to prepare inputs. Many organizations have found that the nuisance of purchasing, punching, and storing cards is great. Devices are available that permit information to be entered directly onto a small reel of magnetic tape or a small disc. This reel of magnetic tape or disc can be either mounted directly on a tape or disc drive that is a part of the computer system, or combined off-line into a standard size tape or disc which then is mounted on a drive that is a part of the computer system.

The use of key-to-tape or key-to-disc devices tends to shift the major burden of the editing of input sets onto the computer. This is because punched cards can be checked and corrected by people, whereas tapes and discs must be read and edited by a computer. However, these devices can produce a typewritten copy of the input that both provides a readable copy of the input and assists in editing.

With the development of a standard for the representation of characters, typewriters to reduce the problem of computer input to that of typing may be more readily available. In addition, some scanners can

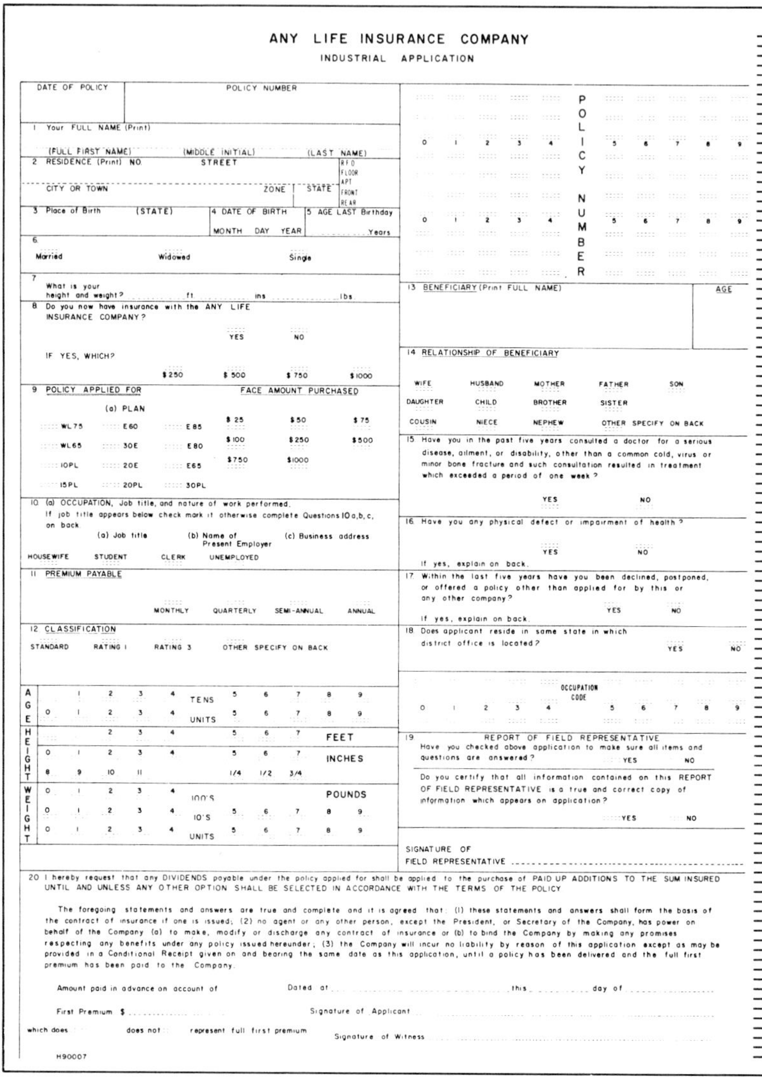
ANY LIFE INSURANCE COMPANY
INDUSTRIAL APPLICATION

DATE OF POLICY — POLICY NUMBER

1 Your FULL NAME (Print) (FULL FIRST NAME) (MIDDLE INITIAL) (LAST NAME)

2 RESIDENCE (Print) NO. STREET — R.F.D. FLOOR APT FRONT REAR — CITY OR TOWN ZONE STATE

3 Place of Birth (STATE) — 4 DATE OF BIRTH MONTH DAY YEAR — 5 AGE LAST Birthday Years

6 Married Widowed Single

7 What is your height and weight? ft ins lbs

8 Do you now have insurance with the ANY LIFE INSURANCE COMPANY? YES NO — IF YES, WHICH? $250 $500 $750 $1000

9 POLICY APPLIED FOR (a) PLAN: WL75 E60 E85 WL65 30E E80 10PL 20E E65 15PL 20PL 30PL — FACE AMOUNT PURCHASED: $25 $50 $75 $100 $250 $500 $750 $1000

10 (a) OCCUPATION, Job title, and nature of work performed. If job title appears below check mark it otherwise complete Questions 10a,b,c, on back. (a) Job title (b) Name of Present Employer (c) Business address — HOUSEWIFE STUDENT CLERK UNEMPLOYED

11 PREMIUM PAYABLE: MONTHLY QUARTERLY SEMI-ANNUAL ANNUAL

12 CLASSIFICATION: STANDARD RATING 1 RATING 3 OTHER SPECIFY ON BACK

AGE: TENS 1 2 3 4 5 6 7 8 9; UNITS 0 1 2 3 4 5 6 7 8 9

HEIGHT: FEET 2 3 4 5 6 7; INCHES 0 1 2 3 4 5 6 7 8 9 10 11 1/4 1/2 3/4

WEIGHT: POUNDS 100'S 0 1 2 3 4; 10'S 0 1 2 3 4 5 6 7 8 9; UNITS 0 1 2 3 4 5 6 7 8 9

POLICY NUMBER 0 1 2 3 4 5 6 7 8 9

13 BENEFICIARY (Print FULL NAME) AGE

14 RELATIONSHIP OF BENEFICIARY: WIFE HUSBAND MOTHER FATHER SON DAUGHTER CHILD BROTHER SISTER COUSIN NIECE NEPHEW OTHER SPECIFY ON BACK

15 Have you in the past five years consulted a doctor for a serious disease, ailment, or disability, other than a common cold, virus or minor bone fracture and such consultation resulted in treatment which exceeded a period of one week? YES NO

16 Have you any physical defect or impairment of health? YES NO — If yes, explain on back.

17 Within the last five years have you been declined, postponed, or offered a policy other than applied for by this or any other company? YES NO — If yes, explain on back.

18 Does applicant reside in same state in which district office is located? YES NO

OCCUPATION CODE 0 1 2 3 4 5 6 7 8 9

19 REPORT OF FIELD REPRESENTATIVE — Have you checked above application to make sure all items and questions are answered? YES NO — Do you certify that all information contained on this REPORT OF FIELD REPRESENTATIVE is a true and correct copy of information which appears on application? YES NO

SIGNATURE OF FIELD REPRESENTATIVE

20 I hereby request that any DIVIDENDS payable under the policy applied for shall be applied to the purchase of PAID UP ADDITIONS TO THE SUM INSURED UNTIL AND UNLESS ANY OTHER OPTION SHALL BE SELECTED IN ACCORDANCE WITH THE TERMS OF THE POLICY.

The foregoing statements and answers are true and complete and it is agreed that: (1) these statements and answers shall form the basis of the contract of insurance if one is issued; (2) no agent or any other person, except the President, or Secretary of the Company, has power on behalf of the Company (a) to make, modify or discharge any contract of insurance or (b) to bind the Company by making any promises respecting any benefits under any policy issued hereunder; (3) the Company will incur no liability by reason of this application except as may be provided in a Conditional Receipt given on and bearing the same date as this application, until a policy has been delivered and the full first premium has been paid to the Company.

Amount paid in advance on account of First Premium $ — which does / does not represent full first premium

Dated at ____ this ____ day of ____

Signature of Applicant

Signature of Witness

H90007

Fig. 6.21 Form used to prepare inputs for optical scanner

recognize hand-printed inputs. The ability to recognize a variety of handwritings reliably, which is still a subject of research, will provide an even greater breakthrough in the input bottleneck.

6.12 COMMUNICATION AND ITS IMPACT

Communication between remote terminals and computers and among computers linked together in a network is a significant aspect of computer utilization. Signals must be transmitted from one location to another. This usually is done in three steps: 1) first, the information is converted to signals (a form suitable for transmission); 2) then the signals are sent to their destination; and finally 3) each signal is converted once again so that it can be utilized at its destination. Since the information is going either to or from a computer, at least one of the conversions involves digital encoding or decoding. The middle step in the procedure — the transmission of the information — has the greatest impact on how the computer can be used. In this section, we will discuss the principal organizations providing communications services and the types of services that they provide.

The organizations that provide communications services in the United States are one type of *common carrier*. Common carriers are organizations that provide a transportation or communication service and are operated as near-monopolies. Since the major common carriers are monopolies or near-monopolies, the government must regulate their activities. The Federal Communications Commission (FCC) regulates interstate communications services. Services of common carriers must be available at standard rates to anyone requesting the service, and the owner or operator cannot interfere with what is being transmitted. (Thus, for example, TV stations are not common carriers.)

In connection with their regulatory function, the FCC requires common carriers to file with them *tariffs* which contain detailed descriptions of the services they provide and the charges associated with these services. One company may use tariffs supplied by another company. Reference 16 in the Annotated Supplementary Bibliography contains a description of virtually all the companies providing data transmission services. We shall discuss only three of the most important carriers here.

The principal supplier of communications service in the United States is the American Telephone and Telegraph Company and its subsidiaries and associates. This network of telephone, data, and other communication facilities is called the Bell System. The Bell System offers a Telegraph Exchange Service (TWX) which permits users of subscribing teleprinters to dial any other subscriber and transmit messages. It also provides a wide variety of line connections which are especially important to computer users.

Nearly all of the Bell System communications facilities that we will discuss can be used for either voice or data communication; that is, for transmitting conversations or numbers. Ordinarily, communication between individual telephone sets passes through a *switching facility*. The switching can be done manually, by an operator at a switchboard, or automatically, in which case the user dials his own connection. Switching facilities are connected to each other via a *trunk line* (see Figure 6.22). In most calls that go over the public telephone network, the communications pass through a complex sequence of switching

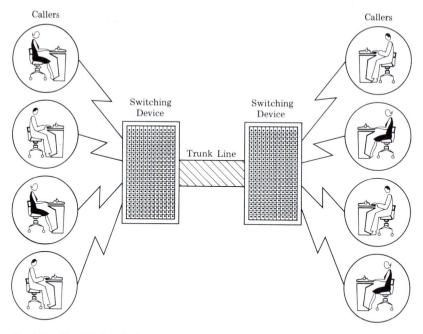

Callers

Callers

Switching
Device

Switching
Device

Trunk Line

Fig. 6.22 Simplified depiction of the links made in completing a telephone connection

facilities and trunk lines. A trunk line can transmit many telephone conversations simultaneously. A *tie-line* is a private, leased, trunk connection. Many large companies have tie-lines that connect various locations. Typically, such private tie-lines are capable of carrying about 60 telephone conversations simultaneously.

The capacity of an ordinary voice-grade telephone line ranges from a few hundred to a few thousand bits per second. (Some people use the term *baud* as if it were synonomous with bits per second. However, these terms are synonomous only if the transmission network is such that the line can be in only two different conditions. If the line can be in more than two conditions, the number of bits that can be transmitted per second is greater than the baud rating of the line.) Special facilities must be added to obtain the upper range of transmission speed. *Wide-band lines*—for example a tie-line that uses several of the voice-grade connections for data transmission—can transmit tens or even hundreds of thousands of bits per second. The medium used in such wide-band communication facilities may be wire, coaxial cable, microwave, or even satellite. Wide-band capabilities are very expensive. *Narrow-band lines,* transmitting at tens of bits per second (typical speeds range from 50 to 250 bits per second), also are available. These lines are not capable of transmitting voice communications.

A second important common carrier is the Western Union Tele-graph Corporation. It provides a full range of narrow, voice-grade, and wide-band communications facilities. These facilities were developed in connection with telegraphy but have been especially adopted to computer needs. Western Union also operates a direct dial-up tele-printer connection service called the American Telex System.

A third common carrier is the General Telephone and Electronics Company Network, known as the General System. This is the second largest telephone company in the United States, accounting for about 5 to 10 percent of the market. The General System offers a wide range of services, including interconnected, direct dial-up teleprinter facilities.

The available data transmission services largely are based on modifications of other types of communication networks: voice and telegraphy. These transmission facilities are adequate for low-cost, narrow-band communications. They can deal effectively with keyboard inputs, character printers, and cathode-ray tube outputs; but fast card readers and high-speed printers are another matter. A low-cost trans-mission facility with a capacity ranging from 10,000 to 20,000 bits per second could be used effectively by the computer industry; however, it is not yet available.

The error rate in transmission equipment is considerably greater than that in computer equipment, probably because the redundancy in voice communication is such that a little noise in the line is tolerable. This is not true of data communication; again, it appears that only makeshift solutions to problems are available to the computer-oriented user of transmission facilities.

6.13 SOFTWARE—AN OVERVIEW

There are at least three kinds of software and related facilities that a computer manufacturer might be expected to supply with his equip-ment: 1) an operating system; 2) some application programming pack-ages; and 3) a service that facilitates the documentation and exchange of software among different computer centers.

Some kind of operating system is available with almost all computers, even minicomputers. Section 1.3 mentioned that operating systems maintain the smooth flow of job execution with a minimum of operator intervention. They also help implement multiprogramming and time sharing (to the extent that they are available), and may contain applica-tion programming packages. A computer's capabilities are determined mainly by the effectiveness and efficiency of its operating system.

We already have discussed several programming languages: FOR-TRAN and WATFIV, PL/I and PL/C, and BASIC. Many other programming languages have been developed (see Reference 24 in the Annotated Supplementaty Bibliography) whose availability can enhance a computer's usefulness.

At one time, most manufacturers provided all software with their equipment at no additional charge. In recent years, some components, especially compilers and applications packages, have been made available only at an additional charge. The term *proprietary software* has been associated with programs that are available for sale or lease. Many software vendors offer special programming packages. Some of these are worthwhile; others may be overpriced or not very useful. However, the cost of developing a program is great enough to warrant a review of the proprietary software that is available before proceeding with a programming effort.

A users' group can be a valuable resource. This is especially true for computer centers, such as those at universities, that service a wide variety of customers. Useful operating system components and application programs may be available from other centers. A users' group or clearing house that certifies program acceptability and arranges for the exchange of programs is useful; however, if their capabilities are widely known, well-documented programs can be circulated without these special arrangements. For example, the especially efficient FORTRAN compiler for student use called WATFOR (and in later versions WATFIV), which was developed at the University of Waterloo, has gained widespread acceptance. The user-oriented facilities of any computer manufacturer apparently were not needed to achieve this wide dissemination.

Application programming packages are now available in many areas, such as statistical calculations, information storage and retrieval, linear and non-linear programming, payroll processing, banking applications, hospital accounting, and simulation. Some of these are proprietary software; others are available without additional charges. Frequently, the application packages must be adapted to the special needs of a particular user. A user should be certain that the software vendor will help him complete this adaptation, and that the combined cost of the original package and the additional effort is justified. We shall say more about application packages in the last two sections of this chapter. First we will discuss the use of the computer as a translator from one language to another, and then we will provide an overview of higher-level languages.

6.14 THE COMPUTER AS A TRANSLATOR

Machine-language programming is extremely difficult. Operations codes must be memorized; the contents of every address in storage must be noted and modified as changes take place; and every process must be broken down into its most elementary components. Quite early in the development of computers, computer scientists thought that the computer itself might be used to translate instructions from a more easily mastered programming language into machine language. That is, computer programs could be written to accept instructions which a human could easily generate as input, and to produce the corresponding machine-language instructions as output.

These translating programs are called assemblers or compilers. The most elementary translator, an *assembler,* permits the use of languages, called *assembly languages,* that are just one step removed from machine languages. Assembly languages use mnemonics, such as "A" or "M" for the operation codes "add" and "multiply," and labels such as "AGE 1," "AGE 2," and "PAY" for the operands. The computer keeps track of where everything is, and, upon request, will provide a key to the storage locations used for the various operands in the form of a symbol table. For example, the assembly-language instruction corresponding to the machine-language instruction 21 11234 11236, discussed in Section 6.5, could be

A   AGE1,AGE2

where (11234) is denoted by the symbol AGE1, and (11236) by the symbol AGE2.

Higher-level languages carry this procedure a step further. Assembly languages generally have one instruction for each machine-language instruction. A single higher-level language instruction would generate several machine-language instructions. For example, the FORTRAN instruction:

X=(A+B+C)*D

would generate machine-language instruction in the IBM 1620 computer like those shown in Figure 16.23. So would the PL/I instruction:

X=(A+B+C)*D;

and the BASIC instruction:

100 Let X=(A+B+C)*D

Figure 16.24 contains a description of the procedure involved in processing programs written in higher-level languages. Note that there are two steps. The first, *compilation,* accepts the *source deck* containing the *source program* and *control cards* as inputs, and produces a corresponding machine-language program, called the *object program.* The second step, *execution,* accepts the machine-language program and input data as inputs, and produces the desired outputs. A programmer has this second step in mind when he writes a program to be

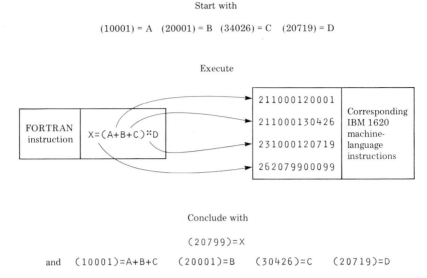

Start with

(10001) = A (20001) = B (34026) = C (20719) = D

Execute

		211000120001	Corresponding IBM 1620 machine-language instructions
FORTRAN instruction	X=(A+B+C)*D	211000130426	
		231000120719	
		262079900099	

Conclude with

(20799)=X

and (10001)=A+B+C (20001)=B (30426)=C (20719)=D

In order to preserve A, it is likely that
the machine-language instructions would
begin with, say

261085010001

So we would also conclude with

(10850)=A

Fig. 6.23 Illustration of one-to-many relation between higher-level and machine languages

implemented by a computer. Both these steps ordinarily are carried out on the same computer. The machine-language program produced in the first step may be kept in auxiliary storage, pending the execution of the second step.

6.15 OVERVIEW OF HIGHER-LEVEL LANGUAGES

There are many (some might say too many) higher-level programming languages. Most of these languages were developed to satisfy special needs, but a few were developed for general use. We have already discussed FORTRAN and WATFIV, PL/I and PL/C, and BASIC, and have said a little about the origins of these languages and how they are being used. In this section, we will talk about the nature and use of two

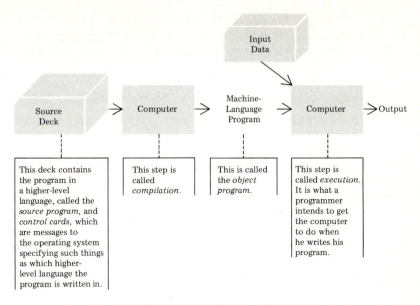

Fig. 6.24 Processing programs written in higher-level languages

other widely used languages—COBOL and ALGOL—and conclude with a discussion of three special-purpose languages—GPSS, which is used in simulation; LISP, which is used in list processing; and SNOBOL, which is used in string processing. These last three languages have been chosen because they are probably the most widely used special-purpose languages in each of the three important application areas.

COBOL

In 1959, the Department of Defense recognized that a programming language designed for use in business data-processing applications was needed. These applications were expected to require large files of information to be processed with some arithmetic calculations, but also with a great deal of information transfer from one file to another and to printed output. A Defense Department committee was organized to develop specifications for this kind of language, which was to use ordinary English terminology as much as possible. The product of the committee's efforts, COBOL (COmmon Business Oriented Language), was first described and made available in 1960 in a version called COBOL 60. Later versions appeared, and a standard version, called ANS COBOL, was established.

An interesting development in connection with COBOL was the Navy Department's creation of a series of programs called *The*

COBOL Compiler Validation System, which tests COBOL compilers. A description of the preliminary version of this facility appears in 14 volumes that were prepared in the mid-1970s and are available from the National Technical Information Service.

COBOL permits files of information to be processed record-by-record, in a direct manner. For example, the statement

```
READ CUSTOMER RECORD; AT END GO TO ADDRESSOR.
```

reads the records in the file called CUSTOMER one by one (and probably processes each record in accordance with subsequent statements). The program branches to the statement labeled ADDRESSOR when all the records in the CUSTOMER file have been processed.

COBOL also contains features that enable the same program to be used on different computers or on differently equipped versions of the same computer. A section of the program, called the *environment division,* includes such things as the name of the computer on which the program is to be compiled and the one on which it is to be executed, the input/output components used during execution and, perhaps, the main storage capacity of the computer on which the program is to be executed.

The English-like nature of COBOL can be seen from the following COBOL statement, which adds together OVERHEAD, FRINGE-COST, and SALARY, and calls the sum TOTAL.

```
ADD OVERHEAD,FRINGE-COST,SALARY GIVING TOTAL.
```

However, do not be mislead by the English-like nature of this statement. COBOL is a programming language and its rules must be followed strictly. For example, the words ADD and GIVING cannot be replaced by synonyms. ADD must be the first word and GIVING must precede the name for the sum. However, a formula-like version of this statement also is permitted. It would be:

```
COMPUTE TOTAL=OVERHEAD+FRINGE-COST+SALARY.
```

COBOL has become the most widely used programming language in business applications. This is a testimony to its success as a specialized language.

ALGOL

Computer scientists and other specialists in the use of computers recognized in the late 1950s that FORTRAN was not especially well-suited to the implementation of complex algorithms, even those required in scientific applications. FORTRAN had some facilities that were useful and worth retaining, but it lacked facilities to build a program by combining separate program units. (We shall say more in Section 8.11 about building algorithms piecemeal in complex applications.) These facilities were incorporated into ALGOL; the separate program units were called *procedures*. The procedural facilities of ALGOL served as a model for the same facilities that were incorporated into a language that later was developed in the mid-1960s, PL/I.

FORTRAN lacked other facilities that were incorporated into ALGOL, including the ability to carry out logical operations and comparisons. A facility which permitted branching to be contingent on these comparisons and, if necessary, on several comparisons involving several variables, was thought desirable. For example, suppose that we wished to compare X with Y and also to compare X with Z in order to determine which statement to execute next. More specifically, suppose that we wished to branch to statement S3 if $X > Y$ no matter what Z is, and to statement S2 if $X \le Y$ and $X > Z$, but to S1 if $X \le Y$ and $X \le Z$. We could write in ALGOL:

```
T1: IF X > Y THEN S3
    ELSE IF X > Z THEN S2;
S1: . . .
    :
    :
S2: . . .
    :
    :
S3: . . .
    :
    :
```

T1 is a label for the first statement. A colon is used to separate labels from the rest of the statement. Note that statements conclude with a semicolon. The ELSE clause in the second line of the statement T1 functions in much the same way as it would in ordinary English language. The ELSE clause makes the branching contingent on several comparisons.

The pressures that led to the development of COBOL and ALGOL also resulted in the improvement of FORTRAN. So, for example, logical comparisons were added to newer versions of FORTRAN, as was the ability to process files record-by-record.

ALGOL has become one of the most widely used programming languages in Europe, as well as in some American universities.

Simulation and GPSS

Simulation, a crucial area of computer applications, is a technique involving experimentation with a model of a real-world system that has been stored in a computer. Business enterprises, economic systems, and social and political systems are being simulated to help people understand how these systems function. Especially dangerous or expensive activities are being simulated to provide training for personnel who may be required to carry out these activities in reality. War games are being used to train military personnel; aircraft pilots are being trained in computer-controlled flight simulators.

In modeling real-world systems on a computer, the system can be viewed as changing smoothly from one state to another or as jumping or changing in a stepwise fashion from one state to another. In the former case, the system is viewed as continuous, and in the latter as discrete. Digital computers are most widely used in discrete simulations. Consider, for example, the operator of a desk calculator in a statistical laboratory. Although he is in motion continuously, for simulation purposes, his activities can be viewed as a series of discrete steps. He presses a series of buttons; makes marks on paper; reads from the paper; presses a series of buttons again; and so on. As an example of a continuous system, consider an airplane in flight. The power of the engines, the direction and speed of the wind, the positions of the control surfaces, and the position and velocity of the airplane are continuous variables which take on a continuous series of values. Although the flight of an airplane could be described in a series of discrete steps such as taking off, cruising between landmarks, and landing, such a model would not be useful to evaluate the flight characteristics of the plane or to train pilots. However, a discrete model might be useful for studying air traffic.

Because discrete simulations are the principal type implemented on digital computers, we will discuss a language that implements discrete simulations, GPSS. The General-Purpose Simulation System, or GPSS, is one of the oldest and most widely used discrete simulation languages. Many versions of GPSS have been produced. We will discuss GPSS/360; more recent versions of GPSS do not differ markedly.

The design of GPSS departs radically from that of statement-oriented languages. A fundamental element in GPSS is a transaction. A transaction might be a customer in a bank, a ship in a port, or an airplane in flight. Transactions are created and destroyed, as required, during simulation. A transaction could be created as a customer entered a bank, and destroyed when that customer left the bank. Activities are caused by the interaction of transactions with other system components, as the transactions flow through the system. Customers might write out a deposit slip, wait in line to see a teller, and be serviced by a teller. Each transaction carries with it a set of parameters that determine the transaction's attributes. Such things as the purpose of the customer's visit to the bank and whether or not that customer needs to fill out a deposit slip could be noted with parameters.

System components that service transactions can be used in GPSS. *Facilities,* for example, are used to simulate equipment that processes one transaction at a time. Equipment that can service more than one transaction at a time is called a *storage*. For example, if we were simulating a bank, a single teller would be a facility and a set of tellers could be viewed as a storage. GPSS automatically maintains statistics on the utilization, average contents, and other aspects of facilities and storages. The final values for these statistics automatically are output at the end of the simulation.

The operational functions are carried out within blocks. GPSS blocks, which are equivalent to statements, determine the logic of the system by controlling the flow and interaction of the transactions. For example, some blocks control the ways in which a transaction can use equipment. Other blocks affect the parameters associated with the transaction. Still others control inputs, and others control the direction of transaction flow. About 40 different types of blocks are available in GPSS. The essence of GPSS simulation lies in the actions which occur as blocks interact with transactions. The GPSS block is laid out in an 80-column format. Columns 8–18 contain the keyword or words that define the block's function. Beginning in column 19, there are a series of operands, separated by commas, that specify functions of the block. Columns 2–7 are used for reference labels. Comments may be inserted at the end of each block after the last operand, but one or more blank columns must separate the last operand from the comment.

The birth and death of transactions are controlled, respectively, by the GENERATE and TERMINATE blocks. The function of the TERMINATE block is to destroy any transaction that enters the block, along with all parameters associated with that transaction. This block also is used to control termination of the run, by halting the run after a pre-set number of transactions have been terminated. For example, the block

```
                 TERMINATE 1
```

immediately will remove from the system any transactions that enter this block. Each time a transaction is terminated, the operand 1 is subtracted from a counter that was set initially to a value prescribed by the programmer. When this counter is reduced to zero, the simulation run is terminated.

Among the operands that can be used in a GENERATE block are parameters that specify the rate at which transactions should be generated. For example, the block

```
                 GENERATE 22,12
```

will create transactions in intervals that are uniformly distributed from 10 to 34. That is, a number from 10 to 34, inclusive, will be selected at random to determine when the next transaction is to be created. If, for example, the number 14 is selected, the next transaction will be created 14 time units after the creation of the current one. The range 10 through 34 is decided on by both adding and subtracting 12 from the first parameter (22).

Simulation of the usage of an equipment usually requires three blocks. Two blocks are used to identify the equipment that is to be used or freed, and the third block is used to indicate how long that equipment is to be occupied. The third block is the ADVANCE block. For example, the block

```
ADVANCE 15,5
```

would force any entering transaction to be delayed in this block for a time interval selected randomly from the range 10 to 20, inclusive (that is, 15, plus or minus 5). If no ADVANCE blocks are included anywhere in the system, each transaction will flow through all blocks in zero time.

The two other blocks used to simulate equipment usage vary with the type of equipment. The SEIZE and RELEASE blocks are used for facilities. Thus, usage of a facility named PHONE for 10 to 20 time units could be simulated by the blocks:

```
SEIZE      PHONE
ADVANCE    15,5
RELEASE    PHONE
```

When a transaction enters the SEIZE block, the facility PHONE is recorded as being in use. The PHONE remains in use as long as the transaction is in the ADVANCE block. After the specified delay time, the transaction enters the RELEASE block, and the facility is freed from use.

General-purpose languages also are widely used in simulations. In fact, probably more simulations have been programmed using FORTRAN than any other language. However, for an extensive, sophisticated, discrete simulation, special-purpose languages such as GPSS can substantially reduce the programming effort that is required.

Lists and LISP

Ordinarily, a computer program is written to manipulate numbers. Mathematically oriented languages readily permit extensive computations with these numbers, and business-oriented languages permit sets of these numbers to be computed and manipulated conveniently. In many applications, the computer processes entities other than numbers—for example, positions on a checkerboard, segments of graphic images, or statements in plane geometry. Such entities are appearing more and more in computer programs.

These entities usually are structured in a prescribed way. For example, the statements in geometry are grouped and sequenced to form a proof. The segments of graphic images also are grouped and sequenced, forming graphic entities which, in turn, can be grouped and sequenced to form a picture. The segments could be small squares of various shades of gray; the graphic entities might be a man, a tree, an X-ray machine, or a table; and the picture might be a landscape or an operating room in a hospital. In the latter instance, the picture has a *hierarchical structure* in which whole lists of graphic images are single elements in the list of graphic entities.

Consider as a second example of a *hierarchical list* a set of hands in a game of bridge. The highest-level list consists of the symbols North, East, South, and West, standing for the frequently used points-of-the-compass designation of bridge hands. Each symbol refers to another list containing cards (e.g., the ace of spades or the ten of hearts). Each hand contains 13 cards.

To preserve structure as a part of a list, each element listed must contain not only the symbol for the element but also connecting links to the next element in the list and, if it is a hierarchical structure, links to another list containing all items that make up this element. These connecting links are called *pointers*.

A list-processing language that has become one of the most widely used in recent years is called LISP (*LIS*t *P*rocessor). Work on LISP was started by J. McCarthy and his associates at the Massachusetts Institute of Technology in 1959, and the first manual was published in 1960. LISP comes in a variety of versions. The most recent version, LISP 2, is really a general-purpose language, with origins both in LISP and ALGOL. We shall discuss only LISP 1.5 here.

LISP is rather different from, and perhaps more difficult to understand and use than, other programming languages. For example, sets of nested parentheses frequently appear in LISP programs. The number of sets of parentheses is important in determining the significance of the program. Our discussion will define only a few of the functions that are used in LISP to build new lists from old ones.

The CAR and CDR (pronounced "couder") functions of a list help analyze the content of a list and break it into components. The CAR, essentially, is the first element of a list, and the CDR of a list is itself a list which consists of all the elements, in their original order, after the CAR. For example, the CAR of the list (North East South West) is North, and the CDR is (East South West). Note that lists are enclosed in parentheses in LISP, and that list elements are separated by blanks. There also are functions that create a new list in other ways. The

CONS function builds a new list by adding elements to the beginning of a list. For example, if L = (Hearts Diamonds Clubs) and S = Spades, then CONS (S L), read as CONS the atom S onto the list L, is the list (Spades Hearts Diamonds Clubs). The original list L is unchanged.

List elements which are not themselves lists are called atoms in LISP. Names can be used to denote atoms and lists; in this case, S denotes the atom Spades, and L the list (Hearts Diamonds Clubs).

Hierarchical lists are lists consisting of lists. For example, a bridge deal is made up of four hands; each hand is itself a list. We could, for example, represent one specific deal in the following way. If we denote the deal by D, we have:

```
D = (N E S W)
```

where

```
N = (S1 S2 S4 S10 H2 H4 H5 D1 D9 D12 C4 C6 C8)
E = (S3 S11 S12 H1 H3 H6 D2 D3 D4 D5 C2 C3 C5)
S = (S5 S6 S7 H7 H8 H11 H12 H13 D6 D7 C7 C9 C10)
W = (S8 S9 S13 H9 H10 D8 D10 D11 D13 C1 C11 C12
     C13)
```

so that

```
D = ((S1 S2 S4 S10 H2 H4 H5 D1 D9 D12 C4 C6 C8)
     (S3 S11 S12 H1 H3 H6 D2 D3 D4 D5 C2 C3 C5)
     (S5 S6 S7 H7 H8 H11 H12 H13 D6 D7 C7 C9 C10)
     (S8 S9 S13 H9 H10 D8 D10 D11 D13 C1 C11 C12
     C13))
```

A card in a hand is denoted by a letter to signify the suit, followed by a number indicating the value of the card (1 = ACE, 2 = DEUCE, . . . , 11 = JACK, 12 = QUEEN, 13 = KING). LISP uses this notation because atoms must begin with a letter.

We see, for example, that

```
CAR(N) = S1
```

and that

```
CDR(W) = (S9 S13 H9 H10 D8 D10 D11 D13
          C1 C11 C12 C13)
```

There are functions that permit comparisons of atoms and lists. For example EQ compares atoms. EQ is true if the atoms are identical and false if they are not. Thus, given the bridge hands above,

```
EQ(CAR(N) S1)
```

is true.

Strings and SNOBOL

We already have mentioned character and bit strings in discussing PL/I and BASIC. In this section, a string will be viewed as a sequence of characters from among a certain prescribed set. String manipulation is especially useful in non-numeric computer applications. It also is used in constructing compilers and in other activities associated with developing the systems software.

Two characteristics of a string are especially important: 1) the actual length of the string—that is, how many characters it contains; and 2) whether the string is permitted to vary in length or is fixed in length.

Since string manipulation typically is required in processing text, we will concentrate on this area of application. Three of the basic capabilities required in processing text are:

1. Creating a new string;

2. Joining two strings to form a new one (called *concatenation*); and

3. Determining the length of a string.

The first requirement is satisfied in the usual way. We can store a string in a storage location by assigning a constant to a variable. (This is how we stored numbers in storage locations; it works just as well for strings.) The problem now is how to represent character string constants. A typical way is to embed a character string between punctuation marks of some kind. Single apostrophes are often used so. For example:

```
'LAUGH'
```

represents the character string constant *laugh*.

Concatenation and string-length determination occur in different ways in different languages. Generally, some kind of symbolic operator or function that has character strings as operands is used.

The first string-processing language was COMIT and the most widely used string-processing language is SNOBOL. COMIT was developed by a team under the direction of Dr. V. Yngve at the Massachusetts Institute of Technology in the late 1950s. SNOBOL was developed by D. J. Farber, R. E. Griswold, and I. P. Polonsky at the Bell Telephone Laboratories in the early 1960s. We shall use SNOBOL to illustrate string-processing languages.

In SNOBOL we can use SIZE (name-of-string or character-string-constant) to determine the length of a character string given as its argument. For example:

```
SIZE ('LAUGH') = 5
```

Concatenation in SNOBOL is obtained by merely joining strings with no specific operator indicated. The strings must be separated by at least one blank. Thus, for example:

```
WORD = 'LAUGH' 'ING'
```

causes the string 'LAUGHING' to be assigned to WORD.

SNOBOL has many additional facilities. There are four types of basic statements: 1) assignment; 2) pattern matching; 3) replacement; and 4) the end statement. A program consists of a sequence of statements. They may be one statement to a line, or several statements can be separated by semicolons on one line.

Assignment statements in SNOBOL are much like those in FORTRAN. Their form is: variable = expression. Enclosing strings in quotes distinguishes them from variables. Floating-point numbers, integers, and strings can be operands in SNOBOL expressions.

A novel feature of SNOBOL is that input and output are done using assignment statements. The variable INPUT is used to read an 80-character string from the next card in the card reader. The variable OUTPUT is used to print, and the variable PUNCH to punch, string or integer-valued outputs. For example,

```
OUTPUT = 'THE TEXT FOLLOWS'
```

prints the character-string constant, THE TEXT FOLLOWS in the next line of the printed output at this point in the execution of the program. Similarly,

```
OUTPUT = 'THE POINT COUNT IS'; OUTPUT = N
```

prints the heading **THE POINT COUNT IS** and then the value of the integer variable, N. Finally,

```
PUNCH = INPUT
```

punches out a duplicate of the input card.

Pattern matching is requested by writing the string that is to be scanned, followed by one or more blanks, and then the pattern that is being sought. So, for example,

```
'LAUGHING'   'AU'
```

results in a "hit." The pattern AU is present in 'LAUGHING'. Similarly, if we had:

```
WORD = 'MATILDA'
```
then
```
WORD    'AU'
```

would result in a "miss."

Pattern matching makes conditional substitutions in character strings by means of the *replacement statement,* which consists of two parts — a pattern matching and a substitute string — separated by an equal sign. The substitute string replaces the pattern if a hit is obtained in the pattern matching. Thus, for example, the statements

```
WORD = 'MATILDA'; WORD 'ILDA' = 'CH'
```

replace the contents of WORD (which was 'MATILDA') with 'MATCH'. If the pattern fails to match, no substitution is made.

6.16 APPLICATION PACKAGES

Nearly all computer manufacturers provide a set of computer programs designed to carry out scientific and statistical calculations. Most of these programs are available without charge. They include programs to carry out such complex calculations as inverting a matrix, determining the roots of a polynomial, fitting a function to a set of data by least squares, and carrying out an analysis of variance — as well as programs to carry out simpler calculations, such as calculating a frequency distribution, and means and standard deviations. In addition, scientific and statistical application packages are available from a variety of other sources. Some of the most widely used packages include the scientific and statistical programs available from IMSL (International Mathematical and Statistical Libraries) located in Houston, Texas, and the SPSS, SAS, and BMD statistical packages. SPSS is available from the National Opinion Research Center at the University of Chicago; SAS from the Institute of Statistics at the North Carolina State University at Raleigh, North Carolina; and BMD from the Health Sciences Computing Facility at the University of California at Los Angeles. Reference 20 in the Annotated Supplementary Bibliography contains a survey of 37 statistical packages.

Libraries, research centers, and business data-processing organizations all require capabilities to store and retrieve large volumes of information. Some organizations have attempted to develop their own programs for this purpose — usually, since the task is formidable, without too much success. In recent years, packages to carry out information storage and retrieval have been made available by the computer manufacturers as well as other sources.

Reference 25 in the Annotated Supplementary Bibliography contains a detailed description of the capabilities of interactive information systems. These include systems which are available from the computer manufacturers, such as STAIRS and IMS/360, available from IBM; IMS-8, available from UNIVAC; and MARS III, QUERY UPDATE, and MARS VI, available from Control Data Corporation.

Other systems can be obtained from vendors of time-sharing services; for example, DML from Computer Sciences Corporation; OLIVER from On-Line Systems; and FLEXIMIS from the General Electric Company and universities (GIPSY from the University of Oklahoma, LEADEMART from Lehigh University, and PIRETS from the University of Pittsburgh). Software vendors and research-oriented corportions also are active in this area. Systems available from these sources include BASIS from the Batelle Memorial Institute; ORBIT III, DS/3, and COMIS from the System Development Corporation; D.R.S. from A.R.A.P., Inc.; GIM from TRW Systems Group; INQUIRE from Infodata Systems; MARK IV from INFORMATICS; and MICROTEXT from the MITRE Corp.

6.17 A CHECKLIST FOR APPLICATION PACKAGES

The choice of an application package can be a difficult, time-consuming task. Many packages are available in a variety of sizes and prices. A checklist is given below to help determine whether a particular package is likely to satisfy your needs. Of course, before the checklist can help you, you must establish a needs specification, which should include a set of representative application problems.

The checklist reviews four As and an E for each package: the package's Availability, Applicability, Accessibility, Accuracy, and Efficiency should be checked. The checklist appears as a series of questions, each of which is followed by an example of a difficulty, enclosed in parentheses, that might be encountered if the answer is wrong. Some questions also have a comment following them.

Availability

1. Is this package available from a reliable source? (You encounter a difficulty and the vendor will not help you.)

2. Has this package been implemented on a computer like the one you have? (Pioneers pay a price in delay and inconvenience.)

3. Is there documentation and is it well-written — especially the programmer's and user's manuals? (You may not be able to get the package to work, and/or users may be stymied when they attempt to make use of the package.)

Applicability

4. Does this package contain all the capabilities that you now require? (Users may not be able to solve their problems.)

5. Does this package contain all the capabilities you will require in the next few years? (The package becomes obsolete quickly and you must get another one.)

6. Does this package do all that the vendor claims it does? (You may not be able to solve the users' problems after all.) It may be advisable to speak to people who have used the package for a while about applications similar to your own in connection with this question and others.

7. What are the limitations on such things as the amount and kind of data that can be processed and the media on which these data can be stored? (You have extensive data sets on magnetic tape and the package will not process them because there is too much data, or the data are formatted in an unacceptable way on the tape, or the package just doesn't accept magnetic tape input.)

Accessibility

8. How difficult is it for a user to learn about the package? (Users refuse to use the package because the documentation is confusing.)

9. What are the allowable formats for entering data? (A user has to repunch all his cards.)

10. How does a user tell the package exactly what the user wishes to do? (Potential users are discouraged because they would have to write the equivalent of a computer program to get the desired result.)

Accuracy

11. What algorithms does the package use to obtain its results, and are they correct? (A user gets an incorrect answer and holds you personally responsible, or a user gets an incorrect answer and doesn't even know it.)

12. Is the output formatted in a clear way and effectively labeled? (A user gets a correct answer but he cannot find it in the output.)

Efficiency

13. What is the running time for some representative applications of the package? (The first monthly report of computer use after

the package has been made widely available creates a series of nasty memoranda about your inability to select packages.)

14. How many resources—main storage space, auxiliary storage space, card cabinet drawers—does the package require? (You are billed for an additional 48,000 characters of main storage capacity after the package has been installed.)

15. How much user effort and other resources are required to use the packages? (A user has to apply several procedures to get a solution to a problem with this package, whereas the same user previously solved a similar problem using only one procedure with another package.) This question relates to applicability and accessibility, too, of course.

Exercises

1. Define: bistability, cycle time, access time, and execution time.

2. What is the principal difference between the way in which main storage and auxiliary storage function?

3. Why is reading from core storage said to be destructive?

4. Why are main storages that are computer circuits said to be volatile?

5. Define the terms "track" and "cylinder," as used in connection with disc storage media.

6. In what ways may especially important items in storage be protected from accidental erasure?

7. Name the principal auxiliary storage devices and compare their speeds and capacities.

8. Name the principal card-processing devices, and describe the function of each.

9. List five kinds of printers and compare their speed, versatility, effectiveness, and cost.

10. Why does the use of key-to-tape devices for input, in place of card input, shift some of the editing function to the computer?

11. What are the principal kinds of remote terminals?

12. Define: switching facility, narrow-band line, and tie line.

13. List the principal common carriers of data, and describe the facilities that each of them offers.

14. Define: proprietary software.

15. List the most widely used scientific and statistical packages available from sources other than the computer manufacturers, and the source for each of them.

16. What are the four As and an E that should be considered in selecting application packages?

17. What statements are used to set up and eliminate transactions in GPSS?

18. Write a series of GPSS statements that will occupy a facility called MACHINE for from 5 to 11 time units, and then free it.

19. Using the notation of LISP and the one used for bridge hands in Section 6.15, set up a list of the following four poker hands; that is, a list for:

Hand 1	Hand 2	Hand 3	Hand 4
ace of hearts	nine of diamonds	ten of clubs	ace of spades
king of clubs	eight of diamonds	nine of hearts	ace of diamonds
jack of clubs	four of clubs	eight of hearts	five of hearts
deuce of hearts	three of hearts	four of spades	three of clubs
deuce of diamonds	three of spades	deuce of clubs	deuce of spades

20. What is the CAR of Hand 1 and the CDR of Hand 2?

21. Write a series of SNOBOL statements that first assigns the string 'INPUT' to the variable A, then replaces 'INPUT' with 'OUT-PUT' (using the replacement statement), and finally outputs the contents of A.

*22. Referring to machine-language programming in the 1620 computer, suppose that $(11234) = \bar{1}234$, $(11236) = \bar{9}6$, $(11241) = \bar{0}0001$, and $(11246) = \bar{1}2212$ before the execution of the first instruction. What are the contents of these locations and the contents of the product area (i.e., of locations 00099 on back) after the execution of the following two instructions?

```
INSTRUCTIONS:  32 11245 59822
               23 11246 11236
```

*23. Referring to machine-language programming in the 1620 computer, suppose that main storage contains the following digits at the indicated addresses (we are not referring to the formal contents of addresses here but merely to a list of the elements in storage from location 06000 forward to location 06059):

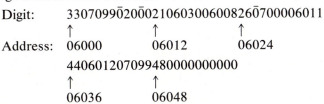

Suppose also that the address of the first instruction to be executed in a program is 06000. What can you say about the contents of storage after this program has been completed?

24.   An important consideration in using computers from remote terminals is the limited amount of printing that can get done when relatively inexpensive facilities are used. The printing capability of most terminals is specified in terms of the number of lines that are printed per minute or the number of characters printed per second, and the user frequently wishes to know how many pages will be printed per workday. For example, several terminals are available that print at about 200 lines per minute. A user who requires about 2000 pages of printing in a 16-hour workday wishes to know if these teriminals can accommodate his needs. Write a computer program that will help users make these decisions. That is, write a program in FORTRAN, PL/I, or BASIC that accepts as input the number of lines printed per minute and produces as output the number of pages printed in a 16-hour day. Assume that the time required to print a page is the same as that required to print 60 lines.

25.   The ability of a particular terminal to meet a user's needs is a function of its printing speed, the length of the workday, and the number of lines of printing per page. Write a program that is more versatile than the one you wrote to solve the previous exercise in that it considers the actual length of the workday. That is, write a program in FORTRAN, PL/I, OR BASIC that accepts as input both the printing speed in lines per minute and the length of the workday in hours, and prints out the number of pages printed per day. Continue to assume that the time required to print a page is the same as that required to print 60 lines.

26.   Write a computer program that accepts as input the number of characters printed at a terminal per second and the length in hours of the workshift, and prints out the number of pages printed per day. Assume that the time required to print a page is equal to that required to print 6000 characters.

ANNOTATED SUPPLEMENTARY BIBLIOGRAPHY

Most introductory computer science books contain one or more chapters about computer components and the way they function. Since such information would add little to what already has been discussed in this chapter, it is not included in the bibliography that follows. Instead, the bibliography lists reference materials that provide more detailed discussions of the topics covered in this chapter. The bibliography is organized by topics, which are listed according to the order in which they were discussed in the chapter.

Processor, Main, and Auxiliary Storage

1. Manuals prepared by the computer manufacturers are the best source for detailed information on a particular processor or storage unit. They are readily available, especially if you are a potential purchaser of the equipment. However, with one notable exception (Digital Equipment Corporation), they tend to be poorly written.

2. Bell, C. G., and Newell, A., *Computer Structures: Readings and Examples* (New York: McGraw-Hill Book Company, 1971). Comprehensively describes the capabilities of nearly all the major processors developed up to the late 1960s. A concise notation—called PMS, for Processor-Memory-Switch—is used to describe the organization of computer components, and a second, succinct notation—called ISP, for Instruction-Set Processor—is used to describe the programming level capabilities of the computer. Once these notations have been mastered, this book becomes a readable, useful reference.

3. Articles that present a brief survey of the capabilities of a new computer or software development appear from time to time in such publications as *Datamation*. For example, the September 1972 issue of *Datamation* contained an article entitled, "IBM's Virtual Memory 370s."

4. Hilleguss, J. R., "The Minicomputer—Getting It All Together," *Computer Decisions:* 34–39 (October 1972). This contains a useful listing of the names and addresses of the minicomputer manufacturers, and a table summarizing the major characteristics of the 67 minicomputers.

5. Foster, C. C., "A View of Computer Architecture," *Communications of the ACM,* Vol. 15, No. 7:557–65 (July 1972). This article is in the excellent 25th anniversary issue of the *Communications* of the principal professional computer society in the United States, the Association for Computing Machinery (ACM). The article contains a nicely illustrated review of the future of very small computers.

Input/Output

6. Levy, J., *Punched Card Data Processing* (New York: McGraw-Hill Book Company, 1967). A comprehensive review of punched cards and the principal machines which processed them in the mid-1960s can be found here.

7. Andersson, P. L., "OCR Enters the Practical Stage," *Datamation:* 22–27 (December 1971). This contains a useful list of the names and addresses of the principal manufacturers of optical scanning equipment, and a description of the major characteristics of 49 optical scanners.

8. Peters, J., Bakey, T., and Sloan, D., *Printer/Plotter Considerations* (Palo Alto, Ca.: Varian Data Machines, 1972). This book has a well-written, useful description of the way printers and plotters work. In discussing electrostatic matrix printers, it especially emphasizes the Varian type printer.

9. Dolotta, T. A., "Functional Specifications for Typewriter-Like Time-sharing Terminals," *ACM Computing Surveys,* Vol. 2, No. 1: 5–31 (March 1970). The specifications given are comprehensive and detailed. The article also contains a useful list of 25 references to publications on specific terminals, and to standards and specifications for terminals.

Communications

10. Martin, J., *Telecommunications and the Computer.* (Englewood Cliffs, N.J.: Prentice-Hall, Inc., 1969). This excellent introduction to tele-communications describes the facilities that are available, how they are used, and how they work.

11. Gourley, D. E., "Data Communications: Initial Planning," *Datamation:* 59–64 (October 1972). This is the first of three useful articles on data communications. The next two references, Nos. 12 and 13, complete the series.

12. Pyres, N. R., "Planning a Data Communications System," *Datamation:* 74–81 (November 1972). A checklist of remote terminal requirements and a brief summary of the characteristics of 15 programmable communications processory are included.

13. Deal, R. L., and Wood, P. C., "Data Communications: Putting It All Together," *Datamation:* 72–80 (December 1972).

14. Farber, D. J., "Networks: An Introduction," *Datamation:* 36–39 (April 1972). This provides a brief introduction to the major networks linking computers in the United States.

15. "Networks for Higher Education," *Proceedings of the Educom Spring Conference* (Princeton, N. J.: EDUCOM, The Interuniversity Communications Council, Inc., April 15, 1972). This review of networks and their present and potential impact on the university is quite detailed.

16. Gaines, E. C., "Specilized Common Carriers — Competition and Alternative," *Telecommunications,* Vol. 17, No. 9: 15–26 (September 1973). This survey article on common carriers includes a description of virtually all the companies providing data transmission services.

Software

17. *Communications of the ACM,* Vol. 15, No. 3 (March 1972). This whole issue is devoted to papers from the ACM Symposium on Operating System Principles.

18. Presser, L., and White, J. R., "Linkers and Loaders," *ACM Computing Surveys,* Vol. 4, No. 3:149–68 (September 1972). This tutorial article focuses on one aspect of operating systems: the way they link and load programs.

19. Denning, P. J., Third-generation Computer Systems," *ACM Computing Surveys,* Vol. 3, No. 4:175–216 (December 1971). This is a comprehensive discussion of the operating systems which are provided with third-generation computers.

20. Shucany, W. R.; Shannon, B. S.; and Minton, P. D., "A Survey of Statistical Packages," *ACM Computing Surveys,* Vol. 4, No. 2:65–80 (June 1972). This surveys the capabilities of 37 different statistical packages. A convenient table summarizing the characteristics of the packages is included. However, the relative merits (such things as accuracy, efficiency, and ease of use) of the different packages are not well-covered.

21. Martin, W. A., "Sorting," *ACM Computing Surveys,* Vol. 3, No. 4:147–74 (December 1971). This is an excellent tutorial, discussing the most important algorithms for sorting, and providing a list of 37 published algorithms on sorting. Most of these algorithms are available in the Collected Algorithms of the ACM, which are an important source of applications software.

22. Rivest, R. L., and Knuth, D. E., "Computer Sorting: Bibliography 26," *Computing Reviews,* Vol. 13, No. 6 (August 1972). While we are on the subject of sorting, reference is made to this bibliography in *Computing Reviews.* Many of the 30 or so bibliographies in *Computing Reviews* can be expected to include references related to the topics discussed in this chapter, especially software.

23. Rosen, S., "Programming Systems and Languages, 1967–75," *Communications of the ACM,* Vol. 15, No. 7:591–600 (July 1972). Both this article and the next one appear in the excellent 25th anniversary issue of the *Communications of the ACM* that was cited earlier.

24. Sammet, J. E., "Programming Languages: History and Future," *Communications of the ACM,* Vol. 15, No. 7:601–610 (July 1972). This article focuses on the history of the development of programming languages. It includes a comprehensive language history chart.

25. Fife, D. W.; Rankin, K.; Fong, E.; Walker, J. C.; and Marron, B. A., *A Technical Index of Interactive Information Systems.* (NBS Technical Note 819, National Bureau of Standards, March 1974). The capabilities of 46 interactive information systems are described in detail. There are no qualitative evaluations. This publication also provides a list of some of the larger data bases that are available.

26. McFarlan, F. W.; Nolan, R. L.; and Notron, D. P., *Information Systems Administration* (New York: Holt, Rinehart & Winston, 1973). This collection of articles provides a useful perspective on information processing as a resource management problem. There is little on hardware and software, but much on organizing and managing information.

27. Slysz, W. D., "An Evaluation of Statistical Software in the Social Sciences," *Communications of the ACM,* Vol. 17, No. 8:326–32 (June 1974). This article answers questions about the relative efficiency of five statistical packages (SPSS, BMD, TSAR, OSIRIS, and DATA-TEXT) used by social scientists on one computer (IBM 360/s). Unfortunately, since one package is not uniformly more efficient than another, there are no definite answers.

28. Friedman, D. P., *The Little LISPer* (Palo Alto, Ca.: Science Research Associates, Inc., 1974). A delightful introduction to a difficult language, LISP. This short book is written in a question-and-answer format that makes it especially readable and effective.

29. Lindsey, C. H., and Van Der Meulen, S. G., *Informal Introduction to ALGOL 68* (Amsterdam: North-Holland Publishing Company, 1971). This provides the least formal description of ALGOL 68 that was available at the time this book was published. However, it would not be correct to say that this book is easy to read.

30. McCracken, D. M., and Garbassi, V., *A Guide to COBOL Programming* (2nd ed.) (New York: John Wiley and Sons, 1970). This is the most readable introduction to COBOL that currently is available.

31. Maisel, H., and Gnugnoli, G., *Simulation of Discrete Stochastic Systems* (Palo Alto, Ca.: Science Research Associates, Inc., 1972). An excellent description of GPSS and a survey of simulation languages are included.

32. Sammet, J. E., *Programming Languages: History and Fundamentals* (Englewood Cliffs, N.J.: Prentice-Hall, Inc., 1969). Chapter VI, pp. 382–470, is probably the best place to go next for additional information on string- and list-processing languages. It includes more than six pages of references to publications on the subject.

33. Griswold, R. E.; Roage, J. F.; and Polonsky, I. P., *The SNOBOL 4 Programming Language* (Englewood Cliffs, N.J.: Prentice-Hall, Inc., 1968). This is the most comprehensive book published on SNOBOL and a particularly well-written reference.

34. Gottfried, B. S., *A Comparison of Programming Languages* (New York: Quantum Publishers, Inc., 1973). This is a concise, handy, 19-page reference guide that compares the characteristics of FORTRAN, PC/1, BASIC, COBOL, and ALGOL. Gottfried also has prepared similar reference guides from Quantum Publishers on each of these five languages.

Chapter 7

Algorithms

7.1 INTRODUCTION

If you want to learn to develop procedures to solve problems with the aid of a computer, you must work the exercises in this chapter. For Chapters 7 through 11 in general, the exercises within a chapter will concentrate on specific techniques, and the exercises at the conclusion of the chapter will concentrate on preparing complete algorithms, using the language appropriate to that chapter.

The language in which the algorithm is written and the level of detail required are dictated by how the algorithm is to be used. In this chapter, we shall discuss English-language algorithms which a reasonably intelligent person, without any background in the subject matter of the procedures, can execute. In the next chapter, we shall discuss algorithms in the form of flowcharts, usually written as an aid to computer programming. In later chapters, we shall discuss algorithms in the FORTRAN, PL/I, and BASIC programming languages.

The techniques of algorithmic construction associated with the phrase *structured programming* are introduced, as appropriate. The importance of clear, direct algorithmic structure and statements is emphasized. The use of the clearer, more direct, branching statements already has been emphasized in the discussions of FORTRAN, PL/I, and BASIC in Chapters 2, 3, and 4. Top-down solutions, introduced in connection with the payroll problem discussed in Chapter 8, are not emphasized, since they are not the appropriate solution for the majority of problems encountered here. Chapter 12 emphasizes the importance of writing readable programs with sufficient annotation and effective documentation.

137

7.2 DEFINITION

An *algorithm* is an unambiguous, complete procedure for solving a specified problem in a finite number of steps. It must include specific steps for both starting and stopping the procedure. Provision for every possible alternative that might be encountered, including provision for the possible submission of erroneous inputs, also should be made to the maximum extent feasible.

7.3 CONNECTION WITH COMPUTER PROGRAMMING

The preparation of an algorithm is an integral part of the general procedure for writing computer programs. This procedure involves:

1. Specifically stating the problem that is to be solved with the aid of a computer;
2. Formulating an algorithm for its solution;
3. Preparing general and detailed flowcharts;
4. Writing a computer program;
5. Debugging, i.e., testing and correcting, the computer program; and
6. Applying the program to appropriate data and analyzing the results.

In some cases, the problem will be small or simple enough, or the programmer will be proficient enough, to permit the procedure to be telescoped. It even may be possible to write the algorithm (step 2) directly in the form of a computer program, making one step out of steps 2 to 4. In other cases, the problem will be so complex that step 2 must be subdivided into other steps. Flowcharts may be developed jointly with the construction of the algorithm, since they may help clarify the structure of the solution and lead to a better algorithm. This is especially true for those complex problems that lend themselves to a top-down solution (We shall say more about this in connection with the payroll problem in the next chapter). In general, obtaining an algorithm is distinct from writing the program, and precedes it.

Debugging programs can be a difficult, time-consuming task. If at all possible, test data should be constructed and operated on as in the program, but hand calculations or a desk calculator should be used. This is called *hand simulation*. We shall say more about testing algorithms in Sections 7.10 and 7.11.

There is no "cookbook approach" to writing algorithms. This text presents examples of algorithms in the hope that the reader will learn by analogy. A few hints on concluding algorithms are given in Section 7.6 and some hints on recognizing the end of a set of input data are given in Section 7.8.

7.4 THE CALCULATION OF ACCUMULATED SAVINGS

This problem, familiar to anyone who has had a savings account earning interest, will introduce the techniques of algorithm formulation. Suppose that we deposit an amount of money, say P, in a savings account. Suppose also that this money earns interest at an annual rate, R, compounded quarterly. This means that interest is earned each quarter on the principal which is then in the account at a rate of R/4. But since interest is compounded, interest is earned on interest. That is, the interest earned each quarter must be added to the principal. Interest for the next quarter then is calculated using the new principal.

For example, if P = $1000 and R = 4%, then the interest earned each quarter is 4%/4 = 1%. At the end of the first quarter, $10 interest would be earned and the new principal would be $1010. At the end of the second quarter, $10.10 interest would be earned and the new principal would be $1020.10. This process would continue until the money is withdrawn.

Restating the problem (the first step in developing a solution), we have as input:

P = principal that is deposited
R = annual rate of interest (R/4 = quarterly rate of interest)
N = the number of quarters until the money is withdrawn

We wish to compute and output the principal at the end of N quarters.

Suppose that we let I = R/4, and write P_K to indicate the principal at the end of K quarters. This means that $P_1 = (1 + I)P$, and P_N is the value we desire, the output. (We assume that I is converted to a decimal number, so that if I = 1%, it is expressed as .01 in the calculations.) We see that:

$$P_1 = (1 + I)P$$
$$P_2 = (1 + I)P_1 = (1 + I)(1 + I)P = (1 + I)^2P$$
$$P_3 = (1 + I)P_2 = (1 + I)(1 + I)^2P = (1 + I)^3P$$
$$P_4 = (1 + I)P_3 = (1 + I)(1 + I)^3P = (1 + I)^4P$$

and so on, so that finally:

$$P_N = (1 + I)^N P$$

This means that to get the output, we multiply $(1 + I)$ by itself N times and multiply that result by P. If we call the output A, the procedure is:

1. Input the principal, P, the annual interest rate, R, and the number of quarters, N;
2. Let $I = R/4$;
3. Let $A = (1 + I)^N P$;
4. Output A;
5. Stop.

This procedure assumes an ability to accept inputs, carry out arithmetic operations, and produce outputs — reasonable assumptions for an algorithm that is to be implemented on a computer. This procedure also assumes that interest will be stated as an annual rate and that interest is compounded quarterly. These assumptions were made because they are applicable to many American savings banks. But we can generalize the algorithm by assuming that I, the interest rate for each interest period, is input directly. P is the starting principal, as before, and N is the number of interest periods. With these assumptions, we can calculate the amount due, A, as follows:

1. Input the principal, P, the interest rate, I, and the number of interest periods, N;
2. Let $A = (1 + I)^N P$;
3. Output A;
4. Stop.

The algorithm has one less step because the input exists in a more usable form. (We do not have to convert the annual interest rate to a quarterly rate in the algorithm; the user does this in preparing the input.) The algorithm can be applied to a greater variety of problems. For example, if interest were at an annual rate of 6 percent compounded semi-annually, and if we wished to calculate the amount due in 10 years on a principal of $1200, we could use this algorithm with $P = 1200$, $I = .03$, and $N = 20$. We also could use this algorithm to calculate the amount due if interest were compounded quarterly. For example, to calculate the amount due in 1 year on a principal of $1000 earning interest at an annual rate of 6 percent compounded quarterly, we would input $P = 1000$, $I = .015$, and $N = 4$.

7.5 THE SIEVE OF ERATOSTHENES

Algorithms are not a new subject. In about 250 B.C., Eratosthenes constructed one to answer a question that is still of interest to today's mathematicians: "What are all the prime numbers between 1 and some specified positive integer, say N?" The algorithm, called the *Sieve of Eratosthenes*, proceeds as follows:

1. Write all integers in numerical order from 2 through N. Call this the *basic list*.
2. Record, in what we shall call the *prime list* (to distinguish it from the basic list), the first uncrossed number in the basic list. Call it M, then cross it off the basic list and cross off every Mth number thereafter.
3. If M is less than $\sqrt{N}$, return to step 2; if M is $\geq \sqrt{N}$, add all remaining uncrossed numbers to your prime list and stop.

The prime list you have prepared is, in fact, the desired list of primes less than N.

For example, what are all the primes less than 24? We record:

2	3	4	5	6	7	8	9	10
11	12	13	14	15	16	17	18	19	20
21	22	23	24

We record 2 and cross off every even number. Since $2 < \sqrt{24}$, we record 3 and cross off 3, 6, 9, 12, etc. Since $3 < \sqrt{24}$, we go back to the beginning of the basic list, place 5 on the prime list, and cross off every fifth number. At this point, our basic and prime lists are:

Basic   *Prime*

2 3 4 5 6 7 8 9 10   2, 3, 5
11 12 13 14 15 16 17 18 19 20
21 22 23 24

Since $5 > \sqrt{24}$, we add 7, 11, 13, 17, 19, and 23 to the prime list and stop. We conclude that 2, 3, 5, 7, 11, 13, 17, 19, and 23 are the prime numbers less than 24.

Note that 6, 10, 12, 15, 18, 20, and 24 were crossed off twice in this procedure. This might appear to be a waste of effort. However, if we chose not to cross off any number more than once, we would have to spend additional effort keeping track of which numbers we had crossed off previously. Sometimes it is better to solve a problem simply and directly, even though there is some redundancy in the solution.

A variation of this method was used by Lehmer [1]* to produce a list of prime numbers as long ago as 1914. The list was greatly extended with the aid of the electronic digital computer, and the effort took a new turn. Large computer facilities competed with each other to find new largest known primes [2].

Exercises

1. What would be the input to the savings algorithm (Section 7.4) if we wished to calculate the amount in a savings account at an annual interest rate of 5-1/2 percent compounded quarterly, with an initial deposit of $1000 after one year?

2. A well-known problem in connection with interest calculations is the Manhattan Island problem: Suppose that the Indians had deposited the $24 that they were paid for Manhattan in a savings account in 1628. Suppose also that the account paid 4 percent annual interest compounded annually. How much would they have today in this account? What are the inputs to the savings algorithm for this problem?

3. Find all the primes less than 99 using the sieve of Eratosthenes.

*4. Why does step 3 in the sieve algorithm work? Would you improve on this step—that is, could you rewrite the algorithm by modifying its stop rule to obtain a complete list of primes with fewer listings and crossings of numbers?

5. Suppose that we do not assume that the $\sqrt{N}$ is available as input. Rewrite the sieve algorithm so that it could function without this information. Try to do this in two ways: 1) by changing the stop rule; and 2) by comparing M with the square root of N without actually calculating $\sqrt{N}$. (Hint: if 9 is less than 10 then $3 < \sqrt{10}$.)

7.6 LOOPING AND ITERATION

The processes carried out on a computer are often extremely long. Usually, however, a series of instructions must be executed repeatedly with only slight modifications in the instructions or in the data being processed. For example, in calculating a sum, we repeated the sequence

---

*Numbers in brackets are references to a list of books and articles that appear at the end of the chapter. This list is distinct from and precedes the Annotated Supplementary Bibliography. This same practice will be followed in later chapters.

input, sum several times. The algorithm should be constructed to take advantage of this repetition by returning as often as possible to instructions executed previously. This, as we have mentioned, is called *looping*.

There is a loop in the sieve algorithm discussed in the previous section. The third step provides for returning to step 2, a previous instruction, if $M < \sqrt{N}$. Even in the simple numerical example given to illustrate this algorithm, branching occurred twice. More importantly, by constructing the algorithm in this way, allowance has been made for any number of repetitions of the step 3-step 2 sequence.

In many applications, the repetitive calculations are designed to obtain better and better estimates of a desired quantity. Successive estimates of the quantity are obtained by substituting previous estimates in the same procedure. This technique is called *iteration*. Frequently, only the last estimate of the quantity is used to obtain the next estimate. In this case, we would begin with some starting estimate, say E_0. The iterative procedure then is used to obtain the first estimate E_1, using E_0 as an input. E_2 is then obtained using E_1 as input, and so on. The problem is to find a valid procedure, choose an appropriate starting value, and decide when to stop the iteration. We shall say no more about selecting procedures and starting values, since books on numerical methods, which sometimes contain hints on the choice of a starting value, can help you find appropriate procedures (for example, see [3]).

As for stopping, in some applications it is possible, given an estimate of the desired quantity, to check on how good this estimate is. For example, if we were estimating the square root of a number, say X, using an iterative scheme, we could square our estimate and compare it with X. In most applications, however, we are forced to rely on a different checking mechanism. It is reasonable to expect that, as we get closer and closer to the true value, successive estimates will differ by smaller and smaller amounts. We could prescribe some small quantity, ϵ, and stop when the magnitude of the difference between successive estimates was less than ϵ. (The absolute value of the difference between successive estimates is calculated. This means that only the numeral, called the *magnitude* of the number, is used. Any sign is disregarded.) To ensure against making too many iterations, these stop rules almost always are combined with a rule that places an arbitrary, prescribed upper limit on the number of iterations. The iteration is stopped as soon as either this upper limit is reached or the checking criterion is satisfied.

Suppose, for example, that we wish to estimate the square root of 1715. We first must decide on a procedure. A commonly used one is based on Newton's formula, in which the next estimate of the square root of X, say E_n, is obtained from the preceding one, E_{n-1}, and X

$$\text{using } E_n = 1/2 \left(E_{n-1} + \frac{X}{E_{n-1}} \right).$$

(The mathematical properties of the iterative technique based on the use of this formula are discussed in [3].) Now we need a starting value. It is easy to observe that 40 squared is 1600 and that 41 squared is: $(40 + 1)^2 = 1600 + 40 + 40 + 1 = 1681$. Similarly,

$$(40 + 2)(40 + 2) = 1600 + 80 + 80 + 4 = 1764$$

A guess of 41.5 might be reasonable. Finally, we must decide on the error we shall tolerate in terms of the difference between the square of E_n and 1715. We also should set some upper limit on the number of iterations. If we insist that the magnitude of the difference between E_n^2 and 1715 be less than 0.0001, and if we agree to make no more than 10 iterations, we find that:

i	E_i	$E_i^2 - 1{,}715$
0	41.5	7.25
1	41.4126506	0.0076
2	41.4125585	-0.000002

Since 0.000002 is less than 0.0001, we take 41.4125585 as the estimate of the square root. The beginner should not be misled by the fact that a satisfactory result was obtained so quickly. The rapid and sharp reduction in the error, as evidenced by the third column in the table, is not typical of iterative procedures. Newton's formula is especially good, or, as the mathematicians might say, the estimate converges especially rapidly.

7.7 AN ALGORITHM FOR OBTAINING SQUARE ROOTS

Now that we have seen, in rough outline, how we could proceed to estimate the square root of a number, let us write a precise, complete, unambiguous procedure — an algorithm — to do this.

We must begin by specifying the number that we are to work with, as follows.

1. Input X.

The next step is to prescribe a starting value, i.e., a value for E_0. The hunt-and-guess scheme we used in getting the square root of 1715 might be used in general, but it is awkward to prescribe. Instead, we shall use a procedure that is easier to state and that gets us off in the right direction, namely, taking half the value of X as the starting value. So we have:

   2. $E = X/2$.

We must set up a counter to keep track of which iteration we are currently making. This always must be done explicitly. Variables, even if they are subscripts, cannot be introduced into the algorithm without specifying how values are to be assigned to them. So we have:

   3. $n = 1$.

and then:

   4. $E_n = 1/2(E_{n-1} + X/E_{n-1})$.

Now we must provide for stopping this procedure. But we have nothing to use for this purpose; we did not input either ϵ, the greatest tolerable absolute difference between E_n^2 and X, or the maximum number of iterations, say K. We should modify the first step as follows:

   1. Input X, K, and ϵ.

Now we are ready for the next series of steps.

   5. Is the absolute value of $X - E_n^2$ written as $|X - E_n^2| < \epsilon$? If the answer is *yes*, go to 6; if *no*, go to 7.

   6. Output E_n and stop.

   7. Is $n = K$? If the answer is *yes*, go to 8; if *no*, go to 9.

   8. Output E_n and the message that the maximum number of iterations has been executed and stop.

   9. Set $n = n + 1$ and go to 4.

This appears to complete the algorithm, but let us now consider the "provision for every possible alternative" discussed when we defined algorithm. Suppose, for example, that $X = 1/2$. We know that $\sqrt{X} > 1/2$ but that our starting value is actually less than $1/2$. We might modify step 2 as follows:*

   2. $E_0 = (X + 1)/2$.

This gives us a value of E_0 that is halfway between 1 and X. For example, $E_0 = 3/4$ if $X = 1/2$. But what if $X = 0$? We would get $E_0 = 1/2$, and

---

*Note that this is the value of E_1 that would be obtained if E_0 were to be taken to be either 1 or X itself.

successive applications of Newton's formula would only serve to halve the estimate. We would waste a lot of effort. We therefore might find it advisable to check on whether $X = 0$ at the start. A negative value of X is even more disastrous, and should be screened out of the computations. Now we can rewrite the algorithm as follows:

1. Input X, ϵ, and K.

2. If $X \leq 0$, output X and stop; if $X > 0$, go to step 3.

3. $E_0 = (X + 1)/2$.

4. $n = 1$.

5. $E_n = 1/2(E_{n-1} + X/E_{n-1})$.

6. Is $|X - E_n^2| < \epsilon$? If the answer is *yes*, go to step 7; if *no*, go to 8.

7. Output E_n and stop.

8. Is $n = K$? If the answer is *yes*, go to step 9; if *no*, go to 10.

9. Output E_n and the message that the maximum number of iterations has been executed, and stop.

10. Set $n = n + 1$ and return to step 5.

Let us apply the algorithm to a few sets of inputs. We shall take $\epsilon = 0.0001$ and $K = 10$ for each input. We start with $X = 1715$. We then get $E_0 = 858$ and

n	E_n	$X - E_n^2$
1	429.9994	More than 158,000
2	216.9939	More than 45,000
3	112.4487	A little less than 11,000
4	63.8500	About 2362
5	45.3549	About 342
6	41.5839	14.2207
7	41.4129114	0.0292306
8	41.4125585	0.000002

We have arrived at the same estimate, but this time we required eight iterations rather than only three. It would appear that we should improve our procedure for estimating E_0. However, computers perform iterations of this kind quite quickly, and the price we are paying, five additional iterations, is a small one. Even more importantly, the hunt-and-compute techniques we used to arrive at the better starting value might produce an even longer overall running time for the estimation of the square root if they were implemented on the computer. However, this is not typical of all iteration procedures. In many applications, the choice of a good starting value is critical — we cannot even get an answer if the starting value is poor.

Suppose that we next try to estimate $\sqrt{1/2}$; that is, we input $X = 1/2$ as well as $K = 10$ and $\epsilon = 0.0001$. This time, $E_0 = 0.75$, and we have

n	E_n	$X - E_n^2$
1	0.708333	0.0017356
2	0.70710784	0.000001497

Finally, if $X = -1715$, we would only execute steps 1 and 2, and would output the value of X.

A sizeable area of applied mathematics, numerical analysis, is devoted to the study of the theory of computational algorithms. Reference [3] is a good introductory book on this subject.

7.8 END-OF-FILE

A problem that frequently arises in writing algorithms is providing a mechanism for recognizing the end of the input. Recall from Chapters 2–4 that the number of values to be summed was input first when this number was allowed to vary from one application of the program to another. However, the actual number of values input and the number specified may not agree. The algorithm should be written to make this recognizable (see Exercise 13 in Chapter 2, 13 in Chapter 3, and 11 in Chapter 4). It may not be convenient, or even possible, to count the number of values beforehand. A mechanism should be provided to recognize the end of the set of input, called recognizing the *end-of-file*.

If the input is a sequence of numbers, then it may be possible to add a number at the end of the input that could not possibly be in the set of input numbers. (This was the approach suggested in Exercises 2.13, 3.13, and 4.11.) Each value that is read in is compared to the number that has been placed at the end of the input. For example, if we marked the end of the input with a value of -999999, and if we were reading in the numbers one at a time and storing them in a location called B, the following steps might appear in the algorithm:

20. Input B

21. If B is equal to -999999, go to 50

In these steps, B is processed appropriately. This section would conclude with:

Go to 20

and the next statement would be statement numbered 50, which would begin the processing that is to be carried out after all the input has been read in.

This is just one way to recognize and respond to the end-of-file. Some operating systems include provision for marking and sensing the end-of-file. For example, most of the operating systems available with the IBM/360 and 370 computers will recognize a card that contains a slash punched in column 1 and an asterisk in column 2 as an end-of-file indicator. However, the action that the operating system takes in response to the presence of this card may not be the one that the programmer wants. Some programming languages permit programs written in that language to use this operating system feature. We shall see an example of this when we discuss the END option in FORTRAN in Chapter 9.

Files that are written on magnetic tape by a computer frequently conclude with an end-of-file indicator of some kind to let the computer recognize the end of a file that is stored on magnetic tape. The payroll algorithm that is discussed in the next chapter will use this.

7.9 CHARACTER STRING MANIPULATION

Applications of computers involve non-numeric as well as numeric information processing. Strings of characters—for example, names of employees or students, English-language text, and bibliographies—more and more are the grist for the computer's mill. Algorithms to process such strings are important.

In some respects, character strings can be treated like numeric data because instructions are available to compare them and to determine which of a pair of strings is lesser (i.e., which precedes the other in alphabetic ordering), or which succeeds the other in alphabetic ordering. Two character strings are said to be equal only if they are identical. In addition, special facilities are available in some languages to process strings of characters. Algorithms should be written so that they take advantage of these facilities.

Consider the following simple example. Three names are to be input and placed in increasing alphabetical order. An algorithm to do this might be:

1. Input the first name; call it A. A is a variable that takes on character strings rather than numbers for its values.

2. Input the second name; call it B.

3. Input the third name; call it C.

4. Is A ≤ B? If so, go on to step 8; if not, go to step 5.

When applied to character strings, the question, "Is A ≤ B?" is equivalent to the question, "Does the character string called A precede or equal the character string called B in alphabetic ordering?" The string called A is compared to the one called B, from the left, character by character, until a different character is encountered in the two strings. When this occurs, alphabetic precedence is determined. For example, if A = 'CODIFY' and B = 'CODIFIED', then the fifth character determines the ordering and B < A. If A = 'EXTENT' and B = 'VIEW', the first character determines the ordering and A < B. Character strings may contain digits and punctuation marks or other special characters. Conventions have been adopted regarding the "alphabetical" sequence of these characters.

5. Set X = A.

The character string called A now also is called X; the string stored in A is unaffected.

6. Set A = B. (Now A is changed.)

7. Set B = X.

The use of X is necessary; without it we would have A = B, followed by B = A. This would leave B unchanged and in both locations. These three steps serve to interchange the contents of A and B and to ensure that A does indeed precede B in alphabetical order.

8. Is B ≤ C? If so, go to step 12; if not, go to 9.

9. X = B.

10. B = C.

11. C = X.

Now we are sure that B ≤ C; however, A may no longer precede B, so we now check that again.

12. Is A ≤ B? If so, go to step 16; if not, go to 13.

13. X = A.

14. A = B.

15. B = X.

16. Output A, B, and C in that order.

17. Stop.

This very simple algorithm shows how character strings can be manipulated in much the same way as numbers. In fact, Exercise 6 asks you to write an algorithm to put three numbers in decreasing numerical order. Your algorithm will be similar to this one.

Algorithms that process character strings also contain some special features. For example, it may be important to search for a particular character, such as a blank space, a period, a comma, or some other punctuation mark that is used to denote important boundaries within the string. This hunting for individual characters frequently is required in text analysis and processing. It is one of the reasons why this type of application is time-consuming.

7.10 TESTING ALGORITHMS

Writing algorithms is a tedious task that offers much opportunity for error. All algorithms should be tested. Ideally, we would like to prove (in the mathematical sense) that, given any input, the result must be correct. However, in most cases a mathematical proof of the correctness of the algorithm is not possible — or at least not readily obtainable. Therefore, the algorithm must be tested using specially chosen test inputs.

Since writing algorithms is the first step in developing a computer program, testing the algorithm could be postponed and, in effect, combined with checking or debugging the computer program. However, experience indicates that errors in logic are the most difficult errors to detect. For this reason, it may be wise to check the algorithm for logical errors before any computer instructions have been written, rather than spending time checking for errors in writing the instructions and for logical errors in the algorithm when the program is debugged.

Testing an algorithm for logical errors begins with a set of *test inputs* which should be constructed such that, as a whole, they cause every step in the algorithm to be executed. They also should be realistic. If they are numeric, both their magnitudes and their signs should cover the range of values that may appear as input. Finally, several exceptional inputs (values that would only appear in the event of input errors) should be included, whether or not they would cause new steps in the algorithm to be executed. They may reveal new alternatives for intermediate results that must be accounted for; i.e., they may cause several steps to be added to the algorithm.

Once a set of test inputs has been established, it is a good practice to give the algorithm and the test inputs to a co-worker who has not seen either of them and ask him to obtain the results. It is surprising how frequently a fresh viewpoint can find dead ends and logical inconsistencies that the person who constructs the algorithm fails to see. Often, just describing your algorithm to a co-worker will give you some useful fresh insights.

Let us try to set up some test data for the algorithm to calculate the principal in the savings account that first was discussed in Section 7.4. Since the algorithm contains no branches, every step will be executed each time the algorithm is applied. A single set of input will ensure the execution of every step. Realistic inputs might include:

Set	P	I	N
1	3642	.015	62
2	43	.0125	14
3	10172	.0175	4
4	642.13	.065	18

An input that would require many digits to be carried in the calculations is:

Set	P	I	N
6	4213641.12	.01125	650

For erroneous inputs we add:

Set	P	I	N
7	0	.015	62
8	−43	.0125	14
9	10172	1.	4
10	3642	0	62
11	43	−.0125	14
12	43	.0125	0
13	43	.0125	−14

Recall that an algorithm should provide for the possible submission of erroneous inputs. We should include steps to check on whether I, P, and N are non-positive. It also might be advisable to check on whether I is unreasonably large. If an erroneous input is found, an appropriate message should be output. With this in mind, we might revise the algorithm as follows:

1. Input P, I, and N.

2. If P ≤ O, go to step 8.

3. If N ≤ O, go to step 10.

4. If I ≤ O or I > .25, go to step 12.

5. Let $A = (1 + I)^N P$.

6. Output A.

7. Stop.

8. Output P and the message that the principal is not positive.

9. Stop.

10. Output N and the message that the number of interest periods is not positive.

11 Stop.

12. Output I and the message that this interest rate is not permitted.

13. Stop.

7.11   A TEST SET FOR THE SQUARE-ROOT ALGORITHM

Let us try to set up test data for the square-root algorithm discussed in Sections 7.6 and 7.7. To ensure the execution of every step, we include the following sets (the reader should determine which step in the algorithm is executed for the first time by each new set of test input):

Set	X	K	ϵ
1	−1	10	0.001
2	0	10	0.001
3	1	10	0.001
4	10	1000	0.001
5	10	3	0.000001

For realistic inputs, we include:

Set	X	K	ϵ
6	1047.26	100	0.001
7	0.062172	100	0.00001
8	1.004131	50	0.0001

For grossly erroneous inputs, we add:

Set	X	K	ϵ
9	10	4.5	0.00001
10	10	−5	0.001
11	10	100	−0.001
12	10	−5	−0.001

Substituting the above inputs in the algorithm probably would cause us to modify the algorithm; thus we first check whether K is negative or zero, and we stop the process if $n > K$ (to accommodate a value of $K = 4.5$). We also probably would choose to output X, K, and ϵ as well as E_n each time an output is made.

Exercises

6. Given three numbers, A, B, and C, write an algorithm which will sort these numbers in decreasing order. Prepare a set of test inputs for this algorithm and substitute these inputs in your algorithm.

7. Write a computer program, using the language that you learned in Part I, that will implement the algorithm you wrote in answering the preceding exercise (Exercise 6).

*7.12   ERRORS IN IMPLEMENTING ALGORITHMS
          ON A DIGITAL COMPUTER

Algorithms implemented on electronic digital computers frequently may give erroneous results. There are three major reasons for these errors: first, the computer does what it is programmed to do; an erroneous algorithm produces an erroneous result. Second, erroneous input data produce erroneous outputs, or more succinctly, GIGO (garbage in, garbage out). Third, the computer can retain only a finite number of digits in its calculations. If, for example, the difference between two nearly equal numbers is divided into a third number, the loss of significance in the digits discarded from the first two numbers can be disastrous.

If we use lower case letters to denote operands and capital letters to denote algorithms, then the procedure X operating on a and b can be denoted by $X(a, b)$. In addition, we use a superscript asterisk to indicate the algorithms and operands actually used, as opposed to the true algorithms and operands. The error in applying X to a and b is then given by:

$$X(a, b) - X*(a*, b*)$$

This can be rewritten as:

$$[X(a, b) - X(a*, b*)] + [X(a*, b*) - X*(a*, b*)]$$

The first difference is the error resulting from applying the right algorithm to the wrong data, and is called the *propagated error*. The second difference results from applying the wrong algorithm to the data actually processed, and is called the *generated error*.

There are many sources for propagated errors. Poor data collection procedures and careless handling of the data in preparing the input can introduce errors. Errors also result from the loss of significance that occurs when input data are truncated or rounded, and from using the erroneous result of a previous calculation in the present calculation. Some authors apply the term "propagated error" only to this last kind of error. They call the other errors simply *input errors.*

Generated errors can result from erroneous models for the process under study, clerical errors in preparing the program, and errors in the program itself.

The techniques of statistical design [4, 5] should be applied to avoid gathering invalid or incomplete data. Quality-control procedures can be applied fruitfully when checking a large volume of input data. For small volumes of data, we recommend a complete check of the final input (usually in the form of a listing of the contents of a deck of punched cards) against the source for the data (c.g., laboratory notebooks, questionnaires, statistical abstracts). Similarly, a complete check of a listing of the program deck should help minimize the number of clerical errors in the program.

Logical errors in programming should be detected in the debugging of the program. There is another class of programming errors, which might be called "sloppy output errors." The organization, labeling, and effective formatting of outputs are essential to avoid misinterpretation or misrepresentation of valid output.

There is no substitute for a penetrating, thorough analysis of the algorithm. A great deal of experience with a wide range of procedures may be required to do an effective job on complex problems. However, a novice who makes full use of the available references will be able to devise and implement algorithms to solve complex as well as simple problems.

Exercises

8. Construct an algorithm to solve the following problem: Given a positive integer N, determine the Nth Fibonacci number. The

first Fibonacci number is 0, and the second is 1. Each succeeding Fibonacci number is obtained as the sum of the two preceding numbers so that, for example, the first few numbers are 0, 1, 1, 2, 3, 5, and 8. Set up a counter, in the form of a variable that takes on the values 1, 2, 3, . . . , N, to indicate how many numbers have been generated, and test the value of the counter against N to determine if the algorithm should be stopped.

9. Write an algorithm to compute $\sum\limits_{i=1}^{N} x_i$, given x_i and N. Use a counter, as in Exercise 8. The symbol $\sum\limits_{i=1}^{N}$ is used to indicate the addition of the elements in the expression following this symbol, with $i = 1$ in the first term of the sum, $i = 2$ in the second and so on until $i = N$. Thus,

$$\sum_{i=1}^{N} x_i = x_1 + x_2 + x_3 + x_4 + \ldots + x_N$$

10. Write one algorithm to compute both the mean and standard deviation of a series of numbers, $x_1, x_2, \ldots, x_N$, given N and the numbers themselves. The formulas for these statistics are given below. Be sure to include a procedure for computing the required square root.

$$\text{Mean} = \frac{\sum\limits_{i=1}^{N} x_i}{N}$$

$$\text{Standard deviation} = \sqrt{\frac{\sum\limits_{i=1}^{N} x_i^2}{N} - \left(\frac{\sum\limits_{i=1}^{N} x_i}{N}\right)^2}$$

In this formula, $\sum\limits_{i=1}^{N} x_i^2 = x_1^2 + x_2^2 + x_3^2 + x_4^2$

$$+ x_5^2 + \ldots + x_N^2.$$

11. Construct a set of test inputs for the algorithm written in Exercise 9. If your algorithm requires N as input, be sure to include a set of data for which N is given erroneously.

12. Write an algorithm to sort a set of five numbers in decreasing order.

13. Construct a set of test inputs for the algorithm written in Exercise 12.

*14. Write an algorithm for computing the point count in a bridge hand (a bridge hand contains 13 cards) using the following point-count scheme:

1) 4 points for each ace.

2) 3 points for each king—but not if the only card in the suit is the king (i.e., not for singleton kings).

3) 2 points for each queen and 1 point for each jack—but not if there are two or fewer cards in the suit. In the case where there are exactly two cards in the suit, the queen or jack counts only if the other card is of higher rank.

4) 3 points for each suit in which you have no cards (i.e., 3 points for each void).

5) 2 points for each suit in which you have one card (i.e., 2 points for each singleton).

6) 1 point for each suit in which you have two cards (i.e., 1 point for each doubleton).

Points for distribution, i.e., points resulting from conditions 4, 5, and 6, are scored independently of the rank or value of the cards held in the suit. For example, a singleton king is worth a total of 2 points (2 for distribution plus none for the king), whereas a singleton ace is worth 6 points (2 for distribution and 4 for the ace). A doubleton king, jack is worth 5 points (1 for distribution, 3 for the king, and 1 for the jack because the king is of higher rank).

*15. Given a pair of integers, I and J, write an algorithm to find the greatest integer that is a divisor of both I and J. (N is a divisor of M if, and only if, a positive integer L exists such that $M = LN$.) It may either encourage you or heighten your frustration to learn that the Euclidean school of Greek mathematics solved this problem thousands of years ago. Their result is known as the *Euclidean algorithm*.
Look at Reference 3 in the Annotated Supplementary Bibliography and try writing algorithms to solve a few of these problems.

REFERENCES

1. Lehmer, D. N., "A List of Primes from 1 to 10,006,721," *Carnegie Institute Publication 164* (1914).

2. Miller, J. P., "The Search for Large Primes," *Proceedings of the Manchester University Computer Symposium* (1951).

3. Conte, S. D., and de Boor, C., *Elementary Numerical Analysis* (2nd ed.) (New York: McGraw-Hill Book Company, 1972).

4. Cochran, W. G., *Sampling Techniques* (2nd ed.) (New York: John Wiley and Sons, Inc., 1963).

5. _____, and Cox, G., *Experimental Designs* (2nd ed.) (New York: John Wiley and Sons, Inc., 1957).

ANNOTATED SUPPLEMENTARY BIBLIOGRAPHY

The literature on how to construct algorithms is sparse. Although most introductory computer-programming texts discuss the subject, their treatment is usually too superficial to supplement this book. A few discussions that are more than superficial and that can help a person faced with a problem in algorithmic formulation are referenced below.

1. Gear, C. W., *Introduction to Computer Science* (Palo Alto, Ca.: Science Research Associates, Inc., 1973). This is a first-rate introduction to computer science that includes extensive coverage of topics in data representation.

2. Knuth, D. E., *The Art of Computer Programming,* Vol. 1: *Fundamental Algorithms;* Vol. 2: *Seminumerical Algorithms;* Vol. 3: *Sorting and Searching* (Reading, Mass.: Addison-Wesley Publishing Company, 1958, 1971, 1973). This monumental work—difficult to read but well worth the effort—is the "last word" on algorithms.

3. Gruenberger, F., and Jaffray, G., *Problems for Computer Solution* (New York: John Wiley and Sons, Inc., 1965). An old collection but still the best available set of problems for computer solution. Try writing algorithms to solve a few of the problems in this book that interest you.

4. Culbertson, J. T., *Mathematics and Logic for Digital Devices* (Princeton, N.J.: D. Van Nostrand Company, Inc., 1958). This reference includes a definition of algorithms, one or two examples of algorithms, and a discussion of the notation for sums and the notation for products. It has been through many new printings since 1958 and is still one of the best references for the most elementary mathematical topics associated with computing.

Chapter 8

Flowcharts

8.1 INTRODUCTION

Flowcharts are an especially convenient form in which to express algorithms before programming a computer. Some programmers do not prepare flowcharts before writing the computer programs but wait until after a program has been debugged, so that they can incorporate the flowchart into the written, detailed description of the program. In many cases, a systems analyst or programmer will not write out a formal, step-by-step algorithm such as those presented in Chapter 7, but will proceed directly to a flowchart.

Flowcharts are used widely because they combine the precision and continuity of an algorithm expressed as text with the visual aid inherent in a plot or diagram. In addition, they pinpoint dead ends, unaccounted-for alternatives, and subsections of the algorithm that are particularly susceptible to errors.

The language used in flowcharts includes some well-known symbols (such as arrows) and some special symbols (which will be described in succeeding sections), as well as ordinary English statements and mathematical formulas. The arrows are used to indicate the path to be followed from one step to another. The special symbols are the boxes used to enclose the steps. The shape of each box categorizes the objective of a particular step. The English and mathematical statements in the box prescribe the operation to be performed. Ordinarily, the flow depicted on a chart proceeds from left to right and top to bottom, as in English text; however, the arrows unambiguously indicate the direction of flow.

When using a flowchart to present the algorithm, the steps in the algorithm must be classified. The major classifications are: input/output, decision, terminal, and processing. Each type of step, and the flowchart symbols used with it, will be discussed in later sections of this chapter.

There is an American National Standard (ANS) for flowchart symbols for information processing [1]. Figure 8.1 contains the principal symbols and their meanings.

The shape of a box determines its function. Large or small boxes of the same shape may be suitable for use in different flowcharts or even in a single flowchart. Each box must be proportioned properly; in particular, the standard for the ratio of its width to its height must be maintained. If this is not done, the shape can be distorted and there may be some confusion in interpreting the step. These proportions will be noted in connection with the discussion of each box, if appropriate. (For example, this would not be necessary for connectors. A circle is a circle.)

First we will contrast systems flowcharts with programming flowcharts, and then we will discuss the distinction between general and detailed flowcharts. The chapter concludes with several examples of programming flowcharts.

8.2   SYSTEM VERSUS PROGRAMMING FLOWCHARTS

Diagrammatic descriptions of real-world processes were used long before electronic digital computers. Among these were descriptions of the ways in which systems function, called *process charts* or *system flowcharts*. Such a flowchart was not intended to represent an algorithm but rather to describe a system; for example, how a manufacturing process for an organization functioned, or how a clerical process was carried out. A standard exists for these system flowcharts [2]. Diagrams also have been used as an aid in designing equipment for information handling. A standard exists for these *logic diagrams* [3] as well.

This chapter will not discuss these other types of flowcharts, but rather the use of flowcharts to describe algorithms. There is only one standard that is applicable, ANS X3.5. All references to flowcharts in the remainder of this book will be to programming flowcharts.

8.3   DETAILED AND GENERAL FLOWCHARTS

Real problems often are complex, and it usually is difficult to construct a detailed algorithm for their solution from scratch. Instead, a general procedure is outlined at the start. This might be called an overview of

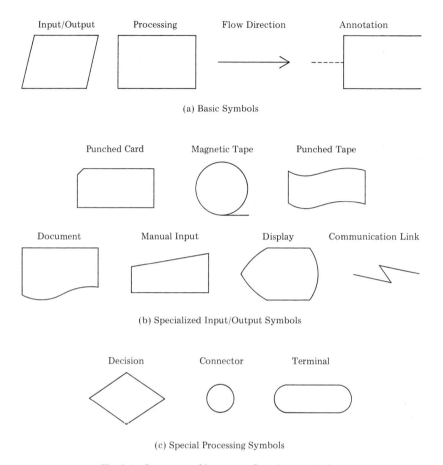

(a) Basic Symbols

(b) Specialized Input/Output Symbols

(c) Special Processing Symbols

Fig. 8.1 Summary of important flowchart symbols

the logic for the solution of the problem. After the general procedure has been reviewed for logical correctness and efficiency, a detailed algorithm is built piecemeal, one piece for each major step in the general procedure. A flowchart depicting the general procedure is called a *general flowchart;* one presenting the details is called a *detailed flowchart.*

Another way to distinguish between general and detailed flowcharts is to ask: "Can I write a computer program directly from the flowchart?" The detailed flowcharts should resolve any question that may arise in writing the computer program; the general flowchart, almost invariably, will leave some questions unanswered.

A third way to distinguish between the flowcharts is to note the kinds of entries that appear in the boxes. Detailed flowcharts usually have a greater number of mathematical formulas and comparisons, whereas general flowcharts have a greater number of broad English-language statements or questions. To put this another way, detailed flowcharts assign symbols or values to each variable that is processed, and relate the variables via formulas. General flowcharts deal with variables in generic terms as subjects or objects of English-language statements or questions.

In a later section, we shall discuss both general and detailed flowcharts for an algorithm that calculates a payroll. We shall see how a complex problem may be attacked by dividing it into more manageable pieces, or *modules*. An algorithm in the form of a flowchart will be developed for each module. This approach is called *modular program flowcharting*. A general flowchart is drawn first, providing an overall (top-down) view of the solution, and is used as a guide in breaking the algorithm into modules. Detailed flowcharts then are prepared for each module. We shall see how the detailed flowcharts resolve questions that may arise in writing a program by posing several important questions that are not answered by the general flowchart but are answered by the modular, detailed flowcharts for the payroll algorithm.

8.4 FLOWCHART SYMBOLS FOR INPUT AND OUTPUT

The slanted parallelogram can be used in a flowchart to represent any input or output operation. Its proportions are, width to height, 1:2/3. This box can be used in any step in which the algorithm requires information from an external source or in which the information is recorded on some external medium. Special symbols also exist that can be used to denote specific input or output media. Thus, for example, if the input or output is to come from or go to punched cards, this step can be enclosed in a box shaped like a card. Similarly, for punched paper tape or magnetic tape, the box looks like a stream of paper tape or a reel of magnetic tape. The proportional dimensions for both the paper tape and the punched card symbol are, width to height, 1:1/2. Symbols for special input/output operations are given in section (b) of Figure 8.1. If output is to go on a document or to be sent to a display via a communication link, there are appropriate symbols to indicate this. This book will use the slanted parallelogram, for the most part, to denote input or output steps. This is a good practice to follow because it makes the algorithm independent of a particular device or medium.

The text enclosed in the symbol should, as a minimum, specify:

1. Whether the operation is an input or an output; and
2. Which variables are to be assigned values or are to be output.

This can be done either by listing the names of each of the variables or, if the data are appropriately structured, by denoting a whole set of variables using a single name, such as an array name, a file name, or a record name.

For example, a box that would input three values required in the algorithm to calculate accumulated savings would look like:

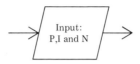

8.5 THE DECISION SYMBOL

A diamond-shaped symbol is used to enclose a step that involves decisions that may lead to branching. Typically, diamond-shaped symbols in general flowcharts contain English-language questions, whereas those in detailed flowcharts contain specific methods for implementing questions. The dimensional proportions of this box are, width to height, $1:2/3$.

Frequently, the method used in detailed flowcharts is to base the branching decision on the contents of two storage locations, say A and B. A is compared to B, and three alternatives are allowed for: $A > B$, $A = B$, and $A < B$. For example, the box that would implement the branching involving a comparison of $A:B$ would look like:

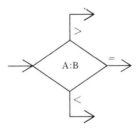

The branching could be based on comparing whole formulas involving many variables. Each formula would appear on either side of the colon. Also, only two outgoing paths might be appropriate; we might branch one way if $A = B$ and another if $A \neq B$. In this case, the decision box would look like:

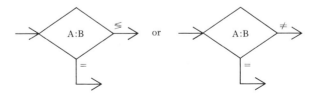

The two boxes are equivalent, and the user is free to choose the notation he prefers for the algorithm he is representing. The entry arrow may not always come from the left; it frequently comes from above, or, in rare instances, from the right or bottom.

8.6 TERMINAL SYMBOLS

There are two types of terminals in a flowchart; a start box and a stop box. Both the beginning and the end of the algorithm should be specifically indicated. Although in most flowcharts the algorithm begins in the upper left-hand corner of the page, it may begin elsewhere. Often it is necessary to use several separate pages to draw a flowchart, and to distinguish the beginning of the whole procedure from the beginning of the procedure on a single page. A terminal box is used to mark the beginning of the whole procedure. A connector is used to mark the beginning of the procedure on a single page.

Terminal symbols are shaped like long rectangles with rounded ends. The dimensional proportions are, width to height, 1:3/8. In the flowcharts we will draw, either the word *start* or *stop* will appear in a terminal box. The terminal box is the first we have seen so far that has a single arrow connected to it. (Arrows may enter or exit from other directions.) So we have:

8.7 CONNECTORS

We already have noted that flowcharts may require several pages. This may be because one-paged charts are impossible (there is no paper in stock big enough to hold them), or awkward (the chart becomes too confusing), or for other reasons (the boss doesn't like them). The exit from one page must be connected to the entry on the next page. An identifier is placed in the exiting connector—for example, a letter of the alphabet. The same identifier is placed in the corresponding entering connector. Frequently the exiting connector appears in the lower right-hand corner of the page and the corresponding entry connector in the upper left-hand corner of the next page. We have:

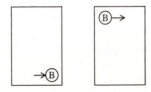

Connectors also may be used on a single page within the flowchart to avoid excessive crossing of lines or long lines from one part of the page to another. Figure 8.3 shows the use of this kind of connector.

8.8 PROCESSING

The rectangular processing symbol is the catch-all for steps that are not otherwise classifiable. Most processing symbols on detailed flowcharts for computer programs contain assignment statements. Ordinarily, only a single step should be placed in each box. If multiple steps are shown in one symbol, they should be read and implemented from top to bottom.

The proportional dimensions of width to height for processing boxes is 1:2/3.

8.9 ANNOTATIONS

Remarks may be affixed to a flowchart by means of a special symbol designed for that purpose. The symbol is a three-sided rectangle, open on either the right or the left. It is connected to the portion of the flowchart that it annotates by a broken line from the closed side of the rectangle. The proportional dimensions for the open rectangle are, width to height, 1:2/3. In general, the annotation box will be open on the left if the box appears to the left of the area of the chart that it annotates, and open on the right if it appears to the right of the area of the chart that it annotates. Annotation boxes, therefore, look like:

Annotation boxes do not contain steps in the algorithm; they merely contain remarks. If an annotation box is removed, the procedure is unaffected. They help to clarify and explicate the content of the flowchart but do not modify the procedure in any way. Examples of annotation boxes can be found in Figures 8.2, 8.5, and 8.8.

Flowcharts should be drawn neatly so that they are legible and unambiguous. Symbols should be drawn carefully and with correct dimensions. A template is a useful aid in drawing flowcharts. Templates frequently are available from the computer manufacturer, and also may be purchased in some stores.

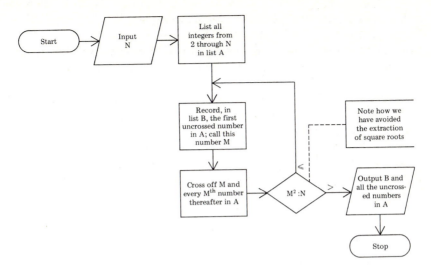

Fig. 8.2   A flowchart for the sieve of Eratosthenes

Exercises

1. Draw a detailed flowchart for calculating the amount accumulated in a savings account. Be sure to include provision for erroneous inputs (see Sections 7.4 and 7.10).

2. Draw a flowchart for finding $\sqrt{N}$ using Newton's formula. This time, use a combination of all three possibilities (a ceiling on the number of iterations, a bound on the error in the results, and a bound on the difference in successive estimates) to obtain a stop rule. That is, stop the procedure as soon as one of the three criteria is met. Be sure to indicate in your output which of the three criteria caused the stop.

3. Prepare a detailed flowchart for finding the Nth Fibonacci number (see Exercise 8 in Chapter 7).

4. Prepare a detailed flowchart for sorting three numbers, A, B, and C, in decreasing order (see Exercise 6 in Chapter 7).

5. Prepare a detailed flowchart for computing the mean and standard deviation of N numbers, X_1, X_2, . . . , X_N (see Exercise 10 in Chapter 7).

8.10   FLOWCHART FOR THE SIEVE OF ERATOSTHENES

Just as with algorithms, one learns how to draw flowcharts by example and by doing. In the remainder of this chapter we shall present examples of flowcharts.

A general flowchart for the sieve algorithm is given in Figure 8.2. Note that this time we are including a specific procedure for comparing M with $\sqrt{N}$. The diamond-shaped decision box contains the procedure. Since we used the notation A:B, meaning compare A with B, we are comparing M^2 with N. If $M^2 < N$, we continue the procedure of listing and crossing numbers; if $M^2 \geq N$, we write out our results and stop.

8.11   THE PAYROLL PROBLEM

We shall be dealing with payroll processing in a somewhat unrealistic way. To concentrate on algorithmic formulation but keep the problem manageable, we are emphasizing the arithmetic aspects of the payroll process and are de-emphasizing the transfer of information and the handling of files and records that are required in an accounting operation of this kind.

The objective of the algorithm is to calculate the pay due each employee who worked in the preceding week, and to update each employee's record in the master payroll file to reflect the week's payroll activities.

A master payroll file consists of a series of records, one for each employee. Ordinarily, the records in the master file will be kept in order of employee number. If not, then the records should be reordered (sorted) so that this is the case.

The master payroll file contains the following information in each record: employee number, employee name, regular hours worked, hourly pay rate, regular gross weekly pay, cumulative gross pay to date in the current year, cumulative social security deduction in the current year, withholding tax deduction class, cumulative withholding tax deduction in the current year, hospitalization deductions, and regular net pay (see Figure 8.3).

A series of cards is punched each week (one for each employee). Each contains an employee's number, name, and number of hours worked during the week (see Figure 8.4). The cards are input to the computer; the program retrieves the matching employee record from the master payroll file and computes:

1. The actual gross weekly pay. (If no overtime was worked, the actual gross weekly pay will be equal to the regular gross weekly

pay; if the employee worked overtime, the hourly rate will be used to determine the additional gross pay to be added to the regular gross pay.)

2. Cumulative gross pay to date.

3. Appropriate withholding tax deduction this week.

4. Cumulative withholding tax deduction.

5. Social security tax deduction.

6. Cumulative social security tax deduction.

7. Actual net pay.

Payroll processing begins by matching the number and the name of the first entry in the master payroll file with the number and the name of the first entry in the weekly file. Normally, a match takes place and the processing goes on to the next step. The abnormal case—no match—is discussed later.

Both the name and number are matched to make errors in input less likely to affect the payroll. Suppose that only the numbers were matched. If a keypunching error were made in preparing the weekly input, the erroneous number might accidentally be a correct number for another employee. This could be costly. Although it is less likely, accidental erroneous matching of names also could occur if only the names were matched.

Remember that both the master and the weekly files are in order of increasing payroll number. This speeds the processing, especially (as is likely) if the master file is kept on magnetic tape. Since the records in the file are ordered according to the sequence in which they are to be processed, there would be no need to waste time spinning tapes in a search for the next record. Files that are organized in this way are called *sequential files*. Files that are stored on magnetic tape should be sequential if processing times are to be minimized.

The number of hours actually worked is used to determine the amount of overtime, if any. For example, comparing the entries in the *hours-worked* field in the weekly file (Figure 8.4) to the entries in the *regular-hours* field in the master file (Figure 8.3), we see that Mr. Masterson worked five hours of overtime. From this, the program determines gross and net pay for the week. (It can use the regular figures in the master file for everyone but Mr. Masterson.) Mr. Masterson's regular hourly rate is $3.20 and, since all overtime is paid at a time-and-a-half rate, his overtime rate is $4.80. This means that his gross pay is

$$40(\$3.20) + 5(\$4.80) = \$152.00$$

The deductions to be made are

$$5.85\% \text{ of gross for social security (FICA)} = \$ \quad 8.89$$
$$18\% \text{ of gross for withholding income tax} \quad = \quad 27.36$$
$$\text{Regular deduction for hospitalization} \qquad = \quad \underline{\quad 2.80}$$
$$\text{Total deductions} = \$ \quad 39.05$$
$$\text{Net Pay} \qquad \qquad = \$112.95$$

The figure of 18 percent used to compute the withholding tax is determined from the number of deductions claimed by the employee. We could have put this figure directly in the master file, but we chose to assume that the number of deductions is in the file. This means that the payroll program must include a table that converts from number of deductions to percentage of gross salary withheld. For example, the table might be

No. deductions:	0	1	2	3	4	5	6	7	8	or more
% withholding:	20	18	16	15	14	13	12	11	10	

The cumulative entries in the master file now would have to be corrected as follows:

Cumulative FICA is now $90.69; that is, $81.80 + $8.89.

Cumulative withheld tax is $279.00; that is, $251.64 + $27.36.

Cumulative gross earnings are $1550; that is, $1398 + $152.

No other changes are made in the master file. A payroll check for $112.95 is printed, along with an itemized report of the employee's earnings and deductions.

Now we shall consider the abnormal case—when the payroll numbers and names in the master and weekly files do not match. In such cases, a message is printed out so that steps can be taken to correct the files, if necessary. There are at least four possible situations:

1. The payroll number for the master file is less than the number for the weekly file, and the names do not match.

2. The payroll number for the master file is greater than the number for the weekly file, and the names do not match.

3. The payroll numbers are different, but the names are the same.

4. The payroll numbers are the same, but the names do not match.

An appropriate message should be printed out in each case, and the process continued. If the master-file number is less than the weekly-file number, we print an appropriate message and proceed to read the next record from the master file. Similarly, if the weekly-file number is smaller, a message is printed and the next record from the weekly file is read. In either case 3 or case 4, a message is printed.

For example, in Figures 8.3 and 8.4, the first entry in the master file is for employee number 12345, which is less than the first employee number in the weekly file, namely, 12347. Case 1 applies, and a message is printed. The record for Paul R. Johnson is drawn from the master file; a match takes place, and his payroll for the week is computed.

How do we attack a problem of this kind? It is usually wise to begin by developing a general flowchart, an overall procedure. A general flowchart is given in Figure 8.5. It was developed directly from the description of the problem.

It is obvious that a great many specific procedures and formulas are not given in the general flowchart. Since the programmer needs to know these procedures, several questions of interest to him, but unanswered by the general flowchart, could be listed immediately. For example: How are the gross pay, deductions, net pay, and cumulative figures computed? What is the "appropriate output" to be given in the event of failure to match entries, and which is the "appropriate file" from which to draw the next entry? Which entries in the MASTR file should be updated? What do we really mean by matching entries? What are the possible kinds of output? How do we go about determining whether or not both files are exhausted?

We can divide the procedure into three major modules. The first is the initialization and conclusion of the algorithm. These steps are linked together through the connector (1). They include the first two boxes in the upper left of Figure 8.5 and the last two boxes in the lower left of this figure. The second is the matching procedure which is summarized in the decision box in Figure 8.5 and includes the output that is to be generated if the match fails (the box below the decision box). The third is the calculation of the payroll, the update of the master file, and the output of a paycheck and report. These are the boxes down the rightmost column of Figure 8.5.

The detailed flowcharts for the payroll problem are given in Figures 8.6 to 8.8. The distinction between the two types of charts should become apparent in comparing Figure 8.5 with these figures. Figure 8.9 contains a dictionary of variable names used in the flowcharts.

The first detailed flowchart, Figure 8.6, describes the procedure for checking whether the files are ended. Note the mechanism used for this purpose. It is assumed that an *end-of-file mark* is entered on the tape. This is a reasonable assumption, since the end of a tape file is marked in a standard way when the file is written by a computer. The variable M is used for the master file, and a W is used for the weekly

Number	Name	Regular Hours	Rate	Regular Weekly Pay	Cum. Gross Pay	Cum. FICA	No. Deduc.	Cum. Tax Deduc.	Weekly Hosp. Deduc.	Regular Net Pay
12345	SMITH, JOSEPH E.	40	3.20	128.00	1280.00	74.90	0	256.00	4.10	90.81
12347	JOHNSON, PAUL R.	40	3.20	128.00	1280.00	74.90	3	192.00	4.10	97.21
12351	FRIEDERICHS, CARL	40	3.60	144.00	1440.00	84.20	3	216.00	4.10	109.88
12353	MASTERSON, JOHN F.	40	3.20	128.00	1398.00	81.80	1	251.64	2.80	94.67
12356	PAULERS, HARRY V.	40	4.03	160.00	800.00	46.80	4	112.00	4.10	124.14
12361	MEYERS, JOAN S.	35	3.00	105.00	1050.00	61.40	1	189.00	0.00	79.96
.	.	.	.	.	.	.	.	.	.	.
.	.	.	.	.	.	.	.	.	.	.
.	.	.	.	.	.	.	.	.	.	.

Fig. 8.3 Typical contents of a master payroll file

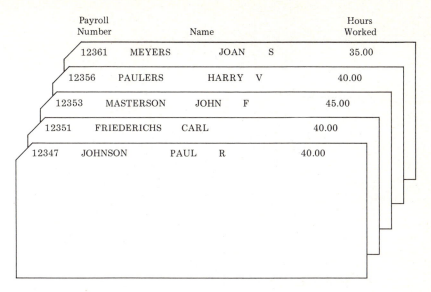

Payroll Number	Name			Hours Worked
12361	MEYERS	JOAN	S	35.00
12356	PAULERS	HARRY	V	40.00
12353	MASTERSON	JOHN	F	45.00
12351	FRIEDERICHS	CARL		40.00
12347	JOHNSON	PAUL	R	40.00

Fig. 8.4 A few cards in the weekly payroll file

file. Each variable is set equal to one when the tape mark is read for the corresponding file. Thus, for example, if W is 1 when the tape mark on the master file is read, all the entries in both files have been read. The normal entry is the START and the normal exit from this chart is connector (8.7). Connector (8.7) is the normal entry to the second detailed flowchart, which provides for the matching of employee names and numbers.

The algorithm is written so that the variable NER will provide a count of the number of times that a match of both the names and numbers in the two files fails. Each time such a match does not occur, an appropriate message is entered in the output. If NER is not zero when both files are exhausted, the operator is instructed to print this output. The use of standard messages facilitates programming by permitting a single output statement to be used repeatedly. Figure 8.10 contains the key to these messages. The normal exit from the chart in Figure 8.7 is connector (8.8), which is the normal entry to the last detailed flowchart.

The last detailed flowchart, Figure 8.8, presents the procedure for calculating the desired payroll figures. Note the way we reduce the withholding tax table to a kind of mathematical function of the number of dependents. The normal exit in this chart is the connector (8.6).

This completes the basic payroll problem. However, it should be pointed out that algorithms (and ultimately computer programs) must be written to supplement the basic algorithm to permit:

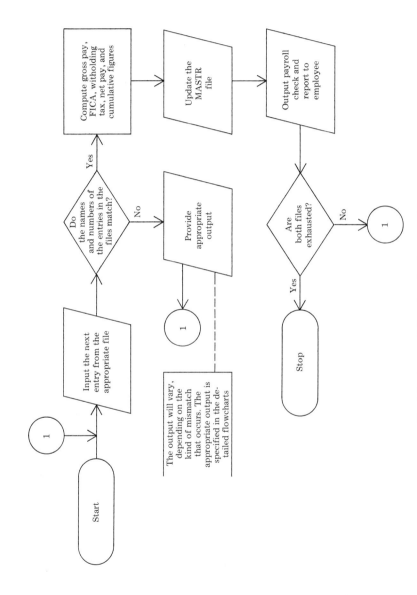

Fig. 8.5 A general flowchart for the payroll problem

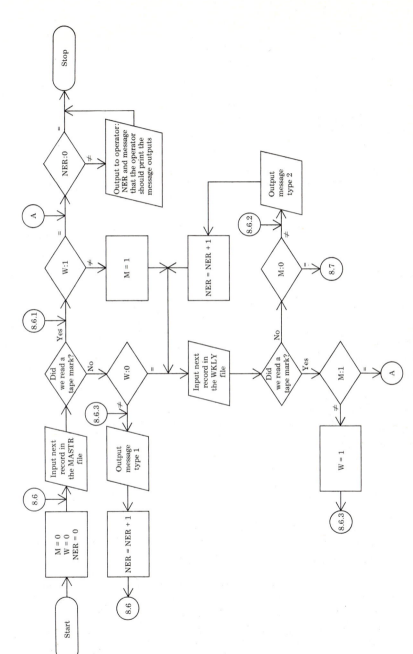

Fig. 8.6 A detailed flowchart for deciding whether to end the processing or to branch to the matching procedure

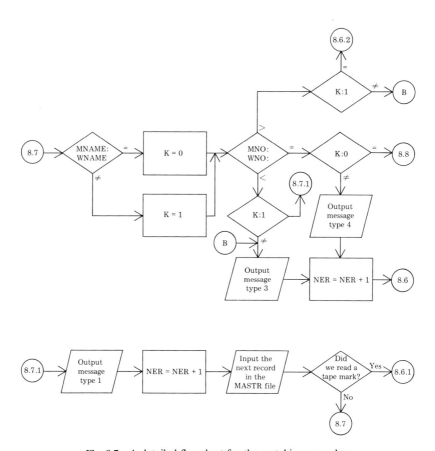

Fig. 8.7 A detailed flowchart for the matching procedure

1. Additional updating of the master file or the weekly file. *Updating* a file refers to any modification – such as correcting a field in a record, deleting an entire record, or adding a new record. Employees may change their addresses or their withholding deductions. These changes should be entered in the file.

2. Initializing the files, especially the master file, at the start of a new payroll year. The major function of this algorithm is to reset cumulative figures to zero. Initializing procedures may also provide for such things as changes in the withholding tax rates or the social security laws.

3. Obtaining special reports from the files such as reports on ab-

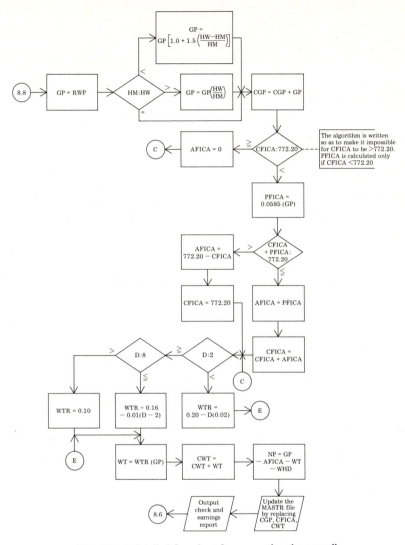

Fig. 8.8 A detailed flowchart for computing the payroll

senteeism, employee turnover, and summary payroll figures by department.

The basic payroll-processing task is really quite simple, but because all alternatives must be considered; and because the task must be broken down into elementary parts, the algorithm is quite lengthy. This is typical of real-life problems.

Variable Name	Meaning
MNAME	The name of the employee in the record in the master file that is being processed
WNAME	The name of the employee in the record in the weekly file that is being processed
MNO	The number of the employee in the record in the master file that is being processed
WNO	The number of the employee in the record in the weekly file that is being processed
HM	The total number of hours ordinarily worked
HW	The total number of hours actually worked in the preceding week
RWP	The regular weekly pay
GP	The actual gross pay for the preceding week
CGP	The cumulative gross pay for the current year
CFICA	The cumulative social security deductions for the current year
PFICA	The potential social security deduction for the preceding week
AFICA	The actual social security deduction for the preceding week
WTR	The withholding tax rate
D	The number of deductions claimed
WT	The tax to be withheld from the pay for the preceding week
CWT	The cumulative tax withheld in the current year
WHD	The deduction for hospitalization insurance
NP	The net pay for the preceding week
M	A variable that is set to 1 to indicate that the master file has been exhausted
W	A variable that is set to 1 to indicate that the weekly file has been exhausted
NER	The number of special messages generated in processing the payroll
K	A variable that is set to 1 to indicate that MNAME does not match WNAME
MSTR	The name for the master file
WKLY	The name for the weekly file

Fig. 8.9 Definitions of the variable names used in the payroll flowcharts

Message Number	Message	Variables That Are Output
1	An entry in the master file is not in the weekly file.	`MNO`, `MNAME`
2	An entry in the weekly file is not in the master file.	`WNO`, `WNAME`
3	The employee names are the same but the numbers differ.	`MNO`, `WNO`, `MNAME`
4	The employee numbers are the same but the names differ.	`MNAME`, `WNAME`, `MNO`

Fig. 8.10 Key to the standard messages used in the payroll flowcharts

Exercises

*6. Prepare a general flowchart for solving the bridge point-count problem given in Exercise 14 in Chapter 7.

7. Prepare a detailed flowchart for the program you wrote to calculate and output the difference between K pairs of numbers (see Exercise 11 in Chapter 2, Exercise 11 in Chapter 3, or Exercise 9 in Chapter 4).

8. Prepare a detailed flowchart for the program you wrote to calculate the mean of a set of values (see Exercise 14 in Chapter 2, Exercise 14 in Chapter 3, or Exercise 12 in Chapter 4).

9. Prepare a detailed flowchart for the program you wrote to calculate gross pay for each of a set of employees with identification numbers (see Exercise 16 in Chapter 2, Exercise 16 in Chapter 3, or Exercise 14 in Chapter 4).

10. Prepare both general and detailed flowcharts for sorting a set of five numbers in decreasing order (see Exercise 12 in Chapter 7).

*11. Prepare a detailed flowchart for the Euclidean algorithm (see Exercise 15 in Chapter 7).

*12. Prepare a detailed flowchart for solving the following problem: Given n and k, compute

$$\sum_{i=k}^{n} {}_nC_i$$

where the symbol ${}_nC_i$ is used to denote

$$\frac{n!}{i!(n-i)!}$$

and $n!$ (read n *factorial*) is the product of the first n integers.

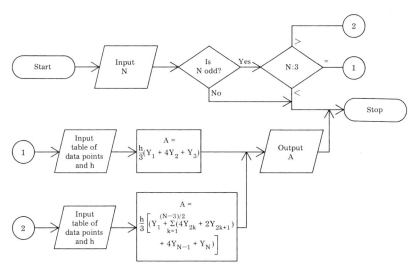

Fig. 8.11 General flowchart for calculating the area under a smooth curve using Simpson's rule

*13. Prepare general and detailed flowcharts for finding the values of X satisfying $AX^2 + BX + C = 0$, the quadratic formula. Recall that they are given by

$$X_1 = (-B + \sqrt{B^2 - 4AC})/2A,$$

and

$$X_2 = (-B - \sqrt{B^2 - 4AC})/2A.$$

Be sure to treat the cases of multiple roots and imaginary roots appropriately. Assume that you will be asked to solve N such problems. The value of N is input first, followed by N sets of A, B, and C.

*14. Given N pairs of data points, (X_1, Y_1), $(X_1 + h, Y_2)$, $(X_1 + 2h, Y_3)$ ... $[X_1 + (N - 1)h, Y_N]$, write a detailed flowchart for finding the area under a smooth curve connecting the values of Y using Simpson's rule; i.e., write detailed flowcharts that would implement the general flowchart given in Figure 8.11.

REFERENCES

1. *Standard Flowchart Symbols and Their Use in Information Processing,* ANS X3.5 (New York: American National Standards Institute, 1970).

2. *Standard Method for Charting Paperwork Procedures.* (New York: American National Standards Institute, 1959).

3. *Standard Graphic Symbols for Logic Diagrams.* ANS YS2.14 (New York: American National Standards Institute, 1962).

ANNOTATED SUPPLEMENTARY BIBLIOGRAPHY

Most references on computer programming discuss flowcharts; in fact, the problem of how to construct an algorithm frequently is absorbed, without too much success, into the discussion of how to construct a flowchart. The references below were chosen because they either discuss flowcharting in a comprehensive manner or provide a novel perspective of some kind.

1. Bohl, M., *Information Processing* (Palo Alto, Ca.: Science Research Associates, Inc., 1971). This book includes an especially lucid discussion of flowcharting.

2. Chapin, N., "Flowcharting with the ANSI Standard: A Tutorial," *Computing Surveys,* Vol. 2, No. 2:119–46 (June 1970). This is an effective, well-written tutorial on flowcharting. It includes suggestions for such things as cross-referencing sections of flowcharts, representing multiple media symbols in a flowchart, process flowcharting, and a series of guidelines for flowcharting techniques.

3. Miller, G. A.; Galanter, E.; and Priba, K. H., *Plans and the Structure of Behavior* (New York: Holt, Rinehart & Winston, Inc., 1960). The application of information-processing models, especially flowcharts, to many areas of psychology is discussed in a delightful manner.

Programming Revisited

INTRODUCTION

In this, the third part of the book, we return to the three programming languages that were first discussed in Part 1: FORTRAN, using WATFIV, PL/I using PL/C, and BASIC. A chapter is devoted to each language, and the chapters are intended to be independent of one another. It is expected that most readers will attempt to master only one of these three chapters in their first reading of this book.

The facilities introduced in Part 1 are reviewed and discussed in greater depth. Other facilities are discussed as well; however, not all the facilities of each of the three languages—especially PL/I—can or should be discussed in an introductory book.

Although the three chapters on programming languages in this part of the book should be independent of one another, they are not meant to be independent of Chapters 2–4. Although references to Part 1 have been omitted, the chapters in Part 1 which discuss each of these three languages should be read before the corresponding chapters in Part 3. Part 3 concludes with a chapter on program effectiveness, efficiency, and documentation.

Chapter 9

FORTRAN IV Using WATFIV

9.1 THE CHARACTER SET

A FORTRAN program is an algorithm which consists of a sequence of statements, or instructions. A statement corresponds to a box in a flowchart or to a step in an English-language algorithm. The sequence helps determine the order in which the statements are to be executed.

The main objective of this chapter is to help the reader state algorithms in the FORTRAN language. We will present a repertoire of statements, the rules for their formulation, their significance, and the significance of their application. However, in order to begin at the beginning, we first shall specify the set of characters that can be used in the words appearing in a FORTRAN statement.

There are three kinds of characters: alphabetic, numeric, and special. The alphabetic characters include all 26 letters, but only capital letters are permitted; there are no lowercase letters in FORTRAN. There are 10 numeric characters, the digits 0 to 9. The special characters permitted in FORTRAN include characters representing arithmetic processes: the plus sign (+), the minus sign (−), a slash for division (/), and an asterisk (∗) for multiplication. Also available are left and right parentheses (()), an equals sign (=), a period (.), and a comma (,). Finally, we must not forget the blank, an important special character. In summary, the 46-character set is:

Alphabetic characters: A B C D E F G H I J K L M N O
                        P Q R S T U V W X Y Z

Numeric characters: 0 1 2 3 4 5 6 7 8 9

Special characters: + − / ∗ ( ) = . , blank

Sometimes, several successive characters are used to denote a single operation. For example, ∗∗ is used to denote exponentiation.

9.2 CONSTANTS

The operands in FORTRAN statements within the scope of the applications discussed in this chapter are constants, variables, or array elements.

FORTRAN *constants* are denoted merely by entering their values in the FORTRAN statement. We will discuss four kinds of constants: integers, real numbers, logical constants, and literal constants.

Integer constants are written without decimal points. The following are valid representations of integers:

$$21463$$
$$100$$
$$-21$$

The following are invalid representations of integers:

$$21463.$$
$$1E2$$
$$-21.$$

Real constants can be specified either by a decimal point or by a floating-point representation. In the latter case, the mantissa must have a decimal point, and the exponent must contain one or two digits but no decimal point. The letter E is used to separate the mantissa from the exponent if the number is to be stored using *single precision*. The letter D is used if the number is to be stored using *double precision*. On IBM 360/370 computers, for example, the mantissa of a single precision number contains about 7 decimal digits, while that of a double-precision number contains about 16 decimal digits. A real constant that requires more than seven significant digits in its mantissa must be stored in double precision. If it is stored in single precision, the value is truncated. Commas should not appear anywhere. The following are valid representations of 7900.02 in floating-point notation:

$$7900.02$$
$$7.90002E3$$
$$7.90002E03$$
$$7.90002D3 \text{ (double precision)}$$
$$790002.E\text{-}02$$

The following are invalid floating-point representations of this same number:

$$7,900.02$$
$$790002$$
$$7900.02E$$

The *logical constants,* true and false, are indicated by the use of .TRUE. and .FALSE. Note that each constant begins and ends with a period.

Literal constants are strings of characters which are to be recorded and processed by a FORTRAN program. They usually appear as messages to be output. Such a constant is identified by an integer number that is equal to the number of characters in the constant, followed by the letter H and, finally, the sequence of characters that constitutes the literal constant.* Be sure to count blank characters. Thus, for example, to write: "The input was in error" we use:

22HTHE INPUT WAS IN ERROR

since there are 22 characters in this string.

9.3 VARIABLES AND ARRAYS

A variable is denoted by any combination of alphabetic and numeric characters, with the following restrictions:

1. The first character must be alphabetic, and

2. There can be no more than six characters in a single variable name.

3. No special characters can appear in a variable name.

Some valid names for FORTRAN variables are:

```
MAST    TOT12    BUDG    HALO
X4      I3END    DOW4    DIMMER
```

Some invalid names are:

```
31END    ITOTS+    BUDGETARY
X*       DOW/4     DIMMEST
```

FORTRAN variables may take on integer, real, or logical values. A given variable name can be used to denote any one type of variable. Logical variables take on the values "true" or "false," and real variables are assigned floating-point values. Integer variables take on only integer values. This may lead to some peculiar arithmetic. For example, although a quotient of two integers generally is not necessarily an integer, in FORTRAN, it always is. This integer result is obtained

---

*There is another way to represent literal constants in WATFIV; however, it is not discussed here because it is not available in ANSI FORTRAN.

by dropping any fractional remainder. This means that, in integer arithmetic, 10 divided by 3 is 3, as is 11 divided by 3.

Any name that can be used for a variable name can be used for an array name instead. Individual elements in an array are denoted by the use of the array name and *subscripts* that pinpoint the element's location. Subscripts are enclosed in parentheses and separated by commas. Thus, for example, A(3,4) refers to the element in the third row and the fourth column of A. The subscripts can take on only positive integer values; that is, real, logical, and non-positive integer subscripts are not permitted.*

The following are valid names for arrays or elements in an array:

DOW4   (This is an element in the one-dimensional array **DOW**.)

DOW(4)   (This is an element in the one-dimensional array **DOW**.)

DOW(3,I)   (Note the use of an integer variable as a subscript. Since a variable must have been assigned a value before being used in FORTRAN, this refers to a single element in DOW. However, by changing the value assigned to I, we can deal with any element in the third row of DOW.)

X3(K,2)
DIMMER(4,29)

The following are invalid names for arrays or elements in an array:

DOW/4
DOW(4.)
DOW(3.E1,I)
DIMMEST(4,29)

9.4 SPECIFICATIONS FOR VARIABLES AND ARRAYS

In the absence of any specification to the contrary, the first letter of the variable or array name serves to specify the type of value stored in that variable or array. If the first letter is any of the letters I through N, the variable or array takes on integer values. If the first letter is any other letter, the variable or array takes on real (i.e., floating-point) values. This is the most frequently used method for specifying the

---

*This is a second instance of the use of an ANSI standard FORTRAN rather than a WATFIV FORTRAN specification. Other kinds of subscripts are permitted in WATFIV.

type of a variable or array, and generally it is adequate if only integer or floating-point numbers appear in a program.

A second means of specifying the type of a variable or array is type statements. The type statement begins with an explicit specification of type, followed by a list of the variables or arrays of that type. Four types that may be specified are: INTEGER, REAL, DOUBLE PRECISION, and LOGICAL. A type statement may use only these words to describe the values that a variable is permitted to assume. DOUBLE PRECISION specifies that the variable will be floating-point and will use the long form of the mantissa. If, for example, we were calculating the sum of a thousand or more five-digit numbers and storing the result in the variable SUM, then SUM would be double precision. The appropriate type statement is:

```
DOUBLE  PRECISION  SUM
```

Other examples of type statements are:

```
INTEGER FIX,UNIT,I3
REAL ITOP,NUT,ZETA
LOGICAL OK
```

Note that the last variable listed in each of the first two type statements given above would have the same type in the absence of this specification. The integer variable I3 begins with the letter I, and the real variable ZETA begins with the letter Z. Although it is not necessary to specify that these variables are INTEGER and REAL, it is permissible to do so.

In addition to specifying the type of value that an array can take on, it is necessary to specify the number of subscripts that an array has and the maximum value of each subscript. This can be done in either a DIMENSION statement or a type statement.

The DIMENSION statement begins with the word DIMENSION. A list of arrays follows, and the array name is given for each array. The maximum value that each subscript of the array can take on is listed in its appropriate position inside the parentheses used to enclose the subscripts. The DIMENSION statement is used for this specification if the type of the array is to be denoted by the first letter which is used for naming the array. If, on the other hand, the array must be typed in an appropriate type statement, the type statement can be used to establish specifications for the number of dimensions and the maximum value for each subscript. This is done by including the array in the list of variables and by indicating the maximum values that each subscript can take on, as with the DIMENSION statement. Type statements and DIMENSION statements must precede the variables listed in these statements. It is a good practice to begin a program with all the type and DIMENSION statements that are required. Some examples of specifications for arrays are:

```
DIMENSION A(20,20),B(200),TIME(3,3,3),I(5)
REAL K(3)
```

A variable cannot be used to specify the maximum value for a subscript. When beginning programmers calculate such things as the sum of a set of numbers (say $X(1) + X(2) + . . . + X(N)$), frequently they are tempted to write DIMENSION X(N). This is not allowed.

9.5 A PROGRAM TO CALCULATE TUITION DUE

At this point we will write a FORTRAN program to calculate the tuition due from a student, given the number of credits that the student is taking. The input consists of the student's identification number and the number of credits that the student is taking, and the output should be the student's identification number and the tuition due. The tuition is calculated as follows:

If the student takes ten or more credits, the tuition is $1500.

If the student takes fewer than ten credits, the tuition is $150 per credit.

We begin by developing an algorithm for the solution of this problem. An algorithm that calculates the tuition correctly is given in Figure 9.1. However, it does not contain adequate provision for the detection of errors. We should "trap" values for the identification number and the number of credits that are not allowable and stop the

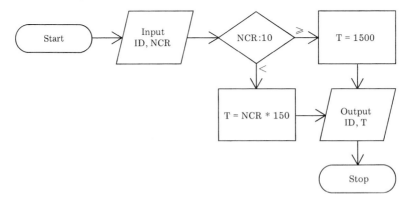

Fig. 9.1 Flowchart for an algorithm to calculate tuition

procedure without producing any output if an illegal value is encountered. An algorithm that does this is given in Figure 9.2.

A FORTRAN program to implement the algorithm in Figure 9.2 is given in Figure 9.3. Note the use of the type statement:

$$\text{INTEGER T}$$

In the absence of this statement, the variable T would be floating-point rather than integer. Variables should be stored and processed in integer form wherever possible because arithmetic operations on integers are faster. Since tuitions can take on only integer values, the tuition is stored in integer form.

The names that were chosen for variables indicate the usage of the variable; e.g., T for tuition and ID for identification. The programmer writes the statements in the program with these names in mind. Since the computer does not "know" which variable is used to denote which kind of data, the programmer determines this implicitly by the way in which he writes the program.

The program's readability can be improved without affecting the result by replacing the IF statements in the third and fourth lines with the single IF statement:

$$\text{IF((ID.LE.0).OR.(NCR.LE.0))GO TO 1}$$

Exercises

1. Which of the following are invalid names for FORTRAN variables? Assume that parentheses always are used to enclose subscripts and that the type of each variable is determined from the first character in its name. Give reasons for your choices.

```
VVV          X*          A4719      N(6.,4)
INTEG 1      1SUM        X/21       INTEG(1)
A(-7,21)     LENGTH      POST       PLUSS
```

2. Suppose that all the variables in Exercise 1 which have valid names are to be used to represent double-precision numbers. Write an appropriate type statement.

3. Suppose that we use the variables A, B, T, F, and L in the following way in a program: A and B denote double-precision, real variables; T and F, logical values; and L, an array of double-precision numbers having at most ten rows and six columns. Write the appropriate type statements.

4. Write a FORTRAN program that calculates and outputs the tuition due from each of K students. Assume that K is input first and that one card then is input for each student. Each card con-

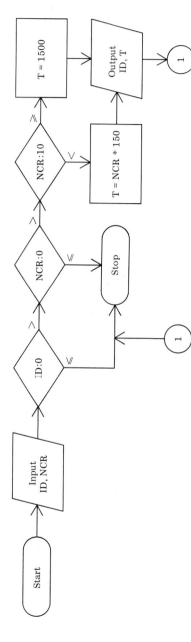

Fig. 9.2 Flowchart for an algorithm to calculate tuition with provision for checking input values

Input

```
 12345678  9
```

Program

```
C  A PROGRAM TO CALCULATE TUITION DUE FOR ONE STUDENT
      INTEGER T
      READ,ID,NCR
      IF(ID.LE.0)GO TO 1
      IF(NCR.LE.0)GO TO 1
      IF(NCR.GE.10)GO TO 5
      T=150*NCR
      GO TO 6
   5  T=1500
   6  PRINT,ID,T
   1  STOP
      END
```

Output

```
 12345678              1350
```

Fig. 9.3 A WATFIV program to calculate tuition due from one student

tains an identification number and the number of credits which that student is taking. If an illegal value for either number that is input is encountered, go on to the next student.

9.6 OPERATIONS, EXPRESSIONS, AND FORTRAN BUILT-IN FUNCTIONS

Figure 9.4 contains the definition of the FORTRAN operations and examples of their use. The operands in the figure are variables, including array elements, or constants in each case. Operations on arrays as a whole are not permitted. The operands in logical operations are either numbers or logical variables. The result of a logical operation is always either true or false.

Arithmetic operations are executed in the following order: all exponentiations first, all multiplications and divisions second, and all additions and subtractions third. Operations at the same level are executed from left to right; but if there are several exponentiations, they are executed from right to left. Expressions in parentheses are evaluated first. For example, if $A = 2.$, $B = 3.$, and $C = 4.$, then:

```
A*B + C = 10.  and  A + B*C = 14.;  also
A/C*B = 1.5,  as does B*A/C.
```

	Symbol	Definition	Example	Value of Operands	Result
Arithmetic	**	Exponentiation	A**B	A=2.,B=3.	8.
	*	Multiplication	A*B	A=2.,B=3.	6.
	/	Division	B/A	A=2.,B=3.	1.5
	+	Addition	A+B	A=2.,B=3.	5.
	−	Subtraction	A−6.	A=2.	−4.
Logical	.GT.	Greater than	A.GT.B	A=2.,B=3.	FALSE
	.GE.	Greater than or equal to	A.GE.B	A=2.,B=2.	TRUE
	.LT.	Less than	A.LT.B	A=2.,B=3.	TRUE
	.LE.	Less than or equal to	A.LE.B	A=2.,B=3.	TRUE
	.EQ.	Equal to	A.EQ.B	A=2.,B=3.	FALSE
	.NE.	Not equal to	A.NE.B	A=2.	TRUE
	.NOT.	Not	.NOT.A	A=1	FALSE
	.AND.	And	A.AND.B	A=1,B=0	FALSE
	.OR.	Or	A.OR.B	A=1,B=0	TRUE

Fig. 9.4 FORTRAN operations

Two operations cannot be written in succession. If two successive operations are to be carried out, they should be separated by parentheses. If, for example, A is to be multiplied by −B, it must be written as A*(−B) rather than A*−B. However, it may be written as −B*A.

Some logical operations are used mainly to check on whether certain inequalities hold. These *comparison operations* are the first six logical operations shown in Figure 9.4. They may have expressions as operands; for example, if A = 2., B = 3., and C = 4., then:

$$(A*B).GT.(B*C)$$

gives the result false;

$$(A/C*B).EQ.(B*A/C)$$

gives the result true; and

$$(A/C).LE.(B/C)$$

gives the result true.

There are three logical operations in FORTRAN that are not comparisons. These are the .NOT.,.AND., and .OR. operations. These logical operations function as follows (examples of their use are given in Figure 9.4):

1. The result of a .NOT. operation is the opposite value of the logical operand that follows it.

2. The result of an .OR. operation is false if and only if both operands associated with it are false.

3. The result of an .AND. operation is true if and only if both operands associated with it are true.

Logical operations may be quite elaborate. For example, if A = 2., B = 3., and C = 4., then

    ((A*B).GT.(B*C)).OR.((A/C*B).EQ.(B*A/C))

gives the result true because the right-hand operand of the .OR. operator is true; that is, A/C*B is equal to B*A/C. However,

    ((A*B).GT.(B*C)).AND.((A/C*B).EQ.(B*A/C))

gives the result false because the left-hand operand of the .AND. operator is false; that is, A times B is not greater than B times C.

In the absence of parentheses, the order of execution of logical expressions requires any arithmetic parts to be evaluated first, and logical operations to be carried out afterwards. Among the logical operations, the comparison operations are executed first. These six operations are of equal priority, and so are executed from left to right in the order in which they appear. .NOT. is executed next, followed by .AND. The operation .OR. has the lowest priority and is executed last. Thus, for example, the numbers under the operations in the following expression indicate the order in which they are to be executed:

    A.GT.B.AND.C.GT.D.OR.A**N-X.LE.B/C*D+F
      6   9   7   10   1 4 8 2 3 5

Certain calculations frequently are required in FORTRAN programs; for example, square roots. To facilitate the programming of these calculations, the FORTRAN compiler contains special subprograms that can be used by merely writing the subprogram name, followed by the argument or arguments in parentheses. To calculate and use the constant which is equal to the square root of 27.4, we need only write SQRT(27.4). SQRT is the name of the built-in function that calculates square roots of single-precision arguments. If the argument is double precision, then the appropriate library subprogram is DSQRT. There are many other built-in functions—trigonometric functions, absolute-value functions, and logarithmic and exponential functions, to name a few.

9.7 THE END OPTION IN A READ

There is a version of the READ statement available in WATFIV that lets a programmer branch to another statement in the program when an end-of-file is encountered. This version of the READ statement looks like:

    READ(5,*,END=50)ID,NCR

The word READ appears, beginning in column 7, followed by three items that are separated by commas and enclosed in parentheses. The first item is the digit which specifies the device from which input will be entered. In most installations, the digit 5 is used to indicate that input will be from the card reader. The second item is an asterisk which indicates that this input operation is format-free. (We shall see in the next section that this second item is used in a different way for formatted output.) The third item is the special entry that provides for the end-of-file: the word END appears, then an equal sign, and then a statement number. The program branches to that numbered statement (50 in the example) when the end of the input file is sensed. The READ statement concludes with the list of variables to be read.

Figure 9.5 contains a program to calculate the tuition due from an unspecified number of students. This program will go on to the next student if either the ID number or the number of credits is not positive. The algorithm stops when the end-of-file is encountered.

9.8 ANNOTATING OUTPUT—THE WRITE AND FORMAT STATEMENTS

All the FORTRAN programs that we have written thus far have had format-free outputs. Numbers are printed without labels, headings, or other descriptions. This is not a good way to present the output; it should have adequate annotation. For example, in the tuition program it would be helpful to label the two numbers that are output. The first number might be called *student ID* and the second *tuition due*. It also would be useful to output a message of some kind if an illegal student number or number of credits were encountered. We shall see how this is done in the next two sections and conclude with a revised, annotated version of the tuition program.

Two FORTRAN statements may be used to provide annotated output.* The first is a WRITE statement. It is *executable*—that is, it results in a series of corresponding machine-language instructions that cause the output to be carried out at that point in the program. The second statement is a FORMAT statement, which is *non-executable* and may be placed anywhere in the program. It contains specifications for the output operation. We shall place our FORMAT statements immediately after the corresponding WRITE statement. Some programmers prefer to place all their FORMAT statements together just before the END statement.

---

*The PRINT statement can be used to annotate outputs. However, this is less versatile than the approach described in this section. The reader should become familiar with the FORTRAN FORMAT statement because it is required in most versions of FORTRAN and is also used to lay out the input in some statistical packages and other application programs.

Input

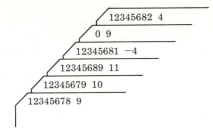

Program

```
C A PROGRAM TO CALCULATE TUITION DUE FOR AN UNSPECIFIED NUMBER OF STUDENTS
      INTEGER T
    1 READ(5,*,END=50)ID,NCR
      IF((ID.LE.0).OR.(NCR.LE.0))GO TO 1
      IF(NCR.GE.10)GO TO 5
      T=150*NCR
      GO TO 6
    5 T=1500
    6 PRINT,ID,T
      GO TO 1
   50 STOP
      END
```

Output

```
12345678        1350
12345679        1500
12345689        1500
12345682         600
```

Fig. 9.5 A WATFIV program to calculate tuition due for an unspecified number of students

A typical **WRITE** statement that outputs values for the variables ID and T in that order looks like:

$$\texttt{WRITE(6,2)ID,T}$$

The word **WRITE** appears beginning in column 7. This is followed by two numbers in parentheses, and then by a list of the variables whose current values are to be output. The first of the two parenthetical numbers designates the output device. We will always use a 6 since, in most versions of WATFIV, this 6 results in printed output. The only missing element is the link between this WRITE statement and the corresponding FORMAT statement. The second number in parentheses—the statement number of the corresponding FORMAT statement—provides that link.

The FORMAT statement corresponding to this WRITE statement might be:

```
2 FORMAT(11H1STUDENT ID,I10,10X,11HTUITION DUE,I6)
```

A FORMAT statement begins in columns 1–5 with a statement number. In this example, the statement number is 2. The word FORMAT then appears beginning in column 7, followed by a series of specifications for the output enclosed in parentheses and separated by commas. These specifications include a code that prescribes the interpretation of each element in the list of variables (I10 and I6 in the example), as well as such things as instructing where to print the line on the page, skipping print positions within a line (10X in the example), and annotating the output. Annotation is entered first in the example because the line begins with annotation. It appears in a literal constant.

In the example above, the literal constants are 1STUDENT ID and TUITION DUE. The 1 that begins the first literal constant is the specification for where to print the line on the page. The specification is called the *carriage control*. It is the first entry in the FORMAT and must always be a single literal character. As in the example, it can be prefixed to an annotation. In most installations, use of a "1" for carriage control causes the line to be printed at the top of a new page. Use of a "0" causes a line to be skipped and printing to begin on the line after the next one (double spacing). Use of a blank character causes printing to begin on the next line (single spacing).

The order of the entries in the FORMAT statement is important because it controls the order of the entries on the printed line. The first entry in a FORMAT statement used with a WRITE statement must be a carriage control character. If the line begins with an annotation, the carriage control character may be embedded in a longer literal constant. If not, the FORMAT begins with 1H and then the appropriate carriage control character. In the example, the carriage control, 1, is embedded in the annotation, and the line is printed at the top of a new page beginning with the phrase STUDENT ID. Note that the carriage control character is not printed. The next item in the FORMAT in the example is I10. Since this is a specification for printing the value taken on by a variable on the list, the value stored in the location denoted by the first variable on the list (ID in the example) would be printed next, according to the I10 code. The specification 10X then causes ten blank characters to be printed; i.e. it causes ten print positions to be skipped. The literal constant TUITION DUE is printed next. Finally the value stored for T is printed using the I6 code. In summary then, the line looks like:

STUDENT ID value-for-ID 10-spaces TUITION DUE value-for-T

A line printed using this FORMAT could be:

```
STUDENT ID 123456789          TUITION DUE  1500
```

The list of variables, rather than the FORMAT statement, controls termination of the output activities associated with a WRITE statement. Numbers are read from the corresponding storage locations named by the list until the list is exhausted. There is one exception to this rule: literal data is printed even if it appears after the last format specification.

9.9   FORMAT CODES

Each variable in the list must have a FORMAT code associated with it. Codes are associated with a variable one by one from left to right in the order in which they both appear. In the example in the preceding section, the first code that is associated with a variable is the code I10. It is associated with ID. The second code is 10X, but since X codes are not associated with variables, the code I6 is associated with the variable T.

We shall discuss the I, F, and X format codes. Other codes exist, but these three, along with the H code, satisfy the data-formatting needs of many FORTRAN applications.

The I format code is used to transfer integer data. It has the form: Iw. The letter I must appear explicitly in the format specifications. The w is replaced by an integer that indicates the width of the field designated by this specification.

If we were printing an integer on output using this specification, then w print positions would be filled one way or another as a result of this format specification. If the number to be printed contains fewer digits than print positions, then the leftmost print positions are filled with blanks. If the number of digits to be printed is greater than w, the action may be any of several—depending on the particular implementation of FORTRAN. In most implementations of WATFIV, asterisks are printed in lieu of output. If, for example, we assume that the I4 specification was used, then:

If the following is stored internally	The printed result is
−7132	∗∗∗∗
64241	∗∗∗∗
0	bbb0
−323	−323
−6	bb−6

The letter b is used here to indicate a blank character. In the printed output this print position would be left blank.

The Iw specification may be multiplied by an integer constant to indicate repeated use of this code. This means that 3I10 is equivalent to the specification I10, I10, I10. The multiplier must be an integer constant, and there must be no blank spaces between the multiplier and the letter I. In general, there should be no blanks between characters associated with a single format item.

The X format code is used to indicate the insertion of blanks in output. The letter X is preceded by an integer that indicates how many blanks to insert in the output. The X format code is not associated with a variable in the list. Illustrations of X-code use will be given in the annotated program to calculate tuitions, presented at the end of this section.

The F format specification is used to transfer real (floating-point) data. The letter F is entered, followed by two integers separated by a period — e.g., F8.4. The first integer indicates the width of the field; the second, the number of digits to the right of the decimal. We might say, then, that the form of the F code is Fw.d.

The use of the F code causes w print positions to be filled, with d digits to the right of the decimal point. Provision should be made on output for a sign and a decimal point. This means that if the output is expected to contain at most k digits to the left of the decimal point, then $w \geq k + d + 2$. As with the I code, if too little space is allowed, the WATFIV version of FORTRAN will print asterisks in lieu of the number. Therefore, it is best to be sure that the inequality is satisfied.

If there are more than d digits to the right of the decimal in the internal value, the last digit that is retained is rounded. That is, the last digit is increased by 1 if the next digit is 5 or greater and is unchanged if the next digit is 4 or less. For example, if the specification F6.2 is used to print an internally stored value of 21.317, the printed result is b21.32. If the stored value is 21.313, the printed result is b21.31.

A program that produces annotated outputs for the tuition calculations is given in Figure 9.6. Typical outputs corresponding to various inputs that were obtained in running this program are:

Input	Corresponding Output
123456 9	STUDENT ID 123456 TUITION DUE 1350
123567 12	STUDENT ID 123567 TUITION DUE 1500
135799 0	NO. OF CREDITS FOR 135799IS ERRONEOUS IT IS 0
-8 12	ID IS ERRONEOUS IT IS -8

Exercises

5. Write a single FORTRAN statement to sum all the elements in each of the arrays listed in the following statement. Call the result SUM in each case and write a separate statement for each array.

    DOUBLE PRECISION X(4),IN,OUT,Y(3,3)

6. Write a single FORTRAN statement to compute the unbiased

Input

```
12345678 9
```

Program

```
C AN ANNOTATED PROGRAM TO CALCULATE TUITION FOR ONE STUDENT
      INTEGER T
      READ,ID,NCR
      IF(ID.LE.0)GO TO 1
      IF(NCR.LE.0)GO TO 7
      IF(NCR.GE.10)GO TO 5
      T=150*NCR
      GO TO 6
    5 T=1500
    6 WRITE(6,10)ID,T
   10 FORMAT(11H1STUDENT ID,I10,10X,11HTUITION DUE,I6)
      GO TO 9
    1 WRITE(6,11)ID
   11 FORMAT(22H1ID IS ERRONEOUS IT IS,I10)
      GO TO 9
    7 WRITE(6,12)ID,NCR
   12 FORMAT(19H1NO. OF CREDITS FOR,I10,18HIS ERRONEOUS IT IS,I6)
    9 STOP
      END
```

Output

```
    STUDENT ID 12345678              TUITION DUE   1350
```

Fig. 9.6 An annotated WATFIV program to calculate tuition due from one student

estimate of the standard deviation, SIGHAT, of a set of N numbers $X_1, X_2, \ldots, X_N$. SIGHAT is given by:

$$\text{SIGHAT} = \sqrt{\frac{N \sum_{i=1}^{N} X_i^2 - \left(\sum_{i=1}^{N} X_i \right)^2}{N(N-1)}}$$

Assume that

$$\sum_{i=1}^{N} X_i^2$$

has been computed and is stored in a variable called S2, and that

$$\sum_{i=1}^{N} X_i$$

has been computed and is stored in a variable called S1. A value for N is stored in the variable called N. Also assume that all calculations, variables, and results are to be double precision.

7. Write a type statement that would appear at the beginning of the program in which SIGHAT (see the preceding exercise) is calculated.

8. Write WRITE and corresponding FORMAT statements that could be used to produce annotated outputs for the programs written in solution to Exercises 9, 10, 11, 14, 15, and 16 in Chapter 2.

9. Write a WATFIV program to calculate tuition due from each of K students (see Exercise 4). This program should provide annotated output and treat erroneous values for the ID number, the number of credits, and K by printing an appropriate message and going on to the next student (if the ID number or number of credits is not positive), or stopping (if the value for K is not positive). This program also should be able to detect other errors in K by counting the number of values actually input and comparing this to K. If there is a discrepancy, an appropriate message, which would appear at the end of the tuition output, should be printed.

9.10 THE COMPUTED GO TO AND ARITHMETIC IF STATEMENTS

Two versatile branching statements available in FORTRAN (in addition to the logical IF statement that was discussed in Chapter 2) are the computed GO TO and arithmetic IF statements. The form of the computed GO TO is:

GO TO (statement-number-1, statement-number-2, . . . , statement-number-n), integer-variable

The integer variable cannot be subscripted. The value of the integer variable is determined — say it is i; the program then branches to statement-number i. For example, if $N = 3$, then:

```
GO TO(43,16,17,21,1005),N
```

would cause the program to branch to statement 17. If the integer variable takes on a value outside the allowable range — for example, a value of 0 or 6 in the above illustration — then, in the WATFIV compiler for FORTRAN, the program proceeds to the next statement.

The computed GO TO is frequently used in FORTRAN programs that are made up of several independent segments, each of which may be executed only once in any one application of the program. For example, if a computer were used to assist in medical diagnosis, the combination of symptoms could be analyzed to determine which of several possible diagnostic algorithms was most appropriate. A separate segment of FORTRAN code would be written for each of the various diagnostic algorithms and the computed GO TO would be used to branch to the appropriate segments. A value for the integer variable in the computed GO TO would be computed first, based on the analysis of the symptoms.

The arithmetic IF statement has the form:

IF (arithmetic-expression) statement-1, statement-2, statement-3

The arithmetic IF statement is performed by first evaluating the arithmetic expression that appears in parentheses. The expression is followed by three statement numbers separated by commas, denoted above by statement-1, statement-2, and statement-3. If the expression is negative, the program branches to the statement that has statement-1 as its label. If the expression is equal to zero, the program branches to the statement that has statement-2 as its label; and if the expression is positive, the program branches to the statement labeled statement-3. Consider, for example, the program given in Figure 9.3. The three logical IF statements in that program (the statements on the third, fourth, and fifth lines of the program) could be replaced by the following arithmetic IF statements:

```
      IF(ID) 1,1,2
  2   IF(NCR) 1,1,3
  3   IF(NCR-10) 4,5,5
```

The next statement would have to be labeled 4, thus becoming:

```
  4   T=150*NCR
```

9.11   THE DO STATEMENT

The DO statement is used to set in motion a powerful looping mechanism. Suppose that we are given a one-dimensional array, A, containing N real elements, and we wish to compute the sum of the elements in the array. We already have seen what an algorithm to accomplish this might look like. We must input N and the array, initialize the sum, loop, and then conclude the summation. We then should output the result. This could be done in several ways, using either an arithmetic or logical IF statement. Three approaches are given in Figure 9.7. Note that the DIMENSION statement implies that the maximum value permitted for N is 1000.

The sum can be obtained more succinctly using the DO statement:

```
      DO 2 I=1,N
```

The DO statement has the form:

DO statement-number-1, integer-variable = initial-value,
test-value, increment

Statement-number-1 determines the *range of the DO* and is the statement number of the last statement to be executed repeatedly. It

```
DIMENSION A(1000)        DIMENSION A(1000)        DIMENSION A(1000)
READ,N                   READ,N                   READ,N
SUM=0.0                  SUM=0.0                  SUM=0.0
I=1                      I=1                      I=1
2 READ,A(I)            2 IF(I.GT.N)GO TO 3      2 READ,A(I)
SUM=SUM+A(I)             READ,A(I)                SUM=SUM+A(I)
IF(I-N)1,3,3            SUM=SUM+A(I)             I=I+1
1 I=I+1                  I=I+1                    IF(I.LE.N)GO TO 2
GO TO 2                 GO TO 2                  WRITE(6,4)SUM
3 WRITE(6,4)SUM        3 WRITE(6,4)SUM          4 FORMAT(5H1SUM=,F16.6)
4 FORMAT(5H1SUM=,F16.6) 4 FORMAT(5H1SUM=,F16.6)  STOP
STOP                    STOP                     END
END                     END
```

Fig. 9.7   Three approaches to calculating a sum of N elements without the use of a DO statement

is 2 in the example. The *integer variable* is called the *DO variable*. It cannot be subscripted and it serves as a counter (I in the above example) in executing the DO. It may or may not appear as a variable in one or more FORTRAN statements within the range of the DO. The *initial value, test value,* and *increment* each must be either an integer constant or a non-subscripted integer variable. Each must be positive. The increment is optional; if it is not given, it is taken to be 1. In the above example, the initial value is 1, the test value is N, and the increment − since it is omitted − is 1.

The DO statement acts as follows: the DO variable is set equal to the initial value, and the statements in the range of the DO are executed. The DO variable is incremented and the statements in the DO are again executed if the DO variable is less than or equal to the test value. The statements are executed for the last time when the DO variable takes on the greatest value that is less than or equal to the test value.

Using the DO statement, the program to compute the sum of the elements of the array, A, becomes the program given in Figure 9.8.

The DO variable need not appear in the statements in the range of the DO; it merely serves as a counter. Suppose, for example, that we wished to calculate the tuition due from a specified number of students using a DO statement. (Exercise 4 asked you to solve this same prob-

```
DIMENSION A(1000)
READ,N
SUM=0.0
DO 2 I=1,N
READ,A(I)
2 SUM=SUM+A(I)
WRITE(6,4)SUM
4 FORMAT(5H1SUM=,F16.6)
STOP
END
```

Fig. 9.8   Calculating a sum of N elements using a DO statement

lem without using a DO statement.) A program to do this (Figure 9.9) contains a statement that we have not yet discussed—the CONTINUE statement.

The CONTINUE statement is called a *dummy statement* because it does not directly implement a step in an algorithm. It is used in a FORTRAN program to avoid breaking a rule for the formulation of the program. It sometimes is inserted as the last statement in a DO loop in order to avoid an error. For example, in the tuition program, we wish to go on to the next student if either the ID number or the number of credits is not positive. However, we cannot branch back to the DO statement (this would start the DO loop all over from

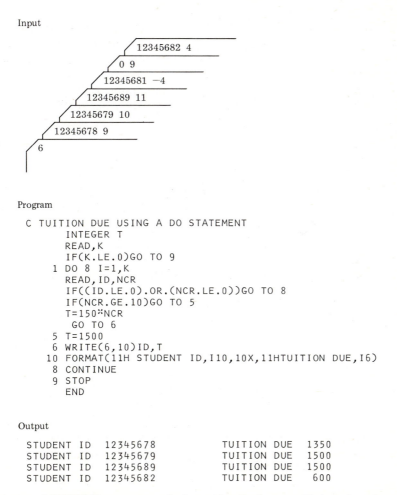

Input

```
                          / 12345682 4
                       / 0 9
                    / 12345681 −4
                 / 12345689 11
              / 12345679 10
           / 12345678 9
        / 6
```

Program

```
C TUITION DUE USING A DO STATEMENT
      INTEGER T
      READ,K
      IF(K.LE.0)GO TO 9
  1   DO 8 I=1,K
      READ,ID,NCR
      IF((ID.LE.0).OR.(NCR.LE.0))GO TO 8
      IF(NCR.GE.10)GO TO 5
      T=150*NCR
       GO TO 6
  5   T=1500
  6   WRITE(6,10)ID,T
 10   FORMAT(11H STUDENT ID,I10,10X,11HTUITION DUE,I6)
  8   CONTINUE
  9   STOP
      END
```

Output

```
STUDENT ID  12345678        TUITION DUE  1350
STUDENT ID  12345679        TUITION DUE  1500
STUDENT ID  12345689        TUITION DUE  1500
STUDENT ID  12345682        TUITION DUE   600
```

Fig. 9.9 A WATFIV program to calculate tuition due for a specified number of students using a DO statement

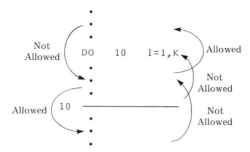

Fig. 9.10 Do's and don't's in branching in and out of DO loops

scratch with I reset to 1), nor can we branch to the READ statement after the DO (this would go on to the next student without incrementing I). The CONTINUE statement is inserted so that we can get the desired result by branching to it.

This example illustrates why it is not permissible to branch back to the DO statement from inside the DO loop. There are some other dos and don'ts with respect to DO loops. They can be summarized as follows:

1. Do not branch into a DO from outside its range.*

2. Branching out of the DO before it is completed is permitted. (These branching dos and don'ts are illustrated in Figure 9.10.)

3. The last statement in the range of the DO cannot be non-executable; so, for example, it cannot be a FORMAT statement.

4. The last statement in the range of a DO cannot be a GO TO, a STOP, an arithmetic IF, or another DO statement.

5. Do not change the values of the initial value, the test value, and the increment within the range of the DO.

As another example of the use of the DO statement, consider the FORTRAN program given in Figure 9.11. This program calculates a square root using the algorithm discussed in Chapter 7. X is the number for which we wish to obtain the square root, TEST is the limit on the error (ϵ in Chapter 7), and K is the limit on the number of iterations. E is the error in the current estimate of the square root. The current estimate is called NEXT and E is obtained in statement 8 using the built-in function DABS which calculates the absolute value of a double precision argument.

---

*More specifically, you may branch to the DO statement itself from outside the range of the DO, but you may not branch elsewhere into the range of the DO.

```
DOUBLE PRECISION E,X,TEST,NEXT,LAST,DABS
E=1.0
READ,X,TEST,K
LAST=(X+1.)/2.
DO 8 J=1,K
IF(E.LT.TEST)GO TO 9
NEXT=(LAST+X/LAST)/2.
LAST=NEXT
8 E=DABS(X-NEXT*NEXT)
9 WRITE(6,2)X,TEST,K,NEXT,J
2 FORMAT(19H1THE SQUARE ROOT OF,F17.8/22H USING A TEST VALUE OF,F17.
18/27H AND AN ITERATIONS LIMIT OF,I10/3H IS,F20.8/29H NUMBER OF ITE
2RATIONS USED IS,I4,10H MINUS ONE)
STOP
END
```

Fig. 9.11   A WATFIV program to calculate a square root

DABS is included in the list of variables in the DOUBLE PRE-
CISION statement. This is a peculiarity of WATFIV; library subprograms are treated like variables with respect to specification of type.

The 2 FORMAT statement in this program is notable for two reasons. First, it requires three cards; this illustrates the lengths to which
we sometimes must go to adequately annotate outputs. Also, it contains several slashes. A slash is used to return the carriage of the
printer to the left margin. A carriage control character must follow
each slash. This character determines on which line the printing is to
take place. In this case, the carriage control after each slash is a blank
character, and so the printing is single-spaced. The input submitted
and the output obtained in each of two runs of this program is shown
in Figure 9.12.

Note that no subscripted variable was used in calculating the square
root. That is, we did not use, say, Y_j for the Jth estimate of the square
root. We might have initialized Y and used a DO loop and WRITE
statement something like:

```
Y(1)=(X+1.)/2.
DO 8   J=2,K
IF(E.LT.TEST)GO TO 9
Y(J)=(Y(J-1)+X/Y(J-1))/2.
8 E=DABS(X-Y(J)*Y(J))
9 WRITE(6,2)X,TEST,K,Y(J),J
```

After some analysis it should become clear that, because the DO variable is incremented after Y(J) has been calculated and before E has
been compared to TEST, we would be attempting to print out a value
we had not yet calculated. For example, if Y(5) resulted in an E that
satisfies the comparison with TEST, then we would attempt to print
Y(6). (The program in Figure 9.11 recognizes this by annotating the
output with the message that the NUMBER OF ITERATIONS
USED IS value-for-J MINUS ONE.) Possibly, we might have

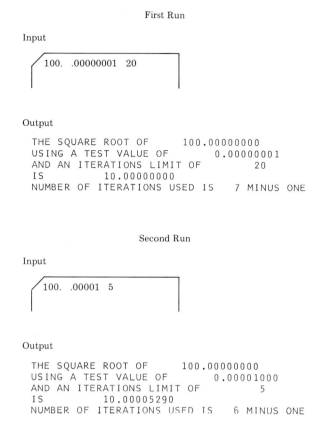

First Run

Input

```
100. .00000001  20
```

Output

```
THE SQUARE ROOT OF      100.00000000
USING A TEST VALUE OF         0.00000001
AND AN ITERATIONS LIMIT OF        20
IS          10.00000000
NUMBER OF ITERATIONS USED IS   7 MINUS ONE
```

Second Run

Input

```
100. .00001  5
```

Output

```
THE SQUARE ROOT OF      100.00000000
USING A TEST VALUE OF         0.00001000
AND AN ITERATIONS LIMIT OF        5
IS          10.00005290
NUMBER OF ITERATIONS USED IS   6 MINUS ONE
```

Fig. 9.12 Input and output for each of two runs of the square-root program

avoided this problem by rewriting the DO loop. However, we then would have gotten an error if all K iterations had been carried out. In this case, because of the way the DO-variable is compared to K, J would take on the value K + 1 with equally disastrous results.*

In general, it may not be wise to use subscripts in iterations. One reason is the difficulty discussed above. Another is that many iterations may be required before a satisfactory result is obtained; if we store all intermediate results (which is what we are doing if we use subscripts), we may run out of space and inhibit the completion of the iteration.

---

*Arrays are stored sequentially in storage. The subscript points to the storage location in which an element is stored. If, for example, the last estimate calculated is Z(10) and we ask for Z(11), we get the contents of the next location in storage after Z(10), no matter what this may be.

9.12 INPUT AND OUTPUT OF ARRAYS

Selected elements in arrays may be listed in a variables list in a READ, PRINT, or WRITE statement, with the aid of a notation similar to that used in the DO statement. The subscript in the array is the DO variable, and the initial value, test value, and increment are used to indicate which elements are to be input or output. Thus, for example,

$$\text{READ,}(X(I),I=1,5,2)$$

results in values being input for X(1), X(3), and X(5).

In dealing with matrices, we must account for two subscripts. We could write:

$$\text{READ,}((X(I,J),I=1,5,2),J=1,7,3)$$

if we wished to assign values to X(1,1), X(3,1), X(5,1), X(1,4), X(3,4), X(5,4), X(1,7), X(3,7), and X(5,7), in that order. Note that the subscript I, which is in the innermost parentheses, is changing most rapidly. That is, we are reading in values column by column. In this particular example, if we wished to assign values to the same elements of X(I,J), row by row, we would write:

$$\text{READ,}((X(I,J),J=1,7,3),I=1,5,2)$$

Now the elements have been assigned values in the order X(1,1), X(1,4), X(1,7), X(3,1), X(3,4), X(3,7), X(5,1), X(5,4), and X(5,7). Just as for DO statements, if the increment is 1 it need not be given.

The word "DO" does not actually appear in the READ, PRINT, or WRITE statement. As a result, the phrase *implied DO* is used to refer to the use of the DO notation in input/output.

An unsubscripted array name also may appear in a variable list. In this case, all the elements in the array are assigned values (input) or printed (output). The DIMENSION statement determines the number of elements to be processed. Elements of matrices are assigned values or printed out column by column, as if the first subscript were in an innermost parenthesis. So, for example, if we had:

```
DIMENSION X(2,3)
READ, X
```

and if the input card contained the six values 1.1, 2.2, 3.3, 4.4, 5.5, and 6.6, the values read into X would be:

```
X(1,1) = 1.1     X(1,2) = 3.3     X(1,3) = 5.5
X(2,1) = 2.2     X(2,2) = 4.4     X(2,3) = 6.6
```

9.13 A PROGRAM TO COMPUTE MEANS
AND STANDARD DEVIATIONS

We now shall develop a FORTRAN program to compute the mean and standard deviation of each of several sets of data. We shall assume that each set begins with a card on which is punched the number of observations in the set—denoted by N in the program—called the *sample size*. This is followed by the observations, eight to a card in free-format form. We shall assume that the observations are real, and have a decimal point punched somewhere in the field.

Given a set of N observations, $X_1, X_2, X_3, \ldots, X_N$, recall that the mean, XBAR, and the unbiased estimate of the population standard deviation, SIGHAT, are given by:

$$XBAR = \frac{\sum\limits_{i=1}^{N} X_i}{N}$$

$$SIGHAT = \sqrt{\frac{N\left(\sum\limits_{i=1}^{N} X_i^2\right) - \left(\sum\limits_{i=1}^{N} X_i\right)^2}{N(N-1)}}$$

We shall compute the sum and the sum of the squares of the observations by adding the value of X_j and X_j^2 to

$$\sum\limits_{i=1}^{j-1} X_i \text{ and } \sum\limits_{i=1}^{j-1} X_i^2,$$

until $J = N$.

The first consideration is whether or not to use double precision variables and arithmetic. The decision depends on the computer on which the program is to be implemented. Recall that with an IBM 360/370 computer, for example, single precision arithmetic retains about seven decimal digits. Both

$$N \sum\limits_{i=1}^{N} X_i^2 \text{ and } \left(\sum\limits_{i=1}^{N} X_i\right)^2$$

can be expected to have more than seven digits in many applications. If we do not use double precision, their difference, and hence SIGHAT, may be zero in those cases when they should not be zero.

The next principal consideration is to conserve storage space in writing the program. If we read all observations into storage before we process any of them, (or even a single set of observations), main storage may be exhausted. Suppose instead that we read in the observations, eight at a time, card by card. We process these eight and use the same storage space (the same variable names in the FORTRAN program) for the next eight. We must, of course, keep a counter that tells us when we have read in all data in a single set. In this program, we would define a new integer variable, M, equal to $(N + 7)/8$. M is the number of cards to be read in if there are N observations. (Recall that when integer arithmetic is carried out, a fractional part of a result is truncated. For example, $(19 + 7)/8$ is 3.) The disadvantage of this approach is that there must be eight numbers punched on all cards, including the last one. If N is not a multiple of eight, $8M - N$ zeroes must be punched on the last card after the Nth entry. For example, if $N = 9$, then two cards will be read in $(M = 2)$ and seven zeroes must be punched on the second card after the ninth data item. If this is not done, an attempt will be made to read seven numbers from succeeding cards. This can result in many different kinds of errors, depending on what is punched on the succeeding cards.

Figure 9.13 contains an annotated FORTRAN program to compute means and standard deviations. The output obtained in a run of this program is given in Figure 9.14.

*9.14   SUBPROCEDURES—STATEMENT FUNCTIONS, FUNCTION
       SUBPROGRAMS, AND SUBROUTINE SUBPROGRAMS

If a series of instructions is executed several times at different points in a FORTRAN program, it may be desirable to use a *subprogram*. The series of instructions is written once as a subprogram and then called in at the different points where it is needed.

Three kinds of subprograms are available in FORTRAN IV; statement functions, function subprograms, and subroutine subprograms. The choice of a subprogram depends on the number of instructions required in it and the number of outputs it is to provide. Figure 9.15 contains a summary of the characteristics of each kind of subprogram.

Subprograms are named in the same way as variables: a statement function or a function subprogram returns a single value, and this value is stored in the location corresponding to the name of the subprogram. Any of the techniques used to declare special properties for variables can be used for statement function or function subprogram names. That is, a name for a subprogram of either of these two kinds can appear in a type statement. Also, function subprograms can be declared to be a special type in the FUNCTION statement itself. This will be discussed later in this section.

Suppose, for example, that we wish to compute repeatedly the sum of five arguments, using this sum in different ways during the execution of the program. We could write:

```
S5(A,B,C,D,E)=A+B+C+D+E
```

Program Statements	Comments
`DOUBLE PRECISION X(8),SUMX,SUMX2,XBAR,SIGHAT,Y,DSQRT`	Note that DSQRT must be included
`WRITE(6,10)`	The table of outputs, beginning at the top of a
`10 FORMAT(12H1SAMPLE SIZE,20X,4HMEAN,20X,9HSIGMA HAT)`	new page, now has a heading
`5 READ(5,*,END=20)N`	The sample size is input
`IF(N.LE.0)GO TO 4`	Branch if N is not positive
`Y=N`	N is converted to a double-precision real number
`SUMX=0.00`	The values in the storage locations that will
`SUMX2=0.00`	hold the sum and sum of squares are initialized
`M=(N+7)/8`	N observations give M cards
`DO 7 J=1,M`	Each card is processed in the same way
`READ,X`	The Jth card is input
`DO 7 I=1,8`	
`SUMX=SUMX+X(I)`	
`7 SUMX2=SUMX2+X(I)*X(I)`	The sum and sum of squares are calculated
`XBAR=SUMX/Y`	The mean is calculated
`SIGHAT=DSQRT((Y*SUMX2-SUMX*SUMX)/((Y-1.DO)*Y))`	The standard deviation is calculated
`PRINT,N,XBAR,SIGHAT`	The results are entered in the table
`GO TO 5`	Go back for another set of data
`4 PRINT,N`	The output if N is not positive. Note that
`20 STOP`	in this case we proceed directly to STOP
`END`	That's all there is; there isn't any more

Fig. 9.13 An annotated program to calculate means and standard deviations

```
SAMPLE SIZE              MEAN                      SIGMA HAT
       112      0.20924107142857140 02      0.5811688215686120D 01
         9      0.50000000000000000 01      0.2738612787525832D 01
        -9
```

Fig. 9.14 Output obtained in a run of the program to calculate means and standard deviations

If we wish to later compute:

$$(SUM+X+Y+Z+F)/(TOP+RHO+SIGMA+SIG2+VAR)$$

and call the result RATIO, we could write:

```
RATIO=S5(SUM,X,Y,Z,F)/S5(TOP,RHO,SIGMA,SIG2,VAR)
```

This illustrates the use of a *statement function*.

A statement function is defined in a single statement that has the form:

$$name(dummy\text{-}arguments) = arithmetic\text{-}expression$$

The *dummy arguments* are nonsubscripted variables separated by commas (the variables A, B, C, D, and E in the example). These variables should appear in the arithmetic expression on the right. They are replaced by other variables when this statement function is used in the program (SUM, X, Y, Z, and F, and also TOP, RHO, SIGMA, SIG2, and VAR in the example). The expression must not contain any subscripted variables. The statement function must precede the first executable statement in the program.

Type	Length	Outputs	Invoked by	Requires in Subprogram
Statement function	One statement	One value	Use of function name, with actual arguments in an expression	Name (dummy arguments) = expression
Function	Several statements	One value	Use of function name, with actual arguments in an expression	FUNCTION name (dummy arguments) . . . RETURN END
Subroutine	Several statements	Any reasonable number of values	CALL name (actual arguments)	SUBROUTINE name (dummy arguments) . . . RETURN END

Fig. 9.15 Characteristics of FORTRAN subprograms

A *function subprogram* is defined in several statements that result in a single output. It is compiled separately from the main program and so must include an END statement. In addition, it must include at least one RETURN statement which serves a purpose similar to that of the STOP statement in the main program. The RETURN statement causes control to be transferred to the main program in much the same way that control is passed to the operating system by the STOP statement.

The first statement in a function subprogram has the form:

FUNCTION name(dummy-arguments)

The arguments ordinarily appear on the right side of assignment statements in the subprogram, and the name ordinarily appears on the left side. These statements assign a value to the function in terms of the dummy variables. Consider, for example:

```
     FUNCTION YTWO(X)
     IF(X)40,40,30
40   YTWO=5.*X+1,0
     RETURN
30   YTWO=.2*X+2.0
     RETURN
     END
```

This function subprogram defines the following function of X:

$$YTWO(X) = \begin{cases} 5X+1.0, & X \leq 0 \\ .2X+2.0, & X > 0 \end{cases}$$

If we wish to compute $(YTWO(B))^2$ in the main program and call it SQUARE, we need only write:

SQUARE=(YTWO(B))*(YTWO(B))

In this example, the function name is YTWO, the dummy argument is X, and the variable in the main program that replaces X is B. B must have been assigned a value in the main program before the statement

SQUARE=(YTWO(B)*YTWO(B))

is executed. The value assigned to B replaces X when the function is executed. A value is obtained for YTWO which replaces YTWO(B) in the above statement when the main program is executed. The execution of the main program triggers the execution of the function subprogram. (This also is true of subroutines.)

Since function subprograms are compiled separately from the main program, it is permissible to use the same names for variables in functions and in the main program. (This also is true of subroutines.) Of course, since the function itself appears in both, this cannot be done with the name of the function.

The type of data stored for the function value can be specified by beginning the FUNCTION statement with the appropriate word for declaring the type. For example,

```
DOUBLE PRECISION FUNCTION YTWO(X)
    INTEGER FUNCTION TOTAL(I,J,K)
```

In the first case, the real value YTWO, returned from the subprogram, is expressed using the long form. YTWO must be declared to be DOUBLE PRECISION in the calling program. In the second case, TOTAL is declared to be an integer function name with three arguments. TOTAL must be declared to be an integer variable in the calling program

Subroutines tend to be more elaborate than functions. Since a subroutine may return several results, the set of dummy arguments associated with it includes output variables as well as input variables. The subroutine (or subroutine name) does not take on a value. A special *CALL statement* is required to use a subroutine. It has the form:

CALL name(actual-arguments)

The actual arguments are variables appearing in the main program that are to be substituted for the dummy arguments in the subroutine. The first statement in the subroutine is the *SUBROUTINE statement*, which has the form:

SUBROUTINE name(dummy-arguments)

Except for the inclusion of output variables in the set of dummy arguments, this statement is much like the FUNCTION statement, but without type specifications. Most programmers list input variables first and output variables last, but this is not required.

Consider, for example, the following subroutine:

```
    SUBROUTINE LARGE(ARR,I,BIG,J)
    DIMENSION ARR(10,10)
    BIG=ABS(ARR(I,1))
    J=1
    DO 70 K=2,10
    IF(ABS(ARR(I,K))-BIG)70,70,71
 71 BIG=ABS(ARR(I,K))
    J=K
 70 CONTINUE
    RETURN
    END
```

ARR AND I are the dummy input variables, and BIG and J are the dummy output variables. Note the use of the FORTRAN library sub-program ABS, which computes the absolute value of its argument. After some analysis, it should be clear that this subroutine, called LARGE, finds the element in the Ith row of the array, ARR, that is largest in absolute value. It assigns the dummy variable BIG to the absolute value of this element and the dummy variable J to the column in which BIG appeared. We might use this subroutine as follows:

```
    DIMENSION COVAR(10,10)
        .
        .
        .

    CALL LARGE(COVAR,J,DIV,ICOL)
    DO 10 I=1,ICOL
 10 COVAR(J,I)=COVAR(J,I)/DIV
        .
        .
        .
```

The values stored in the array COVAR and the variable J are passed to the array ARR and the variable I when the subroutine is executed. The values obtained for BIG and J in executing the subroutine replace DIV and ICOL in the main program. This replaces the elements in the Jth row of COVAR, up to and including the element with the biggest absolute value in the row, with the original element divided by this biggest absolute value. The two variables, I and J, are used to denote different things in the subroutine and in the main program. For example, J is the column in which BIG appears in the subroutine, and J is also the row in COVAR that we are changing in the main program.

Control is passed to the statement immediately after the CALL statement in the calling program after a subroutine has been executed.

There are some dos and don'ts with respect to function programs and subroutines. They include:

1. SUBROUTINE statements and FUNCTION statements may not appear anywhere other than as the first statement in the subprograms.

2. Subprograms may call other subprograms, but a subprogram may not call itself or a subprogram that leads back to itself.

3. The dummy arguments must agree in type and length with the actual variables. Arrays that appear as dummy arguments must have the same dimensions as arrays in the main program. How-ever, it is permissible to assign maximum values to the sub-

scripts in arrays in subprograms using integer variables. This makes the dimensions of dummy arrays adjustable, a feature that is called *adjustable dimensions* or *object-time* dimensions.

Exercises

10. Rewrite the program written in answer to Exercise 11 in Chapter 2 so that it uses a DO statement to implement the loop that is required.

11. Rewrite the program written in answer to Exercise 14 in Chapter 2 so that it uses a DO statement to implement the loop in that program.

12. Write a statement function that calculates the product of three numbers and show how it would be used to calculate:

$$H = (A*B*D)/(E*F*G)$$

13. Write a FORTRAN subroutine that calculates the sum of the diagonal elements in a 5-by-5 matrix of double-precision real numbers. The diagonal elements are those for which the two subscripts are equal. If we call the 5-by-5 matrix X, then the diagonal elements are $X(1, 1), \ldots, X(5, 5)$.

14. Write a FORTRAN program that accepts a 5-by-5 matrix of double-precision real numbers, say Y, as input and produces as output another 5-by-5 matrix, say Z. Each element in Z is obtained by dividing the corresponding element in Y by the sum of the diagonal elements of Y. That is, for all I and J

$$Z(I, J) = \frac{Y(I, J)}{Y(1, 1) + \ldots + Y(5, 5)}$$

Call the subroutine you write in answer to Exercise 13 in this program. You may assume that only five digits are required to the right of the decimal in the output.

9.15 DEBUGGING A WATFIV PROGRAM

The WATFIV compiler and language have several features that a programmer can use in debugging a WATFIV program. However, since debugging a program is really another kind of algorithm testing, Section 7.10 should be reviewed before reading about these special features. It is most important to prepare an adequate set of test data in accordance with the recommendations in that section.

We shall discuss four major aids for debugging WATFIV programs:

1. The diagnostic messages provided by the WATFIV compiler;
2. The substitution of test data in the program;
3. The sectioning of a program into subprograms; and
4. The insertion of additional WRITE and associated FORMAT statements at critical points in the program.

The WATFIV compiler provides diagnostic messages in the output to indicate to the programmer the kind of error that may be present. WATFIV messages are printed in the source listing which is provided as a part of the output of a compilation. WATFIV messages are in straightforward English text. (Many FORTRAN compilers, and other compilers as well, provide codified messages that must be looked up in a manual.) For example, in submitting the program for calculating means and standard deviations, the FORMAT statement labeled 6 inadvertently was omitted. The following message appeared in the program listing, immediately after the END statement:

```
***ERROR***MISSING FORMAT STATEMENT 6
          USED IN LINE 18
```

Line 18 contained the WRITE statement that referred to this FORMAT statement. We shall say no more about WATFIV diagnostic messages. You probably have had a good deal of experience with them by now if you have been working the exercises in this chapter and in Chapter 2.

The WATFIV messages should be very helpful in correcting syntactical errors. However, the errors that remain after the syntactical errors have been corrected frequently are hard to detect. This is particularly true of long, complex programs. One approach is to substitute test inputs and to "play computer." This is called *hand simulation,* or *desk checking.* The contents of every storage location (all the variables) should be recorded as they are known, and the output should be written down as it is generated. Suppose, for example, that we had the following input to the means and standard deviation program:

> Card 1: 9
> Card 2: 1. 2. 3. 4. 5. 6. 7. 8.
> Card 3: 9. 0. 0. 0. 0. 0. 0. 0.

A hand simulation gives the results, shown in Figure 9.16.

One way to simplify the debugging of a complex program is to break the program into smaller, simpler parts. For example, if a long program can be separated into logically distinct sections, it may be advantageous

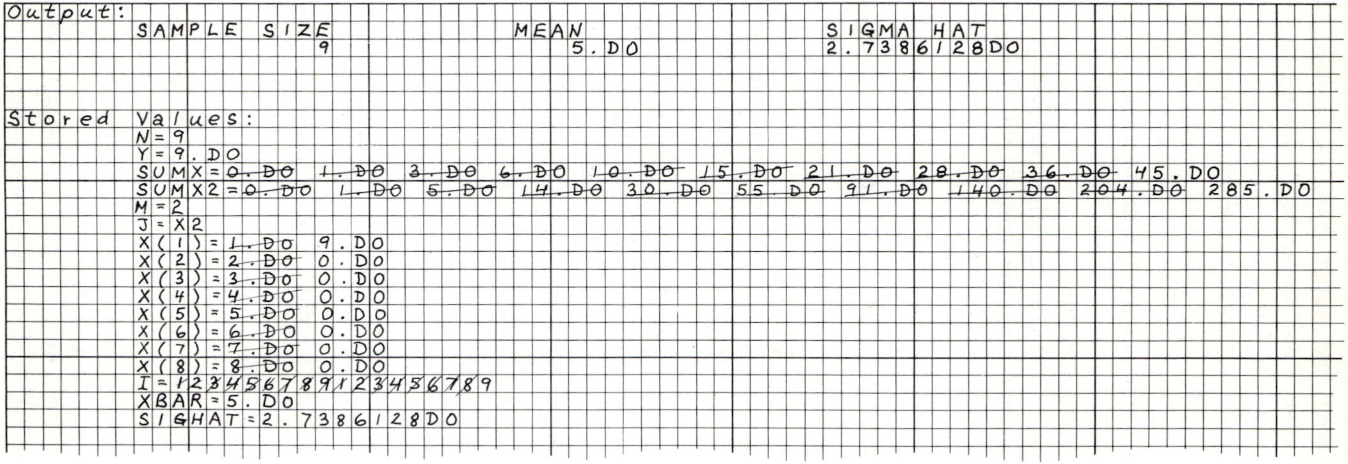

Output:

SAMPLE SIZE	MEAN	SIGMA HAT
9	5.DO	2.7386128DO

Stored Values:

N=9
Y=9.DO
SUMX=0.DO 1.DO 3.DO 6.DO 10.DO 15.DO 21.DO 28.DO 36.DO 45.DO
SUMX2=0.DO 1.DO 5.DO 14.DO 30.DO 55.DO 91.DO 140.DO 204.DO 285.DO
M=2
J=X2
X(1) = 1.DO 9.DO
X(2) = " 2.DO 0.DO
X(3) = " 3.DO 00.DO
X(4) = " 4.DO 00.DO
X(5) = " 5.DO 00.DO
X(6) = " 6.DO 00.DO
X(7) = " 7.DO 00.DO
X(8) = " 8.DO 00.DO
I=123456789123456789
XBAR=5.DO
SIGHAT=2.7386128DO

Fig. 9.16 Worksheet in a hand simulation of the means and standard deviations program

to write the program by using several subroutines. Test data can be inserted and the input and output of each subroutine can be checked separately. Of course, if this approach to debugging is implemented, the program first must be written in modular form and then put together section by section. The technique called *structured programming* incorporates this approach to program design and development. Its use can reduce programming time substantially, both in formulating a correct algorithm and in debugging the program. The major disadvantage of this approach is that it may use more computer time, since each subroutine is compiled separately.

WRITE statements and corresponding FORMAT statements can be added to a program during debugging to obtain intermediate results which, ordinarily, are not written in the output. This approach is recommended because:

1. The statements can be removed easily after the program is debugged;

2. The printout can be conveniently labeled; and

3. The set of variables whose values are written in the output can be modified by changing the WRITE statement.

Consider, for example, the following WRITE and FORMAT statements, which could be added during the debugging phase of the development of the program to compute means and standard deviations:

```
        WRITE(6,100)M
100 FORMAT(3H M=,I8)
```

These statements could be inserted after the statement $M = (N + 7)/8$. Also, the statements

```
    WRITE(6,200)SUMX,SUMX2
200 FORMAT(6H SUMX=,F28.12,20X,6HSUMX2=,F28.12)
```

could be inserted after statement 7 if only the last values of SUMX and SUMX2 were desired. If intermediate values of these sums were desired, these same statements could be inserted immediately before the statement SUMX = SUMX + X(I). (This would cause all sums, except the last to be printed out for each set of input data. If all sums, except the initial value but including the last one, were desired, something else would have to be done. See Exercise 15.)

Excerpts from an output obtained from the means and standard deviations program with a WRITE and a FORMAT statement added are given in Figure 9.17. One set of input was processed. Note that the mean and standard deviation are listed after the sums. This awkward

```
SAMPLE SIZE              MEAN                    SIGMA HAT
M=      3
SUMX=                                            SUMX2=           895.909260032100
        17          32.120910000000    1.889465          7.225034
```

Fig. 9.17 Output obtained in debugging the means and standard deviations program

structuring of the output occurs only in the debugging phase. Recall from Figure 9.14 that a conveniently formatted output is obtained after the special WRITE and FORMAT statements are removed.

Exercises

15. Modify the program to compute means and standard deviations as follows: Using additional WRITE and FORMAT statements, output all values of SUMX and SUMX2, except the initial value, for each set of input data.

16. Write a FORTRAN program to calculate the amount due in a savings account (see Sections 7.4 and 7.10 for a definition of this problem) and apply it to The Manhattan Island problem (see Exercise 2 in Chapter 7).

Exercises 17–21 are given in the table below. In each case, a FORTRAN program should be written to implement the algorithm and/or flowchart which previously was developed in working exercises in Chapters 7 and 8. A brief title for the exercise also is given in the table.

Exercise	Chapter 7 Reference and Title	Chapter 8 Reference and Title
17	8 Fibonacci numbers	3
18	12 Sort five numbers	10
*19	14 Bridge problem	6 But a detailed flowchart is needed
*20	——	13 Roots of a quadratic
*21	——	14 Simpson's rule

ANNOTATED SUPPLEMENTARY BIBLIOGRAPHY

References on FORTRAN IV are listed below, after a manual for WATFIV and a reference on structured programming in FORTRAN have been cited. Many books on FORTRAN are available. The books listed below were selected because they have a special feature or are especially well-written.

1. University of Waterloo Faculty of Mathematics, *I360 WATFIV Implementation Guide* (Ontario, Canada: University of Waterloo, 1969). (Modified and available in more recent editions.)

2. Tenny, T., "Structured Programming in FORTRAN," *Datamation,* Vol. 20, No. 7:110–115 (July 1974).

3. Parker, J. L., and Bohl, M., *FORTRAN Programming and WATFIV* (Palo Alto, Ca.: Science Research Associates, Inc , 1973). This is a well-written, nicely illustrated description of FORTRAN, with special attention to WATFIV.

4. Alexander, D. E., and Messer, A. C., *FORTRAN IV Pocket Handbook* (New York: McGraw-Hill Book Company, 1972). Here is a nicely packaged, inexpensive, convenient summary of the FORTRAN IV language.

5. McCracken, D. D., *A Guide to FORTRAN IV Programming* (2nd ed.) (New York: John Wiley and Sons, 1972). This well-written description of FORTRAN is especially suitable for the engineer and physical scientist.

6. Harris, L. D., *Numerical Methods Using FORTRAN* (Columbus, O.: Charles E. Merrill Books, Inc., 1965). This book describes FORTRAN in the context of numerical methods and very nearly succeeds in "killing two birds with one stone."

7. Kennedy, M., and Solomon, M. B., *Ten Statement FORTRAN Plus FORTRAN IV* (2nd ed.) (Englewood Cliffs, N.J. Prentice-Hall, Inc., 1975). This is a well-written, straightforward introduction to FORTRAN that probably can be mastered without attending a class. Access to a computer for laboratory work is required.

Chapter 10

PL/I Using PL/C

10.1 THE CHARACTER SET

A PL/I program is an algorithm which consists of a sequence of statements, or instructions. A statement corresponds to a box in a flowchart or a step in an English-language algorithm. The sequence helps to determine the order in which the statements are to be executed.

The main objective of this chapter is to help the reader state algorithms in the PL/I language. We will present a repertoire of statements, the rules for their formation, their significance, and the significance of their application. To begin at the beginning, we first shall specify the set of characters that can be used in the words appearing in a PL/I statement.

A PL/I program can be written using either of two character sets, the 60-character set or the 48-character set. However, since the 48-character set is not available in PL/C, we shall restrict our discussion and usage to the 60-character set.

The 60-character set is composed of alphabetic characters, digits, and special characters. There are 29 alphabetic characters, which include the 26 letters in upper case (capital) form; and three additional characters which may be used as if they were alphabetic characters: the dollar sign ($), the number sign (#), and the commercial "at" sign (@). There are 10 digits and 21 special characters (see Figure 10.1 for a listing of the complete set). The special characters permitted in PL/I include characters representing arithmetic processes: the plus sign (+), the minus sign (−), a slash for division (/), and an asterisk (∗) for multiplication. Also available are an equals sign (=), a left and right parentheses (()), a comma (,), a period (.), a quotation mark ('), a percent sign (%), a question mark (?), a semicolon (;), and a colon

221

Special Character Name	Character	Alphabetic Characters	Numeric Characters
Equals, assignment	=	A B C D E F G	0 1 2 3 4 5
Plus	+	H I J K L M N	6 7 8 9
Minus	–	O P Q R S T U	
Asterisk, multiply	*	V W X Y Z $ # @	
Slash, divide	/		
Left parentheses	(		
Right parentheses	)		
Comma	,		
Decimal point, binary point, period	.		
Quotation mark, apostrophe	'		
Percent	%		
Semicolon	;		
Colon	:		
Not	¬		
And	&		
Or	|		
Greater than	>		
Less than	<		
Break character	_		
Question mark	?		
Blank character			

Fig. 10.1 The 60-character set in PL/I

(:). Other special characters are used to indicate comparisons and logical operations. These include the comparisons less than (<) and greater than (>), and the logical operations not (¬), and (&), and or (|). Finally there is a break character (_), which is used to make identification (see next section) more readable; and the important special character, the blank.

Some of these characters serve more than one purpose, as indicated in Figure 10.1. For example, an equals sign is used as an equals sign in comparing two quantities but it is also used in PL/I in an assignment statement. In addition, two characters may be joined to denote a single operation; for instance, ✳✳ is used to denote exponentiation.

10.2 IDENTIFIERS

An *identifier* is a set of not more than 31 consecutive alphabetic, numeric, and/or break characters used to name an entity in a program or to specify the function of a statement. The first character must be alphabetic. Some examples of identifiers are:

```
ADD3
Y
N
X_AXIS
#643
P$4
ANTIDISESTABLISHMENTARIANISM
```

The following sequences of characters cannot be used as identifiers (reason given in parentheses):

2BOLT(first character must be alphabetic)
USER*(asterisk not allowed)
X AXIS(blank not allowed)
T012345678901234567890123456789012345678901(too many characters)

It probably is wise to restrict identifiers to a length of seven characters. Longer identifiers are tedious to write and error-prone. In some situations, PL/C may truncate longer identifiers to seven characters. Except for keywords, we shall limit our identifiers to seven characters in this chapter. Keywords will be defined and discussed in Section 10.4.

10.3 STATEMENT LABELS

A statement label is an identifier. PL/I statements may have one or more labels attached as a prefix to them. Although Section 3.2 showed how this is done, we did not discuss the possibility of having more than one label for the same statement. Since this is allowable,

$$ADD1:ADDONE:X=X+1.;$$

for example, is a valid PL/I statement. This statement has two labels — ADD1 and ADDONE — and can be referred to as either of these.

10.4 KEYWORDS

The function of a statement or the significance of parts of a statement usually are specified by unique identifiers called *keywords*.

There are eight types of keywords, but we shall define only three in this section: separating keywords, statement identifiers, and built-in function names. The other keyword types are conditions, data attributes, file attributes, formats, and options. Data attributes will be discussed in later sections.

There are five *separating keywords,* used to separate parts of a statement. They are:

BY   THEN   WHILE   ELSE   TO

Keywords used to convey the function of statements are called *statement identifiers.* Some of the commonly used statement identifiers are:

BEGIN	DO	GET	READ
CALL	END	IF	RETURN
DECLARE	ENTRY	PROCEDURE	STOP
DISPLAY	FORMAT	PUT	

Built-in function names are keywords which are used to call previously written algorithms that are available to a programmer who is using the PL/I language. The programmer can obtain square roots, trigonometric functions, absolute values, and a variety of other functions merely by employing the appropriate keyword and specifying the arguments for the function (the arguments are enclosed in parentheses).

For example, if we wish to assign to X a value obtained by multiplying the previous value of X by the square root of 2, we need only write:

X=X*SQRT(2);

Keywords are not *reserved* in PL/I; that is, they may appear elsewhere in the program and may be used for other purposes. However, this is an unwise programming practice which may make a program difficult for others to understand and lead to programming errors. Some keywords are reserved in PL/C and cannot be used as identifiers; these are listed in Figure 10.2.

Exercises

1. Which of the following cannot be used as identifiers in PL/C? Give reasons for your choices.

#$ 4IN   BY/TO   ON   IN_FOR
YDOT   IN4   DON'T   CODE   X-

2. Can the identifier RADIX_AXIS be used in PL/C? Is it advisable to use it, and if not, why not?

3. What are the five separating keywords?

4. What are the keywords called that convey the function of a statement?

```
ALLOCATE    END        NO           RETURN
BEGIN       ENTRY      NOCHECK      REVERT
BY          EXIT       NOFLOW       SIGNAL
CALL        FLOW       NOSOURCE     SOURCE
CHECK       FORMAT     ON           STOP
CLOSE       FREE       OPEN         THEN
DECLARE     GET        PROCEDURE    TO
DCL         GO         PROC         WHILE
DO          GOTO       PUT          WRITE
ELSE        IF         READ
```

Fig. 10.2 Keywords reserved in PL/C

10.5 CONSTANTS

The operands in PL/I statements, within the scope of the applications discussed in this chapter, are constants, variables, and array elements.

PL/I constants are denoted merely by entering their values in the PL/I statements. Because PL/I is designed to be a general-purpose language, it may use a wide variety of constants. We will discuss only three of them: decimal fixed-point, decimal floating-point, and character-string.

Decimal fixed-point constants are written in the usual way that numbers are written. A decimal point is optional. If it does not appear, it is assumed to be to the right of the rightmost digit; that is, the number is assumed to be an integer. Commas should not appear. The following are examples of valid decimal fixed-point constants:

```
    5           10.
   13         −4306
  −6.25         .0402
```

Floating-point constants are written by separating the mantissa from the exponent by means of the letter E. The mantissa is a decimal fixed-point constant and the exponent is an integer. The following are examples of valid decimal floating-point constants that are equal to the corresponding decimal fixed-point constant listed above:

```
   5E0          1.E1
  .13E2       −.4306E4
 −.625E1       402.E−4
```

Single quotation marks are used to enclose *character-string constants* in PL/I statements. When a quotation mark appears in a character string, it is represented by a pair of quotation marks. Thus, for example, we write:

```
'I CAN''T READ'
```

If this character string constant is pointed out, it appears as:

I CAN'T READ

10.6 VARIABLES AND ARRAYS

A variable in PL/I is denoted by an identifier. PL/I variables may take on a wide variety of values. We shall limit ourselves to only a few of these types of values: integer, floating-point, character-string, and logical. Logical variables take on the value true or false. A variable is a name for a storage location, and only one type of value can be stored in the location corresponding to a particular variable. We shall see in the next section how to specify the type of value to be stored.

Arrays likewise are named by identifiers. Since every element in the array must be of the same type, the conventions used to specify the type of values for variables also will be applicable to arrays. However, subscripts, which are used to designate a particular element, should take on only integer values.

10.7 SPECIFICATIONS FOR VARIABLES AND ARRAYS

The type of variable stored in a variable or array can be specified either by the choice of the first letter of the variable or array name, or by using a DECLARE statement.

If the variable or array name begins with one of the letters I through N, then the value stored in the variable or the elements of the array should be integers. If the first alphabetic character is not an I through N, the value is stored in floating-point.

Thus, for example, the variables IN4, N, and JOOT would be used to designate integer values, whereas YDOT, $SIGN, and Z would be used to designate floating-point values. Similarly, J(3,4) would be used to designate the element in the third row and fourth column of the matrix of integer values called J, whereas X(K,L) would be used to designate the element in the Kth row and L^{th} column of the matrix of floating-point values called X. Of course, values must have been assigned to K and L as well as to X(K,L), if X(K,L) is to be used in a PL/I program.

The DECLARE statement can be used to explicitly specify the type of value stored in a variable or an array. This statement assigns *attributes* — that is, specifications for their characteristics — to variables and arrays. The DECLARE statement is not executable: it does not carry out a step in an algorithm. It is used merely to describe the characteristics of variables.

The statement begins with the word "DECLARE," which may be abbreviated "DCL" if desired. Next, the name of a variable whose attributes are being specified is given, followed by a list of the attributes. Several variables may be assigned the same attributes in the same statement. In this case, the list of variables should be enclosed in parentheses. So, for example, we might have:

```
DECLARE(IRATE,INDEX,JOG)FLOAT;
```

which makes the variables IRATE, INDEX, and JOG all floating-point variables. In the absence of this statement, these variables would be integer-valued.

For our purposes in this chapter, we will use only the attributes FIXED, FLOAT, and CHARACTER. The attribute CHARACTER should be associated with variables and arrays that are used to store character strings. A DECLARE statement must be used for this purpose since there is no default convention for naming a variable that will establish this attribute.

The DECLARE statement also can be used to modify the precision of the data stored in PL/C variables. More specifically, the number of decimal digits for FIXED variables,* the number of decimal digits in the mantissa of FLOAT variables, and the number of characters in the string for CHARACTER variables can be declared by enclosing this number in parentheses after the attribute. If we wished to store integers up to 10 decimal digits in length in the variable called IDOT, we would write:

```
DECLARE IDOT FIXED(10);
```

In most implementations of PL/C, FIXED variables have a precision of a little more than 4 decimal digits,** and FLOAT variables have a precision of a little more than 6 decimal digits. This can be increased at most to a maximum of 10 and 16 decimal digits, respectively, using the DECLARE statement. Character strings can be from 1 to 32767 characters in length. The length of a character string variable should be set at the length of the longest string that will be stored in it. If, for example, we were storing the last names of students in the variable LASTN, we might use the following DECLARE statement:

```
DECLARE LASTN CHARACTER(15);
```

in order to accommodate names that are up to 15 characters in length.

---

*The precision specification also can be used to fix the number of places to the right of the decimal point for FIXED variables.

**Actually, 15 bits are used. Since $2^{15} = 32768$, we see that 32767 is the greatest integer that can be stored using 15 bits.

Because of the way numbers are stored in the IBM System 360/370 computers, it probably is wise to use either the default specification for the precision of integer and floating-point variables, or the maximum specification. If, for example, we were calculating the sum of a hundred or more five-digit numbers and storing the result in a variable called SUM, the appropriate DECLARE statement would be:

```
DECLARE SUM FLOAT(16);
```

The DECLARE statement, in addition, can be used to establish specifications for arrays. The minimum and maximum values that each subscript in an array can take on must be specified; however, if the minimum is 1, the value need not be specified explicitly. Values are specified by entering these numbers in parentheses in a DECLARE statement immediately after the name of the array.

Minimum and maximum values are separated by a colon, and specifications for different subscripts are separated by commas. Any specification for an array can be combined with specifications for the type of element in the array and the precision of these elements. Recall the array WORK (discussed in Section 5.10) that uses the station number, which varies from 7 to 11, for the second subscript. The longest character strings in this array, HARRINGTON and WASHINGTON, are 10 characters in length. We might DECLARE WORK as follows:

```
DECLARE WORK(3,7:11) CHARACTER(10);
```

If, however, we wished to accommodate future assignments, we should allow for longer names and use:

```
DECLARE WORK(3,7:11) CHARACTER(15);
```

10.8   A PROGRAM TO CALCULATE TUITION DUE

At this point, we will write a PL/I program to calculate the tuition due from a student, given the number of credits that the student is taking. The input consists of the student's last name, identification number, and the number of credits; the output should be the name, identification number, and tuition due. The tuition is calculated as follows:

If the student takes more than ten credits, the tuition is $1500.
If the student takes ten or fewer credits, the tuition is $150 per credit.

We begin by developing an algorithm for the solution of this problem.

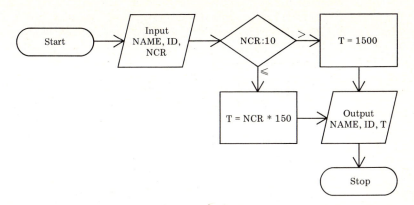

Fig. 10.3 Flowchart for an algorithm to calculate tuition

An algorithm that calculates the tuition correctly is given in Figure 10.3. However, it does not contain adequate provision for the detection of errors. We should "trap" values for the identification number and the number of credits that are not allowable and stop the procedure without producing any output if an illegal value is encountered. The algorithm in Figure 10.4 does this.

In Figure 10.5, a PL/I program to implement the algorithm in Figure 10.4 is given, along with the output obtained in a run of the program. The DECLARE statement illustrates how identical specifications may be given for two or more variables by grouping the variables inside parentheses which are separated by commas. In this case, the variables T and ID are FIXED with a precision of ten decimal digits. In the absence of this specification, ID would be FIXED with a precision of only four digits, and T would be floating-point. Variables should be stored and processed in integer form whenever possible because arithmetic operations on integers are faster. Since tuitions can take on only integer values, the tuition, T, is stored in integer form.

The DECLARE statement also shows that any number of different sets of variables or arrays can be given specifications in the same statement. Again, the comma is used as the separating punctuation mark, and both the set (T,ID) and the variable NAME are given specifications.

Names were chosen for variables that indicate the usage of the variable; for example, T for tuition and ID for identification. The programmer writes the statements in the program with these names in mind; since the computer does not "know" which variables are used to denote which data, the programmer implicitly determines this assignment of data to variables in the way that he writes the program.

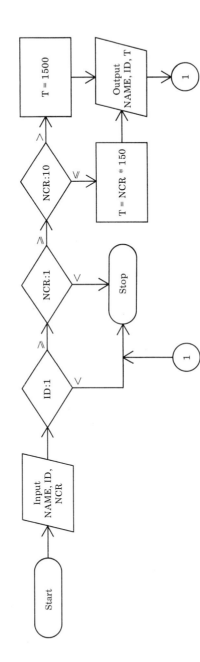

Fig. 10.4 Flowchart for an algorithm to calculate tuition with provision for checking input values

Input

'ABCDEFGHIJKLMN' 87654321 9

Program

```
      /*A PROGRAM TO CALCULATE TUITION DUE */
TUIT:PROCEDURE OPTIONS(MAIN);
      DECLARE(T,ID)FIXED(10),NAME CHARACTER(15);
      GET LIST(NAME,ID,NCR);
      IF ID<1 THEN GOTO ONE;
      IF NCR<1 THEN GOTO ONE;
      IF NCR>10 THEN GOTO FIVE;
      T=150*NCR;
      GO TO SIX;
   FIVE:T=1500;
   SIX:PUT LIST(NAME,ID,T);
ONE:END TUIT;
```


Output

ABCDEFGHIJKLMN   87654321   1350

Fig. 10.5 A PL/I program to calculate tuition due along with the input to and corresponding output from a run of this program

Exercises

5. Suppose that all the valid variables in Exercise 1 are to be used to represent floating-point numbers with a precision of 16 decimal digits; write an appropriate DECLARE statement.

*6. Recall the array CARD introduced in Exercise 15 of Chapter 5. Write a DECLARE statement appropriate for this array.

7. Write a PL/I program that calculates and outputs the tuition due from each of K students. Assume that K is input first and then one card is input for each student. Each card contains a name, identification number, and the number of credits that the student is taking. If an illegal value for either the identification or the number of credits is encountered, go on to the next student.

10.9   OPERATIONS AND EXPRESSIONS

Figure 10.6 defines PL/I operations and illustrates their use. The operands are variables (including array elements) or constants in each case. Although certain operations on arrays as a whole are permitted, they will not be discussed here. The operands in logical operations are either numbers, arithmetic expressions, or logical variables. The result of a logical operation is always either true or false.

Operator			Type of Operator	Example of	
Priority	Symbol	Name		Operation	Result Is
1	¬	Not	Prefix logical	A(A=true)	False
1	**	Exponentation	Arithmetic	A**B(A=2,B=3)	8
1	+	Prefix +	Arithmetic	+A(A=2)	+2
1	−	Prefix −	Arithmetic	−A(A=2)	−2
2	*	Multiplication	Arithmetic	A*B(A=2,B=3)	6
2	/	Division	Arithmetic	A/B(A=6,B=3)	2
3	+	Addition	Arithmetic	A+B(A=2,B=3)	5
3	−	Subtraction	Arithmetic	A−B(A=2,B=3)	−1
4	>=	Greater than or equal to	Comparison	A>=B(A=2,B=3)	False
4	>	Greater than	Comparison	A>B(A=2,B=3)	False
4	¬>	Not greater than	Comparison	A¬>B(A=2,B=3)	True
4	=	Equal to	Comparison	A=B(A=2,B=3)	False
4	<	Less than	Comparison	A<B(A=2,B=3)	True
4	¬<	Not less than	Comparison	A¬<B(A=2,B=3)	False
4	<=	Less than or equal to	Comparison	A<=B(A=2,B=3)	True
5	&	And	Logical	A&B(A=true,B=false)	False
6	|	Or	Logical	A|B(A=true,B=false)	True

Fig. 10.6 PL/I operators

Arithmetic operations are performed in the following order: all exponentiations first, all multiplications and divisions second, and all additions and subtractions third. This priority is indicated in Figure 10.4. For example, if B = 2, C = 6, and D = 2, then A = B + C/D; yields A = 5. For A = B ∗ C / D; we get A = 6, since operations at the same level are executed from left to right. Expressions in parentheses are evaluated first; therefore A = (B + C) / D yields A = 4.

Three of the operators in the table (NOT, prefix-plus, and prefix-minus) affect only one operand. All other operators require two operands. The result of a NOT operation is the opposite logical value from its operand.

An operator, ∗∗, is necessary for exponentiation because all the characters in a PL/I statement must lie on the same line. There is no provision for raising some characters a little above the level of the line or lowering others below the level of the line. The approach is to represent A^B using A ∗∗ B. So, for example, $[2.6(X + Y)]^Z$ is written as (2.6 ∗ (X + Y)) ∗∗ Z. The other arithmetic operators were introduced in Section 3.4.

Comparison operators give the result true or false; that is, the comparison either holds or does not hold. These comparison operators are used to check whether certain equalities or inequalities hold for expressions containing only arithmetic operators; that is, for *arithmetic expressions*. They also may be applied to the comparison of strings, but we will not discuss this application here.

The logical operations & and | function as follows (examples of their use are given in Figure 10.4):

The result of an | operation is false if and only if both operands are false.

The result of an & operation is true if and only if both operands are true.

Suppose, for example, that we wished to test the variables A and B for two conditions. The conditions are: A > B and B < 0. We could use the expression: (A > B) & (B < 0) if we wished both conditions to be satisfied. The expression: (A > B) | (B < 0) could be used if we wished only at least one of the conditions to be satisfied. In each case the expression would be true only if the desired conditions had been satisfied.

The priorities given in the first column of the table indicate the order of execution of arithmetic, comparison, and logical operations. Operations of equal priority are executed from left to right; however, if there are several exponentiations in the same statement, they are executed from right to left. Thus the numbers under the operations in the following expression indicate the order in which the operations are carried out.

$$A>B\&C>D|A**N-X<B/C*D+F$$
$$6\quad 9\quad 7\;10\quad 1\quad 4\quad 8\quad 2\quad 3\quad 5$$

10.10   ANNOTATING OUTPUTS—EDIT DIRECTED OUTPUT

All the PL/1 programs that we have written thus far have had format-free outputs. Numbers are printed without labels, headings, or other descriptions. Tables are not set up, even though a tabular output might be appropriate. A better way to present the output would be to provide adequate annotation and layout. In the tuition problem, it would be helpful to label the three outputs. The first output might be labeled *student name,* the second *ID number,* and the third *tuition due.* It also would be useful to output a message of some kind if an illegal student number or number of credits were encountered. Sections 10.10 and 10.11 will show how this is done. Section 10.11 will present a revised, annotated version of the tuition program.

The PUT EDIT statement can be used to lay out and annotate output. It has the form:

PUT EDIT(variables-list)(format-list);

This variables list is analogous to the variables list used in the PUT LIST statement. Character string constants can be included in the list to annotate the output. The items in the format list are of two types: control-format items and data-format items. *Control format items* specify such things as the spacing within a line, skipping lines, and going on to the next page of printed output. *Data format items* describe the printing format for the items on the variables list. Elements in the variables list are associated, in order, with data items in the format list. Output is terminated when the variables list has been exhausted. Control and data items appearing after the last-matched data item are not processed.

Format items in the format list are separated by commas. They can be preceded by an iteration factor. We shall see several examples of PUT EDIT statements in the next section, including examples of the use of iteration factors. But first we must learn the codes used to express format items.

10.11 FORMAT ITEMS

Many format items are available in PL/I. We shall discuss only those data format items associated with fixed-point, floating-point, and character-string data. We also will discuss a few of the control format items.

Fixed-point data format items can be specified using any one of the following three forms:

$$F(w)$$
$$F(w,d)$$
$$F(w,d,p)$$

The letter F and the parentheses appear in the PL/I statement, as indicated. Integer numbers ordinarily would replace the w, d, and p. The letter w indicates the total number of print positions that this fixed-point number will occupy. For example, F(10) would imply: print the corresponding data item right justified in the next ten print positions. Since no d specification is given, only the integer portion of the number is printed. The result is truncated, not rounded — that is, the fractional portion is discarded without affecting the unit position of the integer. If a d specification is given, then d places to the right of the decimal are printed. A decimal point also is printed if $d > 0$. The p specification is used to print a value equal to the stored value times 10^p. The contents of memory corresponding to the variable are not changed. Suppose, for example, that the value stored for X is 210.22, and that we wished this value to be multiplied by 100 and then printed. If we had the following statements in the program:

```
PUT EDIT (X)(F(10,2,2));
Y=X-100.12;
```

then the printed output would be:

21022.00

and the value stored for Y would be 110.10.

Space should be included for a possible minus sign and a possible decimal point in determining w. The following table shows the value that is printed which corresponds to a stored value of 379.62, when the given fixed-point format item is used. A b is used, as before, to indicate a blank character.

Format Item	Value Printed
F(8,2)	bb379.62
F(8,1)	bbb379.6
F(8,0)	bbbbb379
F(8)	bbbbb379
F(8,3,-2)	bbb3.796

The attributes of a variable need not agree with the format prescribed for the data item. The proper conversion is made to conform to the format.

If data items are too large in magnitude to be represented conveniently by fixed-point notation, the floating-point format item can be used. It has the general form:

E(w,d,s).

The letter E and the parentheses appear in the PL/I statement, and integers replace w, d, and s. As before, w represents the total number of print positions used, and d the number of digits to the right of the decimal (in this case, in the mantissa). The s is optional; it is used to specify the number of significant digits in the mantissa.

The following table shows the value printed which corresponds to a stored value of −2600, if the given floating-point format item is used.

Format Item	Value Printed
E(13,4)	bb−2.6000E+04
E(13,3)	bbb−2.600E+04
E(13,0)	bbbbbbb−2E+04
E(13,4,5)	bb−2.6000E+04
E(13,4,7)	−260.0000E+02

The *character-string data format item* has the general form A(w). The letter A and the parentheses appear in the PL/I statement, and the w indicates the number of print positions occupied by this output. The w can be omitted; the format item could consist solely of the letter A. If w is omitted, the number of characters printed is the current length of the character string that is being written as output. If w is less than the length of the string, the string is truncated in the right. If w is greater than the length of the string, the string in the output has blanks added to the right. The following three statements:

```
PUT EDIT('EXAMPLE ONE')(A(11));
PUT EDIT('EXAMPLE ONE')(A);
PUT EDIT('EXAMPLE ONETWO')(A(11));
```

would give the identical output:

```
EXAMPLE ONE
```

Note that quotes do not appear in the output.

It often is desirable to insert a number of consecutive blank characters in a printed line to separate data items. This can be done with a control format item called a *spacing format item*. The general form is X(w). The letter X and the parentheses appear in the PL/I statement, and the w is replaced by an integer* that indicates how many blank characters are to be inserted.

The other control format items that we will discuss are the PAGE and SKIP items. The PAGE specification causes the printer to go to the top of the next page. It consists of the word PAGE.

The SKIP format item is:

```
SKIP(i)
```

At this point, $i - 1$ blank lines are inserted in the output; the printing skips to i lines after the present one. If $i <= 0$, the next line is printed over the present one. The following illustrates how these control items work:

```
PUT EDIT(X,Y,Z)(PAGE,F(10,2),SKIP(3),F(10,2),X(40),F(10,2));
```

The value stored for X will be printed in the first ten print positions of the first line of a new page. The value for Y will be printed in the first ten positions of the fourth line of the page; and the value for Z will be printed in print positions 51 through 60 of this same fourth line.

Suppose we had the statement:

```
PUT EDIT(X,Y,Z)(PAGE,2F(10,2),SKIP(3),X(50),F(10,2));
```

In this case, X would be printed in the first ten print positions of line 1 of a new page; Y in the next ten positions (because 2F(10,2) is identical to the specification F(10,2),F(10,2)); and Z in print positions 51 through 60 of the fourth line.

---

*In general, the integer values for these control items can be arithmetic expressions. The expression is evaluated and truncated to an integer, say i. Then i blanks are inserted. If $i <= 0$, no blanks are inserted.

Inputs

Program

```
      /*A PROGRAM TO CALCULATE TUITION DUE */
TUIT:PROCEDURE OPTIONS(MAIN);
      DECLARE(T,ID)FIXED(10),NAME CHARACTER(15);
      GET LIST(NAME,ID,NCR);
      IF ID<1 THEN GOTO ONE;
      IF NCR<1 THEN GOTO TWO;
      IF NCR>10 THEN GOTO FIVE;
      T=150*NCR;
      GO TO SIX;
   FIVE:T=1500;
   SIX:PUT EDIT('STUDENT NAME','IDNUMBER','TUITION DUE')(A(15),A(12),
         A(11));
      PUT EDIT(NAME,ID,T)(SKIP(1),A(15),F(10),X(5),F(8));
      GOTO THREE;
   ONE:PUT EDIT('THIS ID NUMBER IS ERRONEOUS.IT IS',ID)(A(35),F(10));
      GOTO THREE;
   TWO:PUT EDIT('NUMBER CREDITS FOR',NAME,'IS ERRONEOUS.IT IS',NCR)(A(
         20),A,A(20),F(10));
   THREE:END TUIT;
```

Outputs

```
STUDENT NAME    ID NUMBER    TUITION DUE
IVAN              12345678        1500

NUMBER CREDITS FOR  HERBERT       IS ERRONEOUS.IT IS         0

THIS ID NUMBER IS ERRONEOUS.IT IS         -26
```

Fig. 10.7   An annotated program to calculate tuition due along with the inputs and the outputs obtained in each of three runs of the program

Now we can rewrite the tuition program so that the output is more neatly set out and annotated (Figure 10.7 gives a program to do this). PUT EDIT statements can be so long that they must be written on two successive cards. In most versions of PL/C, the statement should appear in columns 2 through 72 of the card; but, since the end of a statement is marked by a semicolon, the statement can continue on as many cards as needed until the semicolon is encountered. Figure 10.7 also contains the output obtained in each of three runs of the program. The input can be deduced from the output.

Exercises

8.   Write a single PL/C statement to sum the elements in each of the arrays listed in the following DECLARE statement. Call the result SUM in each case, and write a separate statement for each array.

```
DECLARE (X(4),Y,OUT,IN,T(4:7,3))FIXED(10);
```

9. Write a single PL/C statement to compute the unbiased estimate of the standard deviation, SIGHAT, of a set of N numbers, X_1, $X_2, \ldots X_N$. SIGHAT is given by:

$$\text{SIGHAT} = \sqrt{\frac{N \sum_{i=1}^{N} X_i^2 - \left(\sum_{i=1}^{N} X_i \right)^2}{N(N-1)}}$$

Assume that

$$\sum_{i=1}^{N} X_i^2$$

has been computed and is stored in a variable called S2, and that

$$\sum_{i=1}^{N} X_i$$

has been computed and is stored in S1. A value for N is stored in the variable called N.

10. Modify the programs written in solution to Exercises 9, 12, 14, and 16 in Chapter 3 so that they have appropriately annotated and formatted output.

10.12 THE ON ENDFILE STATEMENT

PL/C offers a statement that lets a programmer branch to another statement in the program when an end-of-file is encountered on input. It is the ON ENDFILE statement, and it looks like:

```
ON ENDFILE(SYSIN)GO TO label;
```

When an appropriate statement label is used, it replaces the word label. In executing this statement, the program branches to the statement with this label when an end-of-file occurs. If, for example, we wished to modify the tuition program given in Figure 10.7 so that it could process an unlimited number of students, we could add the statement:

```
ON ENDFILE(SYSIN) GO TO THREE;
```

to the program. Its location in the program is not critical; no matter where this statement is placed, it will cause the program to branch to the statement labeled THREE when there are no more cards to be read in. In this case, we placed this statement immediately after the input statement:

```
                     GET LIST(NAME,ID,NCR);
```

The GET LIST statement also must be labeled, since the program should branch back to this statement after processing a set of input data. We might label it FOUR, and change the GO TO THREE; statements to GO TO FOUR; statements. A program that does all this is given in Figure 10.8.

SKIP(1) format items were inserted in the PUT EDIT statements labeled SIX, ONE, and TWO to ensure that the output for a new student would be put on a new line. The second card of the PUT EDIT statement labeled TWO begins with the specification of the format items; the first card for this statement is not ended in column 72. If it

Input

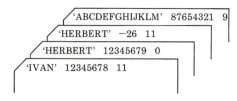

'ABCDEFGHIJKLM' 87654321 9

'HERBERT' −26 11

'HERBERT' 12345679 0

'IVAN' 12345678 11

Program

```
        /*A PROGRAM TO CALCULATE TUITION DUE */
TUIT:PROCEDURE OPTIONS(MAIN);
        DECLARE(T,ID)FIXED(10),NAME CHARACTER(15);
    FOUR:GET LIST(NAME,ID,NCR);
        ON ENDFILE(SYSIN) GOTO THREE;
        IF ID<1 THEN GOTO ONE;
        IF NCR<1 THEN GOTO TWO;
        IF NCR>10 THEN GOTO FIVE;
        T=150*NCR;
        GO TO SIX;
    FIVE:T=1500;
    SIX:PUT EDIT('STUDENT NAME','ID NUMBER','TUITION DUE')(SKIP(1),A(15
        ),A(12),A(11));
        PUT EDIT(NAME,ID,T)(SKIP(1),A(15),F(10),X(5),F(8));
        GOTO FOUR;
    ONE:PUT EDIT('THIS ID NUMBER IS ERRONEOUS. IT IS',ID)(SKIP(1),A(35),
        F(10));
        GOTO FOUR;
    TWO:PUT EDIT('NUMBER CREDITS FOR',NAME,'IS ERRONEOUS.IT IS',NCR)
        (SKIP(1),A(20),A,A(20),F(10));
        GOTO FOUR;
THREE:END TUIT;
```

Output

```
STUDENT NAME    ID NUMBER    TUITION DUE
IVAN             12345678        1500
NUMBER CREDITS FOR  HERBERT        IS ERRONEOUS.IT IS         0
THIS ID NUMBER IS ERRONEOUS.IT IS        −26
STUDENT NAME    ID NUMBER    TUITION DUE
ABCDEFGHIJKLMN  87654321        1350
```

Fig. 10.8   A program to calculate tuition using the ON ENDFILE statement

were filled in all the way to column 72, the keyword, SKIP, would be continued from one card to the next; and it is a bad practice to break up any identifier in this way.

The output obtained in a run of the program (given in Figure 10.8) is not as neatly formatted as it might have been. It probably would have been better to enter the heading just once, and to have the output for each student take up just one line. That is, it would have been better to set up a tabular output format. This approach will be required in Exercise 11.

10.13 THE DO GROUP AND DO LOOPS

Very powerful looping mechanisms are available in PL/I, called the *DO group* and *DO loops*.

Suppose that we are given a one-dimensional array, A, containing N floating-point numbers, and that we wish to compute the sum of the elements in the array. We already have seen what an algorithm to accomplish this might look like. We must input N and initialize the sum. We then loop, inputting an element and adding it to the sum. After the loop is completed, we output the result. The PL/I program given in Figure 10.9 shows one way to do this.

The maximum value for N is 100 because this is the maximum value that we have allowed for the subscript; and the elements of A have 16 decimal-digit precision.

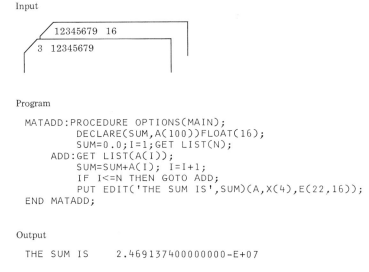

Input

```
12345679  16
3  12345679
```

Program

```
MATADD:PROCEDURE OPTIONS(MAIN);
       DECLARE(SUM,A(100))FLOAT(16);
       SUM=0.0;I=1;GET LIST(N);
   ADD:GET LIST(A(I));
       SUM=SUM+A(I);  I=I+1;
       IF I<=N THEN GOTO ADD;
       PUT EDIT('THE SUM IS',SUM)(A,X(4),E(22,16));
   END MATADD;
```

Output

```
THE SUM IS     2.469137400000000-E+07
```

Fig. 10.9 A program to sum the elements in an array

This program can be carried out using a DO to implement the loop. The loop is initiated by a statement containing the keyword DO. A WHILE clause can be used to indicate how long the loop should be executed. An END statement marks the extent of the loop. The sum of the elements in an array then can be obtained using the program given in Figure 10.10. This program illustrates the use of a DO statement of the form:

DO WHILE (Comparison);

The DO is executed as long as the comparison holds—in the example, as long as I $<=$ N. As soon as the comparison is false—when I $>$ N —the first statement after the END statement, the PUT EDIT statement, is executed.

Another form for the DO statement explicitly names the variable that will be used as a counter (I in the example), the value at which it is to be initialized (1 in the example), and the value against which it is to be tested in order to determine when to conclude the loop (N in the example). The amount by which the counter is to be incremented in each pass through the loop also is given. Using this approach, we would write:

DO I=1 TO N BY 1;

in lieu of DO WHILE (I $<=$ N); in the program to calculate the sum and get the same result. The BY clause is optional; if it is omitted,

Input

```
  12345679  16
3  12345679
```

Program

```
MATADD:PROCEDURE OPTIONS(MAIN);
        DECLARE(SUM,A(100))FLOAT(16);
        SUM=0.0;I=1;GET LIST(N);
    DO WHILE(I<=N);GET LIST(A(I));
        SUM=SUM+A(I); I=I+1;
    END;
        PUT EDIT('THE SUM IS',SUM)(A,X(4),E(22,16));
END MATADD;
```

Output

```
THE SUM IS    2.469137400000000-E+07
```

Fig. 10.10 A program to sum the elements in an array using a DO loop

the increment is assumed to be 1. Thus we also could write:

$$DO \ I=1 \ TO \ N;$$

in lieu of DO WHILE(I $<=$ N);

The WHILE clause can be used along with a counter in those applications where two criteria are to be used to control the execution of the DO loop. In the square root algorithm discussed in Chapter 7, the loop continued either until a maximum number of iterations were completed or until the measure of the error in the result was less than a specified value. If we call the maximum number of iterations K and the specified value for the error TEST, then the DO statement could be:

$$DO \ J=1 \ TO \ K \ WHILE \ (E>TEST);$$

J counts the number of iterations and E measures the error in the estimate. A complete program to calculate a square root using Newton's method, along with an input and corresponding output in a run of this program, is given in Figure 10.11. The output is not as readable as it should be: blank spaces should be entered between the label for each output and the value. The X format code could be used for this purpose. This approach was taken in the programs to calculate sums given in Figures 10.9 and 10.10.

Input

```
100.   .01   20
```

Program

```
ROOT:PROCEDURE OPTIONS(MAIN);
        DECLARE(E,X,TEST,NEXT,LAST)FLOAT(16);
        E=1.0;GET LIST(X,TEST,K);
        LAST=(X+1.)/2.;
    DO J=1 TO K WHILE(E>TEST);
        NEXT=(LAST+X/LAST)/2.; E=ABS(X-NEXT*NEXT);
        LAST=NEXT;
    END;
        PUT EDIT('THE SQUARE ROOT OF',X,'USING A TEST VALUE OF',TEST,
        'AND A MAXIMUM NUMBER OF ITERATIONS OF',K,'IS',NEXT,J,
        'ITERATIONS WERE REQUIRED TO OBTAIN THIS ESTIMATE')(PAGE,A,
        E(22,16),SKIP(1),A,E(22,16),SKIP(1),A,F(10),SKIP(1),A,E(22,16),
        SKIP(1),F(10),A);
END ROOT;
```

Output

```
THE SQUARE ROOT OF1.000000000000000-E+02
USING A TEST VALUE OF1.000000000000000-E-02
AND A MAXIMUM NUMBER OF ITERATIONS OF           20
IS1.000005289564269-E+01
        6ITERATIONS WERE REQUIRED TO OBTAIN THIS ESTIMATE
```

Fig. 10.11 A program to calculate the square root of a number using Newton's algorithm

Subscripts were not used in calculating the square root; instead, we retained the last and next estimate using variables called LAST and NEXT. In general, it is wise to avoid the use of subscripts in iterations to save intermediate results. Many iterations may be required before an adequate result is obtained. If we store all intermediate values, we might run out of storage space and inhibit the computation of the iteration.

10.14 INPUT AND OUTPUT OF ARRAYS

In PL/I, arrays can be input and output as a whole or in part. A whole array is input or output by listing the array name in the variables list of the GET or PUT statement. The specification in the DECLARE statement is used to determine either the number of elements which are to be assigned values on input, or from which values are to be output. Elements in the array are transmitted in row order. This means, for example, that if the array A had two rows and three columns, the order of input or output would be: A(1,1), A(1,2), A(1,3), A(2,1), A(2,2), A(2,3). This is illustrated in Figure 10.12.

Arrays can be input or output in part. If a single element is to be transmitted, then it need only be listed in the variables list. If some but not all of the elements of an array are to be transmitted, these elements can be listed. A DO loop sometimes is a convenient method; separate DO, END, and input or output statements need not be written, since the DO statement simply can be incorporated into the variables list. Suppose, for example, that we wished to output the checked elements in the five-by-five array given in Figure 10.13 in the order indicated by the numbers next to the checks. We could write:

```
PUT LIST(((X(I,J)DO I=1 TO 5 BY 4)DO J=1 TO 5 BY 2));
```

The DO in the innermost parentheses is executed first, so I is incremented before J. This gives the desired result.

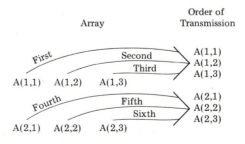

Fig. 10.12 The order of transmission in the input and output of arrays illustrated using a two-by-three array

$$\text{①}X(1,1) \quad X(1,2) \quad \text{③}X(1,3) \quad X(1,4) \quad \text{⑤}X(1,5)$$
$$X(2,1) \quad X(2,2) \quad X(2,3) \quad X(2,4) \quad X(2,5)$$
$$X(3,1) \quad X(3,2) \quad X(3,3) \quad X(3,4) \quad X(3,5)$$
$$X(4,1) \quad X(4,2) \quad X(4,3) \quad X(4,4) \quad X(4,5)$$
$$\text{②}X(5,1) \quad X(5,2) \quad \text{④}X(5,3) \quad X(5,4) \quad \text{⑥}X(5,5)$$

Fig. 10.13 The six elements in a five-by-five array that are to be output and the order in which they are to be output

Exercises

11. Write a program to calculate the tuition due from each of K students. Assume that K is input first and that then the student name, identification number, and number of credits taken are input for each student. If an erroneous student number or number of credits is detected, output an appropriate message and go on to the next student. If the value input for K is erroneous, take some appropriate action and then stop. The output should be in tabular form, with a one-line entry for each student. The table heading should be:

```
STUDENT NAME    ID NUMBER    TUITION DUE
```

12. Rewrite the programs written in answer to Exercises 9, 12, and 16 in Chapter 3 so that they use DO statements to implement the loops that are required.

13. Write a program that reads in a set of employee assignments to the array WORK and then prints out these assignments in a neat, easily interpreted manner.

*14. Write a program that inputs a hand, i.e., a set of zeros and ones, to the array CARD (see Exercise 15 in Chapter 5) and then counts and outputs the number of cards in each suit.

15. What does the following PL/I program segment do:

```
                DECLARE A(10,10);
         DO1:DO    I=1 TO 10;
         DO2:DO    J=1 to 10;
                IF   I=J THEN A(I,J)=1.;
                IF  I¬=J THEN A(I,J)=0.;
  END DO1;
  END DO2;
```

10.15 A PROGRAM TO CALCULATE MEANS
AND STANDARD DEVIATIONS

We now shall develop a PL/I program to calculate the mean and standard deviation of each of several sets of data. We shall assume that each set begins with the specification of the number of observations in the set, also called the *sample size,* denoted in the program by N. This is followed by the observations in free-format form.

Given a set of N observations $X_1, X_2, \ldots, X_N$, recall that the mean, XBAR, and the unbiased estimate of the standard deviation, SIGHAT, are given by:

$$\text{XBAR} = \frac{\displaystyle\sum_{i=1}^{N} X_i}{N}$$

$$\text{SIGHAT} = \sqrt{\frac{N \displaystyle\sum_{i=1}^{N} X_i^2 - \left(\displaystyle\sum_{i=1}^{N} X_i\right)^2}{N(N-1)}}$$

We shall compute the sum and the sum of the squares of the observations by adding the value of X_j and X_j^2 to

$$\sum_{i=1}^{j-1} X_i \quad \text{and} \quad \sum_{i=1}^{j-1} X_i^2,$$

respectively, until $J = N$.

The first consideration is whether or not to use 16-digit precision. Both

$$N \sum_{i=1}^{N} X_i^2 \quad \text{and} \quad \left(\sum_{i=1}^{N} X_i\right)^2$$

can be expected to have more than six digits in many applications. If we do not use 16 digits their differences, and hence SIGHAT, may be zero in these cases when they should not be zero.

The next principal consideration is conserving storage space. If we read all the observations into storage before processing them, main storage may be exhausted. Instead, we will read in the observations one at a time and process them. The same location, i.e., the same variable name, will be used for each observation.

Figure 10.14 contains an annotated PL/I program to calculate means and standard deviations. The output obtained in a run of this program is also given in Figure 10.14. The input is not included because it is quite lengthy. Three data sets were provided: the first with a sample size of 112, the second with a sample size of 9, and the third with a sample size of −9.

10.16 PROCEDURES WITHIN PROCEDURES

Up to now all of our PL/I programs have had the same structure:

Program

```
/*A PROGRAM TO CALCULATE MEANS AND STANDARD DEVIATIONS*/
XBSIGMA:PROCEDURE OPTIONS(MAIN);
    DECLARE(S1,S2,X,XB,SIGHAT)FLOAT(16);
    PUT EDIT('SET','SAMPLE SIZE','MEAN','STANDARD DEVIATION')
        (PAGE,A,X(4),A,X(8),A,X(16),A);
    J=0;
DATA:GET LIST(N);ON ENDFILE(SYSIN)GOTO QUIT; IF N<=0 THEN GOTO ERR;
        S1=0.;S2=0.;J=J+1;
        DO I=1 TO N;GET LIST(X);
        S1=S1+X;S2=S2+X*X;
    END;
        XB=S1/N;SIGHAT=SQRT((N*S2-S1*S1)/(N*(N-1)));
        PUT EDIT(J,N,XB,SIGHAT)(SKIP(1),F(3),F(10),2(X(4),E(22,16)));
    GOTO DATA;
ERR:PUT EDIT('N TOO SMALL,RUN TERMINATED.N IS',N)(SKIP(1),A,X(4),F(6));
QUIT:END XBSIGMA;
```

Output

```
SET     SAMPLE SIZE        MEAN                STANDARD DEVIATION
 1         112      2.092410714285714-E+01    5.811688215686120-E+00
 2           9      5.000000000000000-E+00    2.738612787525831-E+00
N TOO SMALL,RUN TERMINATED.N IS         -9
```

Fig. 10.14   A program to calculate means and standard deviations

```
label:PROCEDURE OPTIONS(MAIN);

                    .

                    .

                    .

             program
                    .

                    .

                    .

      END label;
```

The only complexity that we have added has involved the use of DO groups; thus the structure might contain a number of disconnected DO loops. If the problem is simple enough, only this structure is required. However, more complex structures are permitted in PL/I. We shall describe briefly two types of more complex structures.

We already have seen how a programmer can invoke the same procedure repeatedly and apply it to different arguments by using built-in functions. This same kind of thing can be done for procedures that are supplied by the programmer. Although the procedure is written once, it may be used several times. We will examine this in terms of two situations: when only one value is to be supplied by the special procedure, and when more than one value is to be supplied.

A programmer can write a procedure that supplies a single value and then invoke it in much the same way that a built-in function is invoked. Suppose, for example, that we had to calculate the sum of three numbers repeatedly in a program. Say:

```
A:PROCEDURE OPTIONS(MAIN);
    DECLARE B(4);
    .
    .
    .

    R=S*(R+Y+Z)+T*T;
    .
    .
    .

    Q=V+(R+X+T)/(T+V+U);
    .
    .
    .

    W=(R+Q+V)/Z;
    .
    .
    .

    B(4)=(B(1)+9.3+B(2))/(B(3)+Q+R);
    .
    .
    .

  END A;
```

We could write a procedure, say A3, just once that calculates the sum of any three arguments, and then we might rewrite this program:

```
A:PROCEDURE OPTIONS(MAIN);
  DECLARE B(4);
    .
    .
    .

    R=S*A3(R,Y,Z)+T*T;
    .
    .
    .

    Q=V+A3(R,X,T)/A3(T,V,U);
    .
    .
    .

    W=A3(R,Q,V)/Z;
    .
    .
    .
```

```
.
B(4)=A3(B(1),9.3,B(2))/A3(B(3),Q,R);
.
.
.

END A;
```

The special procedure that adds three numbers must be labeled A3. It can be placed anywhere in the program. It begins with the statement;

```
A3:PROCEDURE (D,E,F);
```

The choice of the variables D, E, and F is arbitrary. They are dummy arguments that are replaced by the arguments for A3, given in the program, in the order in which they appear. In the above example, the first time A3 is invoked, R replaces D, Y replaces E, and Z replaces F. Similarly, the last time A3 is invoked, B(3) replaces D, Q replaces E, and R replaces F. In this particular example the order is not critical. However, for most procedures the order is critical, and care must be taken to list the arguments in the correct order each time the procedure is invoked in the main program.

Because this procedure is so simple, the desired result can be obtained in a single statement. The next statement would be:

```
RETURN(D+E+F);
```

The keyword RETURN says that the result of the expression in parentheses that follows this keyword is the value to be supplied, i.e., returned to the main program. Finally, we must conclude this special procedure with:

```
END A3;
```

The complete program, with the programmer-supplied procedure given just before the END A; statement, now would be:

```
A:PROCEDURE OPTIONS(MAIN);
    DECLARE B(4);
    .
    .
    .

R=S*A3(R,Y,Z)+T*T;
    .
    .
    .

Q=V+A3(R,X,T)/A3(T,V,U);
    .
    .
    .
```

```
W=A3(R,Q,V)/Z;
       .
       .
       .

B(4)=A3(B(1),9.3,B(2))/A3(B(3),Q,R);
       .
       .
       .

A3:PROCEDURE(D,E,F);RETURN(D+E+F);END A3;
END A;
```

In a DECLARE statement following the PROCEDURE statement, it is possible to specify attributes for the value being returned (A3 in the above example). In the absence of a DECLARE statement, the name determines the attributes. In this case, A3 would result in a floating-point variable.

If several variables are to be returned, then a function such as this will not do; a more complex procedure is required. These procedures are invoked by means of a special statement—the CALL statement. The RETURN statement must not have an expression associated with it.

Suppose, for example, that we repeatedly had to calculate the sum of the elements in the rows of a matrix. We could write a procedure that does this once and for all and then invoke it each time it was needed. A procedure that repeatedly calculates the sum of the elements in the rows of a 4-by-4 array is:

```
ROWSUM: PROCEDURE(A,B);
  DECLARE(A(4,4),B(4))FIXED;
  L1:DO K=1 TO 4;S=A(K,1);
  L2:DO I=2 TO 4;S=S+A(K,I);END L2;
  B(K)=S;END L1;RETURN;
END ROWSUM;
```

In this case both arguments are arrays, a 4-by-4 matrix called A, and a four-element, one-dimensional array called B.* The Lth element of the array B will contain the sum of the elements in the Lth row of A.

---

*We could have declared A and B as follows:

```
DECLARE(A(*,*)B(*))FIXED;
```

The use of asterisks in lieu of integer constants is permitted for arrays in procedures that are passed to and from the main program. If asterisks are used, the dimensions of an array in the procedure are the same as those for the corresponding array in the main program. PL/C prefers the use of asterisks, and prints an error message if they are not used. However, the program is executed by PL/C if integer constants are used, providing that these constants are the same as those in the main program.

Nested DO groups, i.e., DO groups within DO groups, are used in this procedure. They were first encountered in Exercise 15.

How might this procedure be used? Suppose we input a 4-by-4 array called X, and then wish to subtract from each element in this array the sum of the elements in the row in which that element appears. If we call the new array Y, a program to do this and output Y would be:

```
MODIFY: PROCEDURE OPTIONS(MAIN);
        DECLARE (X(4,4).Y(4,4),S(4))FIXED;
        GET LIST (X);
        CALL ROWSUM (X,S);
            DO I=1 TO 4; DO J=1 TO 4;
            Y(I,J)=X(I,J)-S(I);END;END;
        PUT LIST (Y);
END MODIFY;
```

Note the use of three END statements. The first two are used to terminate the two DO loops, and the last one to terminate the program.

We could use this same procedure to modify a 4-by-4 array in other ways. For example, suppose that we input an array called T and wish to obtain an array, called D, that adds to each element of T the sum of all the elements in T. The following program does this:

```
ADD: PROCEDURE OPTIONS(MAIN);
     DECLARE (T(4,4),D(4,4),S(4))FIXED;
     GET LIST (T);
     CALL ROWSUM (T,S);
         B=S(1)+S(2)+S(3)+S(4);
         DO I=1 TO 4; DO J=1 TO 4;
         D(I,J)=T(I,J)+B;END;END;
     PUT LIST (D);
END ADD;
```

10.17 DEBUGGING A PL/C PROGRAM

One of the major advantages of the PL/C compiler is that it provides a great deal of assistance in debugging programs; it even will attempt to correct errors and then run the program.

For example, in outputting an array using the DO statement, each use of the DO must be enclosed in a set of parentheses. This means that if two DOs are used, there must be three sets of parentheses around the variables list — two for the DOs and one enclosing the variables list. However, if only two are used, the compiler corrects this. A typical program listing relating to this error is given in Figure 10.15. The last version of statement 2 was used in the program, and the pro-

```
        STMT
         4      1         1              PUT LIST((X(I,J)DO I=1 TO 5 BY 4)DO J=1 TO 5 BY 2);
IN       4                ERROR  SY02 MISSING (
IN       4                ERROR  SY04 MISSING )
PL/C   USES                      PUT LIST (((X (I,J) DO I=1 TO 5 BY 4) DO J=1 TO 5 BY 2));
```

Fig. 10.15 Illustration of the self-correcting feature of PL/C

gram was executed correctly. Note that the compiler provides a statement number for its own reference and uses these statement numbers in its messages to the programmer.

The compiler also provides special assistance in other ways. For example, if main storage capacity is exceeded, not only is that fact noted but the statement that caused the storage capacity to be exceeded is specified. For example, in the program to calculate the sum of the elements in an array (see Figures 10.9 and 10.10), the DECLARE statement originally was:

DECLARE(SUM,A(1000))FLOAT(16);

The statement was numbered 2 by the compiler and the following message was output:

******IN STMT 2 ERROR EX6E STORAGE CAPACITY IS EXCEEDE

The programmer made an adjustment to limit A to 100 elements and the programs ran without error.

Although the errors that we have discussed so far would be relatively easy to correct using any compiler, the PL/C compiler makes the correction unnecessary or trivial. However, logical errors are more difficult to correct. This is particularly true of long, complex programs. One approach—called *hand simulation*—is to substitute test inputs and to "play computer." The contents of every storage location (all the variables) should be recorded as they are known, and the output should be written down as it is generated. Suppose, for example, that we had the following input to the means and standard deviation program:

9 1 2 3 4 5 6 7 8 9

A hand simulation gives the results shown in Figure 10.16. The PL/C compiler also provides special assistance for checking hand simulations. The last values stored for each of the variables in the program can be printed out.*

One way to simplify the debugging of a complex program is to break the program down into smaller, simpler parts. For example, if a long

---

*This is called the DUMP option. Some installations automatically implement the DUMP option; at others, it must be requested. Frequently, the values of individual variables are dumped but the values of array elements are not. The DUMPARRAY option must be invoked to get the values of array elements.

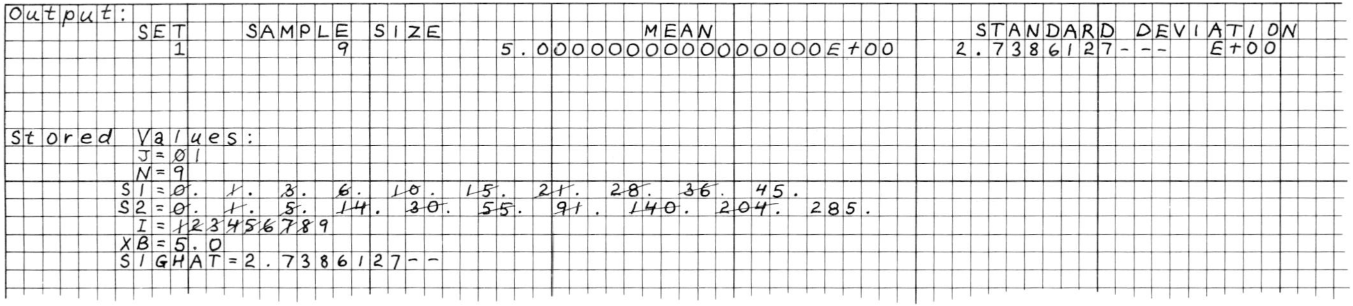

Output:

SET	SAMPLE SIZE	MEAN	STANDARD DEVIATION
1	9	5.0000000000000E+00	2.7386127---E+00

Stored Values:
J=01
N=9
S1=0. 1. 3. 6. 10. 15. 21. 28. 36. 45.
S2=0. 1. 5. 14. 30. 55. 91. 140. 204. 285.
I=123456789
XB=5.0
SIGHAT=2.7386127---

Fig. 10.16 Worksheet in a hand simulation of the means and standard deviations program

program can be separated into logically distinct sections, it may be advantageous to write the program by using several subroutines. Test data can be inserted, and the input and output of each subroutine can be checked separately. Of course, if this approach to debugging is implemented, the program first must be written in modular form and then put together section by section. The technique called *structured programming* incorporates this approach to program design and development. Its use can substantially reduce programming time, both in formulating a correct algorithm and in debugging a program. The major disadvantage is that this approach is somewhat awkward and may use more computer time, since each subroutine is checked first separately and then in combination with the main program.

PUT EDIT statements can be added to a program during debugging to obtain intermediate results which ordinarily are not written in the output. This approach is recommended because:

1. The statements can be removed easily after the program is debugged;
2. The printout can be conveniently placed and labeled; and
3. The set of variables whose values are written in the output can be varied by changing the variables list.

Consider, for example, the program to calculate means and standard deviations. A PUT EDIT statement could be added immediately before the END statement that concludes the DO group. This was done for a run of the program using the same input as for the hand simulation. The modified program, along with the output obtained in a run of the program, is given in Figure 10.17.

Exercises

Exercises 16 through 20 are given in the table below. In each case a PL/I program should be written to implement the algorithm and/or flowchart previously designed in working exercises in Chapters 7 and 8. A brief title for the exercise also is given in the table.

Exercise	Chapter 7 Reference and Title	Chapter 8 Reference and Title
16	8 Fibonacci numbers	3
17	12 Sort 5 numbers	10
*18	14 Bridge problem	6 But a detailed flowchart is needed
*19	————	13 Roots of a quadratic
*20	————	14 Simpson's rule

Program

```
/*A PROGRAM TO CALCULATE MEANS AND STANDARD DEVIATIONS*/
XBSIGMA:PROCEDURE OPTIONS(MAIN);
     DECLARE(S1,S2,X,XB,SIGHAT)FLOAT(16);
     PUT EDIT('SET','SAMPLE SIZE','MEAN','STANDARD DEVIATION')
          (PAGE,A,X(4),A,X(8),A,X(16),A);
     J=0.;
DATA:GET LIST(N);ON ENDFILE(SYSIN)GOTO QUIT; IF N<=0 THEN GOTO ERR;
     S1=0.;S2=0.;J=J+1;
     DO I=1 TO N;GET LIST(X);
     S1=S1+X;S2=S2+X*X;
     END;
PUT EDIT('PARTIAL SUMS AND SUMS OF SQUARES',I,S1,S2)(SKIP(1),A,F(10),
2(E(22,16)));
     XB=S1/N;SIGHAT=SQRT((N*S2-S1*S1)/(N*(N-1)));
     PUT EDIT(J,N,SIGHAT)(SKIP(1),F(3),F(10),2(X(4),E(22,16)));
     GOTO DATA;
ERR:PUT EDIT('N TOO SMALL,RUN TERMINATED.N IS',N)(SKIP(1),A,X(4),F(6));
QUIT:END XBSIGMA;
```

Output

SET	SAMPLE SIZE	MEAN	I	S1	STANDARD DEVIATION	S2
PARTIAL SUMS AND SUMS OF SQUARES			1	1.0000000000000000-E+00		1.0000000000000000-E+00
PARTIAL SUMS AND SUMS OF SQUARES			2	3.0000000000000000-E+005		5.0000000000000000-E+00
PARTIAL SUMS AND SUMS OF SQUARES			3	6.0000000000000000-E+001		1.4000000000000000-E+01
PARTIAL SUMS AND SUMS OF SQUARES			4	1.0000000000000000-E+013		3.0000000000000000-E+01
PARTIAL SUMS AND SUMS OF SQUARES			5	1.5000000000000000-E+015		5.0000000000000000-E+01
PARTIAL SUMS AND SUMS OF SQUARES			6	2.1000000000000000-E+019		1.0000000000000001-E+01
PARTIAL SUMS AND SUMS OF SQUARES			7	2.8000000000000000-E+011		1.4000000000000000-E+02
PARTIAL SUMS AND SUMS OF SQUARES			8	3.6000000000000000-E+012		2.0400000000000000-E+02
PARTIAL SUMS AND SUMS OF SQUARES			9	4.5000000000000000-E+012		2.8500000000000000-E+02
	9	5.0000000000000000-E+00			2.7386127875258331-E+00	
	1	5.0000000000000000-E+00				

Fig. 10.17 A program to calculate means and standard deviations with a PUT EDIT statement added that results in the output of partial sums and sums of squares (note the vertical lines and labels that were handwritten in the output to improve the readability of the special output)

ANNOTATED SUPPLEMENTARY BIBLIOGRAPHY

A manual and two books on PL/I are listed below. The first book is especially well-written; the second, also well-written, covers the essential elements of PL/I in a straightforward way.

1. Conway, R. W., et al., *User's Guide to PL/C, the Cornell Compiler for PL/I* (Ithaca, N.Y.: Department of Computer Science, Cornell University). This PL/C manual is available on magnetic tape to purchasers of the PL/C compiler. It is difficult to obtain a copy in any other way. The guide defines PL/C by comparing it with the corresponding features in version F of PL/I, and a guide to PL/I, F is required to use this PL/C guide effectively.

2. Bohl, M. and Walter, A., *Introduction to PL/I Programming and PL/C* (Chicago: Science Research Associates, Inc., 1973). One of the best written and most comprehensive introductions to PL/I that currently is available.

3. Kennedy, M., and Solomon, M. B., *Eight Statement PL/C (PL/ZERO) Plus PL/I* (Englewood Cliffs, N.J.: Prentice-Hall, Inc., 1972). A well-written, straightforward introduction to PL/I using PL/C. It should be possible to learn PL/I from this book without the assistance of an instructor or a formal course. However, the programming exercises must be worked, and access to a computer is necessary.

Chapter 11

BASIC

11.1 THE CHARACTER SET

A BASIC program is an algorithm consisting of a sequence of statements, or instructions. Each statement corresponds to a box in a flowchart or to a step in an English-language algorithm.

The main objective of this chapter is to help the reader state algorithms in the BASIC language. We will present a repertoire of statements, the rules for their formulation, and the significance of their applications. However, first we shall specify the set of characters that can appear in a BASIC statement.

There are three kinds of characters: alphabetic, numeric, and special. The alphabetic characters include 26 upper case letters; there are no lower case letters in BASIC. There are 10 numeric characters, the digits 0 to 9. The special characters permitted in BASIC include characters representing arithmetic processes: the plus sign (+), the minus sign (−), a slash for division (/), and an asterisk for multiplication (∗). In some versions of BASIC, a vertical arrow is used for exponentiation; in others, two asterisks are used (↑ or ∗∗). Also available are left and right parentheses (()), equals sign (=), period (.), "less than" symbol (<), "greater than" symbol (>), and comma (,). In addition, a dollar sign ($) is available to indicate that a particular variable takes on character-string values. Finally, we have a semicolon (;), quotes (′ in some versions and ″ in others), an apostrophe (′), and a blank character. In summary, the set is:

Alphabetic characters: A B C D E F G H I J K L M N O
                         P Q R S T U V W X Y Z

Numeric characters: 0 1 2 3 4 5 6 7 8 9

Special characters:	$+ - / * ( ) = <> . , \$;$ ' blank
Quote:	' or "
Exponentiation:	$\uparrow$ or $**$

The last entry ($**$) is not a new character but rather a familiar one that is used twice in succession to denote a single operation. There are other instances where two successive characters are used. For example, $>=$ is used to indicate greater than or equal to. The pair must be in that order; $=>$ is not allowed.

11.2   VARIABLES AND ARRAYS

BASIC variables are names for storage locations that contain values associated with the variables. A variable is denoted in BASIC by using one or two characters, with the following restrictions:

1. The first character must be alphabetic.
2. The second character, if present, must be a dollar sign if the variable is used to store character strings; otherwise it must be numeric.

Therefore, special characters cannot be used to denote variables. Some valid variables are:

$$M \quad T1 \quad H4 \quad Y \quad B\$$$

Some invalid variables are:

$$4H \quad T/ \quad YEK \quad EE \quad \$B$$

Any name that can be used for a single-data item can be used for an array instead. An individual element in an array is denoted by the use of the array name and one or two subscripts that pinpoint the element's location. Arrays with more than two subscripts (i.e., with three or more dimensions) are not permitted in most versions of BASIC. Subscripts are enclosed in parentheses and separated by commas. Thus, for example, A(3, 4) refers to the element in the third row and fourth column of the array A. Subscripts may take on only integer values. In most implementations of BASIC, if a subscript takes on a non-integer value, the fractional part is truncated. This means that X(5.4) and X(5.9) both would be X(5).

Most versions of BASIC permit only one subscript for arrays that contain character strings. Arrays with only one subscript are called *lists* in BASIC. Arrays with two subscripts are called *tables* or *matrices*.

The following are valid names for elements in an array:

```
El(3,1)   X(4)   K3(I,2)   D$(3)   (this is the
                                    third element
                                    in a list of
                                    character
                                    strings)
```

The following are invalid names for elements in an array:

```
    E/(3,1)   1X(4)   K3(I,2,3)   D$(3,4)
```

We already have noted that the use of a $ as the second character in a variable serves to specify that the values stored will be character strings. Since no other conventions exist for indicating the kinds of values stored, variables used to represent integer numbers cannot be distinguished from those used to represent floating-point numbers.

11.3 THE DIM STATEMENT

If an array is used in a BASIC program, the maximum value that each of its subscripts can take on must be specified. This is called *dimensioning* the array. It is done by using a DIM statement, which has the form:

statement number DIM specifications

The specifications consist of a list of array names with the maximum value that each subscript can take on placed in parentheses where that subscript otherwise would appear. Some examples of correct DIM statements are:

```
10 DIM I(20)
10 DIM X(4,4), A(100), B$(5)
```

Several arrays can be dimensioned in the same statement. Since every array must be dimensioned before it is used, each program should begin with a DIM statement that dimensions all the arrays used in that program. It also is advisable to estimate the dimensions of an array as precisely as possible to avoid wasting storage space. If you use:

```
10 DIM X(1000)
```

and the maximum value that the subscript takes on is only 10, then 990 storage spaces have been allocated wastefully to the array X.

11.4 OPERATIONS AND BUILT-IN FUNCTIONS

Six *arithmetic operations* are available in BASIC. These are described, along with examples of their use and their priority, in Figure 11.1.

Priority	Symbol	Name	Example of		
			Operation	Values	Result Is
			Arithmetic Operations		
1	↑OR ⁂	Exponentiation	A↑B	A=2, B=3	8
1	–	Prefix minus	–A	A=2	–2
2	⁑	Multiplication	A⁑B	A=2, B=3	6
2	/	Division	A/B	A=6, B=3	2
3	+	Addition	A+B	A=6, B=3	9
3	–	Subtraction	A–B	A=6, B=3	3
			Comparison Operations		
4	=	Equal to	A=B	A=6, B=3	False
4	< >	Not equal to	A<>B	A=6, B=3	True
4	<	Less than	A<B	A=6, B=3	False
4	>	Greater than	A>B	A=6, B=3	True
4	<=	Less than or equal to	A$<=B$	A$='HERB',B$='DON'	False
4	>=	Greater than or equal to	A$>=B$	A$='HERB',B$='DON'	True

Fig. 11.1 The operations in BASIC

Six comparison operations involving the symbols >, <, and = are permissible. These also are summarized in Figure 11.1. The result of an arithmetic operation is a number, whereas the result of a comparison is that the comparison either holds (is true) or does not hold (is false). The last two examples in Figure 11.1 indicate how comparisons can be used with character strings.

An expression is any algebraically valid combination of variables and operations. Some valid expressions are:

$$(A + B + C)/D$$
$$(R(I,J)*Z(I,J))/(K*L)$$
$$(-B + SQR(D))/(2.*A)$$

Expressions are evaluated by first evaluating quantities enclosed in parentheses. In the absence of parentheses, the priority of executions are those given in Figure 11.1. Except for exponentiation, operations of equal priority are executed from left to right. Multiple exponentiations are executed from right to left. In the last expression, a BASIC *built-in function* is used. It is the square root function, which is invoked merely by writing SQR, followed by an argument enclosed in parentheses. That is all that is needed to calculate the square root of any argument. The argument itself may be an expression. It should not take on negative values. Other built-in functions are available in BASIC, the selection of which tends to vary from installation to installation. However, trigonometric and logarithmic functions are widely available. BASIC has a particularly powerful repertoire of built-in functions to process matrices.

11.5 A PROGRAM TO CALCULATE TUITION DUE

At this point we will write a BASIC program to calculate the tuition due from a student, given the number of credits that the student is taking. The input consists of the student's last name, identification number, and the number of credits; the output should be the name, identification number, and tuition due. The tuition is calculated as follows:

> If the student takes ten or more credits, the tuition is $1500.
> If the student takes fewer than ten credits, the tuition is $150 per credit.

We begin by developing an algorithm for the solution of this problem. An algorithm that calculates the tuition correctly is given in Figure 11.2. Names were chosen for variables that indicate the usage of the variable. Tuitions are stored in the variable T, I$ stores the student's last name, I the student's identification number, and N the number of credits that the student is taking. The programmer writes the statements in the program with these names in mind. The computer does not "know" which variable stores which data. This is determined implicitly by the programmer in the way he writes the program.

The algorithm does not contain adequate provision for the detection of errors; we should "trap" values for the identification number and number of credits that are not allowed, and stop the procedure without producing any output if an illegal value is encountered. An algorithm that does this is given in Figure 11.3.

A BASIC program to implement the algorithm in Figure 11.3 is given in Figure 11.4, along with the input and corresponding output obtained in executing this program. The output is given in two lines: identification information is given in the first line, and the tuition due is given on the second. This should improve the readability of the output.

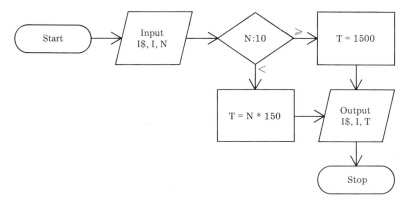

Fig. 11.2 Flowchart for an algorithm to calculate tuition

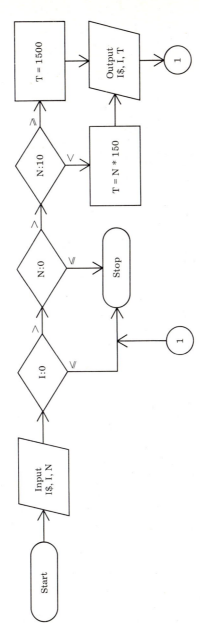

Fig. 11.3 Flowchart for an algorithm to calculate tuition with provision for checking input values

Input

MAIS.12345678.9

Program

```
1 REM TUITION CALCULATION
10   INPUT I$,I,N
20 IF I=<0 THEN 9999
30 IF N=<0 THEN 9999
40 IFN>=10 THEN 100
50 LET T=150*N
60 GO TO 20
60 GO TO 200
100 LET T=1500
200 PRINT I$,I
210 PRINT T
9999 END
```

Output

MAIS   12345678
1350

Fig. 11.4 A program to calculate tuition

Exercises

1. Which of the following are invalid names for BASIC variables? Assume that parentheses are used to enclose subscripts. Give reasons for your choices.

    ```
    V1          SUM  Y(4)    U* N(6.,4.)  I
    A(1,2,3)  X     Y4(4)   U$ 1X          U$(1,2)
    ```

2. Write a single BASIC statement to sum the elements in each of the arrays listed in the following DIM statement. Call the result S in each case and write a separate statement for each array.

    ```
    10 DIM X(4),N(4,2),Y(2,3)
    ```

*3. Recall the array CARD introduced in Exercise 15 in Chapter 5. Write a DIM statement which is appropriate for this array.

4. Write a single BASIC statement to compute the unbiased estimate of the standard deviation, SIGHAT, of a set of N numbers X_1, X_2, . . . , X_N. SIGHAT is given by:

$$\text{SIGHAT} = \sqrt{\frac{N \sum_{i=1}^{N} X_i^2 - \left(\sum_{i=1}^{N} X_i\right)^2}{N(N-1)}}$$

Assume that $\sum_{i=1}^{N} X_i^2$ has been computed and is stored in a variable called S2, and that $\sum_{i=1}^{N} X_i$ has been computed and is stored in S1. A value for N is stored in the variable called N.

5. Write a BASIC program that calculates and outputs the tuition due from each of K students. Assume that K is input first and then one input is made for each of the K students. Each input for a student contains the student's last name, identification number, and the number of credits that the student is taking. If an illegal value for either the identification number or the number of credits is encountered, go on to the next student without any output.

11.6 ANNOTATING OUTPUTS

All the BASIC programs that we have written thus far have had a format-free output. Numbers are printed without labels, headings, or other descriptions. Tables are not set up, even though a tabular output may be appropriate. This is not a good way to present the output; adequate annotation and layout should be provided. In the tuition problem, it would be helpful to label the three outputs: the first output might be labeled *student name,* the second *ID number,* and the third *tuition due.* It also would be helpful to output a message if an illegal student number or number of credits were encountered.

The PRINT statement can do this if literal constants are added to it. These literal constants are printed at the terminal just as they appear in the statement, and in the same order. Thus, for example, we can revise the output of the tuition problem to annotate the output. The revised version in Figure 11.5 includes statements that serve to annotate the input as well as the output. (This will be discussed in the next section.)

Literal constants are enclosed in quotation marks. The quotation mark is a single, short vertical stroke, ', in most implementations of BASIC. In some implementations, a double quotation mark, ", is used. Literal constants also are called *character string constants.*

11.7 ANNOTATING INPUTS

The INPUT statement requests inputs by printing a question mark. The user must know which values to enter. The programmer facilitates this by adding PRINT statements that ask the user for the data in a natural way. For example, the input to the tuition problem could be requested in a natural way using the following statement:

Inputs and Outputs

```
ENTER STUDENTS LAST NAME
? >HERB
ENTER STUDENTS ID NUMBER
? >12345679
ENTER THE NUMBER OF CREDITS STUDENT IS TAKING
? >12
NAME            HERB
ID NUMBER       12345679
TUITION DUE     1500
```

```
ENTER STUDENTS LAST NAME
? >HERBERT
ENTER STUDENTS ID NUMBER
? >12345666
ENTER THE NUMBER OF CREDITS STUDENT IS TAKING
? >-3
TUITION NOT CALCULATED NO. OF CREDITS IS    -3
```

Program

```
   1 REM TUITION CALCULATION ANNOTATED I/O
  10 PRINT 'ENTER STUDENTS LAST NAME'
  11 INPUT I$
  12 PRINT 'ENTER STUDENTS ID NUMBER'
  13 INPUT I
  14 PRINT 'ENTER THE NUMBER OF CREDITS STUDENT IS TAKING'
  15 INPUT N
  20 IF I=<0 THEN 1000
  30 IF N=<0 THEN 2000
  40 IF N>=10 THEN 100
  50 LET T=150*N
  60 GO TO 200
 100 LET T=1500
 200 PRINT 'NAME',I$
 210 PRINT 'ID NUMBER',I
 220 PRINT 'TUITION DUE',T
 230 GO TO 9999
1000 PRINT 'TUITION NOT CALCULATED ID NUMBER IS',I
1010 GO TO 9999
2000 PRINT 'TUITION NOT CALCULATED NO. OF CREDITS IS',N
9999 END
```

Fig. 11.5 Annotated program to calculate tuition

```
9 PRINT'ENTER STUDENTS NAME, ID NUMBER, AND NUMBER OF CREDITS'
```

It would be even better to restructure the whole input operation, using the following sequence of statements in lieu of statement 10 (or statements 9 and 10):

```
10 PRINT'ENTER STUDENTS LAST NAME'
11 INPUT I$
12 PRINT'ENTER STUDENTS ID NUMBER'
13 INPUT I
14 PRINT'ENTER THE NUMBER OF CREDITS STUDENT IS TAKING'
15 INPUT N
```

11.8 THE READ AND DATA STATEMENTS

If the programmer wishes to execute a BASIC program immediately, he enters the input to the program as a part of the program itself. Alternatively, it may be convenient to delay execution of a program until later. The input may be so voluminous that it is convenient to punch it on a paper tape offline and then enter it from a reader when the program is executed. The READ statement can be used in conjunction with the DATA statement to facilitate either of these approaches.

The READ statement lists the variables that will be assigned values and the DATA statement lists the values to be assigned to these variables. When the first READ statement is encountered in executing a BASIC program, the program is scanned, and the first DATA statement that appears is used to assign values to the variables appearing in that READ statement. For example:

```
10 READ A,B
20 DATA 16,4
      .
      .
      .
```

would result in the value 16 being assigned to A and 4 to B. So, too, would the pair:

```
10 DATA 16,4
20 READ A,B
      .
      .
      .
```

The DATA statements may appear anywhere in the program, since they are not steps in an algorithm. However, the READ statements are. In ordering the DATA statements, values must be assigned to variables in the order in which they appear in the DATA statements. Changing the order of the DATA statements in a program can change the assignment of values to variables.

Suppose that we were writing a BASIC program to add 1127, 983, and 104. We could use:

```
   1 REMARKS SUM3 CLOSED
  10 READ A,B,C
  20 LET X=A+B+C
  30 PRINT 'THE SUM IS',X
  40 DATA 1127,983,104
9999 END
```

The DATA statements could be modified in each run of the program to add three other numbers.

To ask the user to insert the numbers to be summed, we could write:

```
   1 REMARKS SUM3 OPEN
  10 PRINT 'ENTER THE 3 NUMBERS TO BE SUMMED'
  20 INPUT A,B,C
  30 LET X=A+B+C
  40 PRINT 'THE SUM IS',X
9999 END
```

The difference in the usefulness of these two approaches is clear. In the first case, a particular problem is to be solved and the BASIC program is written to solve that particular problem. In the second case, any of several problems can be solved.

If there are several READ and DATA statements in the same program, the items in the DATA statements are set up in a single continuous list and assigned to successive variables in the READ statements one by one, in the order in which they appear. For example:

```
 10 READ A
 20 READ B
 30 READ C
100 DATA 10,15,20
```

results in assigning 10 to A, 15 to B, and 20 to C. The same result would have been obtained using:

```
 10 READ A,B,C
100 DATA 10,15,20
```

and also:

```
 10 READ A,B,C
100 DATA 10
110 DATA 15
120 DATA 20
```

Another useful function of the READ and DATA pair is that large volumes of input can be punched offline and entered. Suppose, for example, that we had 1000 items to be read into an array, X. We could use the following:

```
10 DIM X(1000)
20 MAT READ X
```

We could have entered the 1000 items of data on paper tape previously, using a paper tape punch or a teletypewriter terminal which was not linked to a computer. In most installations, when entering a BASIC program, it is possible to switch the terminal so that it accepts parts of the program from punched paper tape. The punched paper tape might contain a series of statements, beginning with:

```
999 DATA 1.64,8.31,100,27.643. . .
1000 DATA −8.21,44,63. . .
```

In this case $X(1) = 1.64$, $X(2) = 8.31$, $X(3) = 100$, $X(4) = 27.643$, and so on. Many DATA statements would be required to enter all 1000 numbers, but this is one way of dealing with large volumes of data.

The READ statement contains the word MAT, which permits us to read data into all the elements of an array. The DIM statement which precedes the READ statement specifies how many elements are read in. The word MAT (which stands for matrix) makes this statement an array operation. Some versions of BASIC do not have MAT operations. Also, MAT operations may be used in connection with other statements in BASIC. For example, we could write 30 MAT PRINT X to print out all the elements in the array X after they have been read in.

It should be clear by now that, except for the MAT option, the form of the READ and DATA statements are:

number READ list of variables separated by commas
number DATA list of constants separated by commas

Exercises

6. Rewrite the programs you wrote in answer to Exercises 10, 12, and 14 in Chapter 4 so that the input and output are properly annotated. Use PRINT and INPUT statements for the input.

7. Rewrite the program you wrote in answer to Exercise 12 in Chapter 4 so that it can process large volumes of input via paper tape — i.e., so that it uses the READ, DATA approach.

8. Write a BASIC program to obtain and output the product of 4.38, 2.176, and .0713.

9. Rewrite the program that you wrote in answer to Exercise 5 so that the input and output are annotated properly. Try to set up the out-

put in tabular form. (You may wish to insert character string constants in the output consisting only of blank characters in order to align the table entries properly.)

11.9 THE FOR AND NEXT STATEMENTS

The pair of statements, FOR and NEXT, are used to set in motion a very powerful looping mechanism in BASIC. Suppose that we are given a list, A, containing N elements, and that we wish to compute the sum of the elements. We already have seen what an algorithm to accomplish this might look like. We must input N, initialize the sum, and then loop. In each step in the loop, we input an array element and add it to the sum. We then conclude the loop and output the desired result. This could be done in several different ways using the IF statement; one way is to use the program given in Figure 11.6. Note that the maximum value for N is 100 because of the DIM statement.

The same program can be implemented using the FOR, NEXT statements. For example, the FOR, NEXT pair:

```
100 FOR I=1 TO N
       .
       .
       .
1000 NEXT I
```

causes the statements between the FOR and the NEXT (those with statement numbers >100 and <1000) to be executed repeatedly; first for I = 1, then for I = 2, and so on until I = N.

More generally, FOR, NEXT statements have the following form:

number FOR variable=expression-1
TO expression-2[STEP expression-3]
       .
       .
       .
number NEXT variable

In most applications, each expression is a single integer or a single variable that takes on integer values. The variable in the NEXT statement should be the same as that in the FOR statement. The brackets around the STEP clause indicate that this clause is optional. If it is omitted, the step size is one—that is, the value for expression-3 is assumed to be 1.

The FOR, NEXT pair operates as follows: the variable is set equal to the value given by expression-1. All statements between the FOR

```
   1 REMARKS SUM VIA IF
  10 DIM A(100)
  20 PRINT 'ENTER THE NUMBER OF NUMBERS TO BE SUMMED'
  30 INPUT N
  35 LET S=0
  40 LET I=1
  50 PRINT 'ENTER THE NEXT NUMBER TO BE SUMMED'
  60 INPUT A(I)
  65 LET S=S+A(I)
  70 IF I=N THEN 150
  80 LET I=I+1
  90 GO TO 50
 150 PRINT 'SUM IS', S
9999 END
```

Fig. 11.6 Calculating the sum of the elements in a list using the IF statement

and NEXT are executed. The variable is incremented by the step size. This incremented value is compared to the value given by expression-2. If the incremented value is greater than the value given by expression-2, the loop is completed and the statement immediately after the NEXT is executed. If the incremented value is less than or equal to the value given by expression-2, the series of statements is executed again and we go back to incrementing the variable.

A program to calculate the sum of the elements in an array using this pair of statements is given in Figure 11.7.

The variable that appears in both the FOR and NEXT statements serves as a counter, and need not appear in the statements between these two. Suppose, for example, that we wished to calculate the sum of W elements without using arrays. We would delete statement 20 in the program given in Figure 11.7, and change the correspondingly numbered statements as follows:

```
10 REM SUM WITHOUT ARRAYS
70 INPUT A
80 LET S=S+A
```

```
  10 REM SUM VIA FOR NEXT
  20 DIM A(100)
  30 LET S=0
  40 PRINT 'ENTER THE NUMBER OF NUMBERS TO BE SUMMED'
  50 INPUT N
  60 FOR I=1 TO N
  70 INPUT A(I)
  80 LET S=S+A(I)
  90 NEXT I
 100 PRINT 'SUM IS',S
9999 END
```

Fig. 11.7 Calculating the sum of the elements in a list using the FOR, NEXT pair of statements

11.10   THE INPUT AND OUTPUT OF ARRAYS

The FOR, NEXT pair also is useful in inputting, manipulating, and outputting arrays. The subscripts of the array frequently appear as variables in the FOR, NEXT statements.

Suppose, for example, that we wish to input a table of values—a matrix. The table contains three rows and five columns. Suppose also that we wish to calculate the sum of the elements in each row and output these three sums. The program given in Figure 11.8 does this.

Note that the program contains nested sets of FOR, NEXT statements. The statements for the J loop (statements 50 through 80) are contained entirely in the I loop (statements 20 through 90). This causes the program to process a row at a time, as it should. If we wished to obtain column sums, rather than row sums, we would input a column at a time, calculate the sum of the elements in the column, output the result, and go on to the next column. In that case, the loop for the variable I would be contained inside the loop for the variable J.

The BASIC program could be generalized to process a table that contained, say, I1 rows and J1 columns. We would have to add some statements and modify others. For example, in statement 20, we should replace the 3 with I1; and in statement 50, we should replace the 5 with J1 (see Exercise 11).

Exercises

10. Modify the program to calculate a sum without using arrays so that it can sum as many as, say, 1,000,000 numbers. Assume that the number 0 never will be input, and use this number to mark the end of the input.

11. Generalize the BASIC program given in Section 11.10 (Figure 11.8), so that it can calculate row totals for a table with I1 rows and J1 columns. Assume that both I1 and J1 are always less than 20.

```
   1 REM TABLE ROW TOTALS
  10 DIM X(3,5),S(3)
  20 FOR I=1 TO 3
  30 LET S(I)=0
  40 PRINT 'ENTER THE ENTRIES IN ROW',I
  50 FOR J=1 TO 5
  60 INPUT X(I,J)
  70 LET S(I)=S(I)+X(I,J)
  80 NEXT J
  85 PRINT 'THE SUM OF THE',I,'TH ROW IS',S(I)
  90 NEXT I
9999 END
```

Fig. 11.8   A program to calculate the sum of the elements in the rows of a three-by-five table

11.11 A PROGRAM TO COMPUTE MEANS AND STANDARD DEVIATIONS

We now will develop a BASIC program to calculate the mean and standard deviation of a set of numbers, $D_1, D_2, \ldots, D_N$. We shall assume that the number of observations in the set, N, is input first. N is called the *sample size*. We also will assume that the volume of input is sizeable enough to justify the DATA approach, and that the upper limit for the sample size is 100.

Recall that the mean and unbiased estimate of the standard deviation, SIGHAT, of the numbers $D_1, D_2, \ldots, D_N$ are given by:

$$\text{SIGHAT} = \sqrt{\frac{N \sum_{i=1}^{N} D_i^2 - \left(\sum_{i=1}^{N} D_i\right)^2}{N(N-1)}} \qquad \text{Mean} = \frac{\sum_{i=1}^{N} D_i}{N}$$

Figure 11.9 contains an annotated BASIC program to compute means and standard deviations, along with a set of input. The output obtained in executing this program is:

```
THE MEAN IS 50.5
THE STANDARD DEVIATION IS 29.011492
```

11.12 SUBROUTINES IN BASIC — THE GOSUB AND RETURN STATEMENTS

If a series of instructions are to be executed several times at different points in a BASIC program, it may be desirable to use a subroutine. The series of instructions is written once, and this subroutine is invoked whenever it is needed. We already have seen how this can work in connection with the use of built-in functions. The programmer can write a kind of built-in function by using the GOSUB and RETURN statements.

For example, suppose that we wished to read in a set of three numbers and calculate their sum at different points in a BASIC program. We could write:

```
                .
                .
                .
70 PRINT'ENTER THE NEXT THREE NUMBERS'
71 INPUT A,B,C
72 LET S=A+B+C
80 — — —
```

Program	Comments
`10 REMARKS MEAN AND STANDARD DEVIATION`	A suitable beginning
`11 LET S1=0`	The sum and sum of squares are initialized.
`12 LET S2=0`	
`20 DIM D(100)`	The sample size is limited to 100.
`25 READ N`	The sample size is read.
`26 FOR I=1 TO N`	A loop is initiated.
`27 READ D(I)`	The Ith observation is input.
`30 NEXT I`	The loop is ended.
`40 FOR I=1 TO N`	Another loop is initiated.
`50 LET S1=S1+D(I)`	The sum is incremented appropriately.
`60 LET S2=S2+D(I)*D(I)`	The sum of squares is also incremented.
`70 NEXT I`	This loop is ended.
`80 LET X=S1/N`	The mean is calculated.
`90 LET S=SQR((N*S2-S1*S1)/(N*(N-1)))`	The standard deviation is calculated.
`100 PRINT'THE MEAN IS',X`	The mean is output.
`110 PRINT'THE STANDARD DEVIATION IS',S`	The standard deviation is output.
`200 DATA 100`	The sample size
`210 DATA 1,2,3,4,5,6,7,8,9,10,11,12,13,14,15,16,17,18,19,20`	The data
`222 DATA 21,22,23,24,25,26,27,28,29,30,31,32,33,34,35,36,37,38,39,40`	
`333 DATA 41,42,43,44,45,46,47,48,49,50,51,52,53,54,55,56,57,58,59,60`	
`444 DATA 61,62,63,64,65,66,67,68,69,70,71,72,73,74,75,76,77,78,79,80`	
`555 DATA 81,82,83,84,85,86,87,88,89,90,91,92,93,94,95,96,97,98,99,100`	
`9999 END`	That's all there is.

Fig. 11.9 An annotated BASIC program to calculate means and standard deviations

```
110 PRINT'ENTER THE NEXT THREE NUMBERS'
111 INPUT A,B,C
112 LET S=A+B+C
120 — — —
        .
        .
        .

240 PRINT'ENTER THE NEXT THREE NUMBERS'
241 INPUT A,B,C
242 LET S=A+B+C
250 — — —
        .
        .
        .

650 PRINT'ENTER THE NEXT THREE NUMBERS'
651 INPUT A,B,C
652 LET S=A+B+C
660 — — —
        .
        .
        .
```

Or we could get the identical result by writing:

```
        .
        .
        .
 70 GOSUB 999
 80 — — —
        .
        .
        .

110 GOSUB 999
120 — — —
        .
        .
        .

240 GOSUB 999
250 — — —
        .
        .
        .

650 GOSUB 999
660 — — —
        .
```

```
998 GO TO 9999
999 PRINT'ENTER THE NEXT THREE NUMBERS'
1000 INPUT A,B,C
1001 LET S=A+B+C
1002 RETURN
9999 END
```

The GOSUB 999 statement causes the program to branch to statement 999 immediately and, beginning with 999, to execute all statements until a RETURN is encountered. The program then branches back to the statement immediately after the last GOSUB that was executed. This means, for example, that the program would branch back to statement 80 after the subroutine invoked by statement 70 was executed, and to statement 660 after the subroutine invoked by statement 650 was executed.

The subroutine is placed at the end of the program and is preceded by a GO TO statement which branches around it so that it is not executed at the wrong time.

The GOSUB and RETURN statements also could be used to insert a variable number of blank lines in the output. For example, the following subroutine could be used to insert from one to five blank lines.

```
1001 REM SUBROUTINE TO INSERT BLANK LINES
1010 PRINT
1020 PRINT
1030 PRINT
1040 PRINT
1050 PRINT
1060 RETURN
```

Thus five blank lines would be inserted in the output each time GOSUB 1010 appeared in the program, and one blank line each time GOSUB 1050 was used.

11.13   DEBUGGING A BASIC PROGRAM

Debugging a program really is another kind of algorithm testing, and Section 7.10 should be reviewed before you read about the special considerations involved in debugging BASIC programs. It is most important to prepare an adequate set of test data in accordance with the recommendations in that section.

We already have seen, in Section 4.10, how error messages can be helpful in debugging BASIC programs. However, the bugs that remain after the syntactical errors have been corrected frequently are hard to detect. This is particularly true of long, complex programs. One ap-

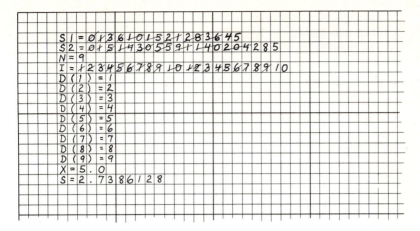

Fig. 11.10 Worksheet in a hand simulation of the means and standard deviations program

proach—called *hand simulation*—is to substitute test inputs and to "play computer." The content of every storage location (all the variables) should be written down as it is generated. Suppose, for example, that we had the following input to the means and standard deviations program:

```
200 DATA 9
210 DATA 1,2,3,4,5,6,7,8,9
```

A hand simulation gives the results shown in Figure 11.10.

One way to simplify the debugging of a complex program is to break the program down into smaller, simpler parts. For example, if a long program can be separated into logically distinct sections, it may help to write the program by using several subroutines. Test data can be inserted, and the input and output of each subroutine can be checked separately. Of course, if this debugging approach is implemented, the program first must be written in modular form and then put together section-by-section. The technique called *structured programming* incorporates this approach to program design and development. Its use can substantially reduce programming time, both in formulating a correct algorithm and in debugging the program. The major disadvantage is that this approach may use more computer time, since each subroutine is checked separately first, and then in combination with the main program.

PRINT statements can be added to a program during debugging to obtain intermediate results which ordinarily are not written in the output. This approach is recommended because:

1. The statements can be removed easily after the program has been debugged;
2. The printout can be labeled; and
3. The set of variables whose values are written in the output can be varied by a simple modification in the PRINT statement.

Consider, for example, the program to calculate means and standard deviations. The following print statement can be inserted in the program in the run made with the data used for the hand simulation. The output that was obtained is shown in Figure 11.11.

```
45 PRINT 'PARTIAL S1 AND S2',I,S1,S2
```

Exercises

12. Write a subroutine that would input X, Y, and Z and calculate P3, the product of X, Y, and Z.

13. Write a program that uses the subroutine written in answer to Exercise 1 to calculate

$$A = \frac{B*C*D + E*F*G}{X*Y*Z}$$

where values for each of the variables B,C,D,E,F,G,X,Y, and Z are to be input.

14. Write a BASIC program to display a table that a traveler could use to help him convert from one currency to another. Make the table convert from yen to dollars at the rate of 300 yen per dollar. Compute and tabulate the number of yen corresponding to from 1 to 10 dollars in increments of 1 dollar, and from 20 to 100 dollars in increments of 10 dollars. Also tabulate the number of dollars corresponding to from 100 to 1000 yen in increments of 100 yen, and from 2000 to 10,000 yen in increments of 1000 yen.

```
PARTIAL S1 AND S2          1          0          0
PARTIAL S1 AND S2          2          1          1
PARTIAL S1 AND S2          3          3          5
PARTIAL S1 AND S2          4          6         14
PARTIAL S1 AND S2          5         10         30
PARTIAL S1 AND S2          6         15         55
PARTIAL S1 AND S2          7         21         91
PARTIAL S1 AND S2          8         28        140
PARTIAL S1 AND S2          9         36        204
THE MEAN IS       5
THE STANDARD DEVIATION IS        2.7386128
```

Fig. 11.11 Output obtained in a run of the means and standard deviations program with a special PRINT statement added

15. Rewrite the program written in answer to Exercise 14 so that it will accept the number of yen per dollar as input and produce the same table of outputs.

Exercises 16 through 20 are given in the table below. In each case, a BASIC program should be written to implement the algorithm and/or flowchart which previously was developed in working exercises in Chapters 7 and 8. A brief title for the exercise also is given in the table.

Exercise	Chapter 7 Reference and Title	Chapter 8 Reference and Title
16	8 Fibonacci numbers	3
17	12 Sort 5 numbers	10
*18	14 Bridge problem	6 But a detailed flowchart is needed
*19	——	13 Roots of a quadratic
*20	——	14 Simpson's rule

ANNOTATED SUPPLEMENTARY BIBLIOGRAPHY

The three references on BASIC cited below were chosen for their special features.

1. Skelton, J. E., *An Introduction to the BASIC Language* (New York: Holt Rinehart & Winston, Inc., 1971). This gives an introduction to BASIC which is especially suitable for the physical scientist and engineer.

2. Sass, C. J., *BASIC Programming for Business* (Boston: Allyn & Bacon, Inc., 1972). This introduction to BASIC is especially well-suited to the business student.

3. Smith, R. W., *A Visual Approach to BASIC* (Control Data Corporation, 1972). A self-instructional text on BASIC, written with a nice, light touch.

Chapter 12

Program Effectiveness, Efficiency, and Documentation

12.1 DEFINITIONS AND DEBUGGING

Effectiveness

A program is *effective* to the extent that it satisfies the needs of the users of that program. Therefore, the requirements that a program must satisfy in order to be considered effective are a function of the way it is to be used. Programs that a user writes solely for his own use probably can be made more effective with less effort than those which are developed for a variety of users.

Correctness

To be effective, a program must be *correct;* it must provide the right output for any set of inputs which are submitted to it. Hence, in preparing the program, the complete range of inputs must be defined. Even when a program is written solely for its developer, this may be difficult; it may be impossible when a program is to be used by many persons.

Correctness can be ensured by one or more of the following techniques:

1. Debugging,
2. Proving, and
3. Maintenance.

Debugging

We have said a great deal about techniques that are useful in debugging a program, and have stressed that a set of test data must be designed carefully. The program should be run with these data, the results analyzed, and the program corrected as necessary. If the set of test data encompasses the set of inputs that will be encountered, debugging may be enough. However, this is rarely the case.

Debugging would be a relatively straightforward task if it were always possible to design a complete, representative set of inputs and to simulate the program for each of these inputs. In many applications, it is not possible to anticipate all the inputs that might be submitted, and frequently the calculations are so extensive that they cannot be hand simulated. Part of the burden of debugging must be shifted to program maintenance (Section 12.2).

In addition to the difficulty of designing a set of test data and checking results for this set, there is another, more subtle, problem associated with debugging. Computers use a finite number of digits to represent a number, usually in a base other than base ten. The value stored in the computer for a floating-point number frequently is only an approximation of the true value. In business applications, for example, where floating-point notation is used to store monetary quantities, fractions of pennies may be lost, accumulating over enough calculations to become significant. To avoid this problem, it is better to store quantities using a fixed-point binary coded decimal notation, and to carry out all calculations in this way.

12.2   STRUCTURED PROGRAMMING AND PROGRAM PROOF

One way to ensure a program's correctness is to prove it mathematically. A proof of correctness almost always requires establishing that the algorithm is invariant to the class of inputs that will be submitted. E. W. Dijkstra of the Netherlands and his associates have been especially active in promoting this approach, combined with structured programming, to establishing program correctness [1]. They recommend developing the algorithms using modules, each of which solve only part of the problem. (See the discussion of payrolls in Chapter 8 for an example of this approach.) The input required and the output produced by each module is determined. Then each module is checked, using hand simulation, logical verification, and, to the maximum extent feasible, a few mathematical theorems, to establish the conditions for invariance in the program design—in other words, building in correctness by using procedures that have been shown to be invariant. Some programmers believe that the effort required to establish invariance is like that required to establish correctness by more heuristic means. Establishing the correctness of programs by proof is not now a widely used technique. In any case, the modular approach to the development of complex programs is a useful technique, and structured programming is a sound programming methodology.

Maintenance

If we cannot anticipate all inputs and debug the program in consideration of them, if the proof of correctness becomes a greater task than the development of the program and its debugging, if users modify the objectives of a program while it is in use, then what are we to do? Provision must be made for *program maintenance* from the outset. This means that each program should be developed with its maintenance in mind. Documentation is essential for effective maintenance. In addition, programming staff familiar with the applications currently in use should be available to determine why any errors in output occur. In most instances, errors that occur during the regular use of the program are more difficult to trace and eliminate than those found during the debugging. Well-qualified personnel are needed, particularly in organizations in which several people use the same program over long periods of time. All too often, program maintenance is given low priority by computer programmers and their supervisors, and adequate program maintenance facilities are not established.

There are some aids which can help reduce the effort required to develop and maintain a program. For example, more extensive and clear debugging messages and special debugging facilities have been incorporated into PL/C, a version of PL/I developed by the Computer Science Department at Cornell University. In addition, PL/C, like WATFIV, substantially reduces compilation time and is ideal in a school environment, where most runs require compilation. Compilers that reduce compilation time also should be used through the debugging phases of program development.

12.3 PROGRAM EFFECTIVENESS

Ease of Use

In addition to being correct, an effective program should be easy to use. This implies that the user must be given clear, precise instructions, with examples, for the preparation of his input. His output must be presented in a way that is useful to him. This may increase the complexity of the programming effort substantially, but it is well worthwhile if the program is to be used many times.

Efficiency

To satisfy the needs of the user in the best possible way, the program should be efficient. A program's *efficiency* should be a rather simple thing to define; a computer program is, after all, a tool. It is efficient to the extent that it gets its work done at a minimum "cost." The first problem arises in defining the "cost" of a computer program.

Costs and Savings

There are at least four measures of cost that might be used:

1. The time required to compile the program,
2. The time required to execute the program,
3. The amount of storage space used by the program, and
4. The amount of effort required to develop and maintain the program.

The compilation and execution of a program are, of course, carried out on a computer. Using whatever accounting procedures are employed at a given installation, it should be possible to associate a dollar cost with measures 1 and 2, above. At some installations, a program is compiled prior to each execution; that is, it is never stored for reuse in its object form. Clearly, in this case, the second cost includes the first, and is probably the only measure of the use of computer time. However, this may be an inefficient way to use a program.

The compiler itself may be a major consideration in reducing the compilation and execution times of a program. Compilers that can reduce these times (sometimes dramatically) are called *optimizing compilers*. Special compilers also are available for special needs. For example, in a school environment, most student jobs compile but do not execute; the compiler should minimize compilation times. The programming staff at the University of Waterloo developed a compiler that does this for FORTRAN (called WATFOR in its earlier version, and WATFIV in its more recent version). Reductions in the time required to process student jobs by a factor of ten or more have been experienced, using WATFOR and WATFIV. The University of Waterloo has developed a similarly efficient compiler for COBOL and other languages.

The cost of the use of storage space is more difficult to assign. In some installations, costs for the use of auxiliary storage and main storage have been allocated. Where such allocations have not been made, this factor is likely to be considered only insofar as the storage demands for a program outstrip the capabilities of the computer on which it is to be run, or require special services at the computer installation. For example, the demand for disk space may require a new disk pack to be mounted each time the program is run. Similarly, tape demands may necessitate that several reels of tape be mounted during the running of the program, in which case the cost of storage would become a cost of executing the program and be measurable in that way. At other times, the program may require so much main storage that it must be run overnight, or according to some other special arrangement. Because many installations charge less for overnight runs, it may seem less costly to use more main storage in this kind of environment. The user may find it hard to determine the cost to him of having to wait a day rather than an hour or two for the results of his program. Such hidden costs should be considered; but since they cannot be quantified, they often are neglected.

The cost of developing and maintaining a program for the most part consists of personnel costs. Examinations of the budgets of computer facilities indicate that more money is spent on salaries than on hardware. Savings can be effected in this area if the development of computer programs is instituted more efficiently. However, there is a tradeoff between the amount of programming effort and the efficiency of a program, as measured by each of the other criteria. In other words, a programmer — especially a relatively inexperienced programmer — has to work harder (and therefore longer) to make his program more efficient (for quantitative results on these and other matters relating to software efficiency and effectiveness, see [2]). Some installations have found it advantageous to spend more on execution and less on program development. This can be done in some application areas by using special information storage and retrieval software rather than developing application programs. The programming becomes rather stereotyped; it may be necessary only to complete a series of forms, and the running time may be less efficient (in some instances, and with some packages, it may be more efficient), but the amount of effort spent in developing and documenting a program almost certainly is less than would be required otherwise. Unfortunately, the information storage and retrieval packages are uneven in quality, and great care must be exercised in selecting them.

We shall say more about programming efficiency later in this chapter when we discuss some considerations regarding the choice of instructions used to write efficient computer programs. However, the savings that can result from these program improvements probably are substantially less than those that result from more effective supervision and recruitment of the programming staff.

12.4 DOCUMENTATION

Introduction

Program documentation serves three essential purposes: it permits a user to determine whether or not he wishes to use a program; if he decides to use it, the documentation gives him access to it; and it serves as a reference for the programming staff responsible for maintaining the program.

At least six kinds of information are needed in documenting a program. Three are intended mainly for the user, and three are for the programming staff.

The documentation of a program should include:

1. An abstract;
2. A description of the real-world problem that is being solved with the aid of the program; and
3. Information, especially relating to input and output, that a potential user of a program needs.

The reference material for the programming staff should include:

1. A heavily annotated source listing and source deck;
2. Run decks and test data; and
3. A description of the logic of the program, preferably in the form of a flowchart.

Abstract

The purpose of an abstract is to allow a potential program user to determine whether or not he is interested in it as quickly as possible. It should be concise; a length of approximately 30–50 words is recommended.

Problem Description

The problem description should indicate, in specific terms, the nature of the real-world problem that is being attacked, and how the computer program contributes to the solution of that problem. In some instances, this can be done in one or two paragraphs; in other cases, several pages are required. Where necessary, references should be given to descriptions and techniques that appear in books or periodicals that are readily available.

User Information

As a minimum, the information for the user must tell how to prepare all inputs and how to interpret outputs. The exact structure that is permitted for inputs to the program should be described, and examples given. Similarly, the structure of all possible outputs should be described, with at least one example for each, including punched and plotted as well as printed output. If error messages or other special messages are not self-explanatory, they should be listed and explained. The user must be told what to do—what steps to take—in response to error messages.

Every program has limitations of one kind or another, whether on the type or amount of input that can be accommodated, or on the accuracy of the results. These limitations should be described candidly.

The user should be given formulas to estimate the time required to execute a program and, if a great deal of storage is required, to estimate the amount of storage that may be used in executing a program. Although it probably is true that most users will not care very much about their main storage requirements as long as the program can fit (as long as it can be run), these formulas should be provided. It is especially important to discuss main storage requirements for programs that might be run at installations which can provide better service if a program uses less main storage.

Control cards are required to execute most programs. The layout of all the required control cards should be specified; the user should not have to guess what to do in order to run a program.

Source Deck

A source deck—the deck of cards on which the statements in the program are punched—must be submitted and heavily annotated to make it readable (see, for example, [3]). Variables should be described where they are declared or first used. The program should be broken into logical paragraphs or sections. Each paragraph should be introduced by a conspicuous comment of some kind. The documentation should include a listing of this source deck.

Run Decks

Decks used in making sample, timing, or debugging runs may be provided with the documentation. At least one such deck with a realistic set of inputs and a complete set of job control statements is highly advisable. Whether or not the decks are provided, the output obtained in the runs made using the test data should be attached as an appendix to the documentation.

Flowcharts

General and detailed flowcharts should be provided with the program. Programs are available that will produce flowcharts directly from the source code; however, these usually are not much help, and hardly improve the information already available in the source code itself. There is no substitute for a good flowchart prepared by a person with an expert knowledge of the program's logic. Templates should be used in preparing all flowcharts; no one should attempt to draw documentation flowchart boxes free-hand.

The documentation should provide a list of the variables used in a program and their definitions. This might be given in the flowcharts or in a separate table. If the list is long, it probably is best to list the variables in alphabetical order, for easy reference. If the list is short, it may be preferable to list the variables in the order in which they appear in the program.

12.5 AN EXAMPLE

An example of the documentation of a program is introduced at this point to illustrate some of the recommendations made in the preceding section. To fully appreciate the considerations involved in documenting a program, the reader should try to understand the program as though he had written it himself. With this purpose in mind, we will document a program that has been used as an exercise throughout the book: the calculation of the point count in a bridge hand. We will assume that the program was written in FORTRAN. The changes required to write the program in another language can be interpolated easily from this example. All the parts of the documentation that would appear as printed text are included (none of the decks of cards are given, of course).

Abstract

This program calculates the point count that would be assigned to a 13-card bridge hand using a system similar to that developed by Goren. It accepts an unlimited number of hands as input; the hands must be encoded, using a three-digit number for each card.

Problem Description

In arriving at bids in a game of bridge, many players use an aid based on a point score assigned to the hand, an approach developed and popularized by Charles Goren. This computer program calculates a point count for a hand based on the following scheme:

1. 4 points are assigned for each ace in the hand.
2. 3 points are assigned for each king but not if the only card in a suit is a king. A king that is a singleton does not earn any points.

3. 2 points are assigned for each queen and 1 point for each jack, but not if there are 2 or fewer cards in a suit. In the case where there are exactly 2 cards in a suit, the queen or jack counts if the other card is of higher rank. An ace is considered to be of highest rank, followed by the king, then the queen, then the jack. Otherwise the queen and jack do not earn any points if they are a singleton or part of a doubleton.

4. 3 points are assigned for each suit in which there are no cards (3 points for each void).

5. 2 points are assigned for each suit in which there is only one card (2 points for each singleton).

6. 1 point is assigned for each suit in which there are two cards (1 point for each doubleton).

Points for distribution (conditions 4, 5, and 6) are scored independently of the rank of the cards held in the suit. For example, a singleton king is worth a total of 2 points (2 for distribution plus none for the king), whereas a singleton ace is worth 6 points (2 for distribution and 4 for the ace). A doubleton consisting of a king and a jack is worth 5 points (3 for the king, 1 for the jack because the king is of higher rank, and 1 for the doubleton).

Input Format

The input consists of a deck of punched cards. Each punched card contains a single bridge hand. Each playing card in the bridge hand is represented using a three-digit number. The first digit indicates the suit, and the next two digits the rank. A blank space should appear between the codes for successive playing cards in the hand. Suits are codified as follows:

Suit:	SPADES	HEARTS	DIAMONDS	CLUBS
Code:	1	2	3	4

Ranks are codified as follows:

Rank	ACE	DEUCE	TREY	FOUR	FIVE	SIX	SEVEN	EIGHT
Code	01	02	03	04	05	06	07	08

Rank	NINE	TEN	JACK	QUEEN	KING
Code	09	10	11	12	13

For example, the bridge hand:

SPADES	HEARTS	DIAMONDS	CLUBS
ACE, QUEEN	KING, TEN	EIGHT, SEVEN	JACK
SIX, DEUCE	NINE, TREY	FIVE, FOUR	

would be codified as follows:

COLS.	ENTRIES	COLS.	ENTRIES	COLS.	ENTRIES	COLS.	ENTRIES
1–3	101	13–15	102	25–27	209	37–39	307
4	blank	16	blank	28	blank	40	blank
5–7	112	17–19	213	29–31	203	41–43	305
8	blank	20	blank	32	blank	44	blank
9–11	106	21–23	210	33–35	308	45–47	304
12	blank	24	blank	36	blank	48	blank
						49–51	411
						52–80	blank

The codes for playing cards need not be entered in any special order, as long as they are given in three-digit fields beginning in column 1, and separated by blanks.

Output Format

The output from this program is a two-column table. The first column contains a sequence of integer numbers, beginning with 1, that serves to identify the hand number. The second column contains the point count or some message to indicate that an error in the hand was detected. An example of a set of input and the corresponding output illustrates these formats.

Input Deck:
```
101 112 106 102 213 210 209 203 308 307 305 304 411
101 112 210 209 208 207 308 307 306 411 309 310
111 106 105 201 211 306 304 410 409 408 407 406 405
112 111 201 202 203 204 205 213 411 410 409 408 407
114 112 210 209 208 207 310 309 308 307 306 411 404
501 112 210 209 208 207 310 309 308 307 306 411 404
101 112 210 209 208 207 310 309 308 307 306 411 404 403
```

Corresponding Output:
```
HAND NO.    POINT COUNT
    1       11
    2       MISDEAL TOO FEW OR TOO MANY CARDS
    3       8
    4       13
    5       NO COUNT A CARD IS 14
    6       NO COUNT A SUIT IS 5
    7       MISDEAL TOO FEW OR TOO MANY CARDS
```

The program can detect four kinds of errors in the input. If a blank or a zero appears in column 49, the message "MISDEAL TOO FEW OR TOO MANY CARDS" is output. If neither a blank nor a zero appears in column 52, the same message is output. If a suit is outside the allowable range, the message "NO COUNT A SUIT IS" is output along with the erroneous suit value. If the rank of a card is outside the allowable range, the message "NO COUNT A CARD IS" is output along with the erroneous card value.

```
C A PROGRAM TO CALCULATE POINT COUNTS IN BRIDGE HANDS
C ALL VARIABLES ARE INTEGER AND WE USE FIVE ARRAYS
      IMPLICIT INTEGER(A-Z)
      DIMENSION HAND(4,13),CARD(14),SUIT(14),RSUM(4),CSUM(13)
C KK IS THE HAND NUMBER
      KK=0
      WRITE(6,31)
   31 FORMAT('1HAND NO.    POINT COUNT')
C THE MAJOR LOOP BEGINS HERE
   55 READ(5,2,END=50)(SUIT(I),CARD(I),I=1,14)
    2 FORMAT(14(I1,I2,1X))
      KK=KK+1
      POINT=0
C THE CHECK FOR TOO FEW OR TOO MANY CARDS
      IF(SUIT(14).NE.0.OR.SUIT(13).EQ.0)GO TO 10
C ARRAYS ARE INITIALIZED
      DO 1 I=1,13
      DO 1 J=1,4
      RSUM(J)=6
      CSUM(I)=0
    1 HAND(J,I)=0
C THIS LOOP CHECKS FOR ERRORS IN SUIT OR CARD VALUES AND CALCULATES SUMS
      DO 5 I=1,13
      IF(SUIT(I).LT.1.OR.SUIT(I).GT.4)GO TO 8
      IF(CARD(I).LT.1.OR.CARD(I).GT.13)GO TO 9
      K=SUIT(I)
      L=CARD(I)
      HAND(K,L)=1
      CSUM(L)=CSUM(L)+1
    5 RSUM(K)=RSUM(K)+1
C THIS LOOP AND STATEMENT FOLLOWING IT COMPUTES POINT COUNT
      DO 3 M=1,4
      IF(RSUM(M).EQ.0)POINT=POINT+3
      IF(RSUM(M).EQ.1)POINT=POINT+2
      IF(RSUM(M).EQ.2)POINT=POINT+1
      IF(HAND(M,13).EQ.1.AND.RSUM(M).GE.2)POINT=POINT+3
      IF(HAND(M,12).EQ.1.AND.(RSUM(M).GE.3.OR.HAND(M,13).EQ.1.OR.HAND(M,
     11).EQ.1))POINT=POINT+2
      IF(HAND(M,11).EQ.1.AND.(RSUM(M).GE.3.OR.HAND(M,13).EQ.1.OR.HAND(M,
     11).EQ.1.OR.HAND(M,12).EQ.1))POINT=POINT+1
    3 CONTINUE
      POINT=POINT+4*CSUM(1)
C OUTPUT IS PRINTED
      WRITE(6,20)KK,POINT
   20 FORMAT(1H ,I6,I14)
      GO TO 55
    8 WRITE(6,21)KK,SUIT(I)
   21 FORMAT(1H ,I6,7X,'NO COUNT A SUIT IS',I4)
      GO TO 55
    9 WRITE(6,22)KK,CARD(I)
   22 FORMAT(1H ,I6,7X,'NO COUNT A CARD IS',I4)
      GO TO 55
   10 WRITE(6,23)KK
   23 FORMAT(1H ,I6,7X,'MISDEAL TOO FEW OR TOO MANY CARDS')
      GO TO 55
   50 STOP
      END
```

Fig. 12.1   Listing of a program to calculate the point count in a bridge hand

Control Cards

The following control cards are required to run this program at the Georgetown University Academic Computation Center.

> a job card
> ```
> // EXEC BRIDGE1
> //GO.SYSIN DD *
> ```

The input deck should consist of these control cards, then a set of input data, and finally, a /∗ card.

Running Time

If the point count for H hands is to be obtained, the running time of the program is estimated to be:

$$time(in \ seconds) = 40 + 4H$$

Program Listing

A FORTRAN program listing suitable for this program is given in Figure 12.1. This program contains some features, such as the IMPLICIT statement and the END option in the READ, that may not be available in some versions of FORTRAN.

Flowcharts

A general flowchart for this program is given in Figure 12.2. A detailed flowchart is given in Figures 12.3 and 12.4.

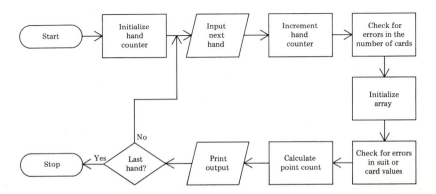

Fig. 12.2 General flowchart for calculating the point count in a bridge hand

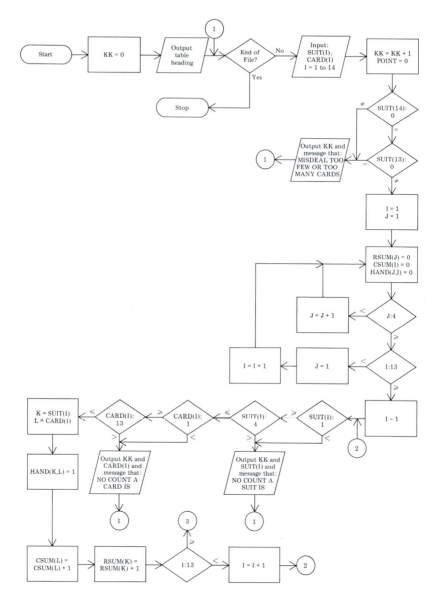

Fig. 12.3 Detailed flowchart for the bridge point-count problem

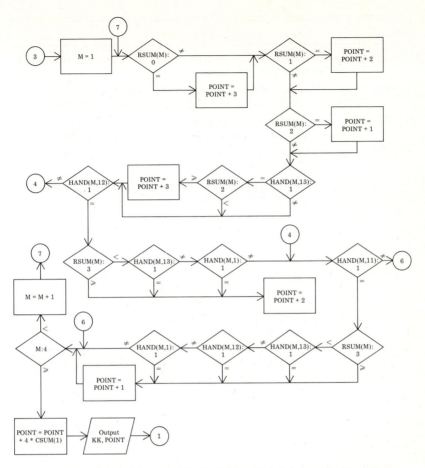

Fig. 12.4   Detailed flowchart for the bridge point-count problem (cont'd)

Variables

A list of the variables used in the program and their description is given in Figure 12.5.

Variable	Description
HAND	A 4×13 matrix that contains zeroes and ones and indicates which playing cards are in the hand
CARD	An array containing up to 14 elements. The Nth element of CARD is the rank (i.e., ace, deuce, trey, etc) of the Nth card.
SUIT	An array containing up to 14 elements. The Nth element of SUIT is the suit (i.e., spades, hearts, etc) of the Nth card.
RSUM	An array with 4 elements. The Nth element indicates the number of cards in the hand in the Nth suit.
CSUM	An array of 13 elements. The Nth element indicates the number of cards in the hand in the Nth rank.
KK	The hand number. KK takes on the values 1, 2, 3, 4 and so on.
POINT	Accumulates the point count. This is the value that is desired.
I, J	Integer variables used in DO loops to process cards, suits and ranks. They may be used in different ways in different parts of the program. For example, I is used to indicate which card is being read in statement 55 and which card has an illegal suit in statement 8.
K	The suit for a particular card (K = 1, 2, 3, or 4).
L	The rank of a particular card (L = 1, 2, 3, ... , 13).
M	A variable indicating suit (M = 1, 2, 3, or 4) that is used in checking on whether to count points for kings, queens and jacks.

Fig. 12.5 Descriptions of the variables in the bridge program

Exercises

1. Write an abstract suitable for the documentation of a program to calculate the tuition due (see Sections 9.5, 10.8, or 11.5).

2. Write a problem description suitable for the documentation of a program to compute means and standard deviations (Sections 9.13, 10.15, or 11.11).

3. Write a description of the input and output associated with one of the programs that you wrote in Chapters 9, 10, or 11. Select a problem near the end of the problem set with a complex enough input and output to make this a reasonably challenging exercise.

4. Make a series of runs of the program you used in answer to Exercise 3, so that you can provide the user with a formula to estimate the running time.

5. Draw a general and detailed flowchart for this same problem suitable for inclusion in the documentation.

12.6 MORE ON EFFICIENCY

In general, a program can be made more efficient if it is tailored to the organization which it is to serve and the installation on which it is to be run. The more generally useful the program, the less efficient it tends to be. It may be desirable to write programs that are to be run repeatedly at one installation in the assembler language of that computer. Although substantial reductions in running times can be obtained, it is more difficult to write this program than one in a high-level language, and it will have to be rewritten when the computer is replaced. For this reason, the tendency in recent years is to write in high-level languages rather than in assembler languages.

Efficient programmers have learned to write programs well—they are proficient in at least one programming language. Good writers do more than write; they also read frequently and well, to master their craft. The importance of reading computer programs has been neglected. Weinberg [4] has been especially active in trying to promote this activity, which affects program quality. It is especially important that first-level supervisors of programming staffs read the programs their staffs write. They should read them frequently and fluently to get insight into the programming's quality, and to guide the supervisor in improving that quality.

A Few Special Considerations in Improving Program Efficiency

In order to write efficient programs in a high-level language, the programmer must be familiar with how the compiler, and perhaps the operating system, treats his programs. This varies from compiler to compiler, and sometimes from installation to installation. Some examples of the considerations that can affect the programmer's decisions, which also serve as tips on technique, are given in this section. The considerations set forth in the preceding sections of this chapter are both more important and, perhaps, more subtle.

Recall the example involving the summation of the elements of an array which has been used throughout this book to illustrate loops. If we were going to add many numbers, the use of an array would waste storage space. If the numbers were input one-by-one or a record at a time, and if the input step were put inside the loop, then we would need at most one record's worth of storage.

Given N, suppose that we had to add N numbers. Assume that these numbers are input one at a time. We can write the program so that it proceeds as follows (each step concludes with a semicolon):

```
Initialize S; input N;
Loop N times; input X; S = S + X; end loop;
Output S; stop algorithm;
```

We used only one location to store the operands, X, and we can still sum N numbers, where N can take on any of a wide range of values.

This summation problem also illustrates some considerations relating to program effectiveness and efficiency. A program to sum numbers is likely to be applied to summing very large sets of numbers. Floating-point numbers are approximated in a computer. Summations may accumulate round-off errors leading to erroneous results. Some schemes for calculating summations require less computer time than others. For example, in comparing three summation schemes, Gregory [5] points out that the straightforward scheme (similar to the one above) is subject to a great deal more error but slightly faster than the second scheme, and very much faster than the third.

In most computers, multiplication is slower than addition, and it is more efficient to compute $A + A$ rather than 2 times A. Similarly, since exponentiation generally is slower than multiplication, A^2 is best calculated as A times A. These considerations have been recognized and built into some compilers. Those which always square via multiplication and double via addition tend to generate more efficient programs in terms of these operations.

It is efficient to introduce values for variables in the form in which the values will be stored. In the absence of special type statements, the use of $A = 4$ or $I = 4$. in FORTRAN is inefficient because 4 is an integer constant and A is a floating-point variable, whereas 4. is a floating-point constant and I is an integer variable. Similarly, if we have X(R) in a PL/I program, it should be preceded with the statement:

```
DECLARE R FIXED BINARY;
```

since subscripts in PL/I are stored in this form.

Blocks or other formal program segments should not be introduced in programs unless they are needed, to save the cost of the overhead expended in setting up and monitoring blocks. In PL/I, it is better to group statements using the structure:

```
DO; ...END;
```

rather than

```
BEGIN; ...END;
```

The use of BEGIN; initiates a more formal programming block than the use of DO; more overhead is expended in setting up and processing BEGIN blocks.

Exercises

Exercises 6 and 8 are very broad and might be assigned as term papers.

6. Discuss the considerations that would enter into planning for the development of the payroll program discussed in this text. Consider both effectiveness and efficiency.

7. Rewrite, to improve its efficiency, one or two of the programs you wrote in answering the problems at the end of Chapters 9, 10, or 11. Obtain measures of the running time or other appropriate quantities for the program, both as originally written and as modified.

8. Suppose that you are the manager of the data-processing center at a university. The center plans to develop a new, largely automated system for registration. Discuss the considerations that would enter into plans for developing this kind of system.

REFERENCES

1. Dahl, O. J.; Dijkstra, E. W.; and Hoare, E. W., *Structured Programming* (New York: Academic Press, Inc., 1972).

2. Boehm, B. W., "Software and its Impact: A Quantitative Assessment," *Datamation:* 48–59 (May 1973).

3. McCracken, D. D., and Weinberg, G. M., "How to Write a Readable FORTRAN Program," *Datamation:* 72–77 (October 1972).

4. Weinberg, G. M., *The Psychology of Computer Programming* (New York: Van Nostrand Reinhold Company, 1971).

5. Gregory, J., "A Comparison of Floating-point Summation Methods," *Communications of the ACM,* Vol. 15, No. 9:838 (September 1972).

ANNOTATED SUPPLEMENTARY BIBLIOGRAPHY

One would expect program efficiency and effectiveness to be so central to computer functioning that computer literature would contain many, many references on this subject. Unfortunately, this is not the case. Knuth's multi-volume work, (cited previously—see Chapter 8, Annotated Supplementary Bibliography, Reference 2), is difficult to read but extremely rewarding in its discussion of efficiency and effectiveness as an integral part of constructing and implementing algorithms. Boehm's article (Reference 2, above) is useful, especially for supervisors of programming staffs; and McCracken and Weinberg's article (Reference 3, above) should be cited in any discussion of the documentation of FORTRAN programs.

A brief summary article on the subject of the proof of program correctness is available that includes a comprehensive bibliography. It is:

Lanzarone, G. A., "Proof of Program Correctness," *Honeywell Computer Journal,* Vol. 6, No. 1:38–42 (January 1972).

Prentice-Hall has a comprehensive and expensive manual of documentation standards. It is:

Kuehne, R. S.; Lindberg, H. W.; and Baron, W. R., *Manual of Computer Documentation Standards* (Englewood Cliffs, N.J.: Prentice-Hall, Inc., 1973). This manual is priced at $75 in the regular edition and $150 in the deluxe edition, which includes reproducible, usable forms.

An issue of the *ACM Computing Surveys* devoted to articles on the writing of good structured programs is:

ACM Computing Surveys, Vol. 6, No. 4 (December 1974).

Finally, and perhaps most significantly, a well-written book on programming style that is an effective guide to good programming and contains many examples of both good and bad programming is:

Kernighan, B. W., and Plauger, P. J., *The Elements of Programming Style* (New York: McGraw-Hill Book Company, 1974).

Applications

INTRODUCTION

The next four chapters discuss computer applications. Chapter 13 contains an overview of computer applications that emphasizes the computer's impact on U.S. culture. Chapters 14 and 15 first describe applications, with little or no reference to the computer, and then describe how the computer is used in the applications, emphasizing *what* is being done with computers, rather than *how* it is being done. The algorithms are not given: they are extremely complex and would do little more than decorate the pages of a book intended as an introductory text. However, sources for these algorithms are referred to. One application, the simulation of the district office network, is discussed in great detail.

Part 4 concludes with a discussion of computer centers—the installations at which applications are implemented. The computer center is described as it might appear to a user who was trying to understand how a computer center functioned, so that he could use it more effectively.

Computer applications have been discussed throughout the book: payroll processing, the calculation of square roots, the calculation of means and standard deviations and tuitions. The reader who would like to investigate still other applications is referred to the Annotated Supplementary Bibliography at the conclusion of each of the next three chapters.

Chapter 13

Cultural Impact

World War II was the catalyst in the development of two discoveries that have reshaped the modern world—atomic energy and computers. Of the two, the computer probably will be recognized as the more significant scientific product of that war because of its impact on our day-to-day activities. Even today, the impact is substantial; by 1990, the computer will have affected almost everyone in developed nations greatly.

Humans always have sought aids for menial tasks. One of these tasks is computation, the manipulation of numbers. The Chinese merchant flicking the beads on his abacus, the Western merchant operating a modern cash register, and the statistical clerk working a desk calculator are using computational aids. However, each aid is being applied to one problem or a single class of problems. Each is only one or two orders of magnitude faster and more reliable than a human calculator. None of these aids is called upon to make decisions —much less to implement them. The electronic digital computer is not similarly bound with respect to application, speed, reliability, or function. Its application to human computational and information-handling problems will be revolutionary.

13.2 THE SECOND INDUSTRIAL REVOLUTION

The second industrial revolution is taking place now. Today, computers are recording airline reservations, maintaining customer accounts in single central locations of banks with many branches, assisting in the analysis of electrocardiograms, helping control traffic in large cities, assisting in the review of income tax returns, and controlling networks of interlocking electrical supply lines. We already can see some effects of the revolution, and we should be able to predict most of the remaining effects. Record-keeping, the control of manufacturing processes, and even some instructional and supervisory tasks are routinely assigned to the computer. Still more menial mental tasks that traditionally have been performed by humans will be relegated to the computer.

What has been the effect of this revolution on our day-to-day working activities? It is easier to make airline reservations; we have access to all flights, and the likelihood of error is small. We are permitted to bank at any one of a large number of branches of a commercial bank, with more efficiency and fewer errors. More electrocardiograms can be processed in less time, and more factors can be considered in their analysis: data from many electrocardiograms (from both normal and diseased patients) can be analyzed systematically and thoroughly, and results can be incorporated into the analysis of a single electrocardiogram. It now takes twenty rather than thirty minutes to drive into Toronto from its suburbs via routes whose traffic lights are controlled by a computer. We have been convinced in no uncertain terms that we must be more thorough in reporting our income and more careful in claiming deductions, because all of our income will be reported to and summed by a computer that can detect idiosyncrasies in our deduction patterns. Finally, and perhaps most dramatically, the northeastern United States was subjected to a blackout of electrical service in the fall of 1965 that probably would have been more widespread if the electrical supply systems had not been computer-analyzed. However, the computer-analyzed system has reduced electrical cost substantially by allowing certain localities and suppliers to avoid duplicating facilities and to rely on neighboring facilities—in fact, on a whole network of facilities—for reserve supplies of electricity.

Several developments that surely will come are needed to complete the second industrial revolution. Among these are another sharp drop in the cost of computers, the widely implemented ability to communicate with computers by handwriting, and a broadly based capability to write instructions for computers. The third of these developments may come last—we may have to wait until a new generation grows to adulthood, a generation that takes computers for granted because it learned about base two in elementary school and about algorithms and problem-oriented languages in high school. The first two developments, natural consequences of technological effort now underway, perhaps are less than a decade away.

13.3 INFORMATION SYSTEMS, PRIVACY, AND EFFICIENCY

A major area of computer application—record keeping—has progressed from a straightforward computer reproduction of the forms and procedures used in keeping records by hand, or with punched-card equipment, to more sophisticated approaches. These approaches employ extensive files, called *data bases,* that contain a substantial portion of the records of an organization. A major objective of these approaches is to be responsive to management, so that management can determine the current state of a variety of the organization's departments and activities quickly, in order to control them more effectively, and to plan for future needs. Such systems are called *management information systems.*

This abstract characterization of information systems will seem more concrete when a hospital information system is discussed later in this section and in Chapter 14. Information systems are discussed here to provide some insight into their cultural impact.

This new approach to record-keeping can be expected to have (and, to a certain extent, already has had) at least three important effects: first, the management of the organization's operations are centralized; second, detailed information on a wide variety of objects and people now can be quickly retrieved and utilized; and third, increased standardization of the forms, procedures, and products of the organization are anticipated.

What impact will these results have on the organization, its customers, and the public at large? There will be fewer management positions and more staff positions in the organization. The chief executive and his staff will concentrate most of their efforts on what will happen in the future—not in terms of short-range decisions on pricing, marketing, and manufacture, but rather in terms of implementing major policy changes in a representation, stored in the computer, of that portion of the economy that is significant to the organization. Management will be able to anticipate the effects of policy changes, if implemented, and to compare them with the extrapolated effects of current policies. Competitors also will be doing this, and such terms as "simulation," "strategies," and "optimization" soon will be widely used by executives.

There is real danger that information on the lifestyles and personal habits of employees, customers, and other individuals that now is freely available to insurance and credit companies will be even more accessible. This threat to privacy is a real one. Also, government records, particularly if they are centralized, will contain a substantial amount of personal information on many of our citizens, in a convenient, accessible form. Without adequate provision for the privacy of these data, they can be used to deprive people of property and liberty without due process.

What other effects can be anticipated? There should be a marked improvement in service and responsiveness. Most applications in record-keeping begin with billing operations. Despite the often-heard complaint, "I just can't get the computer to correct its errors!" it is, in fact, true that fewer errors are being made and that, once an initial break-in period has been completed, the billing operation is extremely smooth and efficient. The ability to correct billing errors should be included in all programs written for this purpose. If the computer won't correct the errors, it is because the people who designed and wrote the instructions for the computer did not include this feature. People, not computers, are responsible for the way computers are utilized. A computer that is used effectively can improve both the organization's operations and the services it provides substantially.

Consider, for example, a hospital information system. Patient billing is almost always the first application to be computerized, resulting in increased efficiency. But the greatest benefit in the use of computers results when a comprehensive, hospital-wide information system is functioning. Hospitals, like businesses, are complex; constant attention to a series of important details is required. Because a hospital operates around the clock, and because errors literally may be fatal, the computer may serve a vital life-saving function.

In summary, record-keeping on the computer has developed to the point where centralized, readily accessible files on all aspects of an organization's operation are available, creating more centralized and effective management, improved planning, more accessible personal information, and greater efficiency of operations.

13.4 COMPUTERS IN THE FEDERAL GOVERNMENT

The federal government is the greatest single user of computers in the United States. Within the government are at least five agencies that use the computer extensively in their operations: the Department of Defense, the Social Security Administration, the Internal Revenue Service, the Bureau of the Census, and the Central Intelligence Agency.

Little is known about the number of computers employed by the Central Intelligence Agency and the ways in which they are used. Informal contacts with their employees and items appearing in the newspapers indicate that this agency uses a great many computers in their operation and maintains a significant volume of files.

The other four agencies use the computer primarily for record-keeping. Computers enable the Department of Defense to maintain its huge personnel and supply files; the Social Security Administration to maintain its file of Social Security records and its claims file; the Internal Revenue Service to maintain tax files; and the Census Bureau to conduct population and business censuses.

Although the computer has become a necessary tool in each agency which uses it, many applications are merely computerized versions of manual methods that were in use before the advent of the computer. Information systems are being developed, but their effective implementation is a more serious challenge than was anticipated. This is due in part to the enormous number of individual records in each file (tens of millions, in several cases), and the difficulty of efficiently updating, indexing, and retrieving records from such a large data base. Resources at each agency that might be devoted to the development of sophisticated systems are tied up in the agency's day-to-day operations. However, information systems are being developed, and easier, more widespread accessibility to information inevitably will result.

In addition, a centralized government data base to be shared by all federal agencies, and perhaps by some state and local governments as well, has been proposed. The potential for centralization of information and control is clear. What a centralized file might "know" about individuals is illustrated in Figure 13.1.

MRS. A. — A government employee	MR. B. — A politically active veteran	MR. C. — Retired
1. Employment and earnings in positions covered by Social Security	1. Employment and earnings in positions covered by Social Security	1. Employment and earnings in positions covered by Social Security
2. Employment and earnings in government positions	2. Income tax records for recent years	2. Claims records as a claimant for Old Age Retirement Benefits
3. Employee evaluations, health and identification records and other information from government employment	3. Census data	3. Recent income tax records
4. Income tax records for recent years	4. Arrest records in a Washington demonstration	4. Census data
5. Census data	5. Health and identification records and other information obtained while in the military service	

Fig. 13.1 Information about three representative individuals that might be present in a centralized file

13.5 EDUCATION AND TEACHING MACHINES

The Socratic dialogue has long been described by many educators as the ideal method of teaching. Because classes at all educational levels are large, this approach has been difficult to implement. The computer now offers educators the opportunity to utilize the Socratic approach in their teaching.

This section will focus on the computer's impact on teaching methods; the impact on teaching facilities will be discussed in a later section. Educationally oriented terminals were discussed in Chapter 6. The special emphasis placed on education as an area of application is not merely the result of the author's interest in education; a greater share of the resources of the United States probably will be devoted to education in future years, because it is both necessary and desirable. Educational activities are a beneficial, enjoyable way to spend our increased leisure time. More important perhaps, in a rapidly changing, technologically oriented society, adult education is a necessity. [1]

Elementary school students in many districts are sitting at terminals and conversing with computers. The computer is a patient tutor with total recall, thus enabling the pupil to obtain repeated practice in basic skills to an extent that otherwise would not be possible. The instruction can be individualized, so that the slow pupil is not dazzled by the speed with which he is confronted with new material, and the fast pupil is not held back while others in his class catch up to him. Also, extensive use of computer facilities permits the critical resource —the teacher—to devote more and more time to tutoring small groups. This teaching method should be better than the common-denominator, class-wide approach.

However, there are at least two impediments to widespread use of this approach. First, cost—computer facilities are still relatively expensive—and, second, the development of suitable teaching materials. Because most elementary education syllabi do not change rapidly, a sufficient supply of teaching materials are expected to build up in time. Cost reductions are a natural consequence of technological improvements.

Computers are an integral part of the educational process at most colleges and universities. Their most frequent use at this level is assigning of realistic homework problems in engineering, the sciences, statistics, the social sciences, and computer science itself. Computer-based instruction involving a student-computer dialogue is increasing. Again, cost and the development of suitable teaching materials are the major impediments. [2]

13.6   THE POTENTIAL IMPACT ON HEALTH CARE

The computer already has had a substantial impact on health care in the United States and some other developed nations. We shall discuss some applications of computers to health care in Chapters 15 (medical diagnosis) and 14 (hospital information systems). This section will emphasize the potential impact that a computer might have, rather than the impact it already has had.

The computer can be a more effective servant than a human being in promoting health care. Consider from two points of view a computer system that contained the medical history of almost every person in the United States: the support it could offer the diagnostician, and the information it could provide the medical researcher. Complete medical histories would be available to assist in making a diagnosis, even though the patient might have had several different doctors and have resided in several different areas. Once the diagnosis was established, information on the effectiveness of alternative methods of treatment also would be available. The medical researcher would be able to draw data pertinent to many areas of medical research from these files. Duplication of expensive research effort could be avoided. Breakthroughs in diagnoses and treatment of rare diseases could be anticipated, if for no other reason than that this computer system would offer the only possible source for a large body of information on these.

If we are willing to expend the necessary resources, even today we can start developing such a system; present computer technology permits it. Such a system is very likely to be in operation within two or three decades. With appropriate provision for security and privacy, such a system can substantially add to our well-being.

Consider also an automated diagnostic facility in which special instrumentation is used to record body functions. The signals resulting from this instrumentation could be converted automatically to sequences of numbers (i.e., digitalized) and transmitted to a central file. Computer programs then could analyze the data, and compare these results with previous results for this patient, and with norms for all similar patients, to suggest areas meriting the physician's further investigation. Once again, current technology permits the development of such a system; in fact, intensive-care units now record and digitalize data much in this way. The analytical programs providing comparisons with previous history and diagnostic guidelines are less widely available, and the instrumentation in intensive-care units frequently concentrates on just one body system (e.g., circulatory) and one area of diagnosis (e.g., malfunctions of the heart).

13.7 COMPUTERS AND THE LAW

Much emphasis has been placed in recent years on the need to reduce the frequency and impact of crime in American society. Technology has been enlisted in this effort, and computers are one element in this attempt to achieve a technological breakthrough.

The computer has been used primarily in two ways: as a research tool, and as an efficient, responsive record-keeper.

Computers offer much promise for the automatic storage and retrieval of legal precedents and the consequent simplification of legal activities. Since many judicial systems have enormous backlogs that impede the legal process, any improvement in this area should reduce the frequency and impact of crime. However, progress has been slow, and only a few jurisdictions are using this approach.

The computer has been used effectively in research projects that attempt to determine significant factors in the increase of crime. Typical studies have examined the impact of addictive drugs on crime (a substantial one), the rehabilitative effectiveness of our penal system (poor), and pretrial detention patterns (extremely long, in some jurisdictions). Facts are an important weapon in fighting crime; political rhetoric is no substitute for effective study and correction of problems.

One of the most dramatic applications of the computer in law enforcement has been the development of a centralized file, maintained by the National Crime Information Center, containing master lists with complete identification of stolen and missing merchandise. If a law enforcement officer suspects that an automobile he has stopped or a weapon he has taken from a suspect may be stolen of missing, he now can request information on these items from this file. In a matter of minutes, often while he is still confronting the suspect, he can determine whether the item is indeed stolen or missing property. This on-the-spot information service has been acclaimed by some law enforcement officers as potentially very beneficial.

Computers also have been used to identify fingerprints and analyze speech patterns. Tens of millions of fingerprints have been accumulated by law enforcement and military agencies. The computer has been used to help classify, store, and retrieve these fingerprint files. Computers can identify fingerprints more speedily and accurately than manual methods. In addition, computers have helped analyze speech patterns, both for purposes of identification and to indicate whether stress (associated with making a false statement) might be present.

13.8 URBAN IMPACT – THE WIRED CITY

The electrification of our cities in the early twentieth century brought an extremely useful source of energy to our urban population. Rural electrification proceeded more slowly but it, too, gradually was accomplished, to a great extent. In much the same way, the wiring of our cities will bring to urban populations the benefits of an information explosion by permitting the free exchange of huge volumes of information at rates greater than can be accommodated by telephone lines. Each improvement has exacted and will continue to exact its price. The generation of electrical energy produces substantial amounts of pollution, and crippling blackouts can result from accidents or because the demand for electricity exceeds the supply. An information explosion can be both a boon and a bane; [3] however, if it is carefully controlled, it can bring the best in artistic performances, education, and even our work activities within easy reach, in our homes. [4]

Consider, for example, the impact on education. First-rate course materials soliciting interactive responses from the student can be presented directly to the home. A color television set and a typewriter-like keyboard can serve as the basic system in the home. Once connection can be made to a studio that provides educational material on a selective basis and that has a computer to monitor and evaluate a student's performance, first-rate advanced education should be within easy reach. As always, cost and the nonexistence of suitable materials are the major impediments. However, it is reasonable to expect that both of these obstacles will be overcome and that a revolution in mass education will occur. It also is reasonable to expect that colleges and universities will continue to provide person-to-person educational experiences that will not be duplicated by these wired facilities, and that their services will be much in demand—both for these purposes, and to generate educational materials for home projection.

The computer will affect many other aspects of urban and suburban living. We already have referred to computer-controlled traffic lights, management information systems in organizations such as municipal and county governments, and law enforcement aids. In addition, computer-controlled transit trains are expected to take over new intra-metropolitan area systems, and computer-controlled turnpike traffic and railroads are anticipated.

13.9 INTELLIGENT MACHINES AND THEIR IMPLICATIONS

Such questions as "Can computers think?" and "Do computers exhibit intelligence?" indicate people's reactions to automatons that might replace some human activities. People do, of course, have qualities that cannot be duplicated by machine, but we need not duplicate all human qualities in order to perform some human tasks by machine. Since certain well-defined (and usually undesirable) tasks are given over to automatons, people need not worry about being replaced entirely.

Serious discussions of whether computers can think almost inevitably arrive at problems of artificial intelligence, or heuristic programming. [5] Computer specialists have attempted to attack difficult tasks that defy solution in a straightforward way by providing *heuristics* (empirically based aids), or by permitting the computer to "learn" (to modify its solution procedure after applying it to a series of specific examples). Given our American culture, what is the potential impact of truly intelligent machines?

One consequence is that they can dehumanize our self-image seriously. Weizenbaum discussed this possibility. [6] Analogies between computers and the brain can be useful in developing models for one or the other system. [7] The critical issue is that we must not think of ourselves as living computers (the first industrial revolution led people to think of themselves as living machines with engines); we are uniquely human beings, and must not confuse ourselves with our tools.

The computer is our tool, and it should remain so always. This means that it must be asked to do only what we cannot or do not choose to do for ourselves. The danger that the computer will become the controller rather than the tool, either by default or by design, is a real one; to avoid such an outcome, the user must continue to synthesize, test, guide, decide—and communicate with other human beings. Although the computer probably will take on more and more routine "creative" activities, the choice of the activity, the scope of the computer's contribution, and this activity's impact on related activities, must remain under human control.

We already have noted that the business executive will use simulations, consider strategies, and try to achieve optimization with the aid of the computer. What of the scientist, secretary, office manager, laboratory technician, machinist, or barber? There certainly will be changes in the working activities of some of these people. The scientist will function more and more creatively; the secretary will become a kind of administrative assistant; and the office manager will become a computer specialist. The job of machinist probably will become obsolete, but demand in other areas will increase—for example, guides in the National Park Service, technicians assisting conservationists in field activities, and technical assistants to college instructors. The barber probably will be around for quite a while, although he might be called a hair stylist.

In one vision of the future, we ultimately can become a society of teachers and students, philosophers and artists, writers and actors, gardeners and artisans, and scientists and executives. Many of us can become missionaries, following the example of the Peace Corps. This happy picture can come true if we are alert to the computer's potential and are realistic about its inevitable place as our most widely used tool. We also should consider seriously such things as guaranteed annual wages and adult schooling, and we should recognize and encourage everyone's capacity to contribute creatively to our culture.

Topics for Discussion

The material in this chapter can be realized most effectively by starting a free-wheeling classroom discussion of the computer's impact on society (after the student has read the chapter). Topics for discussion include:

1. What are the positive and negative effects that computers have had on our culture up to now?
2. Will we be better off after the information revolution?
3. What will education be like in the twenty-first century?
4. Use Topic 3, substituting health services, or our legal system, or our work environment for education.
5. Can we function without checks or cash, after the information revolution?
6. What will life in the United States be like in the year 2000? Try to emphasize the total societal future, not just our information environment. Can we now foresee what life might be like in 2050?
7. A computer simulation of the whole earth was developed by Dennis and Donella Meadows and discussed in their book, *Limits to Growth* (published in paperback by Universe Books and Potomic Associates). Relate this book to Topic 6, and also discuss the book itself as an application of computers.

REFERENCES

1. Vaughan, T. R., and Sjoberg, G., "The Politics of Projection: A Critique of Cartter's Analysis," *Science*. 177:142–47 (July 14, 1972).

2. Carnegie Commission on Higher Education, *The Fourth Revolution: Instructional Technology in Higher Education* (New York: McGraw-Hill Book Company, 1972).

3. Maisel, H.; Lee, R. E.; and Ferkiss, V., "Responsibility in Computer Communications," In Winkler, S. (ed.), *Computer Communication Im-*

pacts and Implications (The First International Conference on Computer Communications, 1972.)

4. Porter, E. B., and Dunn, D. A., "Information Technology: Its Social Potential," *Science.* **176**:1392–99 (June 30, 1972).

5. Feigenbaum, E. A., and Feldman, J., *Computers and Thought* (New York: McGraw-Hill Book Company, 1963).

6. Weizenbaum, J., "On the Impact of the Computer on Society," *Science.* **176**:609–14 (May 12, 1972).

7. Arbib, M. A., "Toward an Automata Theory of Brains," *Communications of the ACM.* Vol. 15, No. 7:521–27 (July 1972).

ANNOTATED SUPPLEMENTARY BIBLIOGRAPHY

Popular magazines frequently refer to the impact of the computer. Rather than attempting to list such articles in this bibliography, we list a few articles and books for professionals that discuss whole areas of impact. There are several periodicals that cover areas of computer applications which have societal implications, such as *Law and Computer Technology* and *Computers and the Humanities.*

1. Weiner, N., *The Human Use of Human Beings: Cybernetics and Society* (Boston: Houghton Mifflin Company, 1950). The first cybernetician gives an early warning of the coming of automation.

2. Pylyshyn, Z. W. (ed.), *Perspectives on the Computer Revolution* (Englewood Cliffs, N.J.: Prentice-Hall, Inc., 1970). A far-ranging discussion of the impact of the information revolution, this book includes some historically interesting early documents on computers, some fictional, imaginative accounts of man-machine confrontations, and many nonfictional accounts of individual and societal relations to the information revolution. As might be expected in a collection of separate articles, the quality of writing is uneven and there are temporary losses of focus; but even so, this book is worth reading.

3. Rothman, S., and Mosmann, C., *Computers and Society.* (Palo Alto, Ca.: Science Research Associates, Inc. 1972). This is a whole book on the impact of the computer on society that amplifies the discussion which we began in this chapter.

4. Gerbner, G.; Holsti, O. R.; Krippendorff, K.; Paisley, W. J.; and Stone, P. J. (eds.), *The Analysis of Communication Content* (New York: John Wiley and Sons, Inc., 1969). This book summarizes the application of computers to document analysis, with special emphasis on its value to this historian. It is obvious, however, that these techniques also could be applied to such fields as literature, intelligence operations, military operations, and psychology.

5. Stevens, M. D., "Non-numeric Data Processing in Europe – A Field Report," *Technical Note 462* (Washington, D.C.: U.S. Government Printing Office, 1968). This is a good summary of the state of the art of non-numeric data processing in the mid-sixties in Europe (including the USSR). This is also an example of a product from an excellent source for publications – the U.S. Government Printing Office. Try to keep one of their recent catalogues handy.

6. National Commission on Technology, Automation, and Economic Progress, "Report of the National Commission on Technology, Automation, and Economic Progress," available in an abridged version from the U.S. Government Printing office as "Technology and the American Economy." This is one of the first and best government studies on the impact of computers.

7. Duggan, M. A., "Law, Logic and the Computer: Bibliography with Assorted Background Material," *Computing Reviews,* Bibliography 9, Vol. 7, No. 1 (January–February 1966). Also in *Computing Reviews: March–April* Supplement B, Bibliography 21, Vol. 11, No. 4.

8. "Computer Utilities – Social and Policy Implications," *Computing Reviews,* Bibliography 17, Vol. 9, No. 10 (October 1968).

9. Anderson, R. E., and Fagerlund, E., "Privacy and the Computer: An Annotated Bibliography," *Computing Reviews,* Bibliography 30, Vol. 13, No. 11 (November 1972). This is a comprehensive, well-annotated bibliography. Certainly it's the first place to go if you are interested in the subject of computers and privacy.

10. Ware, W. H., "Records, Computers, and the Rights of Citizens," *Datamation,* Vol. 19, No. 9:112–14 (September 1973). This summarizes the report prepared by the Advisory Committee on Automated Personal Data Systems of the Department of Health, Education and Welfare. This same issue of *Datamation* contains a description of information systems used in law enforcement.

Chapter 14

APPLICATIONS IN BUSINESS AND MANAGEMENT

14.1 INTRODUCTION

The electronic digital computer has become an integral part of most large business enterprises. Smaller businesses also make extensive use of computer facilities. Record-keeping has been relegated to the computer, and accounts are stored on magnetic tapes and disks rather than in filing cabinets. Further, the nature of the record-keeping function is changing from routine work to a management information system. This system generates summary reports to management on the status of its different departments, reviews the effects of policy changes, provides measures of productivity, and assists in market research. A sophisticated system can help analyze the effects of future policy changes, and can provide condensed predictions of the company's market position. Such questions as "What are the probable consequences of a price decrease on the part of my principal competitor?" and "What can I expect to happen if Company B makes a strong pitch for the market in area A?" can be answered with the aid of these systems.

Three specific applications of computers in business and management will be discussed in this chapter:

1. A management and operating information system for hospitals,
2. The operations of a national wholesale supplier of equipment parts, and
3. The simulation of a Social Security district office.

The general discussion of simulation contained in this chapter is intended to introduce this important area of computer application.

312

14.2   HOSPITAL INFORMATION SYSTEMS

As we already have remarked, hospitals, like businesses, are complex, and constant attention to important details is required. Because a hospital operates around the clock and because errors may be fatal, the computer may serve a vital time-saving and life-saving function in a hospital.

A *hospital information system* often consists of a series of files, and computer programs to process these files. A typical system might include the following files:

1. Scheduled admissions file,
2. Current patient file,
3. Former patient file,
4. Hospital space inventory file,
5. Medical staff file,
6. Nursing staff file,
7. Other professional staff file,
8. Non-professional staff file,
9. Pharmaceuticals file,
10. Laboratories file, and
11. A file containing the names of all other files. This file is part of a special program that controls the manipulation of the other files.

The computer programs that might be included are:

1. Patient billing program,
2. Payroll program,
3. Laboratory scheduling and reports program,
4. Surgical scheduling and reports program,
5. Pharmaceuticals prescription and administration program,
6. Admissions program,
7. Special diet program, and
8. The special control program.

Before discussing these files and programs further, let's consider the equipment setup. At a university hospital, the computer might be a very large one shared by the medical school and other schools in the university. The computer also might be a large one located at one hospital and servicing several other hospitals. Finally, it might be a medium-sized computer dedicated to serving only the hospital information system at one hospital. A typical system includes remote terminals, located at a distance from the computer at nurses' stations, in the admissions office, in the pharmacy, in the dietician's office, and in the laboratories. These remote stations might contain teletypewriter terminals, cathode-ray-tube devices with keyboards, or even card readers (see Figure 14.1). In addition, administrative personnel might have cathode-ray-tube devices permitting them to obtain summary data on various aspects of the hospital functions. Extensive computer output equipment in the computer center itself could provide payroll checks, special reports for research use, space inventories, and similar large-scale outputs.

Two typical problems — patient admissions and drug prescriptions — may illustrate how a hospital information system functions. First, consider a patient who appears in the admissions office for a previously scheduled surgical procedure. The surgeon already has entered into the scheduled admissions file such things as the nature of the surgery and the time for which it is scheduled; identification of the patient and the physician; and special considerations, such as whether or not the patient is a diabetic or has allergies. On arriving at the hospital, the patient fills out a standard admissions form with identification and billing information; information on previous admissions; medical history; special diet for personal or religious reasons, and so on. This form might have been filled out earlier and input by the doctor's staff. This

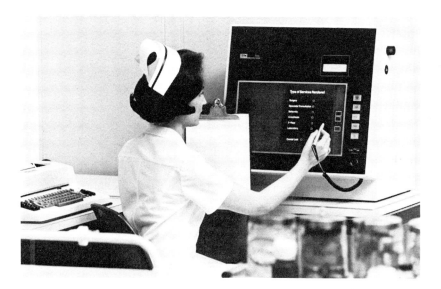

Fig. 14.1   A computer terminal at a nurses' station

information immediately is entered into the computer network by an admissions clerk, who refers to the scheduled admissions file and the former patients file to verify the information. Any discrepancy is detected immediately. Next, the admissions program invoked by the admissions clerk calls up the space inventory file, assigns a bed to the patient, updates the space file to account for this new occupancy, and reports the result. Then it initiates a new record in the patient's file and reports the admission to the appropriate nurses' station. Finally, the admissions program calls the surgical scheduling program to enter information regarding the surgery in the current patients file and the space inventory file. Reminders will be issued to the medical and nursing staff at appropriate times, and the availability of the surgical facility at the scheduled time for surgery will be ensured.

The second problem can occur when a doctor prescribes a drug for a patient. After the doctor has prepared the order in the usual way, the nurse enters the order on a typewriter-like entry board. Before it is released as input, the order is displayed on the screen or printer of the terminal for verification. The pharmaceuticals prescription and administration program examines the order to make sure that the dose being requested is not lethal. This program then calls in information from the patient's file to make sure that the order does not grossly violate standard practices. If it does, a message to the nurse indicates that the program has rejected the order temporarily, and cites the reasons for rejection. The nurse may check with the physician and, on his orders, override the rejection. The pharmaceuticals program then makes entries in the pharmaceuticals file, thereby giving the pharmacy a prescription, reminding the nurses to administer the drug according to the prescribed schedule, and sending a message to the nurses at the appropriate time to cease administering the drug. A nurse, in turn, makes an appropriate entry at a station after each administration of the drug, and the patient's file is modified to include information on the drug that has been administered.

Let us use Figures 14.2 and 14.3 to review these two uses of a hospital information system. Figure 14.2 shows that the physician (1) requests the scheduled admission of a patient for a surgical procedure. The patient appears at the admissions office (2), fills out an admissions form (3), which is reviewed by the program for exceptions (4). After appropriate corrections have been made, the space inventory file (5) is used to assign space to the patient, and this assignment is reported to the appropriate nurse's station (6). Surgical scheduling and appropriate space assignments are completed (7), and special messages are generated. For example, the dietician may be sent a message (8) to the effect that this patient must be put on a salt-free diet.

In Figure 14.3, we see that the physician orders the administration

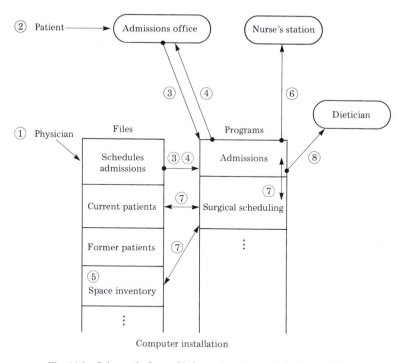

Fig. 14.2 Schematic flow of information in an admission problem

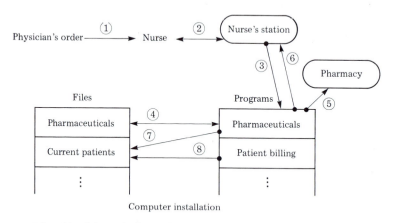

Fig. 14.3 Schematic flow of information in a pharmaceutical problem

of a certain drug to a specified patient (1). The nurse enters this information and verifies it at her keyboard (2) before passing it to the computer (3). The pharmaceuticals program first verifies that the order is neither lethal nor extraordinary (4). It then transmits the prescription to the pharmacy (5), sends messages to the nurses to administer the medicine at the appropriate times (6), and makes entries in the patient's file to reflect administration of the drug (7). Entries also are made in the patient's billing section of the patient's file for the cost of the pharmaceuticals (8).

14.3   NATIONAL PARTS WHOLESALER

Let us next consider a nationwide supplier of equipment parts or similar supplies. Since this application is hypothetical and is not modeled after an existing system, we shall construct an artificial company with the following characteristics:

1. The company's customers and suppliers are scattered throughout the continental United States.
2. The inventory of the company's merchandise includes thousands of items that vary greatly in price and size.
3. The company uses an elaborate computer-controlled communication system to carry out its operations.

Figure 14.4 presents a schematic summary of the company's operations. From his office (which can be anywhere in the country), a customer places an order, which is fed directly into the customer-service program (1). The customer-service program calls in the files it needs to service the order (2), reviews the credit status of the customer, and, if his credit status is satisfactory, selects a warehouse from which to ship the order to the customer. The customer-service program then calls in the order and shipping program to place the order with the warehouse for shipping (3). The order is verified and the warehouse makes the shipment (4). Information regarding the shipment is sent to the computer (5); and, when the shipment arrives, the customer acknowledges receipt (6).

As an integral part of the operation, the customer files and warehouse files are revised to permit billing and adjust warehouse inventory. A field in each record of the parts file will contain the standard reorder quantity, and another field will contain the critical inventory level. Immediately after the inventory has been adjusted, the computer determines whether this shipment depleted the inventory sufficiently to set a reorder mechanism in motion.

Let us assume that a critical inventory level was reached. The inventory-review program determines that more supplies are needed and, by using the qualified-manufacturers file and the standard reorder quantity, it transmits an invitation to bid to the appropriate manu-

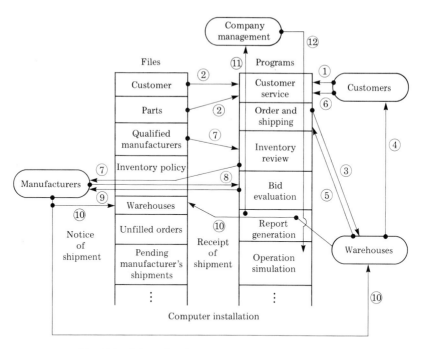

Fig. 14.4 Schematic of operation of a wholesale supplier

facturers (7). The bids are submitted (8) to the bid-evaluation program. This program evaluates the bids and chooses the suitable manufacturer or combination of manufacturers. The award is made (9), and the manufacturer ships the supplies directly to the warehouse (10) and bills the company. Management receives regular and special reports on such things as inventory and customer status and outstanding invitations to bid via terminals located in their offices (11).

Potential policy changes may be transmitted to an operation-simulation program (12), which inserts these changes in the existing policy, and uses the actual operational experience of the past six months or the anticipated experience of the next six months to predict the effects of these changes on the company's operations. This prediction is reported to management, which decides which, if any, of these changes to put into effect.

Implementation of a system such as the one described in this section is complex and expensive. About one-quarter of a million dollars would have to be invested in terminal equipment alone if, in the above example, we were servicing 100 customers using 10 warehouses. Also, the computer programs might—in total—involve as many as one-quarter of a million instructions; and though computers are virtually error-free, programmers are not. The programming costs, both in time and dollars, would be very great.

14.4 SIMULATION—GENERAL CONSIDERATIONS

Simulation is a numerical technique for conducting experiments on a digital computer involving certain types of mathematical and logical models that describe the behavior of a business, or an economic, social, biological, physical, or chemical system (or some component thereof) over extended periods of real time.

Much of the efforts of physical and life scientists are devoted to developing mathematical models of natural processes, and some of these models have been subjected to numerical experimentation. Simulation is most widely used, however, in the social and behavioral sciences and in business, because the activities in these areas cannot be modeled on strictly determined, unvarying relations. Though some underlying relations may be present, substantial deviations from these relations can be expected to appear. For example, the orbit of a planet can be predicted quite precisely, using an explicit mathematical relation; however, the sales of a firm cannot. Even if management makes no changes in the policies of the firm, fluctuations in the economy, changes in the buying habits of the firm's customers, and many other factors make it impossible to predict sales precisely. This is not to say that a good prediction cannot be made; but it is, at best, an "educated guess," and a difference between the actual sales and the predicted sales can be expected. It is important to know how great this difference can be. Simulation permits experimental studies of the firm that provide for the natural fluctuation in sales. Estimates of the differences associated with the prediction can be made.

Up to now, we have said nothing about computers and their place in simulation. One can simulate without using any mechanical or electronic aids. Certain simple manual war games or business games are examples of such simulations; more complex games might require mechanical computational assistance. However, once the simulation attempts either to reflect subtle, complex interrelationships realistically, to consider many factors in the model, or to deal with a large number of basic units individually, the number of calculations and the extent of record-keeping become enormous, and an electronic computer is needed.

In Chapter 6, we introduced simulation briefly in connection with the discussion of a programming language (GPSS) especially designed for use in simulations. In the remainder of this section we shall discuss how simulations are developed, and in the next we will give a specific simulation.

There are at least five major steps in developing a simulation:

1. Defining the problem,
2. Gathering and analyzing pertinent data,

3. Constructing the model(s),
4. Writing and debugging the computer program(s), and
5. Testing and applying the simulation.

Defining the problem should include the preparation of an extensive list of questions that the simulation is to help answer. Simulations of business enterprises are management tools; management should be asked, "If you had this tool today, how would you use it?" and "What questions do you want to answer, using this tool, over the next three and four or more years?" Responses should be forced, if necessary, and as detailed as possible. This step too often is ignored or inadequately pursued, with disastrous consequences — management often is disappointed by the final result, and much of the work often must be redone.

Lists of the activities and events to be simulated and a list of the parameters — the variables — to be used in the simulation should result from this definition stage. The lists of activities and events may take the form of a set of diagrams of the process being simulated. These diagrams may include the connections among the events and activities, and some rough estimates of the time between events and the duration of the activities. (An example of one such diagram will be given in the next section when the simulation of Social Security district offices is discussed.)

The list of parameters is very important: a simulation cannot retain all of the features of the process being simulated. The developer of a simulation always adopts a point of view — sometimes deliberately, sometimes inadvertently — which determines the features to be included, and the list of parameters implements this choice.

All parameters must be listed and defined, and the definitions should include specifications for the units to be used. The relationships among the parameters should be defined as far as possible, not in terms of specific mathematical functions, but rather in terms of which parameters are related to which other parameters.

The second phase of the development of the simulation, gathering and analyzing pertinent data, should not even be designed until after the first phase has been completed. (However, a pilot data-gathering project might be conducted during the first phase to determine what difficulties might be encountered in this kind of enterprise, and to acclimate both field and study personnel to data-gathering techniques. This project should be very brief and the acquisition of definitive data should not be expected.) There are at least three sources for pertinent data:

1. Historical records,

2. Expert opinion, and

3. Field studies.

Historical records may be useful if the process is changing very slowly, or if recent or current records are available. Many historical records are really reports to management. Since the person preparing the record wishes to present the best possible picture, it may be necessary to edit these records carefully before using them. In some cases, the picture may be so distorted that the records are useless.

Expert opinion should not be ignored as a source for data. Subject-matter specialists should be a part of the team developing the simulation because frequently they can provide estimates of the values taken on by some of the parameters, and can help check historical records and set up field studies.

Field studies are the most expensive source for data, and should be undertaken only to fill gaps left after other sources have been exhausted. To be most effective, at minimal cost, they must be designed carefully. During the planning of field studies:

1. Representative, approachable field activites should be selected;

2. Specific sites and dates should be determined;

3. Data-gathering personnel should be selected and trained (these people actually will conduct the field studies); and

4. Special forms for recording data should be designed and printed, and equipment to be used in the field studies should be obtained.

The choice of the units to be studied and the dates of the study should take into consideration the need to estimate the effects of seasonal factors, account for regional and local idiosyncrasies, and estimate the "observer effect." (Working patterns change when people know that they are being observed. If possible, some measurements should be made without letting people know that they are being observed. If this is impossible or unethical, historical information may prove helpful. An example is given in the next section.)

If a field study is well-designed, the data-gathering itself should go smoothly. If it is poorly planned, some serious obstacles may be encountered. For example, poorly designed forms may be filled out erroneously, and poorly trained study teams may confuse field personnel.

The data gathered in this phase of the study must be thoroughly analyzed. This procedure should include not only the usual reduction of the data to obtain means and standard deviations, but also special statistical analyses to determine the underlying nature of the parameter distributions and to fit functions relating the parameters, as well as other tasks. Frequently, the analysis reveals gaps in the data that require some additional data-gathering activities.

The third phase is the construction of models of the process. Actually, the models are being built during the first two phases as well; however, now is the time to be specific and unambiguous, and to reduce these models to algorithms that can obtain outputs for the process under study, given the inputs to the process. Since the models will be implemented in the form of computer programs, the programmer should join the simulation team.

A set of test data should be constructed concurrently with the development of the algorithms. Computer programming will overlap the development of the models—indeed, the third and fourth phases may be indistinguishable. The last phase, the testing and application of the simulation, should begin only after the programmer has debugged his programs. The set of test data then is processed in a simulation run. After any required corrections have been made, other subject-matter specialists and management might be called in for a demonstration of the simulation. If the simulation is a good one, the applications will follow soon thereafter.

The development of computer simulations often is an expensive and time-consuming process. For example, a simulation of land combat required for its development about a hundred man-years of effort, and 3000 hours of time on an IBM 7090 computer over a period of two-and-a-half years. The district-office simulation, discussed in the next section, required about 25 man-years of effort, and several hundred hours of time on IBM 360/65 and GE 245 and 265 computers before its development was completed—three years after it began.

14.5 SIMULATION OF THE OPERATIONS OF THE SOCIAL SECURITY DISTRICT OFFICE NETWORK

The Social Security Administration has several hundred district offices scattered throughout the United States and Puerto Rico. These offices are the principal contact points with the public. Social security account numbers are assigned there, claims are filed, and questions are answered. The efficient and effective operation of these offices is essential to the functioning of the Social Security Administration.

The Bureau of Field Operations and the Operations Research Staff in the headquarters of the Social Security Administration began a joint study of district-office operations in 1966. This study was intended to provide a simulation of district-office operations.

District offices come in a variety of sizes and shapes. The largest ones, called *class-A offices,* are located in metropolitan centers. The smallest, called *class-D offices,* are located in rural or small urban areas. Intermediate-size offices—classes B and C—can be found in a wide variety of locations. Often, smaller offices carry out much of their work in the field rather than the office. Contact stations are established in post offices and similar central locations in small communities throughout the area serviced by the district office. These stations are staffed once or twice a week by special district-office employees, called *field representatives,* or by other employees, called *claims representatives.* These field activities were omitted from the study deliberately; the scope of the simulation was limited to the activities in the district office itself. However, studies of the functioning of district offices indicated that the ratio of the number of claims taken in the field to the total number of claims processed may be an important variable in characterizing the activities of the office.

The simulation was developed in accordance with the approach outlined in Section 14.4. Management, which in this case includes district-office managers as well as key personnel in the regional and headquarters offices, were asked how they would use the simulation. (Line supervision of district offices is provided by 11 regional offices. The staff in a regional office establish policies for, and directly supervise, all district offices in their region. At the top, in the headquarters of the administration, is the Bureau of Field Operations, which is responsible for the overall supervision of the district offices.) Activities of several typical district offices were flowcharted, and lists of activities and parameters were prepared.

A layout of a typical class-C or class-D district office is given in Figure 14.5, along with a mapping of the path that a visitor might follow through the office, and a description of how the claim he might submit would be processed. There are several categories of employees in the office. These include the manager (M in Figure 14.5), assistant manager (AM), administrative clerk (AC), claims representatives (CR), field representatives (FR), service representatives (SR), claims-development clerical personnel (CDC), receptionists (R), and clearance-service clericals who work in the clearance-service unit (CSU).

The manager and assistant manager share the supervisory and policy-making activities of the office. In addition, they frequently make public appearances to present social security policies. Field representatives also make public appearances from time to time. The administrative clerk helps the manager and assistant manager in carrying out the administrative details associated with their activities. The scope of the simulation did not include these management activities. However, the simulation did include the fact that management helps process claims from time to time.

Claims representatives and field representatives are responsible for taking and developing a claim—the former in the district office and the latter in the field. Field representatives also have desks in the district office, and occasionally they assist the claims representative by conducting interviews or reviewing evidence in the district office.

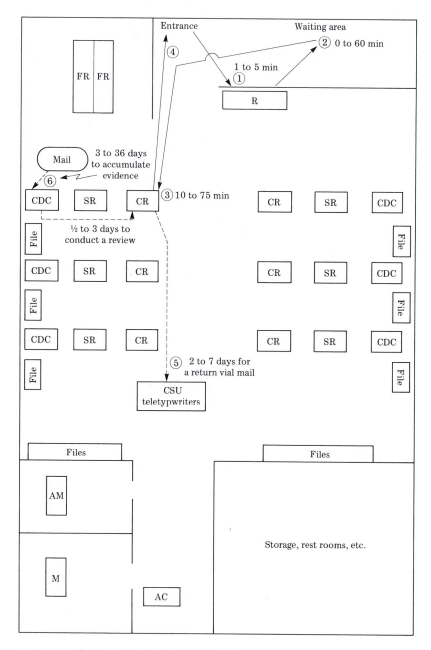

Fig. 14.5 A floor plan of a district office showing the flow of activities. (Solid lines indicate the movements of the claimant and dotted lines the movements of the claim. The scale is approximately 1 in. = 10 ft.)

Claims taken in the field are developed in the district office. The service representatives and claims-development clerical personnel also assist the claims representative. Service representatives handle telephone contacts, answer questions about the status of claims or changes and delays in benefits, and evaluate routine evidence. Claims-development clerical personnel gather the evidence, prepare routine requests for additional material, and forward it to the claims representative for evaluation.

The receptionist is the first person to be contacted by a visitor to the office. In most offices, she issues account numbers and answers simple questions, but she refers a visitor to a claims representative or service representative for interviews regarding the submission of a claim, the development of a previously submitted claim, or delays or changes in benefit checks. The clearance-service unit prepares requests for earnings reports, which are transmitted via teletype to the headquarters of the Social Security Administration. The earnings records are maintained in magnetic-tape files and are processed by a computer. The district-office teletypes are connected to headquarters, which records requests for earnings reports directly on magnetic tapes. These tapes then are removed from the recording device and mounted directly on tape drives in the computer center, where they are processed.

In many offices, much of the work is carried out over the telephone, and the scope of the study included this. Service representatives frequently are assigned to handle telephone inquiries.

Let's return to Figure 14.5. On entering the office, a visitor speaks to the receptionist (1), who determines the purpose of the visit. If the receptionist cannot satisfy the visitor, she determines whom he should see and, if that person is busy, asks the visitor to wait (2). Let us assume that the visitor wishes to submit a claim. He is interviewed by a claims representative (3) and leaves the office (4).

Now we turn our attention to his claim; the visitor has become a claimant. A record of the claimant's earnings is requested via the teletypewriter at the clearance-service unit (5). The earnings report is mailed to the district office and entered in the folder established for the claim by the corresponding* claims-development clerical em-

---

*Claims representatives, service representatives and claims-development clerical personnel often are organized into teams. This is the case in the office described in Figure 14.5. Ordinarily, a single team handles a claim from submission through development and evaluation; it is not passed from one team to another. An account number or the first letter of the claimant's surname is used to guide the receptionist in assigning initial interviews to a claims representative's team. Another approach is to maintain separate pools of claims representatives and claims-development clerical employees. The service representatives and claims-development clerical employees do the work as it comes to them, regardless of which claims representative originally took the claim, or of whether they have worked on the claim before.

ployee (6). When sufficient evidence has accumulated, the clerical employee turns the file over to the claims representative for evaluation (7). This frequently creates further correspondence among the claimant, the district office, and headquarters. The new, incoming mail is entered in the appropriate file (6), and the file again is forwarded to the claims representative for evaluation (7). This process (steps (6) and (7)) may be repeated several times if the claims representative is not satisfied with the evidence that has been submitted.

Solid lines have been used to indicate the path of the visitor, and dotted lines the path of the claim. The range of times required to carry out the processing of the claim associated with steps (5) to (7) also has been entered. For example, it takes from 2 to 7 days to get a response from headquarters to the request for an earnings report (this is noted at step (5)) and from 3 to 36 days to accumulate the evidence associated with a claim.

Historical sources for data were limited to periodic reports to management on district-office operations. Since these reports either were not sufficiently detailed or were prepared with other objectives in mind, they could not, by themselves, supply the data required for the simulation. In addition, since expert opinion also was of limited use, a field study was deemed necessary. Forty-four district offices, studied in the summer and fall of 1967, were located in each of the 11 regions in each of the four classes. Members of the study team were trained in the late spring and summer of 1967. An instructional booklet was prepared in July 1967 and, after the first series of studies which were done in August, revised. Extensive analyses of the results of the study were made; many of these statistical calculations were carried out via a teletypewriter terminal located in the offices of the Operations Research Staff, and linked to a GE 245 computer.

The models were developed by a team which included subject-matter specialists from regional and district offices and from the Bureau of Field Operations, mathematicians, operations analysts from the Operations Research Staff, and computer programmers from the Bureau of Data Processing in the administration headquarters.

Debugging was accomplished by constructing sets of test inputs and running them through the computer programs. Both intermediate and final outputs were monitored. In some cases, exact values for the output were known; in other cases, it was necessary to conclude that the programs were correctly programmed if the data made sense. As is usually the case in debugging, a great deal of additional output was obtained in these runs, to check various details and options of the model. The test data used were entirely hypothetical; they were chosen to ensure that each branch of the program was executed, that erroneous data could be screened out of the models, and that representative data would be processed correctly.

Debugging is not a check on the validity of the model; it merely checks on whether the program correctly implements the model. It does not evaluate the extent to which the program satisfies the desired objectives; however, checks on the validity of the simulation can be made in several ways.

The field study was the major source of performance data against which the district office simulation was checked. To help ensure the validity of the field study results, some of the data obtained in the field study were compared with corresponding data from the district office weekly reports. For example, the weekly reports included data on incoming workloads and number of items processed. These data, as well as a great number of other and more detailed data, were obtained in the field study. A series of statistical analyses was made to compare the results of the field studies to the data in the weekly reports.

A second check to ensure validity involved expert review of results obtained in debugging. The subject-matter experts were given the input for the debugging runs and asked to predict the outputs that could be expected. A special analytical team then resolved any differences between the predictions and the actual results, deciding that either 1) the programs needed further debugging; 2) the submodel was invalid; or 3) the subject matter experts could not predict results efficiently. Some — but only a very few — modifications in the subelements were made as a result of this review.

The simulation record tape is one of the principal devices that is used to ensure validity. This tape, containing a history of the results of all simulation runs, is used in different ways. The major one is to analyze periodically results obtained for what might be called "the standard district office network." In most applications with network or subnetwork-wide objectives, a series of runs is made of the present system, and results are compared with the modified hypothetical system. Because the district office network is reasonably stable, runs of the current system made at different times can be expected to give similar results or to vary in a prescribed way. Such variance can be predicted from a knowledge of the ways in which the system is supposed to have changed since the last simulation application. After each application of the simulation, a calibration analysis is made to determine if there is any significant drift in the standard district office network. This analysis uses function-fitting techniques; most often, the independent variable is time. Clearly, the calibration improves as additional reference data are added — in other words, as more simulations are made.

The district office weekly reports also are compared with the results of the standard network, to see if the real system has drifted in directions which were not anticipated by the group responsible for maintaining the validity of the simulation.

The simulation counted the time in the district office in units of a minute. However, a long period of activity in the district office could be simulated in a short time on the computer. For example, in one early application, a week's activities (about 2500 minutes of activity) of a district office like that depicted in Figure 14.5 were simulated in 15 minutes on an IBM 360/65 computer.

ANNOTATED SUPPLEMENTARY BIBLIOGRAPHY

In addition to the references cited below, there are several periodicals that discuss computer applications in business and management. Three readable periodicals — *Datamation, Computer Decisions,* and *Data Management* — contain many articles relating to business data processing. The periodical *Simulation* is devoted to its title subject; and two other periodicals, the *Journal of the American Society for Information Science* and *Information Storage and Retrieval,* feature articles on information storage and retrieval.

1. Sanders, D. H., *Computers in Business: An Introduction* (2nd ed.) (New York: McGraw-Hill Book Company, 1972). This is a well-written description of computers and how they are used in business organizations.

2. Dearden, J.; McFarlen, F. W.; and Zani, W. M., *Managing Computer-Based Information Systems* (Homewood, Ill.: Richard D. Irwin, Inc., 1971). This is a practical guide to the effective use of the computer and management information systems in a business environment. It includes several case studies.

3. Naylor, T. H., "Simulation and Gaming: Bibliography 19," *Computing Reviews,* Vol. 10, No. 1 (January 1969). This is a useful bibliography on publications in simulation.

4. Maisel, H., and Gnugnoli, G., *Simulation of Discrete Stochastic Systems* (Palo Alto, Ca.: Science Research Associates, Inc., 1972). This provides an excellent summary of simulation methodology, languages, and applications.

5. Madeo, L. A., and Schriber, T. J., *FORTRAN Applications in Business Administration,* Vol. III (Ann Arbor, Mich.: University of Michigan, Graduate School of Business Administration, 1963). A set of 17 well-documented FORTRAN programs for business and management are presented. A reader who is familiar with FORTRAN can see the details, including program listings and flowcharts, of a variety of business applications.

6. Giese, R. L.; Peart, R. M.; and Huber, R. T., "Pest Management," *Science* **187**: 1045–52 (March 21, 1975). Simulation is applied to the control of agricultural pests. Terminals connected to computers use simulations and other tools to help develop strategies for pest control for implementation on farms.

Chapter 15

Applications in Engineering and the Sciences

15.1 INTRODUCTION

Computers first were applied to problems in engineering and the sciences, and such applications continue to be of great importance. Six applications in engineering and the sciences will be discussed in this chapter—two in engineering, one in biology, one in medicine, one that spans all these areas (function fitting), and one in the social sciences. Simulation, another important application area in engineering and the physical and social sciences, was discussed in the previous chapter.

15.2 BALLISTIC CALCULATIONS

One of the first electronic digital computers, the ENIAC, was used in the Ballistic Research Laboratories of the Aberdeen Proving Ground in an engineering application: the preparation of ballistic tables. Ballistic tables are prepared to help artillerymen determine 1) the direction in which to aim a weapon, and 2) the corrections to be made in the aim, using information provided by spotters. Tables indicate the expected range and the direction of flight of the projectile being fired, as well as such things as the time of flight and the velocity of the projectile on impact.

The flight of a projectile can be described using differential equations which consider such known factors as the angle of elevation of the gun, the velocity of the projectile when it is launched, and metereological conditions. However, each type of projectile has its own drag characteristics depending on its shape, surface materials, and spin. As a result, different tables are prepared for each projectile-weapon combination. The critical parameter in preparing a table is called the drag-coefficient of the projectile. The estimation of the drag-coefficient and its use in developing ballistic tables require extensive calculations.

Firings are made and all of the principal parameters are recorded. The results of these firings then are analyzed by means of statistical procedures to determine the drag-coefficient. Least-squares fits (see Section 15.6) are made to the data to estimate the required parameters. The coefficients then are obtained and substituted back in the equations of flight to prepare the ballistic tables.

Before the ENIAC was delivered to the Ballistic Research Laboratories, a team of about 30 statistical clerks was employed to carry out the calculations associated with the preparation of ballistic tables. The ENIAC not only replaced this battery of human calculators but also permitted the use of somewhat more sophisticated techniques in estimating the drag-coefficients.

The calculations themselves were straightforward substitutions in formulas. Although today they are regarded as merely one of many computer applications, during World War II they were extensive and demanding and served as a major impetus for the development of one of the first electronic digital computers.

15.3   MONITORING SEWAGE PUMPS

The computer is a willing servant that will work around the clock, in good weather and bad, and without paid vacations. It is especially well-suited to monotonous jobs such as equipment monitoring.

The city of Baton Rouge, Louisiana, maintains a network of 130 sewage pumping stations (see Figure 15.1). Because the terrain around Baton Rouge is so flat, gravity flow is not sufficient to carry sewage to the treatment plant. At one time, a dozen men were employed to roam around in trucks, checking the pumping stations for malfunctions. Actually, many more men were needed, since only a skeletal force was maintained on nights and weekends, when problems would develop and go unnoticed unless they led to an emergency and a telephone call.

An automatic monitoring system was installed—using an IBM System/7 computer—to control the monitoring function. Now, each of the 130 stations is polled once per hour via a telephone line. Sensors located in the stations monitor such things as fluid level and pump power and generate tone patterns over the telephone line. A program in the System/7 matches the reported patterns with the normal one. Exceptions are reported immediately, both on the system printer (the program also prints out its diagnosis of the problem) and on a TV screen at the waste disposal plant, by means of a color-coded alert pattern.

Fig. 15.1 A sewage pumping station

This program is more effective then the original monitoring system, and costs less. Its success has caused the city of Baton Rouge to extend it in two ways: first, additional functions at each station will be sensed and monitored. Second, some of the activities of the waste treatment plant itself will be sensed and monitored. Ultimately, it is expected that this network of widely dispersed stations will be used to monitor such things as air quality. The computer then could analyze this information in order to obtain patterns, and also could be used to relate these patterns to metereological conditions, traffic flow, industrial activities, etc.

15.4 NUMERICAL TAXONOMY

Taxonomy, the orderly classification of plants and animals according to their natural relationships, has long occupied biological scientists. Some taxonomists would call this *classification,* and would reserve the word "taxonomy" for the theoretical study of the mechanism of classification itself, including its procedures and rules. Until recently, the nature of the work was so subjective that even devoted amateurs could contribute substantially to the field. Quite recently, more elaborate, objective techniques for classification have been developed. Numerical taxonomy, which uses mathematical reasoning in its classification procedures, is one of the new techniques used.

In general, the taxonomist is concerned with either the classification of a large number of organisms or the assignment of a single organism within a pre-existing classification structure. We shall discuss only the way in which a numerical taxonomist attacks the former problem.

When faced with the problem of classifying a large number of organisms, the numerical taxonomist first develops a list of pertinent criteria or characteristics. (Chapter 5 of [1] discusses considerations affecting the choice of characteristics.) Data then are obtained for each characteristic and each organism. These data may indicate merely the presence or absence of a given characteristic (whether a characteristic is present strongly, mildly, weakly, or not at all) or a numerical measurement such as length or weight. The problem is to determine, given all of the data, how best to group the organisms.

Since a realistic problem in taxonomy may involve 500 to 1000 organisms and 100 to 200 characteristics for each organism—about 100,000 pieces of information—automatic assistance clearly is required.

Consider a situation in which we have, say, 500 organisms and 200 characteristics for each organism. One first might code the data for each characteristic numerically, and then summarize the results in a rectangular array, or matrix, in which each organism occupies a single row and each characteristic a single column, thus creating an array with 500 rows and 200 columns. A few of its entries might look like this:

	Char. 1	Char. 2	Char. 3	$\cdots$	Char. 200
Organism 1	1	26.7	3	$\cdots$	1
Organism 2	0	15.8	3	$\cdots$	1
.	.	.	.		.
.	.	.	.		.
.	.	.	.		.
Organism 500	1	21.2	1		0

For characteristics 1 and 200, we have presence or absence; and for characteristic 3, we have four levels of presence or absence. The code used is:

For Char. 1 and 200		For Char. 3	
Code	Meaning	Code	Meaning
0	Absent	0	Absent
1	Present	1	Weakly present
		2	Mildly present
		3	Strongly present

Finally, for characteristic 2, we have a measurement—for example, length in millimeters.

The numerical taxonomist then would compute some sort of measure of the degree of similarity among the different organisms. The simplest of these is the ratio

$$S = \frac{m}{n}$$

where n is the total number of characteristics being compared and m is the number of characteristics that match. To employ this measure, the taxonomist first might reduce all scores to zeros and ones. He might, for example, assign a 1 to a score of 3 or 2 and a 0 to a score of 1 or 0 when dealing with scores in the range 0 to 3. When dealing with measurements such as length, he probably would choose a length arbitrarily to act as the cut between long and short organisms. In this example, he might decide that a length of 20 millimeters or less should be short, and we might code short with a 0 and long with a 1. This means that the entries would become:

	Char. 1	Char. 2	Char. 3	$\cdots$	Char. 200
Organism 1	1	1	1	$\cdots$	1
Organism 2	0	0	1	$\cdots$	1
.	.	.	.		.
.	.	.	.		.
.	.	.	.		.
Organism 500	1	1	0	$\cdots$	0

For this example, n = 200. We could use a computer both to convert the original measurements to 0,1 scores and to compute S for every pair of organisms. We then would get a different kind of array as an output. This time, both the rows and the columns would refer to organisms and the entries would be similarity scores. For example, if we got the array of S scores given below, organism 1 and organism 2 would have a similarity score of 0.245, and organisms 2 and 500 a score of 0.555.

	Organism 1	Organism 2	$\cdots$	Organism 500
Organism 1	1.000	0.245	$\cdots$	0.315
Organism 2	0.245	1.000	$\cdots$	0.555
.	.	.		.
.	.	.		.
.	.	.		.
Organism 500	0.315	0.555	$\cdots$	1.000

The next task would be to group organisms with the largest similarity measures together. This could be done by merely listing all pairs of organisms that had, say, similarity measures greater than 0.80 along with the actual similarity measure. Hopefully, a non-overlapping classification of some subset of the original 500 organisms could be obtained in this way. The critical value of the coefficient then could be reduced to 0.70, and a further classification could be obtained. This process would continue in this way until it became advisable to group the organisms that remained unclassified into a kind of "misfit" classification.

There are many ways to measure the degree of similarity, other than the very simple measure discussed above. Among them are other types of similarity ratios, distance functions, and correlation coefficients. For definitions and discussions of these measures, see [1]. No matter which measure is used, extensive computation and data manipulation are required, and a computer is a necessary tool.

15.5 MEDICAL DIAGNOSIS

Although physicians in research have used computers for a number of years, the physician in regular practice has made little or no use of the computer. This situation slowly is changing, and the direct application of the computer to the treatment of patients is increasing. One such application, the fundamental problem of diagnosis, still is being attacked, for the most part, by research physicians. However, there have been a few applications of the computer to real diagnostic problems.

In addition to quantifying the diagnostic procedure, the computer also uses all of the information in an unbiased way. (It is not, for example, prejudiced by recent experience or personal feelings.) The computer can consider more factors than humans can, does not make computational errors, and is very fast. It has not been applied widely to diagnostic problems yet because it cannot accept easily narrative histories, physical findings, or laboratory reports. When large volumes of medical records can be put routinely into machine-processable form, the techniques of computer-aided diagnosis probably will be applied more widely.

In performing a diagnosis, the physician arrives at a categorization of the patient's state of health from the observations he has made of the patient and his environment. In attacking the problem with the aid of a computer, a specific state is chosen from among a number of mutually exclusive disease states, using information obtained from the patient's medical history, from laboratory tests and physical examinations, and from such things as the relative prevalence of the different disease states in the community at the time that the diagnosis is being made. We shall use the term *symptoms* generically to denote all facts regarding the state of the patient. This means that the term will be applied to information obtained from histories, laboratory tests, and examinations.

The problem can be restated as follows: "Given the patient's symptoms and information about the local incidence of various diseases, what conclusions can be drawn about the chances that the patient is in each of the various disease states?" Note that a probabilistic approach is used. Several probabilistic models have been applied, but the one based on Bayes' theorem is probably the most widely used approach. Bayes' theorem permits us to estimate the probability of the illness, given the symptoms, from the probability of observing the symptoms when the illness is known to be present. Any one of the models lets the physician obtain quantities indicating the probability that each of the different possible diagnoses is the correct one.

Suppose that we are dealing with only two disease states, as follows:

$$d_1: \text{Asian flu}$$
$$d_2: \text{not Asian flu}$$

In this situation, we are concerned only with whether Asian flu is present or absent. This is not a realistic example, since the category d_2 should be further subdivided into other disease states, but it serves our purpose. Let us suppose that we have two patients. One patient, Mr. A, has a set of symptoms, including headache, fever, chills, and general malaise, such that the probability is .95 that if he had the Asian flu he would have these symptoms and only .05 that if he did not have the Asian flu he would have these symptoms. Mr. B, on the other hand, has headache and fever but no chill or general malaise, and the corresponding probabilities in his case are .50 and .50. Let us also assume that it is winter and the Asian flu is "going around," so that the probability of Asian flu in the local population is an appreciable .25. Bayes' theorem now can be applied to estimate the probability that Mr. A and Mr. B are in disease state 1. It turns out that these probabilities are .86 and .25, respectively. This would lead us to conclude that Mr. A probably has the flu but that Mr. B probably does not.

Next let us suppose that Mr. A and Mr. B present the same symptoms but that this time the Asian flu is not "going around," so that the probability of Asian flu in the local population is only .001. Applying Bayes' theorem to these data, we determine the probability that Mr. A is in state 1 to be .02, and the corresponding probability for Mr. B to be .001. Now we would conclude that neither Mr. A nor Mr. B has the flu.

We see that the local incidence of a disease can strongly affect our diagnosis. Note that Mr. B's symptoms cannot differentiate between

d_1 and d_2 (there is a 50-50 chance that either one is appropriate based on his symptoms), so that it is the incidence of the disease in the community that determines the probability of the different disease states in his case.

The preceding example only serves to illustrate the application of Bayes' theorem to medical diagnosis and does not indicate the processing and computational effort needed to apply this approach. Real problems might have 10, 20, 30, or more disease states. The number of different symptom sets that might be observed is enormous.

An algorithm first must be written to reduce the information on symptoms and their relation to disease states to a precise quantity—namely, the probability that a certain symptom will be observed if a given disease state is present. An algorithm also must be written to reduce information on the locale, time of year, and other factors to an estimate of the probability that each of the possible disease states is present in the community at that time. The computation of the diagnostic probabilities (the probability of the various disease states in view of the symptoms) follows from Bayes' theorem, and is the least demanding computational step.

To be successful, this approach requires a great deal of quantified information that is not readily available. The various probabilities of disease states and of symptom sets corresponding to disease states might be estimated from a national medical-information file. Without such a rich source of data, probabilities estimated in this way can do little more than offer some guidance to the diagnostician. The diagnostician must continue to combine such estimates with his own experience and non-quantified observations to arrive at a valid diagnosis.

15.6 FUNCTION FITTING—LEAST SQUARES

The problem of how best to describe or summarize data that seem to follow a smooth pattern when they are plotted has long plagued scientists and engineers. In many applications, the scientist is willing merely to draw a smooth curve through the data and to use the resulting graph to represent his function. Frequently, however, it is desirable to specify mathematically some functional relation between the plotted variables. This presents two problems: 1) how to determine what type of mathematical function is best to use; and 2) given the type of function to be used, how to choose from among all functions of this type the one that fits the data best. Scientists sometimes rely on a mathematical model of the process being studied to decide on the appropriate type of function, and then use *least-squares techniques* to choose the one best function of this type. The least-squares criterion involves choosing that function which minimizes the sums of the squares of the differences between the observed values and the fitted function.

At times, a scientist could choose to use some other criterion for selecting the best function—for example, minimizing the maximum difference between the fitted function and the observed data. This is called *Chebyshev's* (or the *minimax*) *criterion*. The minimax procedure might be appropriate when a scientist was calculating a relation (such as a planetary orbit) or a known mathematical function, in which case minimizing the greatest possible error in a table might be his goal. However, when fitting functions to experimental data, it probably would be preferable to use the least-squares criterion, because a body of statistical methodology has been developed that is applicable when least-squares are used. This theory permits the scientist to make such statements as "chances are 95 in 100 that a yield of this chemical at a temperature of 84°C will be between 6.14 and 6.32 grams," or "chances are less than 1 in 20 that the economic model that we are proposing could have accounted for these data." In short, there is a framework which enables the scientist to state in probabilistic terms the inferences that he draws from his experiments.

Suppose that we wish to fit a function by least squares to the points plotted in Figure 15.2. Suppose also that it was decided that a straight-line fit of the form $y = ax + b$ would be appropriate. The next step would be to determine a and b in order to minimize the sum of the squares of the vertical distances of the points from the fitted line. These distances, with sign, are called residuals (all this is illustrated in Figure 15.2). As the values of a and b are changed, so too are the residuals and the sum of their squares. Clearly, estimating a and b by trial and error could be a long, drawn-out procedure. Fortunately, mathematicians have been able to determine explicit formulas for a and b as a function of the observations (the coordinates of the observed data). A computer can be applied to the problem; programs have been written that will calculate not only a and b, but also all residuals, estimates of the standard error of a and b, and other statistics. Some of these programs even will plot the results.

The calculations for fitting a straight line can be extensive, especially if the additional information is obtained, and the use of a computer is justified. However, the availability of a computer has made it possible to consider fitting even more extensive, complex relationships. Program libraries often contain a variety of programs for fitting functions to data. These frequently include:

1. A program to fit a straight line,

2. A program to fit a multiple linear regression,

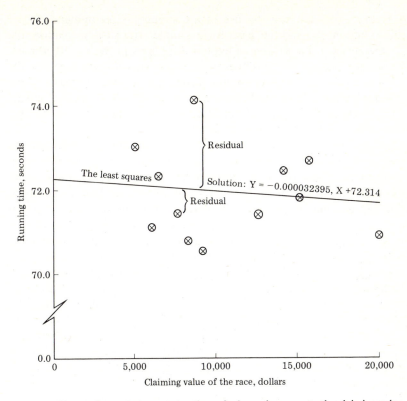

Fig. 15.2 Observations relating running time of a horse in a race to the claiming value of that race, illustrating getting a straight line by least squares

3. A program to fit a series of multiple linear regressions in order to pick the best one, and

4. More general least-squares programs that can handle other types of relationships.

The first of these functions was discussed above. We now will define each of the other three types of functions, and discuss the computer programs that have been used to implement them.

A multiple linear regression is the simplest relation which can be used in the case of several independent variables. The dependent variable is assumed to be a weighted sum of the independent variables, with a constant added. More specifically, the function is:

$$y = a_0 + a_1x_1 + a_2x_2 + \cdot \cdot \cdot + a_jx_j$$

The parameters to be fitted are the coefficients $a_0, a_1, \ldots, a_j$. If the number of parameters to be estimated $(j+1)$ is large, the calculations are very extensive and the use of a computer is recommended. For this function, as was the case for a simple straight-line relation, the coefficients can be written as explicit functions of the observed data. Computer programs have been written to provide estimates of the $j + 1$ coefficients. These programs frequently provide estimates of the standard error of the coefficients and other statistics, such as partial correlation coefficients, that indicate how well the dependent variable fits subsets of the independent variables.

Frequently, a researcher uses the observed data to understand the relationship between a dependent variable and a large number of independent variables. He wishes to allow the data to tell him not just what the relationship should be but which variables contribute to that relationship in a meaningful way. He wants not only to fit a function, but also to screen out variables that are not relevant. One way to do this is to fit multiple linear regressions using subsets of the independent variables, establish criteria for adding or deleting variables, and proceed to fit to many such subsets until the relevant group of independent variables are found. Computer programs can do this in a variety of ways. For example, the dependent variable can be fitted to the most relevant independent variable, and then variables can be added one at a time until an additional variable makes no important contribution to improving the fit. Another way is first to fit to all variables and then delete variables one at a time, as long as the effect of deleting a variable has no significant impact on the relationship. A third way is to fit to all possible combinations of variables, selecting from the totality of fits the one that seems to make the best sense. Clearly, the third approach is a feasible alternative only if there are relatively few independent variables — say, no more than five or six.

Many program libraries contain a generalized linear least-squares program or some similarly named program that can be used to fit other kinds of relationships. In some cases, this may be the only least-squares program in the library, and it would have to be used for fitting such simple relations as a straight-line or a multiple-linear regression with a very few independent variables. This is not desirable because the generalized linear least-squares program is difficult to use, and a user who has a relatively simple relation frequently has to master complex notations and input procedures. It is better to have separate programs for fitting straight lines and multiple linear regressions.

What are the computer programs that are used to fit functions like? Their characteristics are demonstrated by a program to fit multiple linear regressions in a stepwise fashion. This program, developed by M. A. Efroymson [2], proceeds by adding variables one at a time. Because a variable thought to be significant at first may not be significant after several variables have been added to an equation, this program back-checks and deletes such variables from the equation.

The program has been coded to minimize its storage requirements. If M is the number of observations and N is the number of variables, this program requires approximately $3M$ words of storage for data and $N^2 + 5N + 2M$ words for intermediate results. In addition, the program itself requires about 3000 words of storage.

The running time of the program is estimated to be:

$$2(N + 2)^2[M(\nu + \mu) + N(\nu + \mu + \omega/2)]$$

where ν is the addition time, μ the multiplication time, and ω the division time. Thus, for example, if we used 100 observations to fit 10 variables, we should expect that 3650 words of storage would be required and that the time required to carry out 31,680 additions, 31,680 multiplications, and 1440 divisions would be used to complete these calculations.

15.7 CONTENT ANALYSIS

Content analysis has been defined as "the use of replicable and valid methods for making specific inferences from text to other states or properties of its source."[3] The objective is to examine a text in some systematic way to answer questions about its source. Content analysis has been used to help to resolve authorship of the Federalist Papers [4], to explore the concept of style in literature [5], and to determine the attitudes and beliefs of political leaders [6]. Books, magazines, newspapers, and even pottery fragments and psychoanalytical interviews have been grist for its mill. We will discuss just one example of content analysis in this section—Holsti's work determining the attitudes and beliefs of political leaders.

The key to the approach used by Holsti is a dictionary of words which the investigator believes are particularly indicative of an author's attitudes. Each word is evaluated on a scale of from +3 to −3 with respect to each of three criteria. The first criterion can be thought of as good or favorable (+3) versus bad or hostile (−3); the second as strong (+3) versus weak (−3); and the third as active (+3) versus passive (−3). Thus, for example, the word *accost* is scored as −3, 2, 2; that is, it is a very hostile, strong, and active word.

The text is searched for words that appear in the dictionary and analyzed to be sure that the meaning is understood clearly. Since the presence or absence of a word by itself may not indicate the author's attitude, the way in which a word is used must be considered. The investigator simplifies the analysis by precoding the text by hand. The text is scanned, and parts of speech (e.g., subject, verbs, objects, and modifiers) are labeled, thus permitting these keywords to be connected properly.

Tables then are prepared summarizing the perceived qualities of subjects using the dictionary and the scales that were assigned to the words in the dictionary. All positive and negative scores associated with dictionary terms that appear with the subject in the text are added. In examining a text prepared by Dag Hammarskjold, for example, Holsti found that a total of 78 good or favorable scores and only 1 negative score was associated with descriptions of the United Nations. Similarly, 113 strong points and only 3 weak points, and 86 active points and 25 passive points were associated with this same subject in the text.

Tables also are prepared that summarize attitudes towards objects. Outputs are available that summarize the author's attitudes toward a subject and each of the objects with which that subject is connected in the text.

An investigator has many options in using this program. For example, he can add to the dictionary arbitrarily in a particular analysis. This is especially useful, since the program automatically lists all words in the text that do not appear in the dictionary. The investigator can look at this list to see whether he should add some of these words to the dictionary and rerun the program to improve his insight.

It is clear that use of this program requires a major effort in data entry. The whole text must be encoded manually. The computer time required, once this has been done, is variable. In one case, analysis of 16 documents totaling 92,000 words required about 17 minutes on an IBM 7090. This run produced a total of 416 summary tables for a variety of combinations of subjects and objects.

REFERENCES

1. Sokal, R. R., and Sneath, P. H. A., *Numerical Taxonomy* (San Francisco: W. H. Freeman and Company, 1973).

2. Efroymson, M. A., "Multiple Regression Analysis," in Ralson, A., and Wilf, H. S. (eds.), *Mathematical Methods for Digital Computers* (New York: John Wiley and Sons, Inc., 1960).

3. Krippendorff, K., in Gerbner, G.; Holsti, O.; Krippendorff, K.; Paisley, W. J.; and Stone, P. J. (eds.), *The Analysis of Communication Content* (New York: John Wiley and Sons, Inc., 1969).

4. Mosteller, F., and Wallace, D. L., *Inference and Disputed Authorship: The Federalist* (Reading, Mass.: Addison-Wesley, 1964).

5. Sedelow, S. Y., and Sedelow, Jr., W. A., "A Preface to Computational Stylistics," in Leed, J. (ed.), *The Computer and Literary Style* (Kent, O.: Kent State University Press, 1966).

6. Holsti, O., *Content Analysis for the Social Sciences and the Humanities* (Reading, Mass.: Addison-Wesley, 1969).

ANNOTATED SUPPLEMENTARY BIBLIOGRAPHY

Sokal and Sneath's book, above, is one of the best introductions to the methods of numerical taxonomy currently available. *The Analysis of Communication Content* is one of the best overviews of content analysis that currently is available. Six additional references are given below, in order of discussion in this chapter — two on monitoring and controlling industrial processes, a third on numerical taxonomy, two on function fitting, and the last one on numerical techniques for solving problems in engineering and the sciences.

1. Cornish, H. L.; Horton, W. L.; et al., *Computerized Process Control* (New York: Hobbs, Dorman and Company, 1968). This provides an overview of the use of computers in monitoring and controlling industrial processes, and includes a six-industry survey of the state of the art at that time.

2. Smith, C. L., "Digital Control of Industrial Processes," *Computing Surveys,* Vol. 2, No. 3:211–42 (September 1970). This is a good survey article on process control, which concludes with a comprehensive bibliography.

3. Maisel, H., and Hill, L. R., *A KWIC Index of Publications in Numerical Taxonomy in the Period 1948–1968* (Washington, D.C.: Academic Computation Center, Georgetown University, 1969). This is a useful, keyword in context, indexed bibliography to 20 years of taxonometric publications.

4. Acton, F. S., *Analysis of Straight Line Data* (New York: Dover Publications, 1966). (This is a paperback version of a book originally published by John Wiley and Sons, Inc., in 1959.) If you wish to fit a straight line to data, this is the most comprehensive source for guidance.

5. Draper, N. R., and Smith, H., *Applied Regression Analysis.* (New York: John Wiley and Sons, Inc., 1966). Here is an excellent source for useful information on function-fitting of any kind.

6. Ginsberg, M., "A Guide to the Literature of Modern Numerical Mathematics," *Computing Reviews,* Bibliography 36, Vol. 16, No. 2:83–97 (February 1975).

Chapter 16

Computer Centers

16.1 INTRODUCTION

Computer facilities are an expensive resource which, to be used effectively, require a substantial supporting staff. As a result, most organizations with sizeable computer facilities organize and structure their operation and use by means of a computer center.

In this chapter, we will discuss the computer center from several points of view. First, the organizational structures will be outlined; then the staffing requirements will be discussed; and finally the center will be described as it appears to a user.

The discussion in this chapter is intended to let a user understand computer centers and how they function. Such insight should help him to use his own facility more effectively. This discussion is not intended as a definitive review of computer centers; however, more detailed references are available [1,2].

16.2 BUSINESS COMPUTER CENTERS

Figure 16.1 contains an organizational chart for a typical computer center in a business environment. This center frequently is called the data processing department. The staff of the center provides services in the areas of computer operation, programming support, and other kinds of user assistance. Each kind of service is provided by a separate group. The organization chart in Figure 16.1 reflects this separation.

The director of the center supervises the whole department. He is assisted by a clerical staff and, if the center is large, by an assistant director. In some centers, the clerical staff is concentrated in the director's office, and serves as a pool to be used by all employees of the center.

Two kinds of programming services are provided. One group, composed of *systems programmers*, is responsible for maintaining and adopting the system software, especially the operating system, which usually is provided by the manufacturer of the computers in use. Modern, sophisticated operating systems are well-understood and appreciated by only a few employees of a computer manufacturer, who are not readily available to customers of the manufacturer. To make the greatest possible use of its equipment, an installation should develop its own expertise in the operating system and other manufacturer-supplied software. It may be that only one or two systems programmers are required. However, if data bases and information retrieval systems are to be developed or other novel applications of the computer are to be implemented, a larger systems programming staff is required.

The other service group is the *applications programming* staff, which, as the name implies, writes programs to meet specific data-processing requirements. This staff may be large if many applications are to be programmed, and may be organized on a project basis. A senior programmer serves as the project leader, and several other programmers serve on his team. The leader reports to the supervisor of the applications programming staff who, in turn, reports to the chief of programming services for the center.

The operations group is responsible for running the jobs that the computer is to process. Usually, one supervisor is responsible for each shift, and a group reports to him. Some computer centers maintain operations at several locations; this also may be a basis for grouping the operating staff. For example, in Figure 16.1, the plant computer operations staff is one group within operations.

The user services group provides many other types of user services. It may prepare input via keypunches, key-to-tape devices, optical scanning equipment, or some combination of these approaches. It also may set up routine production runs of functioning programs. The staff must be able to respond to a request for a run from a user — to assemble the necessary input materials and submit them to the center so that they can be run on the computer. This group reviews the output, and ensures that the required information has been obtained and is in a form which suits the user. For example, they might *burst* (separate the pages of) the output and assemble it into reports.

Most computer centers accumulate many magnetic tapes, several disk packs, and a variety of manuals and other publications. Control over these items must be maintained: each tape and disk pack should

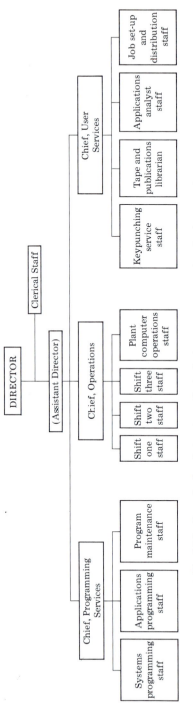

Fig. 16.1 Organizational structure of a typical computer center in a business environment

be numbered; its contents and use should be recorded in a log; and the tape or disk pack should be stored in a safe place. Access to this collection should be limited. A record of where the tape or disk is located should be kept in the log. The log thus should contain, for each tape or disk: identification, a list of the information on that tape or disk, the users of this information, and the current location of the tape or disk. This log-keeping function resembles some of the functions of a librarian. Since publications also are accumulated in a computer center, the computer center librarian frequently maintains control of these, as well.

The *applications analysts* are an especially important component of the computer center. (They also are called *systems analysts* or *applications systems analysts*.) They usually are the first contact a user has with the center, they help him to formulate his problem so that it can be solved by a computer. In some organizations, they are part of the programming staff; in others, they are in the user services group. We have placed them in the user services group in the organization charted in Figure 16.1.

16.3   SCIENTIFIC AND ACADEMIC COMPUTER CENTERS

The organization of a scientific or academic computer center differs from that of a business center in several ways. In the former center, users are better acquainted with such things as programming, the operating system, and the job control language. The volume of data input probably is smaller, and the applications tend to be more sophisticated. These differences should result in an organization something like that in Figure 16.2.

The scientific or academic computer center is likely to be divided into only two major staffing groups: one for programming and one for operations. The programming staff consists of fewer applications programmers and more systems programmers than does a business computer center. A group of consultants is available to assist the user in formulating problems (like the applications analyst in the business computer center), in solving difficult programming problems encountered in developing or debugging the program, and in learning new programming languages. In an academic environment, consultants are available to assist students with routine procedures in using a computer facility.

Although the computer operations staff would be similar to that found in the business computer center, major differences in other user support staff are likely. There may be no keypunching group, or a very small keypunching group may be supervised by the operations

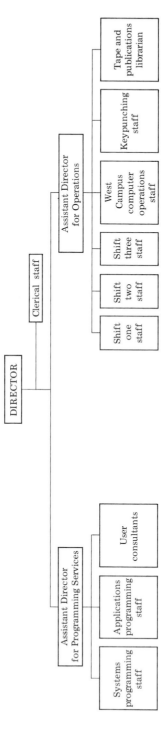

Fig. 16.2 Organizational structure of a typical computer center in a scientific or university environment

supervisor. No job setup staff is needed and, as we already have indicated, the applications analyst would be a part of the programming group.

16.4 STAFFING QUALIFICATIONS

Each systems programmer should be able to program the installation's computer in its assembler language, and be thoroughly familiar with the operating system. As a minimum, he should have completed the relevant training programs offered by the computer manufacturer and should be able to generate the operating system. *Generating an operating system* is the equivalent of installing it. Operating systems are revised and enhanced from time to time, and new versions should be implemented if they contain desirable improvements. Although it may be possible to generate the operating system merely by following the manufacturer's instructions step-by-step, frequently it is necessary to improvise. Each systems programmer should be adept at improvising.

At least one member of the systems programming staff should have more extensive experience, enabling him to modify the operating system successfully so that special features that make the system more efficient or permit users to do as they wish can be implemented. This is especially important at academic and research computer centers. It probably is desirable for systems programmers to have obtained a master's degree in computer science and to have gained some experience in generating and modifying operating systems.

The applications programming staff should know the applications areas with which they must deal, as well as be proficient in at least one high-level programming language. Many companies find that an on-the-job training program can create capable applications programmers. However, formal education leading to a degree in the appropriate applications area, with several courses in computer science or a minor in computer science, is a valuable background for applications programmers. An applications programmer must be able to communicate effectively in order to deal with the user and to document his efforts adequately.

The qualifications of an applications analyst are similar to those of an applications programmer, except that the ability to communicate, both orally and in writing, is even more critical. Since applications analysts deal frequently and directly with the computer facility users, they must be able to help each user formulate his problem and translate the solution into an effective specification for programming.

In some computer centers, the senior applications programmers and the applications analysts are chosen from among the applications programmers. In such centers, most hiring is done at the junior level. Other centers find that the infusion of new senior talent from outside sources frequently introduces new ways of doing things that can improve the center operations. In general, a combination of these approaches is advisable.

In many academic computer centers, faculty members holding shared or full appointments provide consultant services in the areas of systems programming, problem formulation, and applications programming. Many functions of the staff are undertaken by student assistants who are capable of working at a junior level in both the programming and operations groups. For this reason, in some academic computer centers the applications and/or systems programming staffs include only one or two full-time employees who direct the activities of several student assistants.

Figure 16.3 is a summary of the education, experience, and special qualifications associated with the positions of systems programmer, applications programmer, and applications analyst.

There are many training programs for computer operators. Some companies prefer to prepare their better clerical employees for such work via on-the-job training in computer operations and/or classes conducted by the computer manufacturer. Others prefer to hire persons who have completed an intensive six-months to one-year training program, graduates of technical institutes or junior colleges, or persons who have been employed as operators elsewhere.

Most other operations personnel either are promoted from within and given on-the-job training, or hired after having done similar work at another computer center.

16.5 THE USER'S VIEW

A computer center can be a formidable challenge to a potential first-time user of the facility. It contains unfamiliar equipment and personnel; it even may pose a kind of threat, since a new way of doing things is associated with "automating an operation." Experienced users also may encounter difficulties in dealing with the computer center.

Most computer centers publish a guide or some other introduction to facilities and services. If the guide is well-written, it is worth reading. Some centers hold short, informal courses to explain the center's operation and facilities to the novice. Each of these is a good starting point, but sooner or later a user must discuss his needs with a member of the staff. If applications analysts are available, they should be consulted first. If the center has no applications analyst staff or its equivalent, the best first step is to talk with the center director and allow him to suggest the next step.

Position	Desirable Education	Minimum Experience Required to Do Independent Work	Special Qualifications
Systems programmer	Master's degree in computer science	3 years	Thorough knowledge of the whole computer system, especially all aspects of its software. Ability to program in an assembly language.
Applications programmer	Bachelor's degree in applications area with a minor in computer science*	1 year	Knowledge of the applications area and proficiency in at least one high-level programming language. Ability to communicate orally and in writing.
Applications analyst	Bachelor's degree in applications area with several computer science courses	3 years	Thorough familiarity with operating procedures and applications areas of special importance to employer. Thorough knowledge of relevant software, especially program library, available at local installation and elsewhere. Ability to communicate orally and in writing.

*Others might recommend a bachelor's degree in computer science with a minor in the applications area.

Fig. 16.3 Education, experience, and special qualifications associated with three important staff positions at a computer center

Once a contact has been made, the emphasis shifts to getting the application on the computer. Most users have deadlines that, from the point of view of the center staff, are unrealistically short. Using an existing program, if possible, substantially reduces the length of time required to get an application on the computer. The catalog of programs that already have been implemented at the center should be consulted, as well as the catalog provided by the user's group set up by the manufacturer, or one that might be available from another source (for example, the Collected Algorithms of the Association for Computing Machinery). Don't let the staff of the computer center tell you that no catalogs are available; go to a supervisor if you think that the staff is not helping you locate a program that may suit your purposes. As a general rule, if you have a statistical application or a routine scientific calculation, a program is available for your use. But even if you require a somewhat special-purpose program, it may be available.

If a new program is to be developed by the applications programming staff of the center, try to keep in touch with the applications programmer who is responsible for your program. But don't be a pest! If you think he's taking too long to complete your program, talk to him, and then — if he gives you an unsatisfactory response — to his supervisor. Be cooperative. Be prepared to help him develop a set of test data. Maintain sufficient contact with the programmer to make sure that any compromises to your objectives that he makes in developing the program are not detrimental.

Once the program has been written, it must be run on the computer to produce the results you need. If substantial keypunching or other input preparation is required, contact the center staff. Possibly they can arrange to have your keypunching done, if they are not staffed to do it themselves. (This is especially true at academic centers, where students are on-call for part-time keypunching assistance.) If the volume of input preparation is small, you may find it easier to do your own keypunching.

If a job setup staff is available, they will make the runs for you and return the output to you. Of course, they must be told just what it is that you need; that is, you must specify all the options required for your run. Some job setup staffs have developed forms for frequently used programs. It may only be necessary for you to complete the form.

Interpreting the output is usually a straightforward process. However, there are pitfalls: one is that a user may be so inundated with data that he loses track of where he is. To avoid this, logs should be maintained of outputs and their results if a long series of runs is to be made. Similarly, summary tables should be prepared if there is a great deal of output in a single run.

A second difficulty arises when the output is surprising. Usually, if the results are correct, these surprising results are the most important ones; but first, some checks should be made to be sure that the results are correct. Usually it is desirable to do the checking along with an applications analyst, who may in turn call on an applications or systems programmer (depending on the nature of the diagnostic effort required) to be sure that the results are trustworthy.

In summary, a user of a computer center who wants to use a computer to help solve his problem should see that the following steps are completed:

1. Contact the center,
2. Formulate the problem for computer solution,
3. Find or develop an appropriate computer program,
4. Make a series of runs using the program,
5. Interpret and record the output, and
6. Revise the program as necessary and continue to make runs until the objectives of the use of the program are satisfied.

The staff of the center should be able to assist a user in completing each of these steps. However, the user is responsible for making sure that each step is initiated, successfully implemented, and completed. The center staff should not necessarily be made responsible for getting some or all of the user's job done.

Exercises

1. What are the major organizational groups in a business data processing department, and what kind of services does each provide?

2. How do the activities and organizational structure of a scientific or academic computer center differ from that of a business data processing department?

3. If you were promoting from within, what position would you expect your most capable extroverted applications programmers to fill? Why? How about your most capable introverted applications programmers?

4. Which position in a computer center would most probably be filled by persons holding, at most, an associate level degree? Which by those holding a bachelor's degree? Which by those holding a graduate degree?

5. What considerations enter into the choice of an appropriate first point of contact in a computer center by a user?

6. If you need a computer program, what are the major sources for leads to an appropriate program?

7. You are a computer user who was surprised by the results of a run. What do you do next?

REFERENCES

1. Ditri, A. E.; Shaw, J. C.; and Atkins, W., *Managing the EDP Function* (New York: McGraw-Hill Book Company, 1971).

2. Withington, F. G., *The Organization of the Data Processing Function* New York: John Wiley and Sons, Inc., 1972).

ANNOTATED SUPPLEMENTARY BIBLIOGRAPHY

Many articles relating to computer centers and their administration are published each year. For example, *Computing Reviews* has a major classification category called "Administration of Computer Centers," and lists under this heading the following subcategories: General, Administrative Policies, Personnel Training, Operating Procedures, Equipment Evaluation, Surveys of Computing Centers, and Miscellaneous. The annual bibliography and subject matter index published by *Computing Reviews* for 1973 contains a total of about 130 references to these categories. In view of this, an extensive bibliography was not compiled for inclusion in this section. However, a brief bibliography is given below. In addition, it is noted that:

A. The appropriate listings in *Computing Reviews* are probably the best place to find references on a particular aspect of computer centers.

B. References 6, 11, 12, 13, and 19 in the Annotated Supplementary Bibliography for Chapter 6 and the two books referenced above are relevant.

C. An organization called the Data Processing Management Association (DPMA) is concerned with the administration of computer facilities. This organization and its meetings might be of interest to persons who wish to learn more about computer centers.

1. *Datamation*, Vol 17, No. 5 (March 1, 1971). This issue of *Datamation* contains three articles on the nature and management of university computer centers, with special emphasis on the question of centralized vs. decentralized facilities.

2. *Proceedings of the Annual Computer Personnel Research Conferences.* As the title implies, these are comprehensive references on what is cur-

rent in the selection, training, evaluation, and other aspects of the management of personnel employed in computer centers.

3. Rettus, R. C., and Smith, R. A., "Accounting Control of Data Processing," *IBM Systems Journal,* Vol. 11, No. 1:74–92 (1972). This article has been described as the best on the subject of costing out the data-processing function in a business.

4. Van Tassel, D., *Computer Security Management* (Englewood Cliffs, N.J.: Prentice-Hall Book Company, 1972). This is an excellent comprehensive reference on the subject of computer security, and a useful book if you are interested in problems of securing files and facilities.

5. Weinwurm, G. F., (ed.), *On the Management of Computer Programming* (Princeton, N.J.: Auerbach Publishers, Inc., 1970). This book is a collection of articles on the management of one kind of personnel resource in the computer center: the programmer.

Appendix

Powers of 2 from the First Through the Ninety-Third

POWER OF 2				EXPONENT
			2.	1
			4.	2
			8.	3
			16.	4
			32.	5
			64.	6
			128.	7
			256.	8
			512.	9
		1	024.	10
		2	048.	11
		4	096.	12
		8	192.	13
		16	384.	14
		32	768.	15
		65	536.	16
		131	072.	17
		262	144.	18
		524	288.	19
	1	048	576.	20
	2	097	152.	21
	4	194	304.	22
	8	388	608.	23
	16	777	216.	24
	33	554	432.	25
	67	108	864.	26
	134	217	728.	27
	268	435	456.	28
	536	870	912.	29
	1 073	741	824.	30
	2 147	483	648.	31
	4 294	967	296.	32
	8 589	934	592.	33
	17 179	869	184.	34
	34 359	738	368.	35
	68 719	476	736.	36
	137 438	953	472.	37
	274 877	906	944.	38
	549 755	813	888.	39
1	099 511	627	776.	40
2	199 023	255	552.	41
4	398 046	511	104.	42
8	796 093	022	208.	43
17	592 186	044	416.	44

Powers of 2 from the First Through the Ninety-Third

POWER OF 2   EXPONENT

Power of 2	Exponent
35 184 372 088 832.	45
70 368 744 177 664.	46
140 737 488 355 328.	47
281 474 976 710 656.	48
562 949 953 421 312.	49
1 125 899 906 842 624.	50
2 251 799 813 685 248.	51
4 503 599 627 370 496.	52
9 007 199 254 740 992.	53
18 014 398 509 481 984.	54
36 028 797 018 963 968.	55
72 057 594 037 927 936.	56
144 115 188 075 855 872.	57
288 230 376 151 711 744.	58
576 460 752 303 423 488.	59
1 152 921 504 606 846 976.	60
2 305 843 009 213 693 952.	61
4 611 686 018 427 387 904.	62
9 223 372 036 854 775 808.	63
18 446 744 073 709 551 616.	64
36 893 488 147 419 103 232.	65
73 786 976 294 838 206 464.	66
147 573 952 589 676 412 928.	67
295 147 905 179 352 825 856.	68
590 295 810 358 705 651 712.	69
1 180 591 620 717 411 303 424.	70
2 361 183 241 434 822 606 848.	71
4 722 366 482 869 645 213 696.	72
9 444 732 965 739 290 427 392.	73
18 889 465 931 478 580 854 784.	74
37 778 931 862 957 161 709 568.	75
75 557 863 725 914 323 419 136.	76
151 115 727 451 828 646 838 272.	77
302 231 454 903 657 293 676 544.	78
604 462 909 807 314 587 353 088.	79
1 208 925 819 614 629 174 706 176.	80
2 417 851 639 229 258 349 412 352.	81
4 835 703 278 458 516 698 824 704.	82
9 671 406 556 917 033 397 649 408.	83
19 342 813 113 834 066 795 298 816.	84
38 685 626 227 668 133 590 597 632.	85
77 371 252 455 336 267 181 195 264.	86
154 742 504 910 672 534 362 390 528.	87
309 485 009 821 345 068 724 781 056.	88
618 970 019 642 690 137 449 562 112.	89
1 237 940 039 285 380 274 899 124 224.	90
2 475 880 078 570 760 549 798 248 448.	91
4 951 760 157 141 521 099 596 496 896.	92
9 903 520 314 283 042 199 192 993 792.	93

INDEX

academic computer center 347–49
access time **86**
ALGOL 118–19
algorithm 13, 137, **138**–57
alphameric **69**–70
alphanumeric **65**
American National Standards
   Institute (ANS) **80**
amortization problem 3, 14
applications 297–355
  amortization problem 3, 14
  ballistic calculations 330–1
  bridge point-count 155–56, 177
  problem 219, 253, 277
  classification in biology **332**
  combinational problem 177
  content analysis **341**–42
  diagnosis with a computer 335–37
  educational 108–9, 304
  Euclidean algorithm 156, 177
  federal government 302–3, 322–28
  Fibonacci numbers **154**–55, 165, 219,
    253, 277
  function fitting 337–41
  gross pay problem 9, 14, 30, 46,
    61–62, 177
  health care 305, 313–17, 335–37
  hospital information system **313**–17
  information storage and retrieval
    packages 127
  information systems **301**–2, 313–17
  intelligent machines 307–9
  inventory control 318–19
  law 306
  leasts squares **337**–41
  Manhattan island problem 142, 219
  means and standard deviations 155,
    165, 198–99, 208–9, 219, 238,
    244–45, 262–63, 271–72
  medical diagnosis 335–37
  monitoring sewage pumps 331–32
  multiple linear regression 338–41
  Newton's formula for square
    root **144**, 205–6, 242
  numerical taxonomy 332–35
  payroll problem 74–76, 166–77
  privacy 301–3
  programming packages 127–30
  proprietary software **114**
  quadratic roots problem 178, 219,
    253, 277
  savings problem 139–40, 151–52,
    165, 219

scientific packages 127
second industrial revolution 299–300
Sieve of Eratosthenes **141**–42, 166
Simpson's rule problem 178, 219,
   253, 277
simulation **119**–20, 319–28
software overview 113–14
sort **75**, 150, 153, 155, 165, 177, 219,
   253, 277
square root problem 143–47, 152–53,
   165, 204–6, 241–43
statistical packages 127
sum 16, 23–25, 30, 34, 40–44, 48,
   53–57, 61
taxonomy **332**
tuition problem 188–90, 200, 228–31,
   233, 238–40, 244, 260–61, 263
wired city 306–7
applications analyst **347**, 349–50
applications programmer 345, 347, 349
applications programming packages
   127–30
array **75**–79, 186–87, 226, 257–58
ASCII **69**–70, 73, 80
assembly languages **115**
auxiliary storage 8, **84**, 90–5

ballistic calculations 330–1
base 66
BASIC 47–62, 256–77
  annotating inputs 264–5
  annotating outputs 263–4
  arrays 257–8
  arrays, input and output 270
  assignment statement 50
  built-in functions **259**
  character set **256**–7
  comparisons 55, **259**
  constant 49
    character string **263**
    literal **263**
  corrections 48
  DATA statement 265–7
  debugging 274–6
  DIM statement 258
  dimensioning arrays **258**
  END statement **49**
  errors 57
  expressions 259
  FOR statement **268**–69
  format-free input/output **52**
  GOSUB statement **271**–74
  IF statement **55**

input/output overview 51
INPUT statement **51**, 53
LET statement **50**
lists **257**
loop 268–69
matrices 257–58
NEXT statement **268**–69
off-line input operations 267
   arithmetic 258
   comparison 259
   priority of execution 259
PRINT statement **52**, 275–6
READ statement **265**–7
REM statement **49**
remarks 49
RETURN statement **271**–4
skipping lines 274
statement numbers 48–9
subroutines **271**–4
tables 257–8
variable 50, **257**
baud **112**
binary digits **67**
binary representation **66**–7
bits **67**
branching **23, 40**, 53
bridge point-count problem 155–6, 177,
  219, 253, 277
Burroughs B6500 computer 70, 72
bursting of printed outputs **345**
business computer center 344–7
byte **69**

capacities of storage devices and
  media 93
card punch **99**
card reader **99**
card reader/punch 99
cathode ray tube terminals 97, 100,
  107–8
central processing unit 4, **5**
chain printer **101**–2
character printer **101**
Chebychev criterion **338**
classification in biology **332**
COBOL 117–8
combinatorial problem 177
COMIT 125
common carrier **111**
communication facilities 110–3
communications controller **13**
compilation 115–6
compiler 6, **115**–6
compiler validation system for
  COBOL **117**–8
concatenation **125**, 126
connect time **59**
content analysis **341**–2
control cards 115

control statements **94**
conversion among bases 2, 8 and 16
  67–8, 69
conversion to and from base 10 66,
  69, 73
core storage **84**–6
correctness of a program **278**
costs of programs and programming
  281–2
costs of storage devices 86
counter **23, 40, 54**
CPU **5**
cycle time **82**
cylinder printer **102**

data base **74**
data set **74**
data transmission 110–3
debugging
  BASIC **57**, 274–6
  FORTRAN **28**, 215–9
  general 150–3, 278–9
  PL/I **44**, 250–3
desk checking a program **216**
destructive read **85**
detailed flowchart **160**
diagnosis with a computer 335–7
differences in pairs of numbers 30, 46,
  61, 177
disk storage, magnetic 91–3, 96
  cylinder **93**
  track **93**
documentation 282–92
  abstract 283
  example 285–92
  flowcharts 284–5
  problem description 283
  run decks 284
  source deck 284
  user information 283–4
drum storage, magnetic **90**

ease of use of a program 280
EBCDIC **69**–70, 73
educational applications 108–9, 304
effectiveness of a program **278**
efficiency of a program **280**–2, 293–4
electrostatic printer **103**
end-of-file 147–8, 169
end-of-file mark **169**
ENIAC computer 330
enumeration **7**
error checking 27, 43
errors in implementing algorithms 153–4
error rate in transmission 113
Euclidean Algorithm 156, 177
execution cycle **5**, 82, 87
execution time **82**
exponent **20, 38, 49**, 72

federal government, applications in
the 302–3, 322–8
Fibonacci numbers **154**–5, 165, 219,
253, 277
field **74**
file **74**
floating point representation **68**
floating point representation in the
Burroughs B-6500 **72**–3, 74
limits of representation 73
normalized form 73
tag **72**
flowcharts **158**–80
flowchart symbols 161–4
annotation 164
connectors 163–4
decision 162–3
input/output 161–2
processing 164
terminals 163
FORTRAN and WATFIV 15–32,
183–220
adjustable dimensions 214–**5**
arithmetic expression **19**
arrays 186–7
arrays, input and output 207
assignment statement **19**
built-in functions **193**
CALL statement **213**
carriage control **196**, 205
character set **183**
comment **16**
comparisons 25, 192
constants
floating point **18**, 184
integer **18**, 184
literal **185**
logical **185**
CONTINUE statement **203**–4
debugging 215–9
DIMENSION statement **187**–8
DO loops **201**–206
DO statement **198**
DO variable **201**, 205–6
double precision **184**
DOUBLE PRECISION statement
187
dummy arguments **211**
dummy statement **203**
END option in READ **193**–4
END statement **22**
error checking 27
F FORMAT code **198**
FORMAT codes 197–8
format-free input/output **21**
FORMAT statement **187**, 218
FUNCTION statement 209, **212**–3
function subprogram **212**–3
GO TO statement, computed **200**

H FORMAT code 185, 196
I FORMAT code **197**
IF statement, arithmetic **201**
IF statement, logical 25
implied DO **207**
increment of DO **202**
initial value of DO **202**
INTEGER statement **187**
LOGICAL statement **187**
matrices 186–7
object time dimensions 214–**5**
operations **191**–3
arithmetic 191
comparison 192
logical 192–3
priority of execution 192–3
PRINT statement **20**
READ statement 20, 22, **207**
REAL statement **187**
RETURN statement **212**
single precision **184**
statement function 210–**11**
STOP statement **22**
subprogram **209**
subroutine **213**–5
SUBROUTINE statement **213**–5
subscripts **186**
test value of DO **202**
variable 18, 19, **185**
WRITE statement **194**–**5**, 218
X FORMAT code **197**
function fitting 337–41

general flowchart **160**
generated error **154**
generating an operating system **349**
GPSS 120–22, 131
gross pay problem 9, 14, 30, 46,
61–2, 177

hand simulation **138, 216, 251, 275**
handwritten input 109–110
health care applications 305, 313–7,
335–7
heuristics **308**
hexadecimal representation **66**
hierarchical lists **123**
hierarchical structure **74**–5
higher level languages, overview 116–7
Hollerith code 98–**9**
hospital information system **313**-7

IBM 1620, machine language
programming 87–90, 131–2
IBM 360/370 computers 70
IBM 360/370, integer representation
70–2, 74
information storage and retrieval
packages 127

information systems **301**–2, 313–7
inhibit wire **85**
initialization **23**, 26, **41**, **54**, 174
instruction cycle **5**, 82, 87
instruction word **87**
integer representation in the IBM 360/370 **70**–2, 74
intelligent machines 307–9
interactive use of a computer 58–60
iteration 143–4, 205–6
interpretive programming **47**
inventory control 318–9

JOSS 47

key-to-disk input **109**
key-to-tape input **109**
keypunch **99**

laser-based printer **103**–4
law, application in 306
leasts squares function fitting **337**–41
librarian, computer center **347**
light pen **107**–8
line printer **102**
LISP 123–4, 131
    CAR 123
    CDR 123
    CONS 124
list **77**, 122–3
list in BASIC **257**
logic diagrams **159**
logical errors **28**, **44**, 58
looping **7**, 142–3
    BASIC 257–8
    FORTRAN 201–6
    PL/I 240–3
LSI circuits **83**

machine language programming, IBM 1620 87–90, 131–2
    contents of an address **88**
    flag **88**
    P-address **88**
    Q-address **88**
machine language instruction 5
magnetic ink printing and input **109**
main storage **83**-86
maintenance of a program **280**, 282
Manhatten island problem 142, 219
mantissa **49**, 72
mark-sense inputs **97**
matrix **77**
    BASIC 257–8
    FORTRAN 186–7
    PL/I 226
matrix printer 102–4
mean, computation of arithmetic 8, 14, 30, 46, 177

mean and standard deviations problem 155, 165, 198–9, 208–9, 219, 238, 244–5, 262–3, 271–2
medical diagnosis 335–7
memory unit 4
merge **75**
microelectronic circuits 83
microsecond **82**
minimax criterion **335**
modular programming **161**, 279
monitoring sewage pumps 331–2
monolithic systems technology 86
multiple linear regression 338–41
multiprogramming **13**, 86

nanosecond **82**
narrow-band line **112**
Newton's formula for square root 144, 205–6, 242
nonexecutable statements **22**
normalized form **68**–9
numerical taxonomy 332–5

object program **115**
octal representation **66**
off-line operation **104**–5
operating system **11**
operating system, generation of **349**
operations staff 345, 347
operators, computer **350**
optical scanner 97, **109**, 110
optimizing compiler **281**

password protection **94**
payroll problem 74–6, 166–77
photographic film memory **94**
plotters **104**–5
pointer **123**
positional notation 65–7
printers 100–4
privacy 301–3
PL/I and PL/C 33–46, 221–55
    arithmetic expression 36, **232**
    array 226
    arrays, input and output 243
    attributes **226**–8
    assignment statement 36
    built-in functions **224**
    CALL statement 249–50
    character set **221**–2
    CHARACTER attribute **227**
    character string format item **235**–6
    comment 34
    comparison 41, 232
    constant
        character string **225**–6
        decimal fixed point **225**
        floating point 35, **225**
        integer 35

control format item **234**
data format item **234**
DCL statement **227**
debugging 250–3
DECLARE statement **226–8**, 229
DO groups and loops **240–3**
DO WHILE statement **241**–2
DUMP option 251
END statement 35
FIXED attribute **227**, 229
fixed point format item **234**–5
FLOAT attribute **227**
floating point format item **235–6**
format-free input and output 38
GET LIST statement **37**, 39, 239
identifiers **222**–3
IF statement **41**
input/output overview 37
keywords **223**
matrix 226
ON ENDFILE statement **238**–9
operations
    arithmetic 232
    comparison 232
    logical 232–3
    priority of execution 233
PAGE item **230**
procedures 245–50
PROCEDURE OPTIONS (MAIN)
    statement **33**
PUT EDIT statement **233**–7
PUT LIST statement **38**
reserved keywords **224**
RETURN statement **248**
segmenting keywords **224**
SKIP item **236**
spacing format item **236**
statement identifiers **224**
statement labels 34, **223**
variable 35, **226**
process charts **159**
processors 82–3
program
    BASIC 47–62, 256–77
    correctness **278**
    costs 281–2
    debugging 28, 44, 57, 150–3, 215–9,
        250–3, 274–6, 278–9
    documentation 282–93
    ease of use 28
    effectiveness **278**
    efficiency **280**–2, 293–4
    FORTRAN, WATFIV 15–32,
        183–220
    listing 28, 44
    maintenance **280**–2
    modularity **161**, 279
    overview 44
    PL/I, PL/C 33–46, 221–55

proof **279**
    readability 283
programming packages 127–30
propagated error **154**
propriety software **114**
punch cards 97–100
punch card processing equipment
    97–100

quadratic roots problem 178, 219,
    253, 277

radix **66**
read-only storage **94**
record **74**
remote input 10
remote terminals 105–9

savings problem 139–40, 151–2,
    165, 219
scientific computer center 347–9
scientific notation **20, 38, 49,** 68
scientific packages 127
second industrial revolution
    299–300
sense wire **85**
sequential files **167**
Sieve of Erathosthenes **141**–2, 166
Simpson's rule problem 178, 219,
    253, 277
simulation 119–20, 319–28
SNOBOL 125–7, 131
software overview 113–4
sort **75**
    of three numbers 150, 153, 165
    of five numbers 155, 177, 219,
        253, 277
sorter, punched card **99,** 100
sound outputs **97**
source deck **115**
source program **115**
square root problem 143–7, 152–3,
    165, 204–6, 241–3
statistical packages 127
storage unit 4
string processing 125–7, **148–50**
structured programming **137,** 218, 253,
    275, 279
sum
    three numbers 16, 34, 48
    five numbers 30, 44, 61
    ten numbers 23–4, 40–1, 53–4
    variable number of numbers 25,
        42–3, 55–7
switching facility **111**–2
syntactical errors **28, 44, 57**
systems analyst **347**
system flowcharts **159**
systems programmers **345**, 347, 349

table, in BASIC 77
tape storage, magnetic 90–1, 96, 99–100
tariff **111**
taxonomy **332**
teaching machines 304
teaching station 108–9
teletypewriter **106**
test inputs **150**–3
testing algorithms 150–3
thermal matrix printer **102**–3
thin film memory **94**
throughput **86**
tie-line **112**
time-sharing **12**
touch-tone input 97, **106**–7
truncating, truncated **19**, **37**
trunk line **111**–2

tuition problem 188–90, 200, 228–31, 233, 238–40, 244, 260–1, 263
typewriter-like terminals
see character printer

UNIVAC 1108 computer 59
updating **75**, 174
user services group 345
user's view of a computer center 350–3

vector **77**
volatile storage **86**

WATFIV, WATFOR
see FORTRAN
wired city 306–7
word **82**